The Most
Complex Machine

The Most Complex Machine

A Survey of Computers and Computing

David J. Eck
Department of Mathematics and Computer Science
Hobart and William Smith Colleges
Geneva, New York

A K Peters
Wellesley, Massachusetts

Editorial, Sales, and Customer Service Office

A K Peters, Ltd.
289 Linden Street
Wellesley, MA 02181

Library of Congress Cataloging-in-Publication Data

Eck, David J., 1953 -
    The most complex machine : a survey of computers and computing /
David J. Eck.
        p. cm.
    Includes bibliographical references and index.
    ISBN 1-56881-054-7 (hc)
    1. Computer science. I. Title.
QA76.E15 1995
004--dc20   95-32935
                                                                  CIP

Cover photo © Tony Stone Images. Photographed by Andy Roberts.

Printed in the United States of America
99 98 97   10 9 8 7 6 5 4 3 2

Contents

Preface

This book looks at computers, the most complex machines ever created, and at the even more complex programs that those machines execute. In a sense, though, it is complexity itself, rather than the machines and programs, that is the book's real subject. The methods for creating and understanding such complexity are at the core of the field known as **computer science**, and are the major lesson you will take away from what you read here.

As an introduction to computer science, *The Most Complex Machine* is a bit unusual in that it does not follow either of the two most common patterns for such an introduction. It is *not* designed to teach you to program, nor does it seek to make you an expert computer user. Instead, it attempts to introduce you to the fundamental ideas and principles on which the field is built. It was written to be used in a survey course directed mainly to students not currently majoring in computer science. It provides an overview of the field that is appropriate for such students whether or not they continue their study of computer science.

This book might also be used as a supplement in a first course in programming, to broaden student's exposure to the ideas of computer science. It might even make a good required introduction to the major, particularly for students with little previous experience with computer science. Finally, it should also be useful to the individual reader who wants to understand something of what really goes on inside a computer.

There are very few prerequisites for reading *The Most Complex Machine*. I do assume that you have some familiarity with computers, and it would certainly be useful for you to have had some experience using a computer. But all you really need to know is that a computer is a machine that can run programs. A program is a set of instructions for a computer to execute; you can make a computer do a wide variety of different things by giving it different programs. Even if you are fuzzy on these basic ideas, they should become more clear to you as you read.

Some of the discussion in the book is mathematical; some of it is rather technical. But I try to cover everything at a level that can be followed with very little previous mathematical or technical experience—at least if you are willing to do some careful reading and thinking.

The first chapter, titled "What Computers Do," is really an introduction to the subject of complexity. This chapter is fundamental, in that it introduces many of the ideas that are covered more fully in the rest of the book. So, while you don't need to understand in detail everything in this chapter the first time through, you should pay close attention to the main ideas.

The next two chapters explain how computers can be built, step-by-step, out of very simple components. By the end of Chapter 3, you will understand how a physical object can be built to execute an arbitrarily complex set of program instructions. This is the most technical part of the book. If you decide to skip over it, you will not be at a great disadvantage for the rest of the text. However, you will miss some really neat ideas, and I encourage you to browse through at least Section 2.1 and the beginnings of Sections 3.1 and 3.3 at least. And of course, you can read the chapter summaries.

Chapter 4, on "Theoretical Computers," shows that all computers, from the simple model computer constructed in Chapter 3 to the most advanced supercomputer, are really equally powerful except for their speed and the amount of memory they have. Furthermore, they are all subject to certain surprising limitations on the problems they can solve. The idea of "computational universality," covered in Section 4.1, is quite important; the rest of the chapter is interesting but not vital to later chapters.

The next chapter turns for the first time to real computers. It surveys their history, examines their social impact, and discusses how practical machines differ from the simplified model computers considered in the previous chapters.

Chapters 6, 7, and 8 cover computer programming. Chapter 6 introduces the basic concepts, such as variables, loops, and decisions. Chapter 7 concentrates on methods for writing very large or complex programs. And Chapter 8 finishes by looking at some of the many different languages available for writing programs.

The last chapters of the book, Chapters 9 through 12, deal with applications of computing. After a general survey of applications in Chapter 9, the next three chapters cover three of the most important and exciting areas of computer science: computer graphics, parallel and distributed processing, and artificial intelligence. These four chapters can be read in any order.

*   *   *

The book is supplemented with a set of computer programs and with lab worksheets based on those programs. The programs are currently available only for Macintosh computers, but I am working to make them available to run under Windows as well. The programs are closely tied to the ideas covered in the text. They are not essential to understanding the material in the book, but the hands-on experience they give could certainly help to make some of the ideas presented here more accessible. (They are also, as far as I can judge them myself, rather fun.) The programs include:

• *xLogicCircuits*, which lets you build and run simulated circuits made from AND, OR, and NOT gates, like those discussed in Chapter 2;

• *xComputer*, which implements the model computer, xComputer, constructed in Chapter 3;

• *xTuringMachine*, in which you can enter rule tables for Turing Machines, as discussed in Chapter 4, and watch them as they move along their tapes and perform the computations you have programmed;

• *xTurtle*, a programming environment for the programming language xTurtle, which is discussed in Chapters 6, 7, and 10;

• *xSortLab*, a program for experimenting with the sorting algorithms mentioned in Chapter 9; and

• *xModels2D* and *xModels3D*, programs for simple geometric modeling and animation, based on the material on computer graphics in Chapter 11.

The programs and the lab worksheets are available free on the Internet for personal, private use, and they can be freely used in courses that have adopted *The Most Complex Machine* as a textbook. I stipulate that they cannot be used in other courses. You should be able to find the programs in standard Macintosh FTP sites and bulletin boards. If you have access to the World Wide Web, you can get more information at the URL:

`http://math.hws.edu/TMCM.html`

My electronic mail address is eck@hws.edu. I can also be reached by regular mail at the address: David Eck, Department of Mathematics and Computer Science, Hobart and William Smith Colleges, Geneva NY 14456. I encourage comments, questions, and general communication (but do not guarantee a response to every message I receive).

*   *   *

The chapters of the book are divided into numbered sections, which are in turn divided into subsections. When I refer to "Subsection 3.2.4," I mean the fourth subsection of the second section in Chapter 3. If I refer simply to "Section 2," I mean the second section in the current chapter. Figures are also numbered within chapters, so that "Figure 3.7" means the seventh figure in Chapter 3.

There is an annotated bibliography at the end of the book. Bibliographic references within the text are indicated by the author's name enclosed in brackets, with a page number if appropriate. For example, [Eck, p. 42] would refer to page 42 of a book in the bibliography by someone whose last name is Eck.

Each chapter ends with a set of questions. Almost all of the questions are meant to be thought-provoking and to require more than short, straightforward answers. The questions are part of the book and are meant to be read and pondered. My answers to most of the questions can be found in the last section of the book. You should read these answers—after thinking about the questions on your own—since they often provide more perspective on the ideas covered in the chapter itself.

*   *   *

I gratefully acknowledge the help and the encouragement of Kevin Mitchell and Richard Palais, who read large parts of this book when it was less readable than it is now and whose comments have certainly made it a better book than it would have been otherwise. (And you should obviously assume that any parts you don't like are among the parts they didn't get to read in advance.) I would also like to thank the copyeditor, Seth Maislin, and the people at A K Peters Ltd: Joni McDonald, Alexandra Benis, and Klaus Peters.

Chapter 1

Introduction:
What Computers Do

━━━━━━━

WHAT COMPUTERS DO, of course, is compute. That is not the end of
the story, though. The real question is, how can computers do all the
remarkable things that they do, just by computing?

The essence of computing is the *mechanical manipulation of
symbols*. When people compute, in the ordinary sense, the symbols
are numbers, which are mechanically manipulated according to the rules
of arithmetic. For example, a person who memorizes a fairly small set of
rules and applies them correctly can multiply numbers of any size. The
rules include basic facts about the sum and product of any two digits,
along with a procedure that determines the steps to be carried out in
doing the multiplication: "Write down the numbers, one beneath the
other, with the rightmost digits lined up, and draw a line beneath them.
Multiply the top number by the rightmost digit of the bottom number,
writing the result under the line...."

This example reveals several important aspects of computation. First
of all, it is very boring. There are rules to be followed. They tell you
exactly what to do. No creativity. No fun. One small mistake and the
answer will be wrong. (This is what we mean when we say that computation is *mechanical*.) It is no surprise that people find it so difficult to
get through a large multiplication problem without error. Computers,

1

on the other hand, have no such difficulty. They follow the rules without error and without complaint.

Second, computation is, in itself, meaningless. This is hard for people to understand, because people generally compute for a reason. A person who multiplies 16 by 127 is likely to be doing it to find out how much 16 light bulbs cost at $1.27 each or how many calories are in 127 potato chips if each one contains 16. But doing the multiplication involves following the rules, putting aside all thought of calories or light bulbs. It may be that the number "127" being multiplied represents 127 potato chips, but those chips are external and irrelevant to the computation. This is what we mean when we say that a computation manipulates *symbols*. A symbol is something that, while meaningless in itself, can stand in for some sort of external meaning. It is the nature of computation, however, that any external meaning is irrelevant to the computation. Again, this tends to make computation difficult for people, who deal naturally with meaning and find it hard to ignore it.

It is important to understand one other aspect of computation from the start. Although the term commonly refers to the arithmetical manipulation of numbers, it can refer to the manipulation of any sort of symbols according to definite, mechanical rules. For example, the editor who counts the number of words in a book, or who checks each word to see whether it can be found in an official dictionary, is computing in this sense. The symbols being manipulated in this case are words, and the editor's activities are examples of the type of "word processing" that can be done more easily and more accurately by a computer, since counting words or looking them up in a dictionary can be done by applying simple rules that require no understanding of the words' meanings.

All this is just the beginning of an explanation of what computation is, but it is enough to introduce the questions which will occupy us for the remainder of this book: How can a machine be built that can carry out complex computations? How can those computations accomplish things that seem to be much more than the mechanical manipulation of symbols? And what are the limits to what can be accomplished, just by computing?

1.1. Bits, Bytes, etc.

We can start with the question of what sort of symbols it is that computers manipulate. When people do arithmetic, the basic symbols are the digits 0 through 9. It is important to realize that the particular symbols used are arbitrary. It makes no difference, for example, if the symbol 2 is replaced by %, as long as the rules are also changed in an appropriate way ("6 times % is 1%"), and as long as you remember what % stands for when it comes time to interpret an answer ("%03% is an awful lot of calories!").

For a computer, the basic symbols are the two digits 0 and 1. Since there are just two of them, zero and one in this context are called *binary digits*, which is almost always abbreviated to *bits*. Again, it makes no difference if we use different symbols. We might, for example, decide to represent the two possible bits as % and #, or by 7 and 3 for that matter. Since there are two binary digits, they tend to be represented as things that naturally come in pairs, such as true/false, on/off, and black/white. We will use whatever representation seems most natural in context.

Now, two symbols don't seem to give us a lot to work with. For that matter, the ten symbols of ordinary arithmetic might seem a bit inadequate to cover the infinite range of numbers that can be represented. You know how this dilemma is resolved: Any number of digits chosen from 0 through 9 can be strung together to give a *compound symbol*, such as 2032. By stringing together basic symbols, we can represent any number whatsoever. The same principle works when there are only two basic symbols. When we have more than two things to represent, we can turn to strings of bits, such as 10011, to provide us with as many different (compound) symbols as we need. If we are careful, we can represent anything that a computer might have to deal with.

1.1.1. Binary Numbers. Among the most important things computers deal with are numbers. As our first exercise in combining bits, we can construct representations for the most basic type of numbers, the *counting numbers*, or nonnegative integers. Using the digits zero through nine, we write these numbers as

$$0, 1, 2, \ldots, 9, 10, 11, 12, \ldots, 99, 100, \ldots.$$

This way of writing numbers is called the *base ten* or *decimal* representation, since ten digits are used and since the number ten plays such an important role. It is useful to visualize counting in the base ten by thinking of the way a car's odometer keeps track of the number of miles traveled. In a brand new car, the odometer reads all zeros: 000000. Every time the car travels one mile, the rightmost digit increases by one, from 000000 to 000001, up to 000009. At this point you run out of digits;

the rightmost digit goes back to zero and the digit next to it increases by one. This takes you up to 000099. At that point, you've run out of digits in both the first and second places, so the zero in the third place changes to one, giving 000100. (Ordinarily, of course, we don't write the zeros on the left—for one thing, there would be the problem of just how many of them we should write!)

When we use just the two binary digits, 0 and 1, we are working in the **base two** or **binary** system. To avoid confusion, I will subscript any binary number with a 2, so you can tell the difference between 10110_2 (base two) and 10110 (base ten). To count in binary, you just need to imagine an odometer with only zeros and ones: start with 0_2, then 1_2— oops, ran out of digits, so the last digit becomes 0 and the next digit rolls over—10_2, 11_2—ran out of numbers in both places this time—100_2, 101_2, 110_2, 111_2, 1000_2, 1001_2, ... We obtain a translation between binary and decimal simply by matching up the numbers in each system as we count:

0	1	2	3	4	5	6	7	8	9	10	11
0_2	1_2	10_2	11_2	100_2	101_2	110_2	111_2	1000_2	1001_2	1010_2	1011_2

This is not a very satisfactory way to find a translation for, say, the binary number 1001110101_2. However, a little analysis provides a more satisfactory mechanism. I will work through the details of this analysis not because the details are important, but because it shows how a simple idea can be developed into a more complicated, but more efficient, computational procedure. If you are not interested in this, you can safely skip ahead to Subsection 1.1.2.

The first step in our analysis is to find out how many binary numbers there are that are made up of k (or fewer) bits. For $k = 1$, there are only two such one-bit numbers, 0_2 and 1_2. For $k = 2$, there are four two-bit numbers: 00_2, 01_2, 10_2, and 11_2. (It will useful to write some extra zeros on the left, so that each number in the list is a sequence of exactly k bits. If you leave off the leading zeros, you have a list of numbers with "k bits or fewer.") Let's consider the case $k = 3$ more carefully. A sequence of three bits must begin with a 0 or with a 1, so we can divide such sequences into two groups:

Starting with zero: 000_2 001_2 010_2 011_2
Starting with one: 100_2 101_2 110_2 111_2

You can get the numbers in the first group by taking the list of all two-bit numbers (00, 01, 10, and 11) and tacking a zero onto the beginning of each. If you tack on a one instead, you get the second group.

Now, there are two groups of numbers here. Each group contains just as many members as there are two-bit numbers. This is just a way of saying that *there are exactly two times as many three-bit numbers as there are two-bit numbers.* By the same argument, there are exactly sixteen four-bit numbers—just twice as many as the number of three-bit numbers. We can list the four-bit numbers in two groups of eight numbers each as

$$0000_2 \quad 0001_2 \quad 0010_2 \quad 0011_2 \quad 0100_2 \quad 0101_2 \quad 0110_2 \quad 0111_2$$
$$1000_2 \quad 1001_2 \quad 1010_2 \quad 1011_2 \quad 1100_2 \quad 1101_2 \quad 1110_2 \quad 1111_2$$

This argument works for any number of digits. For any number k, there are twice as many $(k + 1)$-bit binary numbers as there are k-bit binary numbers. There are 2 one-bit numbers, 2×2 two-bit numbers, $2 \times 2 \times 2$ three-bit numbers, and so on. In general there are 2^k k-bit numbers, where 2^k is the kth power of 2, that is, $2 \times 2 \times \cdots \times 2$, with k factors of 2.

Now, let's return to the problem of trying to convert a binary number to the base ten. First, note that the binary number consisting of a one followed by k zeros represents the number 2^k. You can see this by noting that, for example, in order to count up to 100_2 you have to count past the four two-bit numbers, so that 100_2 corresponds to 4—that is, to 2^2. (It corresponds to 4, rather than 5, because you start counting with zero; the first four numbers are 0, 1, 2, 3.) Similarly, to get up to 10000_2, you have to count past the 2^4 four-bit numbers, so 10000_2 corresponds to 2^4, or 16. (Note that the rule works even for $k = 0$ or $k = 1$, using the facts that $2^1 = 2$ and $2^0 = 1$.)

The more complicated number 10110_2 corresponds to $2^4 + 2^2 + 2^1$. This can be justified directly by considering how you count up to 10110_2. You must count past 2^4 numbers to get to 10000_2, then past another 2^2 to get to 10100_2 and finally past 2^1 more to get to 10110_2. Alternatively, you could anticipate the meaning of addition for binary numbers and write

$$10110_2 = 10000_2 + 100_2 + 10_2 = 2^4 + 2^2 + 2^1 = 16 + 4 + 2 = 22.$$

The general rule for converting a binary number to the base ten is to add up the powers of two corresponding to each 1 in the binary number. To find the appropriate power, simply count bits from the right, starting from 0 for the rightmost bit. As a final example, we can compute

$$1001110101_2 = 2^9 + 2^6 + 2^5 + 2^4 + 2^2 + 2^0$$
$$= 512 + 64 + 32 + 16 + 4 + 1$$
$$= 629.$$

Binary Number	Power of 2	Decimal Number
1_2	2^0	1
10_2	2^1	2
100_2	2^2	4
1000_2	2^3	8
10000_2	2^4	16
100000_2	2^5	32
1000000_2	2^6	64
10000000_2	2^7	128
100000000_2	2^8	256
1000000000_2	2^9	512
10000000000_2	2^{10}	1024
10000000000000000_2	2^{16}	65,536
$1000000000000000000000000_2$	2^{24}	16,777,216
$100000000000000000000000000000000_2$	2^{32}	4,294,967,296

Figure 1.1. *Some powers of two and their representations as binary and as decimal numbers. Adding a zero onto the end of a base-two number multiplies that number by 2, just as adding a zero to the end of a base 10 number multiplies it by 10.*

After all that, you might be wondering why computers use binary numbers instead of just sticking to the more familiar decimal numbers. In fact, it's sort of an accident. Early mechanical calculating devices generally represented numbers with wheels or gears that could be in one of ten positions, one for each decimal digit. Such calculators worked directly in the base ten. Modern computers are made out of electronic components—for very good reasons involving speed and reliability. The most natural "positions" for a wire in a circuit are **on** and **off**, which correspond in a natural way to the two binary digits. Although it might be possible to represent ten digits by using ten different voltage levels in a wire, such a scheme would have two disadvantages: The inevitable inaccuracy in measuring a voltage would lead to a much higher probability of error than occurs when only the difference between **on** and **off** must be detected. And the complex circuits necessary to work with such a representation would be very difficult to design and build.

1.1.2. Text. If you are like most people, there is something that might be bothering you at this point. You might reasonably point out that you have been working quite happily with computers for years—

typing papers, drawing pictures, or whatever—without ever having heard or thought of binary numbers. Although bits and binary numbers are an essential aspect of the internal workings of computers, it's true that a person who simply wants to use a computer can do so without knowing anything about them. Nevertheless, as you sit there typing on your computer, everything that the computer does is in fact accomplished by manipulating bits. We need to understand how so much can be done with just the two values zero and one.

Let's start with the simple question of how a computer can represent the characters you type as binary numbers. The answer is also simple: Each possible character is assigned a unique binary *code number*. Most computers use a code called ASCII (American Standard Code for Information Interchange). In this code, each character is represented by an eight-bit binary number. For example, the lowercase letter 'a' corresponds to 01100001_2, while the comma ',' is represented by 00101100_2. As we saw above, there are 2^8, or 256, different strings of eight bits, so the ASCII code allows for 256 different characters. Only the first 128 of these are assigned standard meanings; on a particular computer, the extra code numbers are either not used or are used for special characters such as the accented e, 'é'. Of the 128 standard codes, not all of them stand for characters that might appear on your computer screen. Some are used for so-called "nonprintable" or "control" characters, such as a tab or carriage return (which have codes 00001001_2 and 00001101_2, respectively).

An eight-bit binary number is also called a *byte*, so that it takes exactly one byte to specify one character in ASCII. Data is often measured in bytes rather than bits. For example, a document stored on the computer might contain 10,000 bytes. That is another way of saying that it contains 10,000 characters, or 80,000 bits.

Now, any ASCII code number could just as easily be written as a decimal number somewhere in the range from 0 to 255. In base ten, the codes for 'a', comma, and tab are 97, 44, and 9, respectively. In some sense, though, the binary numbers are closer to reality. When you press the letter 'a' on your keyboard, the eight bits 0, 0, 1, 0, 1, 1, 0, 0 are transmitted to the computer. If the computer is storing the letter 'a', then somewhere inside it that sequence of bits is stored in some way. As a user of the computer, you don't have to be aware of any of this—as far as you are concerned, the computer simply understands the letter you type. However, its "understanding" is all based on pushing bits around, and the people who design computers (or who try to understand them) must sometimes deal with things on that level.

The particular code number used for each letter is arbitrary; the code is a *symbol* for the character, whose meaning is established only by convention. As long as everyone knows what convention is being used, no problems arise. In fact, some computers use codes other than ASCII internally, but ASCII is currently used for most communication between computers.[1]

Once individual characters are coded as binary numbers, the step up to representations for words, sentences, or longer pieces of text is easy. To represent a word such as 'cat', just string together the codes for the individual letters 'c', 'a', and 't'. Using the ASCII codes for the individual letters, this would give $011000110110000101110100_2$. An entire document in a word processor could be represented simply as a (very long) string of bits. Special features, such as the beginning of a new paragraph, might be indicated by inserting ASCII codes for non-printing characters. Admittedly, this is not the only, or even the best, way to encode a large document. In fact, each word-processing program tends to use its own encoding. Once again, the person using the program doesn't need to know what that encoding is.

1.1.3. Everything Else. Counting numbers, characters, and text represent only a few of the types of data that computers must deal with. A partial list of other data types would include negative integers, decimal numbers, fractions, dates and times, sounds, pictures, animated images, chess boards, airline flight schedules, computer programs, and textbooks about computers. No matter what type of data is being considered, it must be represented in the computer as a pattern of bits.

For example, when I look at the letter 't' displayed on my computer's screen, what I actually see is a *picture* of a 't'. If I look closely, I can see

---

[1] This might change. A new standard code called Unicode has been proposed (and has been adopted for the new Microsoft operating system Windows NT). Unicode uses a sixteen-bit code number for each character. Thus, Unicode takes up twice as much space as ASCII, but it provides for 2^{16}, or 65,536, different characters. It includes standard code numbers for all the characters available in ASCII as well as the Arabic, Hebrew, and Cyrillic alphabets, complete sets of Japanese, Korean, and Chinese characters, and many mathematical and other special symbols, with room for much more [Custer, p. 42–44]. (As an exercise in developing your "number sense," you might consider how merely doubling the size of the representation gives such a huge increase in the number of different things that can be represented.)

that that picture is just a grid of black and white dots. In fact, the entire screen is simply a grid of dots, each of which can be either `off` (black) or `on` (white). The individual dots are called **pixels**, short for "picture elements." The computer controls what is displayed on the screen by turning each individual pixel `on` or `off`.[2]

This off/on distinction should remind you of the 0/1 of binary numbers, and in fact, the state of each pixel on the screen can be represented by a single bit. From there, representing the entire screen is easy—it can be represented by a string of bits, with one bit for each pixel. On my Macintosh SE/30, with its 512 by 342 grid of pixels, that's a 175,104-bit number! The number that represents the current image displayed on the screen is actually stored somewhere inside the computer, in what we might call **video memory**. When the computer needs to change the image displayed on the screen, it modifies the number in video memory in the appropriate way. (The changes made to this memory are automatically reflected on the screen; we won't worry for now about how this happens.)

For example, to display a 't' on the screen, the bits representing a picture of a 't' are copied to the appropriate place in video memory, depending on where on the screen the 't' is to be displayed. Figure 1.2 shows how 't' might be represented as a grid of pixels, and how that grid is in turn equivalent to a binary number.

Any image that consists of just two colors (black and white) can be represented in the same way. Of course, the amount of detail that can be shown is limited by the size of a pixel. On a typical computer screen, individual pixels are clearly visible. But if small enough pixels are used, the result appears to the eye as a continuous image. The process of representing an image as a string of binary digits is called **digitizing** the image. Color pictures and pictures consisting of shades of gray can also be digitized. Each shade to be used in the image is assigned a binary code number, so that the color of each pixel can be indicated by specifying one of the possible codes. The full image is then represented by stringing together all the codes for the pixels.

---

[2] Most computers now have color screens. Instead of being restricted to `off` or `on`, each pixel can be set to one of some specified number of colors. On one common type of system, each pixel can be one of 256 different colors. Since 256 is 2^8, the color of each pixel can be represented by an 8-bit binary number; we say that such a color image requires one byte per pixel. Systems that use 2^4, 2^{16}, or 2^{24} different colors are also common. Can you guess why the number of colors is generally a power of two?

$$
\begin{array}{ccccc}
0 & 1 & 0 & 0 & 0 \\
1 & 1 & 1 & 1 & 0 \\
0 & 1 & 0 & 0 & 0 \\
0 & 1 & 0 & 0 & 0 \\
0 & 1 & 0 & 0 & 0 \\
0 & 1 & 0 & 0 & 1 \\
0 & 0 & 1 & 1 & 0 \\
0 & 0 & 0 & 0 & 0
\end{array}
$$

$$01000111100100001000010000100100110000000_2$$

Figure 1.2. *A picture of the letter 't', represented as a grid of (big) pixels, as the corresponding grid of bits, and as a binary number. The 40-bit number is obtained by stringing together the rows in the grid of bits.*

You should now see how representations can be built for just about any data using only binary numbers. For data whose possible values are not already numbers, there are really only three basic methods that are needed: combination, enumeration, and digitization.

To represent something that breaks down naturally into a finite number of pieces, find a representation for each of the pieces and *combine* them to represent the whole. This is how we dealt with words—by stringing together codes for each individual character in the word. And to represent a date, we can combine separate codes for the month, the day, and the year.

When you encounter a type of data whose possible values can be listed, you can simply *enumerate* those values and assign each a code number. The ASCII code is just such an enumeration of characters. Similarly, we often represent the months of the year by the numbers 1 through 12. On a somewhat more abstract level, suppose you want to represent the contents of a square on a checkerboard. There are five possible values, which can be enumerated as: empty, red piece, black piece, red king, and black king. One possible binary representation is obtained by encoding "empty" as 0_2, "red piece" as 1_2, and so forth. (Then, of course, given that a checkerboard consists of 64 squares, you can represent a complete board position by combining the 64 code numbers that represent the contents of the individual squares.)

The third method of representation, *digitization*, is used when there is an unreasonably large, or even infinite, number of possibilities to be dealt with. A perfect representation of a picture would specify the color of each of its infinitely many mathematical points; as we have seen, though, specifying the color of points in a finite grid gives an adequate approximation. Note that this can be seen as an approximate application of the first representation method, combination, to the case where the data has an infinite number of parts. If the data has an infinite number of possible values, then an approximate version of enumeration can be used. This is what we do when we encode only a selected finite number of colors out of the theoretically infinite range. Thus, a digitized color image involves both types of approximation.

As a final example, consider digital sound recording, which is used to produce the disks used in compact disk players. A sound can be specified by giving its intensity, or amplitude, at each instant of time. Digitizing the sound involves two approximations: The intensity is recorded at only a finite sample of points in time, and the recorded intensity is limited to only a finite number of possible values. For a compact disk the intensity is sampled 44,000 times per second, and each intensity measurement is encoded as a 16-bit binary number (so a full hour of music on such a disk requires about two-and-a-half billion bits). The fact that the recorded sound is only an approximation has little practical effect. Any recording method will introduce some error, and the errors introduced by digitization are very small and (according to most people) inaudible.

1.1.4. Structured Complexity. We have now seen how all the data to be used by a computer can be represented as a collection of bits, which can then be directly manipulated by the computer. However, we have been sweeping under the rug the issue of how that collection of bits is organized.

Suppose I were to point to some particular sequence of bits inside a computer and ask what it represents. Without further information, the answer could be almost anything—the current date, the color of some particular pixel on the screen, the board position in a game of computer chess, Joe DiMaggio's batting average in 1939.... What it actually means is determined not just by the sequence of bits but also by the physical structure of the computer itself, by the overall structure of the data encoded in the computer, by the program that is running, and by the intentions of the person using the computer. All these things, except perhaps the intentions of the user, are subjects of study in computer science. At this point, you might be thinking that it is hopeless to try to understand such complexity, but in fact, our discussion of data representation holds some clues to how such understanding is possible.

The key is that the data in a computer is not really just a massive jumble of bits. Instead, the data is carefully organized into complex structures. The structure is a natural result of the way that complex representations are made by combining simpler representations.

Consider the problem of representing an airline's flight schedule. Such a schedule could be simply a list of data for individual flights. The data for each flight in turn has a certain structure, perhaps including the date and time of the flight, the names of the cities where the flight originates and terminates, and the flight number. The name of each city is in turn a string of characters, which can be represented in ASCII code. The date consists of a month, a day and a year, and so forth. Furthermore, the flight schedule will itself be only part of an airline's database, which will have its own complex structure. The meaning of any particular part of this structure depends on its role in larger components of the data. Thus, a particular group of bits would represent the year 1993 because it is a certain part of the representation of a date; that date would represent the departure date for a particular airline flight because it happens to be stored in the proper corner of the data for that flight; the flight data can be recognized as such because it occupies a particular place in the list of data for all flights.

In practice, complex data can be managed because it can be viewed as being made up of simpler "chunks," which are combined together in some reasonably straightforward way to give the whole. Of course, each chunk might be made up of even simpler pieces. Eventually, though, the process bottoms out in simple data, such as single characters or numbers, that can be represented directly. Although the overall structure is very complex, it is comprehensible because the chunking that occurs on each level is manageable.

The theme of levels of structured complexity is one that will come up over and over again in this text (starting with the next section). Indeed, it is in some ways the central theme of computer science.

1.2. Transistors, Gates, etc.

What makes a computer such a remarkable machine is its versatility. A single computer can perform any number of different tasks. From another point of view, though, a computer does only one thing: It executes programs. A *program* is nothing but a list of instructions for performing

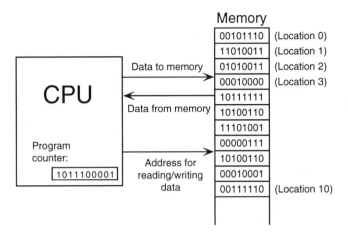

Figure 1.3. *A crude illustration of a computer, showing two of its major components: the memory and the central processing unit. Memory holds data and programs in a sequence of numbered locations. The CPU reads and executes the programs stored in memory. Three connections exist for communication between the CPU and the memory. The first two carry data and program instructions back and forth. The third is used by the CPU to specify which location in the memory it wants to access. A much fuller depiction of a computer is given in Chapter 3.*

a particular task. To get a computer to perform a new task, you just have to give it a new program to execute.

A computer is built to execute programs. From the moment it is turned on, it mindlessly follows instruction after instruction, and it does so because that's the way it is physically put together. In order to understand what is meant by this, you need to have some idea of the main parts of a computer and how they operate. For now, it is enough to know about the computer's **memory** and its **central processing unit** (CPU).

The memory holds a large collection of bits, representing both the data and the programs currently available to the computer, encoded as patterns of bits. Memory is organized as a sequence of **locations**, with each location holding some fixed number of bits. (On most computers, each location holds eight bits, so that the memory can be considered to be a long sequence of bytes.) Each location is identified by a number, which must be specified whenever the contents of that location are to be read or changed.

The central processing unit is the active part of the computer; it actually executes a program stored in memory. The program, remember, is simply a list of instructions stored in a sequence of memory locations. The CPU executes the program by repeating the same two-step procedure over and over: It reads the next instruction from memory and then executes the instruction. This process is called the **fetch-and-execute cycle**. The CPU has a small internal memory called the **program counter** in which it keeps track of which memory location contains the next instruction to be executed. The program counter is automatically updated as part of the fetch-and-execute cycle, so whenever it needs to fetch a new instruction, the CPU simply needs to read the contents of the memory location indicated by the program counter. (If you imagine yourself as the CPU following a list of instructions, the program counter is like a finger that you run down the list to keep track of your place. When you are ready for a new instruction, you just look to where your finger is pointing; after reading that instruction, you move your finger down to the next one on the list.)

Like anything else stored in memory, an instruction read into the CPU is really just a binary number, that is, a pattern of zeros and ones. The CPU doesn't think about what the instruction means or interpret it in any way—it is just constructed in such a way that it will physically react to the pattern by performing the action which the instruction represents. The patterns of zeros and ones understood by the CPU are called the **machine language** of the computer. Each type of computer has its own machine language, and any program for that computer must ultimately be encoded into machine language before it can be executed. Each machine language instruction is very simple and accomplishes very little. The power of the computer comes from its ability to execute millions of such instructions per second.

This short description is a start at understanding how a computer works, but it is by no means obvious how a pile of electronic components can be assembled into a device that will "execute instructions" when it is turned on. It is not easy to design such a device, even when the instructions to be executed are kept very simple. Fortunately, we have already encountered a way of dealing with such complexity: Instead of trying to understand everything at once, we try to see how it can be built up, level by level, out of simpler chunks. We will begin on the very lowest level.

1.2.1. Switches. It is a nice visual image to imagine the processing of data and programs inside a computer as a swirl of zeros and ones being moved around in complex patterns. Of course, in reality the zeros and ones are represented by the absence or presence of currents on wires.[3] Moving the zeros and ones around really means switching the currents on and off. This switching is the fundamental operation on which the overall operation of the computer is based. In modern computers, the switches are *transistors*.

You can think of a transistor as a box connected to three wires: one for input, one for output, and one to control the switch. (What's inside the box is a subject for physics rather than computer science and need not concern us here.) Each wire can be either on or off. The transistor acts like a gate. When the control wire is off, the gate is open, and whatever current is on the input wire will flow through to the output wire; if the control wire is on, the gate is closed, and the output will be off regardless of the state of the input. It is probably more useful to think in terms of a flow of information rather than a flow of current. The input wire carries information (a 0 or 1) into the transistor. If the control wire is off, that information flows through to the output. If it is on, no information about the input gets through—the output will be off, representing a 0, but this will be true regardless of the input, so that looking at the output gives no information about the state of the input. (Remember that turning the control wire *on* closes the gate and blocks the information.)

Note that the input, output, and control of the transistor are really all the same sort of thing—wires that can be either off or on, representing zeros and ones. This has profound implications. It's what makes it possible for patterns of bits to act either as data (input and output) in computations or as instructions in a program (which control the computations). In fact, there is nothing to stop you from hooking up the output of one transistor to the control of another, which is the basis for allowing computations to be controlled by data. The distinction between data and programs becomes a matter of point-of-view, rather than a matter of fact. The same bits that are at one moment being manipulated as data might at the next moment be controlling the manipulation of other bits.

---

[3] This is not quite true. It would be more correct to talk about the "electric potential on the wire being set to -5 or 5 volts" (or some other values). Note also that other physical representations for a bit are possible, such as a static electric charge or the orientation of a magnetic field, and that such representations are used in certain types of computer memory.

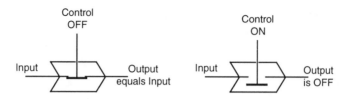

Figure 1.4. *Schematic representations of a transistor, shown with the control wire turned* off *on the left and* on *on the right. These drawings are meant to illustrate that turning the control wire on will break the connection between input and output, cutting off the flow of information.*

We can now form a (slightly) clearer idea of what happens as the CPU executes an instruction. Loading an instruction from memory means turning certain wires in the CPU on or off, according to the pattern of bits in the instruction. This is supposed to bring about the computation that the instruction represents. The computation is performed by transistors, generally in a number of stages. The wires encoding the instruction, along with wires encoding any data to be manipulated by the instruction, are connected to the inputs and controls of transistors, and the resulting outputs from those transistors represent the first stage in the computation. The output wires are connected to other transistors which continue the computation, until eventually the instruction has been completed. While we are still a long way from really understanding this process, this description shows what it means to say that the CPU executes instructions mechanically, simply because of the way it is put together.

As we start building circuits, we need a way of drawing transistors. The picture I will use is not based in the least on the way transistors actually look or work, nor is it the picture used in electrical engineering; rather, it is intended to depict the function of the transistor in a transparent way. Figure 1.4 shows a transistor as we will draw it in its two possible states, with the control wire either on or off.

Since we are so little concerned with the physical nature of transistors, you might guess that other physical objects that have similar behavior could also be used to build computers. You would be right. Some very early computers were built out of **relays**, mechanical devices that really do look a lot like our schematic illustrations of transistors.[4] Computer

---

[4] In a relay, turning on the control wire activates an electromagnet which pulls a metal rod into a position that physically closes the connection between

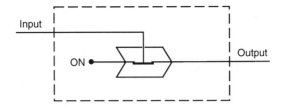

Figure 1.5. *A* NOT *gate constructed from a single transistor. This circuit has one input and one output. The output is determined by the rule that the output is off whenever the input is on, and vice versa.*

designers soon turned to electronic devices, which can be switched on and off more quickly than relays. The first electronic computers used vacuum tubes as their switching element. The basic ideas are the same whether they are implemented in relays, vacuum tubes, or transistors. As we design new circuits, keep in mind that it is the rules that govern the behavior of their components that are important, not the physical details of their construction.

1.2.2. Circuit Building. It's time to descend from generalities to considerations of how we can actually put transistors together into circuits that perform useful computations. We start by building basic circuits for some very simple operations. Later, we will see how to build more complex circuits from these basic building blocks.

The first circuits we consider have one or two input wires and one output wire. The value on the output wire is determined by some fixed rule from the input bits. For a single input and a single output, there are only two possible rules: Either the output is the same as the input, or it is the reverse of the input (on when the input is off and off when the input is on). The first case is rather boring, since the "circuit" could be nothing but a wire connecting the input to the output. A circuit that reverses its input, however, is very useful. It can be built from a single transistor.

Such a circuit is diagramed in Figure 1.5. Note that the input to the *circuit* is used as the *control wire* for the transistor. The transistor's input is connected to a wire that is permanently on. This wire must be connected to the computer's power source, which of course must be

---

input and output. This is different from transistors, in which a signal on the control wire *breaks* the connection, but this difference forces only minor changes in circuit design.

turned on before the circuit can do anything. (All of the circuits we build have such internal connections to a power source, which are not counted as inputs to the circuits since their values never change; they provide the power that drives the computer, but they do not carry information.)

We should check that this circuit behaves as advertised. If the circuit's input is off, then the transistor's control is off, so the transistor's input passes through to its output wire; since its input is on, so is the output, as desired. Turning the circuit's input on will turn on the transistor's control wire, which will cause its output to be off, again as desired.

The circuit we have built is called a **NOT gate**. The use of the term "gate" here is standard, but has nothing to do with gates that open and close, except in the sense that the output can be on or off. The word "NOT" can be justified if we think of a bit as having one of the two possible *logical values*, true or false, instead of a numerical value, one or zero. In logic, "NOT" reverses the truth of a statement: NOT true is false, and NOT false is true. We will have a lot more to say about the relationship between logic and circuits in the next chapter.

We turn now to circuits that have two inputs and one output. Since each input can be separately set to be on or off, there are exactly four possible states that the input can be in: on/on, on/off, off/on, and off/off. The behavior of the circuit is determined by what output it gives in each of these four cases. One such circuit is the **AND gate**, which follows the rule that the output is on if both inputs are on and is off in the other three cases. (The output is on exactly when input 1 is on "AND" input 2 is on.) An AND gate can be constructed from four transistors, as shown in Figure 1.6.

The last basic circuit that we need is the **OR gate**, which also has two inputs and one output. The output of an OR gate is on if either the first input is on, OR the second input is on, OR both are on. The output is off only if both inputs are off. An OR gate can be constructed from three transistors. You might want to construct a table and diagram for an OR gate like those given in Figure 1.6 for an AND gate.

We could go on indefinitely building more and more complex circuits from transistors, but as it turns out we don't have to. In fact, transistors will hardly be mentioned again in this book. The AND, OR, and NOT gates we have built from them will provide the basis for all further work. These gates can already be said to perform simple computations, in the sense that they manipulate bits according to certain rules. We will see

First Input	Second Input	Output of AND Gate
on	on	on
on	off	off
off	on	off
off	off	off

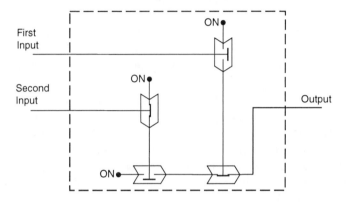

Figure 1.6. *A table specifying the behavior of an* AND *gate, a circuit with two inputs and one output. The diagram shows how an* AND *gate can be constructed from four transistors. In the diagram, the first input is* on, *the second is* off, *and the output is* off, *as specified in the table. You can check that the other three lines in the table are also satisfied.*

that every computation that a computer needs to do can be performed by a circuit put together out of AND, OR, and NOT gates.

The circuits we will build will be very complex. Fortunately, their complexity is structured; that is, complex circuits (like complex data structures) can be viewed as made up of simpler components, which can themselves be made of even simpler components and so on, until the process bottoms out on a level where the components are trivial. In the case of data, the trivial components are individual bits; for circuits, the trivial components are transistors. We have already taken the first step towards complexity by assembling transistors into gates. In Chapters 2 and 3, we will build more and more complex circuits, one (reasonably) easy step at a time, until in the end we see how to build an entire computer.

For now, you should carry away a sense that what's going on inside a computer is a complex flow of zeros and ones, representing data, being manipulated by circuits under the control of other zeros and ones, representing program instructions, with all this activity adding up to useful and meaningful computations—and you should at least be starting to believe that eventually you'll be able to understand the whole process.

1.3. Instructions, Subroutines, etc.

If computers are complex circuits that manipulate data under the direction of programs, then there is one more topic that belongs in this introductory chapter: What are programs and how can they be constructed?

We have already encountered the rather vague idea that programs are lists of instructions, and we have seen that the most primitive program instructions are patterns of bits called machine language. To really understand programs you need to know (1) what types of things machine language instructions can do and (2) what methods are available for building complex programs, starting with simple machine language instructions as a base.

1.3.1. Instructions, Decisions, and Loops.

Although different computers can have very different machine languages, there are certain generalizations that can be made. Every machine language, for example, must include instructions that tell the CPU to perform basic operations such as addition and subtraction. Also required are instructions that move data back and forth between memory, where it is stored, and the CPU, where all calculations are performed. These commands need some way of picking out particular pieces of data in memory. Recall that memory is made up of numbered locations, so picking out data just means specifying which memory location it is in. Typically, a machine language instruction has two parts, a binary code number specifying what operation is to be performed, and a number (also represented in base two) indicating the location of the data to be operated on.

While it is not universal, one common way of building a CPU is to provide it with an *accumulator*. The accumulator provides memory inside the CPU for one piece of data. (Here, "piece of data" means a certain number of bits; the number depends on the computer but is typically thirty-two or sixteen.) An instruction for moving data from memory into the CPU would then say, in effect, "Copy the data from memory location N into the accumulator," where N is the location number included as part of the instruction. Similarly, the machine language would have an instruction that says, "Copy the contents of the accumulator into the memory at location N (replacing what's there now)."

Instructions for arithmetic operations also use the accumulator. An addition instruction, for example, specifies just one address in memory, where one of the numbers to be added is to be found; it is assumed that the other number to be added is already in the accumulator. After the numbers are added, the answer replaces the former value in the accumulator. Thus, adding two numbers together requires three instructions: one to copy the first number from memory into the accumulator, one to add the second number to the accumulator, and finally one to copy the answer from the accumulator back into memory. (The name of the accumulator comes from the fact that it is used to "accumulate" the answer in a step by step computation.)

Besides instructions to move data around and instructions to perform operations on data, there is just one more essential type of machine language instruction that you need to know about: Instructions that change the value in the program counter.

Recall that the CPU uses the program counter to keep track of where it is in the program it is executing. The program counter contains the location in memory of the next instruction in the program to be executed. Now, if all the CPU could do is move down the program at the rate of a few million instructions per second, it would run out of program pretty quickly! It must be able to reuse the same set of instructions over and over. In fact, much of the power of a computer comes from this ability to repeat a task over and over without human intervention. A list of instructions that the computer cycles through more than once is called a *loop*.

The solution is simple. The machine language can include a *jump instruction* whose effect is to change the value stored in the program counter. Since the only way the CPU knows which instruction to execute next is to look at the value stored in the program counter, a jump instruction—by changing that value—says in effect, "Take the next instruction to be executed from memory location N," where N is the (binary) number included as part of the jump instruction. The execution of the program will then continue automatically from the new location, at least until another jump instruction is encountered. A loop can be implemented by putting a jump instruction at the end of the loop to transfer execution back to its beginning.[5]

---

[5] Note again the mechanicalness of all this. Although we might say that the jump instruction *means* "jump to a new location," the way the jump happens

A variation of the jump instruction called a ***conditional jump*** provides another of the computer's essential abilities, by allowing a program to make ***decisions*** between alternative courses of actions, depending on circumstances. A conditional jump changes the value of the program counter only if a certain condition holds. The condition to be tested is built into the instruction, so that a different instruction must be included in the machine language for each type of test it allows. The tests are of a very simple type, such as checking whether the value in the accumulator represents a binary number greater than zero. Such a conditional jump instruction would mean, "If the number in the accumulator is greater than zero, then take the next instruction to be executed from memory location N (and otherwise continue as usual)."

Such a test can be more useful than it might appear at first, if the number in the accumulator is the result of some meaningful calculation. On your tax return, you might see the instructions, "Subtract line 60 from line 53. If the result is greater than zero, send in a check for this amount; otherwise you are entitled to a refund." This could easily be paraphrased in three machine language instructions as something like: "Get the number from memory location 53; subtract the number in location 60; if the answer is greater than zero, then go to the instruction in location number 1375 (or wherever the program for sending in a check is to be found)."[6]

Conditional jumps also play an important role in loops. If they did not exist, the computer would have to continue in the loop forever. In practice, the instructions in the loop would include at least one conditional jump to some memory location outside the loop. Each time through the loop, the condition will be checked; if the test is satisfied, the jump will take place, and the computer will break out of the loop.

1.3.2. Building Programs. The capabilities of individual machine language instructions are extremely limited. Building a program to perform some complex task from such primitive components seems a

---

is entirely automatic. The jump instruction is fetched from memory into the CPU; the resulting activity in the CPU causes a new value to replace the current value of the program counter; when the CPU goes to fetch the next instruction to execute, it takes that instruction from the location indicated by the program counter, just as it always does. The CPU doesn't "know" that it has jumped to a new location.

[6] Perhaps people have trouble filling out tax returns because the instructions for them are more appropriate for computers. People, fortunately for our dinner-table conversation, don't think much like computers.

daunting prospect. I'm sure by now you can guess the solution: Complex tasks can be decomposed into simpler tasks, which themselves might be capable of further decomposition, until the process bottoms out in trivial operations. Although you might find it unlikely now, for any task that can be performed by a computer, this process of decomposition ultimately must bottom out at just the sort of trivial operations provided by machine language.

Loops and decisions provide two ways by which instructions can be "chunked" into larger, meaningful structures. From one point of view, a loop is just a bunch of bits, in which the bits at the end happen to encode a jump instruction. But to the person who designed the program, the instructions *inside* the loop perform some meaningful task, and the loop as a whole performs the slightly more complicated task: "Do *this* [the inside of the loop] over and over." Similarly, decisions can be used to build program chunks that say: "If such-and-such a condition holds, then do `this`; otherwise do `that`," where `this` and `that` are simpler chunks that perform some meaningful tasks.

Most machine languages provide one other mechanism, **subroutines**, to support the construction of programs through chunking. It is inevitable that a programmer will think of certain sequences of instructions in a program as performing certain subtasks in the overall operation of the program. Without subroutines, this breakdown of tasks into subtasks would exist only in the mind of the programmer; with subroutines, it can be reflected in the physical structure of the program.

A subroutine is a list of instructions, which is stored beginning at some location in memory. (It could hardly be anything else.) What makes it special is the availability of a machine language instruction, which we can call **jump-to-subroutine**, that says in effect, "Go execute the subroutine that starts at memory location N, and after it is finished, return to the current location in the program and continue on from there." That is, when a jump-to-subroutine instruction occurs, the entire subroutine will be executed, and then the computer will return to the location in the program where the jump-to-subroutine instruction is located and continue on from there.[7]

---

[7] A jump-to-subroutine is similar to a simple jump to the start of the subroutine except that before the jump is executed, the current value of the program counter is stashed somewhere where it can be found when needed. Restoring the program counter to this value will, in effect, send the computer back to where it was when the subroutine was called. The subroutine must end with another new instruction called **return-from-subroutine**. The effect of this

Note what is happening here: The *single* jump-to-subroutine instruction acts as a stand-in for the *entire* subroutine. You can think of that single instruction as performing the entire task specified by the subroutine, no matter how complicated. It's almost as if a new instruction for performing that task has been added to the machine language. And of course, that's just how the programmer should think of it—the subroutine is a meaningful chunk which, once constructed, can be used as a building block in more complex structures.

Although machine language is the native language of the computer, most computer programmers never write a program in machine language. They write instead in what are called **high-level languages**, such as BASIC and Pascal. The programs they write must be translated into machine language before the computer can execute them, but the translation is itself an automatic process that is done by computer programs called **compilers**. So, the programmer really has no contact with machine language at all—any more than a person using a word processor has contact with the structure of bits that represent a document in the computer.

Machine language tends to be a concern for people designing—or, like you, trying to understand—computers, rather than people who just use them or write programs for them. This book deals with machine language mostly in Chapter 3, where computer design is discussed. In Chapters 6 and 7, we will turn to programming itself as an object of study, and in those chapters we will use a high-level language. Even when we get to that point, though, your experience with machine language won't be wasted. Although high-level languages are much easier to work with than machine language, they are based on the same capabilities we have been discussing in this section, including moving data around, basic arithmetic operations, loops, decisions, and subroutines.

1.4. Handling Complexity

Computers are among the most complicated artifacts that people have ever constructed, and the programs that they execute can be even

---

instruction is to get the stashed program counter value and to restore the program counter to that value; this accomplishes the jump back to proper location. Note that since the computer "remembers" where it is supposed to return to after the subroutine finishes, the same subroutine can be called from several different places in the program. The computer will always to manage to return to the right place.

more complex. Any attempt to understand computers and programs on more than a superficial level must acknowledge that complexity, and must have some method for dealing with it.

We have now seen the same method in three different areas: computers, programs, and complex data structures. In fact, the method we have used may well be the only way people have for dealing with complexity.[8] A person seeking to build or to understand a complex structure must approach it at many different levels, one level at a time. These levels form a hierarchy of increasing complexity. Except for the bottommost level, items on each level are built from items on the level below. The step from one level up to the next must be simple enough to be easily grasped. The final result—on the top level—can be vastly complex yet still comprehensible. The applicability of this approach extends far beyond computer science.

On the bottom level of the hierarchy are things that are not constructed from components simpler than themselves, such as the bits that make up data structures, the transistors that make up computer circuits, or the machine language instructions that make up programs. Everything on higher levels is built out of these fundamental parts, but it is the way that the parts are structured, not just the parts themselves, that makes comprehension possible.

But wait—what's this about machine language instructions being on the bottom level? Aren't machine language instructions made up of bits? So can't they be decomposed into simpler parts? Actually, in practice, what constitutes the bottom level is a matter of *choice*. You are free to choose where to stop analyzing things into simpler parts, and you stop when you judge that further analysis is not necessary or helpful. In this chapter, I chose to take machine language instructions as the fundamental building blocks of programs, because I was interested in the way programs are actually executed by computers. Such a point of view would not be useful to someone writing a program in a high-level language; that person would rightly consider the instructions of the high-level language as basic, even though from the computer's point of view, such instructions must be further decomposed into machine language instructions before they can be executed.

---

[8] All right, I admit to exaggerating here. I can think of at least one other important method for dealing with complexity, that is, by explaining it as arising from the action of simple, generally mathematical laws. This is the canonical approach in physics, for example, but its application elsewhere, even in the other sciences, is more limited than is often appreciated.

The whole idea of levels of complexity is a resource available to you when you need it, not a rigid rule handed down from above that you are forced to obey. Using it well takes practice and ingenuity but offers rewards of great intellectual satisfaction. I think you will find that this is a source of much of the fascination that computers hold.

Chapter Summary

A computer computes by executing a *program*, which is a list of *machine language* instructions. All that the computer does is fetch an instruction from its memory, execute it, and then repeat the same process over and over. It does this *mechanically*: An instruction is a binary number, a pattern of zeros and ones, that causes certain wires in the computer to be turned on and off. These wires turn other wires on and off and so forth, until the net result is that an instruction has been executed—without any awareness or thought about what the instruction means.

Each individual machine language instruction is almost absurdly simple, and the only way that complex programs can be composed from such simple parts is by grouping together instructions into meaningful—to the programmer not the computer!—components, which can themselves be used as parts to build even more complex components, and so forth until programs of extraordinary complexity have been created. The methods available for building structures of instructions include *loops, decisions,* and *subroutines.*

This type of *structured complexity* has many applications besides programming. The data manipulated by a computer are one such application. On one level, all data are made up entirely of zeros and ones. But these are combined into meaningful structures of many different types, including *binary numbers, text, pictures,* and *sounds.*

The computer itself is another application. In one sense, a computer is just a pile of almost absurdly simple components, such as *transistors,* that individually can do very little. But these components are organized into more complex components, such as AND, OR, and NOT *gates.* As you we will see in the next two chapters, these can in turn be assembled, step-by-step, into a complete computer.

At the beginning of this chapter, I said that what computers do is compute. That should mean a lot more to you now than it did then. In a sense, the rest of this book is just filling in details in the picture presented in this chapter. That doesn't mean it will always be easy, but I hope you will find it to be a grand adventure.

Questions

1. The problem of converting a base 10 number to base 2 was not covered in the text. Here is an example of one method. Consider the number 53. Our object is to write 53 as a sum of powers of 2, with each power appearing at most once. Being familiar with the powers of 2 (see Figure 1.1), you recognize that 32 is the largest power of 2 that is less than or equal to 53, so that $53 = 32 + 21$. Similarly, we see that 16 is the largest power of 2 that is less than or equal to 21, so that $21 = 16 + 5$. Finally, $5 = 4 + 1$. To put it all together,

$$53 = 32 + 16 + 4 + 1$$
$$= 2^5 + 2^4 + 2^2 + 2^0$$
$$= 100000_2 + 10000_2 + 100_2 + 1_2$$
$$= 110101_2.$$

Apply this procedure to several other base 10 numbers. Discuss why this method works. Why is it necessary at each step to choose the *largest* possible power of two?

2. When we counted the number of binary numbers with k bits, including possible leading zeros, we found that there are 2^k of them. To be sure you understand this analysis, you might consider a related problem from biology. A molecule of DNA is simply a sequence of simpler molecules called nucleotides. There are four nucleotides, represented as A, T, C, and G. A complete DNA molecule corresponds to a string of such letters, such as AATCCGAC. The number of molecules of DNA containing exactly k nucleotides is thus the same as the number of sequences of k letters, where each letter is A, T, C, or G. How many such sequences are there, and *why*?

3. In a circuit with two inputs and one output, there are four ways to set the input values: on/on, on/off, off/on, and off/off. A table to describe the behavior of such a circuit therefore has four rows, with each row specifying the output for one of these combinations of inputs. Now consider a circuit with k input wires and one output wire. How many different possible ways are there to set the k input wires, and why? Again, if you want to make a table describing the behavior of such a circuit, this is how many rows you will need. Now, here is a harder question: How many different ways are there to fill in the output values in such a table? That is, counting only their input/output behavior, how many different circuits are there with k inputs and one output?

4. A *three-input AND gate* is a circuit with three input wires and one output wire which behaves as follows: If all three of the inputs are on, then the output is on; in all other cases, the output is off. Show how such a circuit can be built directly from six transistors. It is also possible to build the circuit from two normal, two-input AND gates; try to figure out how. Discuss advantages and disadvantages of these two approaches: building the circuit directly from transistors, or building it from two-input AND gates.

5. A subroutine is just a list of machine language instructions. It is possible for that list to include a jump-to-subroutine instruction, which will cause the second subroutine to be executed as if it were part of the first. This possibility makes it a bit tricky to find a place to stash the old program counter value while the subroutine is executing. Why is that? Can you think of any solution? Explain why it is essential for a subroutine to be able to make use of other subroutines, given the role that subroutines play in building complex programs.

6. Computer science is by no means the only field where complexity is dealt with by breaking complex structures into simpler components. In music, for example, every piece of music is made up of individual notes, but there are several levels of structure between these two extremes: measures, themes, and movements, for example. Make a list of different fields and terms they use to describe levels of structured complexity.

Chapter 2

Teaching Silicon to Compute

IN THE NINETEENTH century, an English mathematician named Charles Babbage designed what would have been the first computer, if it had ever been built. It would have been made from metal parts—rods, levers, gears—and powered by steam. Babbage did produce a working automatic calculator, similar in conception to his grand design. One of his colleagues said of it that "the wondrous pulp and fibre of the brain had been substituted by brass and iron; he had taught wheelwork to think" [Swade, p. 88].

Modern computers are built from transistors rather than "wheelwork," and the foundation of their calculating ability is the silicon from which those transistors are made, rather than brass and iron. But we can still understand the awe that a person might feel on first encountering a mechanical device that displays capabilities similar to our own highest reasoning skills. Whether or not such devices actually *think*, they certainly perform difficult computations. The controversial question of thinking machines is left to a later chapter on artificial intelligence. For now, we consider how it can be that silicon can be taught to *compute*.

Over the course of the next two chapters, we will answer this question by designing a working computer. The device we design will be much simpler than real computers in use today, though not all that much simpler than the first working computers built in the 1940s. In this chapter, starting from the three types of logic gates introduced in Chapter 1, we will build an ***arithmetic-logic unit***—a circuit that can perform addition, subtraction, and other operations on binary numbers. Later we will see how logic gates also can be used to construct memory circuits. The circuits we build in this chapter will be used in the computer designed in Chapter 3.

The design of circuits built from logic gates has surprising connections to a branch of mathematics called ***propositional logic*** or ***Boolean algebra***. We will use some basic ideas and notation from this branch of mathematics, without covering it in full detail.

2.1. Logical Circuitry

In the common usage of the term, a ***logical*** person is someone who, like Sherlock Holmes or *Star Trek*'s Mr. Spock, reasons from facts to conclusions using infallible laws of deduction (rather than fallible human emotion). If the facts are true and the rules are followed correctly, there can be no doubt that the conclusions are true.

As shown by the image of the emotionless Mr. Spock, there is something machinelike about logic, and it is perhaps no surprise that logic should have some role in the operation of computers. More surprising, perhaps, is the extent of the role. In a very real sense, logic is all that computers do.

In its simpler applications, logic is easy. Suppose I were to tell you that the statements "Mozart wrote operas" and "Venus is heavier than the Earth" are both true. You could then immediately draw the logical conclusions that the statement "Mozart did not write operas" is false, and that "Mozart wrote operas and Venus is heavier than the Earth" is true. If I then confessed that I lied and that actually, Venus is not heavier than Earth, you would reverse your second conclusion.

Now, these are not great feats of intellect, but having read the previous chapter, you know that very complex structures can be built from trivial beginnings.

Suppose we start with any two statements whose truth or falsity is already known. Rather than pick specific examples, let's just give them names, say A and B. (If you like, you can think of A as standing for "Mozart wrote operas" and B for "Venus is heavier than Earth.") We can then form the statements "A AND B" and "A OR B." Playing a

A	B	A AND B	A OR B	NOT A
true	true	true	true	false
true	false	false	true	false
false	true	false	true	true
false	false	false	false	true

A	B	A AND B	A OR B	NOT A
on	on	on	on	off
on	off	off	on	off
off	on	off	on	on
off	off	off	off	on

A	B	A AND B	A OR B	NOT A
1	1	1	1	0
1	0	0	1	0
0	1	0	1	1
0	0	0	0	1

Figure 2.1. *The logical operations* **and,** **or** *and* **not,** *defined in three equivalent tables. The top table is given in terms of the usual logical values* true *and* false. *The second table, simply replaces these with* on *and* off, *which are appropriate for logic gates thought of as physical circuits. Finally, the third table uses the zeros and ones that are appropriate for logic gates as manipulators of bits inside a computer. You should be able to switch easily among these points of view.*

little loosely with English grammar, we will also say that "NOT A" is a statement, meaning, "It is not the case that A."[1]

Since we know the truth or falsity of A and B, we can immediately deduce whether A AND B is true or false. There are only four cases to consider. Either A and B are both true, A is true and B is false, A is false and B is true, or both are false. Only in the first of these cases is

---

[1] A reminder about the power of mathematics, even in something as simple as notation: By using arbitrary names like A and B instead of specific examples, we can deal with all the infinitely many different possible examples at once. Furthermore, since nothing is known about A and B except whether they are true or false, it is made perfectly clear that for the purposes of propositional logic, all true statements are equivalent, as are all false statements.

the compound statement A AND B true. The statements A OR B and NOT A can be dealt with similarly. The truth values for these statements in all possible cases are shown in the first table in Figure 2.1. This table is worth memorizing. (The English word "or" is a source of some possible confusion. As shown in the table, we take A OR B to be equivalent to "A or B or *both*.")

2.1.1. Propositional Logic.   We have here the whole foundation for propositional logic. A *proposition* is a statement that can be either true or false. Propositional logic deals with *atomic propositions*, represented by individual symbols such as A or B, and all the *compound propositions* that can be constructed from them using the *operators* AND, OR, and NOT.[2] Complexity arises because compound propositions, once formed, can then be used as pieces in larger compound propositions.

In ordinary English, from the three statements "Today is Monday," "Today is Friday," and "I can't work," any number of compound statements can be formed. For example:

- Today is Monday or today is Friday, and I can't work.
- Today is not Monday and I can't work.
- Today is Monday and today is Friday and I can't work.
- Today is Monday and I can't work, or today is not Friday and I can't work.

If we represent the three original statements by A, B, and C, then these compound statements can be expressed as the compound propositions

- $(A$ OR $B)$ AND C
- (NOT $A)$ AND C
- A AND B AND C
- $(A$ AND $C)$ OR $((\text{NOT } B)$ AND $C)$

The parentheses are used here to avoid ambiguity; they indicate which part of the expression should be evaluated first. There is a difference between the statements "$(A$ OR $B)$ AND C" and "A OR $(B$ AND $C)$." (If it happens to be Monday and I *can* work, the first of these would be false, while the second would be true.) English has no foolproof method of avoiding such ambiguity. In the sentences above, I have tried to use punctuation to indicate the intended meaning. Logic has no room for such ambiguity.

---

[2] Statements of the form "If A then B" play an important role in logic. However, we can do without such statements since, in propositional logic, "If A then B" is defined to be equivalent to "(NOT A) OR B."

Mathematicians typically avoid ambiguity in a rather curious way. They say that officially, parentheses are *always* required, but then they immediately give rules for leaving them out in certain cases. The rules determine which operations are done first when parentheses are omitted; in such cases, NOT has first precedence, followed by AND, with OR having the lowest precedence. For example, given the proposition NOT A AND C, the operator NOT has precedence, so the proposition means "(NOT A) AND C" rather than "NOT $(A$ AND $C)$."[3] Similarly, in the fourth example above, all the parentheses could be omitted without changing the meaning. On the other hand, the parentheses in $(A$ OR $B)$ AND C are required; without them, A OR B AND C would be interpreted as A OR $(B$ AND $C)$, since AND has precedence over OR. Generally, it is better to avoid confusion by putting in parentheses even when they are not required.

As a final technical point, consider A AND B AND C. Should this mean "$(A$ AND $B)$ AND C" or "A AND $(B$ AND $C)$"? Here, it turns out that the ambiguity doesn't matter. The two alternatives give the same answer, no matter what the values of A, B, and C. The answer is true only when all three of A, B, and C are true; it is false in all other cases. The general rule is that when AND's are strung together, the order in which they are evaluated doesn't matter. The same rule applies to a string of OR's. A OR B OR C is true if *any one* of A, B, and C is true, and is false if all three are false.

2.1.2. Gates and Circuits.   Now of course, you remember encountering AND, OR, and NOT in Chapter 1. In that chapter, they were used to name certain circuits—the AND gate, OR gate, and NOT gate—constructed out of transistors. You can now see that when we built these circuits, we were "teaching silicon" to perform the most elementary computations of logic. This is just a matter of point of view. Input and output wires in a circuit have two states, on and off. You have already seen that on and off can be interpreted as standing for the binary digits one and zero, but this is just an interpretation. There is nothing to stop us from decreeing, when it is convenient, that on is going to stand for the logical value true, while off represents false.

When the inputs and output of an AND gate are interpreted in this way, it becomes an implementation of the logical meaning of the word *and*. Suppose that A is a statement which is known to be true, while B

---

[3] The proposition NOT $(A$ AND $C)$ is hard to express in English. You would have to say something like "It is not the case that both A and B hold."

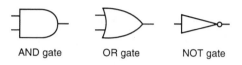

AND gate　　　　OR gate　　　　NOT gate

Figure 2.2. *Standard pictures for the three types of logic gate. Input wires are shown sticking out of the left side of the gate, output wires to the right. Larger circuits can be built out of gates by connecting output wires from some gates to input wires of others.*

is a statement known to be false, and suppose you want to know whether A AND B is true. Instead of working it out for yourself, you can use an AND gate to compute the answer! Just use the first input of the gate to represent A and the second to represent B. Since A is **true**, turn the first input **on**, and since B is false, turn the second input **off**. Sure enough, the output of the gate will be **off**, telling you correctly that A AND B is false. No matter what the truth values of A and B, the AND gate will give the correct answer. Similarly, OR and NOT gates implement the words *or* and *not*, as shown in Figure 2.1.

Because of their relationship to logic, AND, OR, and NOT gates are referred to collectively as **logic gates**, and circuits that are built from them are called **logic circuits**. In diagrams of such circuits, standard pictures are used for the three types of gates. These pictures are shown in Figure 2.2.

I will admit once again that the computation performed by an individual gate is not very impressive, but it really *is* an example of a computation, defined as the mechanical manipulation of symbols. (It is mechanical because the output is determined automatically, without thought, from the inputs. It is dealing with symbols because the inputs and outputs are really just presence or absence of current on wires; it is merely an interpretation to say they are standing for the truth or falsity of certain statements.) By combining a number of gates into a larger circuit, we will be able to teach silicon do more impressive computations.

Circuits can do any computation that can be expressed in propositional logic. In fact, any compound proposition can be used as a blueprint for a logic circuit that can compute the value of the proposition. A compound proposition is built up from atomic propositions using the operations AND, OR, and NOT. The corresponding circuit is built up in a parallel way. Each different atomic proposition corresponds to an input wire of the circuit. These input wires can be turned on or off to indicate

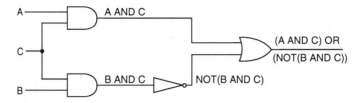

Figure 2.3. *The circuit corresponding to the proposition (A* AND *C)* OR *(*NOT *(B* AND *C)). The output of each logic gate is labeled with the expression that the gate computes.*

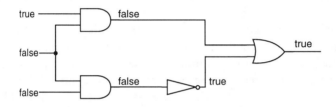

Figure 2.4. *The circuit corresponding to the proposition (A* AND *C)* OR *(*NOT *(B* AND *C)), labeled to show the computation it performs when A is* true *and both B, and C are* false*.*

whether the corresponding atomic propositions are true or false. Each AND, OR, and NOT in the proposition corresponds to a logic gate in the circuit. The structure of the expression determines how these logic gates should be wired together. Finally, the output of the circuit represents the value computed for the expression, depending on the values of the inputs.

The only part of this that might give you trouble is figuring out how to wire together all the logic gates in the circuit. Just remember that the inputs to each gate represent values already computed; the output combines these input values into a more complicated expression. Consider, for example the proposition

$$(A \text{ AND } C) \text{ OR } (\text{NOT } (B \text{ AND } C)).$$

A circuit to compute this expression is shown in Figure 2.3. The inputs to this circuit correspond to A, B, and C, the atomic propositions in the expression. (Note that even though C occurs twice in the expression, there is only one input wire for it; a wire can be connected to the inputs of several gates.) When building such a circuit, it might be easiest to work backwards from the output to the input. It is easy to identify the operator that produces the final answer. (If the expression is fully parenthesized, it is the only operator that is not nested inside parentheses.) In the example, this operator is OR, so the circuit contains an OR gate whose output is the overall output of the circuit. The inputs to this OR gate must represent "A AND C" and "NOT (B AND C)". You can now build smaller circuits to represent each of these expressions and connect their outputs to the inputs of the OR gate. Note that in the circuit for NOT (B AND C), the NOT gate produces the final answer, and it gets its input from the AND gate.

At this point, given any proposition, you should be able to construct a circuit that computes it. Also, given specific values for the inputs to the circuit, you should be able to trace by hand, step by step, the computation that the circuit performs to produce the resulting value of the proposition. A sample computation is shown in Figure 2.4. It would be useful for you to feel comfortable doing such computations whether the values are expressed as true/false, as on/off, or as 0/1. The tables in Figure 2.1 contain all the information you need.

2.1.3. Circuits Made to Order. It might be aesthetically pleasing that there is a relationship between circuits and logical expressions; but to convince you that that relationship is useful, I will have to demonstrate some application to building practical circuits that might find use in a computer.

Suppose you know the exact behavior you want in a circuit. That is, for every possible combination of inputs, you can specify what output should be produced. Is it always possible to build a circuit with the desired behavior? The answer is yes. This can be shown using propositional logic. Furthermore, logic can be used as a tool in designing the circuit, based on its behavior.

Let's start with a simple example in which you have an English description of a circuit's behavior. Suppose you need a circuit with two inputs and one output, such that the output is true when the inputs are *the same*. Let's call the inputs A and B. We can rephrase the requirement as saying that the output should be true if either A and B are both true or if A and B are both false. This is starting to sound more like logic: The output is true if (A is true AND B is true) OR (A is false AND B is false). Now, here is a slightly subtle point. The statement "A is true" is equivalent to the statement "A" by itself. (Just check that they always have the same truth value.) Similarly, "A is false"

A	B	C	output
true	true	true	false
true	true	false	false
true	false	true	false
true	false	false	true
false	true	true	false
false	true	false	true
false	false	true	true
false	false	false	false

A AND NOT B AND NOT C

NOT A AND B AND NOT C

NOT A AND NOT B AND C

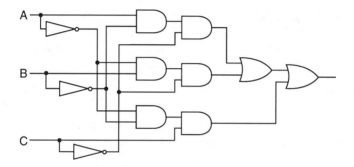

Figure 2.5. *Given any desired input/output behavior for a circuit, it is possible to construct a circuit with that behavior. Here, the table specifies the desired behavior for a circuit with three inputs and one output. Beneath the table is the corresponding circuit. You can check that it has the specified behavior in all cases. The construction of the circuit is described in the text.* Note: *In this and all following diagrams, wires that cross each other do not actually intersect unless a small circle is drawn at the crossing.*

is equivalent to "NOT A". So, finally, we reduce the description of the circuit to saying that the output is given by

$(A$ AND $B)$ OR $((\text{NOT } A)$ AND $(\text{NOT } B))$.

From this description of the output, the circuit can be built immediately.

Translating from English to logic is not always so easy. And errors can easily creep in during the translation, so that it is a good idea to check that any circuit you build in this way gives the desired output for all possible combinations of inputs. Fortunately, there is a more mechanical procedure that is guaranteed to give a correct circuit.

The behavior of a circuit can be described in a table listing all possible combinations of inputs and the resulting output that the circuit should produce in each case. An example of such a table is shown in Figure 2.5. Here, there are three inputs, but the same principle applies no matter how many inputs there are.

How can such a table be used to design a circuit that has the input/output behavior specified by the table? It's just a matter of describing the table "logically"! We really only have to look at the lines in which the specified output is **true**. In English, we could say that the output should be **true** whenever the inputs are those specified in any one of these lines. To make this look more like logic, we would say, in the example from Figure 2.5, that the output is **true** if

(the inputs are those on the fourth line)
OR (the inputs are those on the sixth line)
OR (the inputs are those on the seventh line).

All we need to do is translate "the inputs are those on the nth line" into logic.

Any line in the table specifies that certain of the inputs are true and others are false. That is, it says something like

A is **true** and B is **false** and....

Of course, this can be rephrased in logical notation as

A AND (NOT B) AND....

In Figure 2.5, a translation of the input conditions into a logical expression is shown to the right of each line where the output is **true**. The specification for the entire circuit is obtained by stringing theses conditions together with OR's:

(A AND NOT B AND NOT C)
OR (NOT A AND B AND NOT C)
OR (NOT A AND NOT B AND C)

The circuit built from this expression is also shown in Figure 2.5. The behavior of this circuit happens to have a simple English description: The output is **true** if exactly one of the inputs is **true**. It would be difficult to translate this description directly into a circuit, but it is easy to use it to fill in an input/output table and then to use the table as a guide for building the circuit.

This method can be easily extended to building circuits with more than one output wire. It is only necessary to design a separate circuit for each output.

The important point here is that this method will always work. Given any input/output table, we can always build a circuit that gives the specified output for each possible combination of inputs. To convince yourself that the method works in all cases, consider the expression we constructed corresponding to one line of the table (such as "A AND NOT B AND NOT C" in the example). The circuit specified by this expression is one whose output is **true** for one and only one combination of inputs—the one given in that line of the table. For any other set of inputs, the output value will be **false**.

Now, whenever outputs from several circuits are combined through OR gates, the final output will be **true** if, and only if, at least one of the outputs from the smaller circuits is **true**. The complete circuit we build from the table is constructed in just this way—from smaller circuits, corresponding to each line where the desired output is **true**, with their outputs combined through OR gates. So the overall output of the circuit is **true** precisely for the specified combinations of inputs.

2.1.4. The Laws of Thought. The method described above for building a circuit with a given behavior will often produce very large circuits, much larger in fact than they need to be. It is certainly possible for two circuits that look very different to have the same input/output behavior. In practical situations, the circuit that is simpler—for example, the circuit with fewer gates—would be preferred. In general, finding the simplest possible circuit with a given behavior is a very difficult problem, but some help towards simplifying circuits comes from their association with propositional logic.

In 1854, the mathematician George Boole published a book he called *An Investigation into the Laws of Thought, on Which Are Founded the Mathematical Theories of Logic and Probability.* It is this book that established logic as a part of mathematics. Boole developed an *algebra* of logic, which today is known as ***Boolean algebra***. He designed a mathematical system in which the logical values **true** and **false** would play a role similar to the role played by numbers in ordinary algebra.

You have already seen the notation of Boolean algebra (somewhat modified for our purposes): expressions built up out of "variables" like A and B and the "operators" AND, OR, and NOT. But algebra consists of more than a notation for writing down expressions. It also includes rules for manipulating those expressions. These rules are Boole's "laws of thought." It would perhaps have surprised him to find out that his algebra would one day play a major role in designing circuitry for what

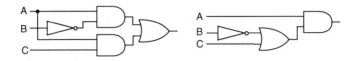

Figure 2.6. *The circuit on the right is obtained from the one on the left by applying the distributive law, (P* AND *Q) OR (P* AND *R)* ≡ *P* AND *(Q* OR *R). The circuit on the left corresponds to the expression (A* AND NOT *B) OR (A* AND *C). In this application, P stands for A, Q for (*NOT *B), and R for C. The circuits are equivalent in that they will always give the same outputs for the same inputs, but the circuit on the right has one fewer gate.*

have been called "thinking machines." But then again, perhaps not; Boole would have understood that in giving a mathematical formulation to logic he was making it possible for logic to be applied mechanically. His algebra can be seen as an attempt to make it possible to reason by computing.

Of particular interest to us are rules that can be used to **simplify** expressions. Two expressions are equivalent if they have the same value for all possible values of the atomic propositions they contain. To simplify an expression means to find an equivalent expression that is shorter than the original. Since the expressions of Boolean algebra correspond to logic circuits, simplifying an expression is the same as finding a smaller circuit with the same input/output behavior.

As a trivial example, consider the algebraic fact that for any proposition P, the expression NOT (NOT P) is equivalent to P by itself. Each NOT reverses the value it is applied to; two consecutive reversals have no net effect. (Note that this applies whether P is an atomic proposition or is itself a complicated expression.) When applied to circuits, this means that two consecutive NOT gates can be eliminated from a circuit—and replaced by a connecting wire—without changing the behavior of the circuit.

Another, less obvious, example is the so-called **distributive law**, which says that for any propositions P, Q, and R,

$$(P \text{ AND } Q) \text{ OR } (P \text{ AND } R) \equiv P \text{ AND } (Q \text{ OR } R)$$

where I have introduced the symbol ≡ to mean "is equivalent to." You can check that this rule is valid by checking that it holds for all possible values of P, Q, and R. Figure 2.6 shows an example of applying this rule to a circuit. Note that the net effect is a reduction in the size of the circuit by one AND gate.

There are many other rules of Boolean algebra that can be helpful in reducing the number of gates in a circuit. I have listed some useful rules in Figure 2.7, but nothing in the rest of this text will require that you memorize these rules or that you develop skill in using them. It is not my purpose here to teach you Boolean algebra. My intent has been to demonstrate that it is possible in principle to build a circuit with any specified input/output behavior, and to indicate the power of Boolean algebra as a tool in building the circuit and as an aid in reducing the size of the circuit without changing its behavior.[4]

2.2. Arithmetic

We are now ready to move on to designing real computer circuits. Any computer must be able to do arithmetic. In this section, we will design circuits to perform some of the basic arithmetic operations.

Recall that numbers in a computer are represented in the base two. Up till now, we have mostly thought of the inputs and outputs of circuits as having the values on and off, or true and false. From now on, it will be more appropriate to think in terms of ones and zero, since the circuits we build are meant to manipulate binary numbers.

To understand these circuits, you will have to learn something about arithmetic with binary numbers. Furthermore, there are certain peculiarities of computer arithmetic that arise because the CPU has a limit on the size of the numbers it can deal with. For example, the CPU might be built to work only with sixteen-bit numbers (possibly including some leading zeros). If you have ever used a calculator to multiply two large numbers and gotten the answer Error, you know what this means: There will be calculations that the CPU cannot do correctly because the answer is too large. We will need to keep in mind the fact

---

[4] One final note on simplifying circuits, which might amount to stating the obvious: When an expression occurs more than once as part of a longer expression, it is not necessary to compute that smaller expression more than once. For example, in

$$((A \text{ OR } B) \text{ AND } C) \text{ OR } (\text{NOT } (A \text{ OR } B)),$$

the subexpression $(A \text{ OR } B)$ occurs twice. A single OR gate can be used to compute the value of $A \text{ OR } B$, and the output of that gate can be used to provide this value at both points where it is needed in the circuit.

Commutative Laws:
> P AND $Q \equiv Q$ AND P
> P OR $Q \equiv Q$ OR P

Associative Laws:
> $(P$ AND $Q)$ AND $R \equiv P$ AND $(Q$ AND $R)$
> $(P$ OR $Q)$ OR $R \equiv P$ OR $(Q$ OR $R)$

Distributive Laws:
> P AND $(Q$ OR $R) \equiv (P$ AND $Q)$ OR $(P$ AND $R)$
> P OR $(Q$ AND $R) \equiv (P$ OR $Q)$ AND $(P$ OR $R)$

DeMorgan's Laws:
> NOT $(P$ AND $Q) \equiv ($NOT $P)$ OR $($NOT $Q)$
> NOT $(P$ OR $Q) \equiv ($NOT $P)$ AND $($NOT $Q)$

Other Laws:
> NOT $($NOT $P) \equiv P$
> P AND $($NOT $P) \equiv$ `false`
> P OR $($NOT $P) \equiv$ `true`

Figure 2.7. *Some laws of Boolean algebra. P, Q, and R are arbitrary propositions.*

that all calculations are to be done with numbers with a limited, fixed number of bits. For definiteness, we will assume the number of bits is sixteen. We could just as easily use eight-bit or thirty-two-bit numbers, and most real computers allow for all these cases by providing separate machine language instructions for each type of number.[5]

I should remark that we know before we begin that it is certainly possible to build circuits to do arithmetic (assuming we already know

---

[5] The use of sixteen-bit numbers is quite common. This allows only 65,535 different numbers to be represented, which is really not a lot. Some serious real-world errors have occurred because of failure to take this limited size into account. Peter G. Neumann in his column *Inside Risks* in the January 1991 issue of the *Communications of the ACM* discusses a plague of computer failures that occurred on September 19, 1989, affecting even the Pennsylvania Wildcard Lotto computer. It seems that these computers represented the current date as the number of days after January 1, 1900. On September 19, 1989, they ran out of bits for this representation. (The *Inside Risks* column is a regular feature of the *Communications of the ACM* and is a good source for cautionary tales about putting too much trust in computers.)

how to get the answers by hand). Suppose we want a circuit that adds two sixteen-bit numbers. That is, we want a circuit whose input represents the two numbers to be added, and whose output gives the sum of those two numbers. Our circuit will need thirty-two input wires, one for each bit of the two numbers to be added, and sixteen output wires to represent the sixteen-bit sum. Given any possible input, we know (or so we are assuming) what the output should be. All we need to do is to fill in a table to represent all the possible inputs and outputs and then build a circuit from it, as described in the previous section, right?

Right—at least in principle. We know that a working addition circuit exists because one *could* be built in the way described. However, in practice, it is not so easy. With thirty-two input wires, a table that includes all the possible combinations of input values would have 2^{32} rows. That's over four billion. Obviously, we need a different approach. As you should expect after reading Chapter 1, our approach will be to construct simpler components that will ultimately be assembled into a complete addition circuit.

2.2.1. Adding Binary Numbers. Before we begin building circuits that do addition, though, you need to know how to add binary numbers by hand. The process is really no different from adding base-ten numbers, except that it's a lot easier. To add base-ten numbers, you must first memorize the sum of each pair of decimal digits: "3 + 5 is 8," "6 + 9 is 5 and carry 1," and so forth through all the other ninety-eight possibilities. In the base two, the only digits are zero and one, and there are only four basic sums you have to memorize:

$$0_2 + 0_2 = 0_2$$
$$0_2 + 1_2 = 1_2$$
$$1_2 + 0_2 = 1_2$$
$$1_2 + 1_2 = 10_2 \quad \text{(or ``0 and carry 1'')}.$$

These are all the rules needed to add two one-bit binary numbers. Note that the answer can be a two-bit number. It will be convenient to add a zero to the front of the first three answers above, so that all the answers have two digits. We call the two digits of the answer the ***carry-digit*** and the ***sum-digit***. In the first three cases, the carry-digit is zero. In the last case, the sum digit is zero and the carry digit is one.

These rules are very simple, simple enough to implement easily in a circuit. What we want is a circuit with two inputs, representing the two digits to be added, and two outputs, representing the two digits of their sum. Figure 2.8 shows a table of the possible inputs and the outputs

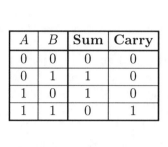

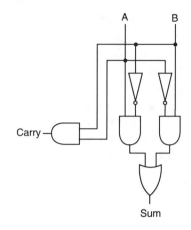

A	B	Sum	Carry
0	0	0	0
0	1	1	0
1	0	1	0
1	1	0	1

Figure 2.8. *A circuit that adds. The table shows the result of adding all possible pairs of binary digits, A and B. The answer is broken into two parts, a sum-digit and a carry-digit. The circuit on the right implements this table. It will compute the sum and carry for any combination of its two inputs.*

they should produce. This table of inputs and outputs is just like the ones we saw in the previous section, except that the values are given in terms of 1/0 instead of `true`/`false`. Applying the methods developed in the previous section to this table, we can write the outputs in terms of the inputs, A and B, as expressions of Boolean algebra:

sum $= ((\text{NOT } A) \text{ AND } B) \text{ OR } (A \text{ AND } (\text{NOT } B))$
carry $= A \text{ AND } B.$

Using these expressions as blueprints, we can build the desired circuit, as shown in the figure. The circuit we have built is called a *half-adder*. We will use it as a basis for constructing more complicated circuits.

The rules for adding single-digit numbers can be applied to longer numbers, using the method you learned in grade school: Write the numbers one above the other, and add the digits in each column; when the sum in one column produces a "carry," the carry should be added into the next column to the left. For example, you might write out the sum of the base ten numbers 3735 and 627 like this, writing any carry produced at the top of the column to which it is added:[6]

---

[6] Such sums can be computed by purely mechanical rules—which is why we can teach computers to add. Unfortunately, some people have been taught

$$\begin{array}{cccc} {}^{1}\;\;{}^{1} & & & {}^{1\,0\,1\,0} \\ 3735 & & & 3735 \\ \underline{627} & \text{or} & & \underline{0627} \\ 4362 & & & 4362 \end{array}$$

On the left, I have followed the usual practices of writing carries only when they are nonzero and of not writing leading zeros in numbers. For a computer, it is useful to regularize things by writing the zeros, as I have on the right.

Binary numbers can be added in the same way. Note that to find the sum of a column that includes a carry of 1 from the previous column, you have to know how to add *three* digits, not just two. The only really new rule for adding three digits is that $1_2 + 1_2 + 1_2 = 11_2$, or "1 and carry 1." With this in mind, here are a few sample additions in the base two:

$$\begin{array}{ccc} {}^{0\,1\,0\,0} & {}^{0\,1\,1\,1\,0} & {}^{1\,1\,1\,1\,0\,1\,0} \\ 1011 & 10111 & 01011101 \\ \underline{0010} & \underline{00011} & \underline{00110101} \\ 1101 & 11010 & 10010010 \end{array}$$

The next step in designing a circuit to perform binary additions is a *full adder*, which can compute the sum (and carry) of three binary digits. One way to build a full adder is from two half-adders. This design is based on the observation that three digits can be added by adding the first two digits, then adding the third digit to the result. The resulting circuit is shown in Figure 2.9. The three inputs represent the three digits to be added. The third input is called carry-in because it generally represents a carry from a previous column. The two outputs, sum and carry-out, represent the sum of the input digits. You should check that this circuit gives the correct outputs for all possible combinations of inputs. Note how it works: The first half-adder adds the first two digits, and then the sum-digit of the result is added to the carry-in by the second

---

these and other mechanical rules as if there were no meaningful justification for them. One way to see why the rules for addition work is to write out the sum as:

$$\begin{aligned} 3735 + 627 &= (3000 + 700 + 30 + 5) + (600 + 20 + 7) \\ &= 3000 + (700 + 600) + (30 + 20) + (5 + 7) \\ &= 3000 + 1300 + 50 + 12 \\ &= 3000 + 1000 + 300 + 50 + 10 + 2 \\ &= 4362. \end{aligned}$$

"Carrying" here is seen as rearranging the numbers so that units, tens, hundreds, etc., can be added separately.

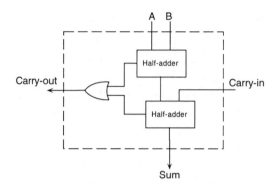

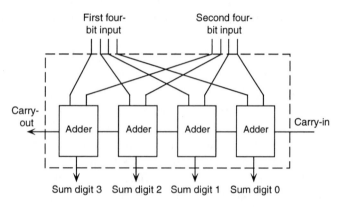

Figure 2.9. *A full adder constructed from two half-adders, and a four-bit-adder constructed from four full adders.*

half-adder. This gives the final sum digit for the full adder. A separate analysis is needed to determine what the carry-out should be, but you can check that the three-digit sum produces a carry of 1 exactly when either the first half-adder or the second half-adder produces a carry of 1. Thus the carry-out can be computed by an OR gate whose inputs are the carries from the two half-adders.

We are now, finally, ready to produce circuits to add multi-bit binary numbers. We will call a circuit that adds two k-bit numbers a *k-bit adder*.[7] A k-bit adder contains k full adders, one for each column in

---

[7] This circuit can be used to add numbers with "k bits or fewer." As usual, if a number has fewer than k bits, you just have to add some leading zeros to bring the number of bits up to k.

the sum. The first two inputs for each full adder come from digits in the numbers to be added. The carry-out produced for each column is simply used as the carry-in for the next column to the left. This leaves the carry-in for the rightmost full adder and the carry-out for the leftmost full adder unconnected. When adding two k-bit numbers, the rightmost carry-in should be set to zero. As for the leftmost carry-out, note that the sum of two k-bit numbers can contain $k + 1$ bits, if the carry-digit in the leftmost column is one. The value of the leftmost carry-out can be used to check whether this occurs; ordinarily, this would represent an error: an answer too large to be represented with the number of bits available.

As stated above, we are trying to design a computer that uses sixteen-bit numbers. That computer will include a 16-bit adder. A 4-bit adder is shown in Figure 2.9, since it is easier to draw, but clearly a 16-bit adder could easily be built in the same way. We have completed a significant step on our way to a working computer!

2.2.2. A Question of Time.

When I first saw a multi-bit adder, I was confused by one point which might be bothering you now. Suppose all the inputs are zero, so that all the outputs, including the carry-out wires, are off. Now imagine turning on the appropriate inputs to the circuit, to represent the two numbers to be added. At the moment you do so, all the carry-out wires will still be off, so it looks like the circuit will not compute the proper sum! In order to compute the sum, all the carries must be set correctly, but in fact, each of them is zero. What's wrong?

The problem with this analysis is that it ignores time (as I have been doing in all of our discussion of circuits so far). A logic gate is a physical device, which always takes some amount of time to change its state from on to off or vice versa. If you turn on one of the inputs to an OR gate, the output does not come on immediately; there is a definite time delay. A complete description of using an OR gate would say: Set the inputs to the desired values. *Wait long enough for the gate to change its state.* Then read the resulting output.

The same comment applies to any circuit built out of gates. The longer the path from the inputs to the outputs, the longer you have to wait to make sure that the effect of changing the input has had time to filter through to the output. If you check the output too soon, it might be wrong.

Let's see what really happens when you set the inputs of a multi-bit adder. At that moment, the output of the circuit does *not* necessarily represent the correct sum. After a short time, the rightmost adder has finished its calculation, and both the rightmost digit of the sum and the rightmost carry-out are correct. It is only now that all three inputs to the second adder—including its carry-in—are correct. After another short time for the second adder to finish calculating, the outputs of the second adder will be correct, and at that point, the third adder from the right will have the correct inputs. This process continues until all the digits of the sum have been correctly computed. So, our addition circuit does work correctly, but it takes some *time* to do so.

Bringing time into the picture allows us to improve our image of the activity inside a computer. Every computer has a clock which "ticks" millions of times per second. (You might have heard the speed of a computer described as so many **megahertz**. Each megahertz stands for one million ticks of the computer's clock per second.) This clock does more than keep time; it is the ticking of the clock that makes the computer go.

Before the clock ticks, all the gates in the computer are in some definite, steady state. The clock has one output wire, which is connected to the computer's circuits. As the clock ticks, it turns this wire on. This event can set off a whole cascade of activity, as gates connected to the clock wire change state, then gates connected to those gates change, and so forth. Eventually, though, the activity dies down, and once again, all the gates are in a steady state. One step of the computer's calculation has just been completed. Then, the clock ticks again, and the next step begins.[8]

2.2.3. Subtraction and Negative Numbers.
After designing a circuit to do addition, it is natural to try our hand at subtraction. When we do so, though, we are faced with an immediate problem. When you subtract a larger number from a smaller, the answer will be negative. We have never discussed how negative numbers can be represented in a computer. There is an obvious representation: Just add an extra bit to a number to indicate whether it is positive or negative, coding, say, "+" as a one and "−" as a zero. As it turns out, the representation we use is nothing like this.

---

[8] Note that the time between ticks must be long enough for the burst of activity set off by the clock's tick to settle down. This is why you can't make a computer run faster simply by using a faster clock. If the clock ticks too soon, the computer will start the next step in the calculation before the results of the previous step are available.

Let's reconsider the analogy between counting and the way a car's odometer keeps track of miles traveled. In Chapter 1, we used a "binary odometer," whose only digits are zero and one, to count in the base two. This time, imagine running the odometer backwards: 000100_2, 000011_2, 000010_2, 000001_2, 000000_2. What happens next? Mathematically, the next number in the sequence should be -1. The number that actually shows up on the odometer would be 111111_2. Is it possible that 111111_2 is -1? Well, not quite. In our computer, numbers are sixteen bits long, and -1 is represented by 1111111111111111_2! (There are 16 ones there; the representation we use for negative numbers depends on the number of bits available. It we were using thirty-two-bit numbers, the representation for -1 would be a string of thirty-two ones.) This might seem silly, but just accept it for the moment and see where it leads.

Starting from -1, we can easily represent other negative numbers. Remember that we are only dealing with binary numbers that can be written with sixteen or fewer bits. For any such number N, we can write

$$-N = (-1 - N) + 1 = (1111111111111111_2 - N) + 1_2.$$

Now, the point here is that $1111111111111111_2 - N$ is very easy to compute. For example, for $N = 221 = 11011101_2$, we could compute:

$$
\begin{array}{r}
1111111111111111 \\
- \ 0000000011011101 \\
\hline
1111111100100010
\end{array}
$$

What makes this easy is that in each column, the lower digit is no larger than the upper digit, so it is not necessary to "borrow" from the column to the left. Furthermore, it is trivial to design a circuit to do the computation. Note that each digit in the answer is the reverse of the digit in the number N on the line above. The circuit that reverses a single digit is the NOT gate. What we want here is a circuit with sixteen inputs and sixteen outputs, where each output is the reverse of the corresponding input. The circuit can be built with sixteen separate NOT gates, each computing one digit of the answer. We call this circuit a *16-bit*-NOT *circuit*.

If the input to a 16-bit-NOT circuit represents the binary number N, note that the output represents $-1 - N$, not $-N$. The representation for $-N$ is obtained by adding one to this output. The output of the 16-bit-NOT is called the *ones-complement* of its input. The name comes from the fact that it is obtained by subtracting each digit of the input number from 1. When 1 is added to the ones-complement, the resulting number is called the *twos-complement*. The name in this case seems to refer to the fact that the twos-complement of a sixteen-bit number could also be obtained by subtracting the number from 2^{16}. Some computers actually use the ones-complement to represent negative numbers. Others use the twos-complement, as do we.

In the above example, where $N = 221$, taking the twos-complement gives 1111111100100011_2 as the representation for -221. Here are two more examples of forming the ones-complement and twos-complement of binary numbers, along with translations into the base ten. In the second example, note that the negative of -221 is 221, as it should be.

1111111111111111	(-1)	1111111111111111	(-1)
$-\,0000000000010100$	$-\,(20)$	$-\,1111111100100011$	$-\,(-221)$
1111111111101011	(-21)	0000000011011100	(220)
$+\,1$	$+\,(1)$	$+\,1$	$+\,(1)$
1111111111101110	(-20)	0000000011011101	(221)

Now, remember that the representations chosen for data in a computer are arbitrary. They are *symbols* for the data that are meaningless in themselves but which can stand for anything we choose. So, we are free to represent negative numbers as described. The question remains, though, is it a good idea? As it turns out, the representation chosen for negative numbers makes subtraction very easy for us. It turns out that when the twos-complement representation for negative numbers is used, $M - N$ can be computed by adding the negative of N to M *using the same circuit we have already designed for addition of positive numbers*, and ignoring any carry-out that is produced by that circuit.[9]

Why should this be true? One way to see it is to think about how addition could be done using a sixteen-bit binary odometer.[10] To add two positive numbers M and N, you could set the odometer reading to M and then advance the odometer N times (by driving N miles, for example). Assuming that $M + N$ is not too large to be represented with the number of digits available on the odometer, the reading would then be the sum of M and N.

---

[9] In the usual base-ten representation, you need a completely new method to do subtraction. While it is still true that $M - N = M + (-N)$, this is used to convert a sum involving a negative number into a subtraction problem, rather than the reverse.

[10] For those with more mathematical background than I am assuming: If you know about "clock arithmetic" or "arithmetic modulo N," you might recognize that all that's going on here is arithmetic modulo 2^{16}. The point is that if you start the odometer at zero and advance it 2^{16} times, it will be back to zero again.

Now consider $M - N$. Assume for definiteness that they are both positive and that $M > N$. (If you like, you can check all other cases as an exercise.)

One way to compute $M - N$ would be to set the odometer to zero, advance it M times, and then turn it back N times. This is essentially the ordinary way of doing subtraction. However, suppose we start with the odometer at zero, first turn it back N times, and then advance it M times. Clearly, the order in which these operations are done doesn't matter, so the answer will be the same for either order. Doing the operations in the latter order corresponds exactly to adding M to the twos-complement representation of $-N$. This is because when you start the odometer at zero and turn it back N times, the number on the odometer will be the twos-complement representation of $-N$. Then, advancing the odometer M times is just adding M to this in the usual way. (Note that, since $M > N$, the odometer will roll over from all ones to all zeros at some point while you are advancing it M times. This corresponds to the fact that a carry from the leftmost bit is produced when M and the twos-complement representation of $-N$ are added. In this case, the carry does not mean that the sixteen-bit answer is incorrect, which is why I said above that it should be ignored.)

It is now easy to build a subtraction circuit. We start with a sixteen-bit addition circuit, but we feed each digit of the second sixteen-bit input number through a NOT gate to compute its ones-complement. We should add one to this to get the twos-complement before doing the addition. However, we can take care of that extra one with a rather cute trick. Recall that the sixteen-bit addition circuit had a carry-in input to the rightmost bit which was unused. If this carry-in is turned on while the subtraction is being performed, the extra one being carried into the rightmost column will add one to the answer. This takes care of the extra one that we needed for the twos-complement. A subtraction circuit constructed in this way is shown in Figure 2.10.

Before leaving the topic of subtraction, it might be a good time to consider the consequences of restricting ourselves to sixteen-bit numbers. There are only 2^{16} different strings of sixteen binary digits, so no matter what we do, we cannot hope to represent more than 2^{16} different numbers. But we *do* have a choice of which numbers we want to represent. It might seem that the most natural choice would be to represent the numbers from zero through $2^{16} - 1$. In this case, a string of sixteen ones corresponds to the number $2^{16} - 1$, or 65,535. However, if we do this, we have no negative numbers to work with at all.

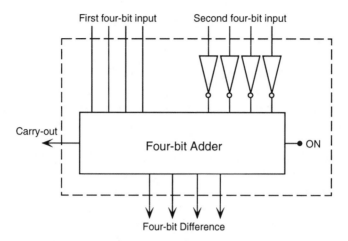

Figure 2.10. *A subtraction circuit, drawn for four-bit inputs rather than sixteen-bit. It uses the addition circuit that was designed previously. Note that the* carry-in *input of the addition circuit is set to* on. *This is required for the subtraction to be done correctly.*

Another choice is to use half of the available representations for negative numbers and half for positive numbers. If we make this choice, we can decree that *a string of sixteen bits represents a negative number if the leading bit is a one.* Thus, bit-patterns from 0000000000000000 to 0111111111111111 correspond to numbers from zero to 32,767, while the patterns 1000000000000000 through 1111111111111111 correspond to the negative numbers from −32,768 to −1, represented using the twos-complement.

In fact, though, we are free to imagine that we are using either of these representations. The computer we are designing will work exactly the same way in either case. If you tell it to add or subtract two numbers, it will do so by feeding those numbers through the appropriate circuit. The bits in the result will be the same, no matter what representation you imagine you are using. However, your interpretation of the answer will be different. Suppose, for example, that your program tells the computer to subtract 5 from 3. The answer, as a pattern of bits, will be 1111111111111110. If your intention is to represent both positive and negative numbers, then this is the correct answer, −2, represented as its twos-complement. If, however, your intention is to represent only positive numbers, then the correct answer cannot be represented at all, and the actual result represents 65,534, which is certainly not correct. If you find it confusing to talk about the result of a computation in the computer depending on the user or programmer's *intentions*, it might be because you are forgetting that the symbols manipulated by the computer never have any meaning in themselves!

2.2.4. Multiplication and Division. Besides addition and subtraction, the other arithmetic operations that a computer must be able to do are multiplication and division. Note once again that circuits to perform these operations can certainly be built, since in principle it would be possible to make a table of inputs and desired outputs. Indeed, some computers do include circuits to perform multiplication and division. The machine languages of such computers include multiplication and division instructions.

Our model computer will not include multiplication and division circuits. However, it will include circuits for certain other simple operations that will make it possible to write *subroutines* to perform multiplication and division.

The method for multiplying binary numbers by hand is the same as that used for ordinary base-ten numbers. It is much easier, though, because the only digits you need to multiply by are zeros and ones. Here are examples of multiplication of base-ten and base-two numbers:

$$
\begin{array}{r}
2731 \\
\times\,508 \\
\hline
21848 \\
0000 \\
13655 \\
\hline
1387348
\end{array}
\qquad
\begin{array}{r}
1101 \\
\times\,101 \\
\hline
1101 \\
0000 \\
1101 \\
\hline
1000001
\end{array}
$$

The numbers between the two lines are shifted to the left to line up the digits properly, and then they are added together to give the final answer. (Although it is not written, you should imagine that a zero is added to the end of a number when it is shifted left.) In the case of binary multiplication, note that each of the numbers being added is either zero or is equal to the top number that is being multiplied, suitably shifted to the left.

It follows that a computer that can perform additions and left shifts can be programmed to do multiplication. It turns out that binary division can be similarly reduced to subtraction, left shifts, and right shifts. We already have circuits to do addition and subtractions. Circuits that do left and right shifts are trivial to design, as shown in Figure 2.11.

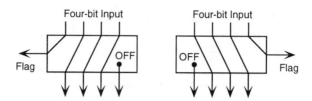

Figure 2.11. *The rather trivial circuits that perform left and right shifts on four-bit numbers. When a number is shifted left, a zero is added to the right end, and one bit is lost from the left end. An extra output from the circuit, labeled "flag" in the diagram, can be used to check whether this lost bit was a zero or one. Similar comments apply to a right shift.*

Our model computer will include 16-bit left-shift and right-shift circuits. With these circuits, we now have in hand everything a computer needs to do all arithmetic operations.

2.2.5. Logical Operators. Besides the usual arithmetic operations on sixteen-bit numbers, our computer will also do the logical operations AND, OR, and NOT on sixteen-bit numbers. Ordinarily, these three operators act on single bits. We have already seen that the ones-complement of a number can be computed by applying a NOT operation to each of its bits. Similarly, we can extend AND or OR to apply to a pair of sixteen-bit numbers by applying the operation to each corresponding pair of bits. For example,

$$
\begin{array}{r} 0001110101011110 \\ \text{AND } 1011000001110101 \\ \hline 0001000001010100 \end{array}
\qquad
\begin{array}{r} 0001110101011110 \\ \text{OR } 1011000001110101 \\ \hline 1011110101111111 \end{array}
$$

Here, the answer in each column is computed separately, by applying AND or OR to the two top bits in that column.

It is, of course, easy to build sixteen-bit AND and OR circuits to do such computations. These circuits have two sixteen-bit numbers as inputs and one sixteen-bit output. Each bit of the output is computed by a separate AND or OR gate.

2.2.6. An Arithmetic-Logic Unit. As a final step in teaching silicon to compute arithmetic and logic operations, we can assemble all the circuits we have developed into a single unit. The resulting multi-purpose circuit is called an ***arithmetic-logic unit***, or ***ALU***. The ALU is the part of the central processing unit that actually performs arithmetic

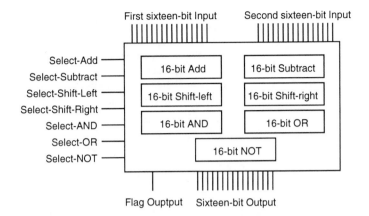

Figure 2.12. *An arithmetic-logic unit that can perform each of the seven basic arithmetic and logical operations. None of the internal wiring is shown here. The input wires along the left side are used to determine which operation it actually performs. When one of these wires is turned on, the result of the corresponding operation is output by the circuit. The extra single-bit output labeled "flag" will represent the carry-out of an addition or subtraction operation, or the "lost bit" of a shift operation.*

and logical calculations. The inputs to the ALU will include two sixteen-bit numbers. It will be able to compute the sum, difference, logical AND or logical OR of those two numbers. It will also be able to compute the logical NOT of the first input, shift that input left, or shift it right. We have designed circuits to do each of these operations. The ALU contains a copy of each of these circuits, with their inputs connected to the corresponding inputs of the ALU.

The ALU outputs a single sixteen-bit result. Since it can do seven different operations, we need some way of telling it which one to do. We do this by adding seven more input wires, one for each operation. These wires are used to *control* the circuit, as opposed to the other inputs, which are used to provide *data* for the operation to be performed. From now on, it will be useful to distinguish between *data inputs* and *control inputs* to circuits. We can say, then, that the ALU has two sixteen-bit data inputs and seven (one-bit) control inputs.

The method for using the ALU is to put the input data for the operation on the data inputs, and at the same time to turn on the control input that corresponds to the desired operation. The answer will appear

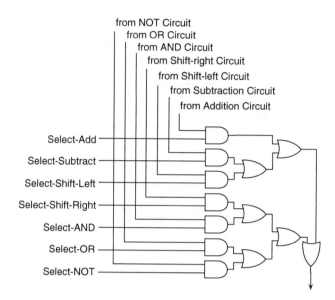

Figure 2.13. *The circuitry used in the ALU to control which operation it performs. In fact, it actually performs all seven operations, but
only one of the results makes it to the output. A circuit identical to the
one shown is used for each of the sixteen bits of the output.*

on the output wires after the short time it takes for the circuit to do the
computation. Note that exactly one of the control wires must be turned
on for the ALU to work properly. If none of these wires is on, the output
of the ALU will be zero; if more than one are on, the output will be
meaningless.

The ALU has a seventeenth output wire, which is used to provide
extra information about the result of the computation performed. If the
operation is addition, for example, this bit represents the carry-out from
the leftmost bit. Our computer will be able to use the value of this
output to make decisions about what to do next in a program. I will say
more about it in the next chapter.

To finish a complete design for the ALU, we need only determine
how to wire up the inside of the ALU to make the control wires work
correctly. The way we do this is surprising in one respect, in that the
ALU actually performs *all seven* computations all the time, no matter
how the control wires are set. The control wires merely determine which
of the seven results gets through to the ALU's output.

We use the same wiring diagram shown in Figure 2.13 for each of the ALU's sixteen output bits. An output bit is connected through such a circuit to the seven control wires and to the corresponding output bit from each of the ALU's seven computational circuits. Understanding this circuit provides a good exercise in understanding how AND and OR gates work.

Let's suppose that Select-Add, the control wire for addition, is turned on and that all the other control wires are off. In that case, the overall output should be equal to the output from the addition circuit. The output wire from the addition circuit is fed through an AND gate along with Select-add. Since Select-add is on, the output of that AND gate is equal to the output from the addition circuit. Also, the other six control wires are off, so the outputs from the other six AND gates in the circuit are definitely off, no matter what the outputs from the other computation circuits might be.

So, of the seven wires coming out of AND gates, six of them are known to be off, and the seventh contains the result from the addition circuit. These seven wires are combined through OR gates to produce the output of the ALU. Whenever values are combined with OR gates, the final result is on if any one of the inputs is on. In this case, six of the inputs to the OR gates are definitely off, and it follows that the final output from the OR gates will be off if the seventh input—from the addition circuit—is off, and will be on if that input is on. That is, the final output is equal to the result from the addition circuit.

We have shown that when the addition control wire is on and the other control wires are off, then the output of the ALU is equal to the output from the addition circuit. The same analysis will work if it is any other control wire that is on. So, our ALU works as advertised.

We have come a long way from the beginning of the chapter. The ALU we have built will be a major part of the computer we design in the next chapter. It will allow our computer to do basic computations with sixteen-bit numbers. It is still not clear how those computations can be controlled by machine language instructions stored in memory, but the outline of a solution can be seen. When an instruction is fetched into the CPU, we must somehow arrange for the data required by that instruction to be fed into the inputs of the ALU, and we must arrange for the correct control input of the ALU to be turned on. Once that is done, the result of the computation can be read from the outputs of the ALU. Getting all the details right will not be easy, but we already have made considerable progress.

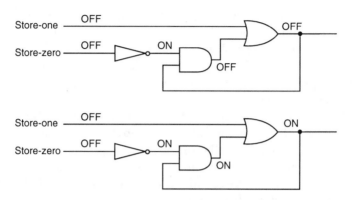

Figure 2.14. *A circuit with a feedback loop, shown in the two states that it can be in when both inputs are off. In the first version, both inputs to the* OR *gate are off, and its output is off. In the second, one of the inputs is on, and its output is on. The circuit is stable in either state, as long as the inputs stay off.*

2.3. Circuits that Remember

Before leaving this chapter, I have to admit that there is a second aspect of logic circuits that I have been avoiding. (The first was the fact that logic circuits take time to do their computations.) All the circuits we have encountered so far share the property that once the values on their input wires are known, the output values are determined. The method introduced in Section 1 for designing circuits was based on this assumption, since it starts with a table of all possible inputs and the desired output for each. There is, however, an important class of circuits for which this assumption does not hold. These are circuits with **feedback loops**.

A feedback loop occurs if the output of some gate is connected, directly or through a sequence of other gates, back to one of its inputs. Figure 2.14 shows a circuit with a feedback loop in which the output of an OR gate is connected through an AND gate back to one of its inputs. For this circuit, looking at the values of the two inputs is *not* enough to tell you what the output will be. As shown in the figure, when both inputs are off, it is possible for the output to have either of the values on or off. The behavior of this circuit cannot be described by any expression of Boolean algebra, since any such expression would assign a single, definite value to the output for any possible input.

The correspondence between Boolean algebra and logic circuits without feedback loops provides a beautiful and useful mathematical theory of such circuits, which we have exploited in designing and understanding them. Once feedback loops are allowed, there is no such simple theory. As a result, circuits with feedback must be "hand-crafted." Their main use is in computer memory circuits. There are only a few basic types of feedback circuits that are used to build memories. In this section, I will describe those that we will need for our model computer.

The lack of a theory for circuits with feedback makes them less interesting from my point of view, since in this text I am more interested in principles than in practice. I will not give all the details of the circuits I discuss here. A much fuller treatment can be found in [Shaffer].

2.3.1. A One-bit Memory Circuit. Let's consider the behavior of the circuit in Figure 2.14 in more detail. Assuming that both inputs are off, this circuit has two possible *states*, as shown in the figure. In one of these states, the output of the circuit is off, and in the other state the output is on. We can think of this circuit as "remembering" the value of a bit—zero if its output is off, or one if its output is on. If we can find a way to tell this circuit *which* of these values to remember, we will have a memory circuit. We will be able to *store* a one-bit number in the circuit and then later *read* the value that was stored there by checking the value of the output. The value in the circuit will not change until we explicitly change it by telling the circuit to store a new bit.

As you might have guessed from their names, the two input wires labeled "Store-zero" and "Store-one" can be used to store a value in the circuit. The procedure for storing a one in the circuit is to turn Store-one on briefly and then turn it off again. The Store-zero wire must be kept off during this process. Turning on Store-one turns on one input to the OR gate. This causes the output of the OR gate to turn on (if it was not already on). Then, since Store-zero is off, both inputs to the AND gate will now be on. The output of the AND gate will then come on, if it is not already. This causes no further changes, since the OR gate is already on. Turning Store-one off turns off one input of the OR gate, but its second input is still on, so its output remains on. The value one has been successfully stored in the circuit.[11]

---

[11] Recall from Chapter 1 that all gates have internal power sources. These internal power sources make it possible for the output of this circuit to be on even though both inputs are off. There is nothing mysterious about the loop in the circuit staying on "by itself."

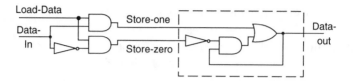

Figure 2.15. *Our official one-bit memory circuit. The value stored in this circuit can be read at any time by checking the value output on the* Data-out *wire. A value can be stored in the circuit by placing that value on the* Data-in *wire and then turning the* Load-data *wire on and off.*

The Store-zero wire works similarly. To store a zero in the circuit, you just need to turn this wire on briefly and then turn it back off. Store-one must be kept off while you do this. Turning Store-zero on turns off the AND gate, which breaks the feedback loop. Both inputs to the OR gate will be off and therefore so will its output. Turning Store-zero off will not change this. The value zero has been stored in the circuit. Note that these procedures for storing a value in the circuit will work no matter which state the circuit starts out in.

The circuit in Figure 2.14 is not quite what we need, because of the inconvenience of using separate wires to store zeros and ones. Figure 2.15 shows the modified circuit that we will use instead. This is a standard circuit, known as a *D flip-flop*. For this circuit, the procedures for storing zero and for storing one are the same. The value to be stored— zero or one—is put on the Data-in wire; then the Load-data wire is turned on and back off. This will store the value in the feedback loop of the circuit. The stored value can be read off the output wire, Data-out. This value will not change until a new value is explicitly loaded into the circuit.

To see how this circuit works, note that the wires Store-one and Store-zero are connected to the outputs of two AND gates, which in turn get their inputs from Load-data and Data-in. Store-one will be on only when both Load-data and Data-in are on simultaneously. Thus, turning Load-data on and off while the value on Data-in is 1 will turn Store-one on and off, which will store a 1 in the feedback loop. (While this is going on, Store-zero stays off because the value of 1 on Data-in passes through a NOT gate and becomes a 0 on its way to the AND gate connected to Store-zero.) On the other hand, if the value on Data-in is 0, then turning Load-data on and off will turn Store-zero on and off while Store-one remains off; this will store a 0 in the feedback loop. Thus, in both cases, the circuit works as it should.

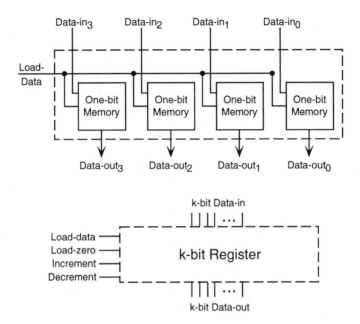

Figure 2.16. *On the top is a four-bit register constructed from four one-bit memories. Below it is a general-purpose k-bit register. This memory circuit stores a k-bit binary number, which can be read off the Data-out wires. The four control wires,* Load-data, Load-zero, *Increment, and* Decrement, *are used to change the stored value.*

Now that we have a working one-bit memory, it is easy to build a memory circuit that can store more than one bit. A circuit to store a k-bit binary number can be built from k one-bit memories. A k-bit memory has k Data-in wires and k Data-out wires. However, it has only one Load-data wire, which is connected to the Load-Data inputs of all k one-bit memories. A k-bit memory therefore stores a k-bit number all at once, as a unit. Its operation is identical to that of a one-bit memory: To store a number, put that number on the Data-in inputs and turn Load-data on and off. This will store each bit of the number in the corresponding one-bit memory. A four-bit memory constructed in this way is shown in Figure 2.16.

2.3.2. Registers. Most of a computer's memory is external to the CPU. However, the CPU itself does include a small number of memory circuits. A memory circuit on the CPU is called a ***register***. For example, the program counter, which I mentioned in Chapter 1, is a register that the CPU uses to store the location in memory of the next machine language instruction to be executed. There are other registers, such as the *instruction register*, which stores a copy of the machine language instruction that is currently being executed by the CPU.

A register is just a k-bit memory circuit. Some registers, including the instruction register, can be designed exactly like the four-bit memory in Figure 2.16. Other registers, such as the program counter, need extra capabilities. A very common operation on the program counter is to add one to the value it contains. Adding one to this value corresponds to moving on to the next instruction in a program, so this operation is part of every fetch-and-execute cycle. So, in addition to its Load-data control wire, the program counter has a second control wire called Increment. Turning Increment on and off will add one to the value in the program counter. (The term *increment* just means "add one to.")

Two more control wires will also be used occasionally. A Decrement wire can be used to decrement (that is, "subtract one from") the contents of the register. A Load-zero wire is used to set the value stored in the register to zero.

A k-bit register with all four possible control wires is shown in Figure 2.16. No single register used in the next chapter will have all the possible inputs shown here.

The implementations of the Increment and Decrement operations are not easy, and I will not discuss them here. They require a more complicated type of one-bit memory than the one introduced above. In any case, we could always use an addition circuit to add 1 or -1 to a number, so you know it is possible in principle; doing it in one step just by turning a wire on and off is the hard part.

In Chapter 3, we will make use of the circuits designed in this chapter. Most of the details of the internal operation of these circuits will not be important. There are some points, however, that you should understand before going on:

- the fact that a circuit (without feedback loops) can be built with any specified input/output behavior;
- the method for using the ALU by giving it two sixteen-bit inputs and turning on a control wire to tell it which operation to perform;
- the purpose of registers and one-bit memories, and the use of their input, output, and control wires.

Chapter Summary

The *ands*, *ors*, and *nots* of logic are reflected in the physical structure of a computer—in its AND, OR, and NOT gates. There is a deep connection between the logical expressions of *Boolean algebra* and the computational circuits in the computer. We can exploit this connection to design a circuit with any desired input/output behavior. Given a table of input/output values, there is a definite, mechanical procedure for writing down a logical formula that expresses the same relationship of output to input; given that formula, there is a definite, mechanical procedure for building a circuit that performs the computation specified by the formula.

It turns out that arithmetic too is deeply related to logic. When dealing with arithmetic, `true` and `false` become one and zero, but the circuits that manipulate the ones and zeros are designed and built in the same way. Starting from simple circuits that manipulate individual bits, and combining them step-by-step into more complex circuits, we arrive eventually at a complete *arithmetic-logic unit*, a kind of calculator that can perform any of several different arithmetic and logical operations on multi-bit inputs.

Computers don't just do computations. They also have *memory*. Data and programs must be *stored* safely away in memory, where the CPU can *read* them as necessary. The CPU itself contains small memory units called *registers* to hold data that the CPU is working with directly. Although memory is very different from computation, it can still be implemented using only AND, OR, and NOT gates, provided that we allow circuits with *feedback*. Although there is no elegant mathematical theory for circuits with feedback, it is possible to design a *one-bit memory* circuit that uses a feedback loop to remember the value of single bit. Such one-bit memories can then be used as a basis for building all the other types of memory circuits we will need.

Questions

1. In Section 2.1, we derived a formula for a circuit with two inputs whose output is **on** whenever the two inputs are the same. Draw the circuit. Use similar methods to design and draw a two-input circuit whose output is **on** when the two inputs are *different*. What simple modification of the first of these circuits would produce a circuit with the same behavior as the second? Now suppose you wanted to design a circuit specified by a table like the one in Figure 2.5, except that most of the outputs are specified as `true`, with only a few specified as `false`. The method given for building a circuit from this table will produce a huge, complex circuit, since each line in the table where the output is `true` adds several gates to the circuit. How could you produce a much smaller circuit with the same behavior?

2. Consider DeMorgan's law, which says that NOT $(A$ AND $B)$ $\equiv$ (NOT A) OR (NOT B). Build a circuit to represent each side of this rule, and check that they have the same behavior for all possible inputs. Make up some examples in English to illustrate this rule. Try to explain in words why it holds.

3. A full adder is a circuit with three inputs (A, B, and *carry-in*) and two outputs (*sum* and *carry-out*). Make a table showing all possible combinations of inputs and the resulting outputs. Use this table to build a full adder directly, using the methods of Section 2.1. Comment on the differences between your circuit and a full adder built from two half-adders. Does it make any difference which version of the full adder is used in building larger circuits, such as a 16-bit adder? (Both "yes" and "no" are possible answers, depending on your point of view. Explain why.)

4. In this chapter, we saw how to construct a one-output circuit from a Boolean algebra expression. The reverse is also possible for circuits that have no feedback loops. That is, given such a circuit, it is possible to write the output as a Boolean expression of its inputs. Give a detailed procedure for finding this expression. Show how it works on some example circuits. What goes wrong with your procedure when you try to apply it to a circuit with feedback loops?

5. The simplest feedback loop that can occur in a circuit is produced by connecting the output of a NOT gate back to its input. How would such a circuit behave? Remember that when the input to a gate changes, it takes some *time* for the gate to change its state. Consider what happens at the moment when the output of the NOT gate is connected to the input, and what happens after that.

6. The ALU developed in this chapter contains two sixteen-bit addition circuits. One of them is inside the subtraction circuit. It would be nice to eliminate this duplication by using the same circuit for both addition and subtraction. For the circuit to do addition, the second sixteen-bit input number must come directly from the second input to the ALU; for it to do subtraction, its second input must come from the circuit that computes the ones-complement of the input to the ALU. Is there any way that the ALU can switch between these two inputs as necessary? In fact, it can be done using **multiplexers**. A multiplexer is a circuit with three inputs and one output. Call the inputs A, B, and *Select*. The output of the multiplexer is defined as follows: If *Select* is on, then the output is equal to A; if it is off, then the output is equal to B. Check that the output can be written in terms of the input as

(*Select* AND A) OR ((NOT *Select*) AND B).

The *Select* wire acts as a switch to determine which of the inputs gets through to the output. With a bank of sixteen multiplexers, we can eliminate the extra addition circuit from the ALU. Show how this can be done. Explain all the modifications necessary to the ALU. Some modifications will be necessary in the circuitry that controls the ALU's output. (One tricky bit you might miss: For the addition circuit to perform a subtraction correctly, the carry-in to the addition circuit must be turned on.)

Chapter 3

Building a Computer

THE WORK DONE in the previous chapter has provided us with the basic materials for building a computing machine. Now we will see how to assemble the pieces into a working computer.

The machine we design in this chapter will, in some ways, seem to be not very impressive. It will understand only a few different machine-language instructions, and it will have very limited memory in which to store data and programs. Only an extremely primitive input/output capability will be provided, so that just getting data and programs into and out of the computer will be almost ridiculously tedious.

But all of that is really beside the point. First of all, many of the limitations are design decisions that could be easily revised. For example, the way we will use sixteen-bit numbers to represent machine-language instructions will force a limitation on the size of the computer's memory. However, using more bits per number would be easy and would allow us to greatly extend the memory size. Other limitations, such as the lack of input/output facilities, are beside the point of this chapter, which is simply to produce a machine that executes programs, without making that machine easy for people to use. A discussion of the problems of making real machines for real people is left to Chapter 5.

Remarkably, though, the limitation that seems most damaging is not a real limitation at all. Real computers can have hundreds or even thousands of different machine-language instructions. Our computer will have a rather anemic set of only thirty-one instructions, and it might seem that this would mean a real restriction on the computations that it is able to perform. This is not the case. Aside from limitations of memory, speed, and difficulty of writing programs for it, our computer will be precisely as powerful as every other computer in existence. This essential equivalence of different computer designs is one of the surprising results of the theoretical study of computation, which will be explained in Chapter 4.

As for this chapter, while it is generally more technical and detailed than other sections of the book, the reward for working through it is substantial: a real understanding of how a purely mechanical device can automatically execute *any* list of instructions written in the machine language it understands. The fact that computers can work at all is surprising. Even more amazing is the fact that their basic operation can be fully understood with a relatively modest effort.

3.1. Basic Design

As we saw in Chapter 1 (Figure 1.3), the two main parts of a computer are its **CPU** and its ***main memory***. The main memory contains a numbered sequence of locations, which hold program instructions and data. The CPU executes programs by fetching instructions one-by-one from memory and carrying out each of those instructions. We can now fill in the details in this description. Details of design can vary greatly among computers, so that the machine we end up with will be different from— and simpler than—any existing real computer. However, our design is very much in the spirit of the design of real computers, and it gives a fair impression of their basic operation.[1]

Most computers have names, and ours should be no exception. We'll refer to it as the "Model X Computer," or, briefly, as the xComputer.[2] The xComputer will be made up of twelve components, connected together by a mass of wires. The wires connected to each component can be divided into three classes: input, output, and control. Input and output wires carry data between components, while the control wires are used to control their operation.

---

[1] That is, it gives a fair impression of the operation of the CPU and main memory, which are the essential components of a computer. Other components, which will be covered in Chapter 5, play supporting roles.

[2] That's xComputer, pronounced "Eck's computer," in case you didn't get the rather weak joke.

One of these components is a *clock*. The clock has one output wire, and as it "ticks," it turns this wire on and off. It is this ticking that drives the whole operation of the computer. (See Subsection 2.2.2.) The clock also has a control wire, which can be used to stop it from running. As long as this wire is off, the clock will continue to tick; if it is turned on, the clock will stop, which will in turn stop the operation of the computer.

The eleven remaining components are circuits. One of these is an ALU to do basic arithmetic and logical operations. Eight of the circuits are registers—small memory units internal to the CPU, each holding from one to sixteen bits. Registers and ALU's were discussed in Chapter 2. That leaves two circuits still to be described. One of these is the main memory unit, which is assembled from a large number of one-bit memories. The difficult part of designing a main memory is dividing it up into locations that can be individually accessed by number. One possible design is discussed below.

The final component is called the *Control circuit* or *Central Control Unit*. It is this circuit that is responsible for controlling all details of the execution of machine-language programs. If there is any part of the computer that "thinks," this must be it! And yet, when we finally get around to it, building this circuit will be simplicity itself. Here is the key: Execution of machine-language programs will be controlled entirely by turning control wires on and off in the right sequence, as the clock ticks. The Control circuit has output wires connected to each of these control wires; we just need to arrange for the Control circuit to turn its output wires on and off as appropriate. Before you can understand how this could be done, you need to know more about the design of the individual components and more about machine-language instructions. By the time we get around to designing the Control circuit in Section 3, it will no longer be a mystery how it can be built.

3.1.1. Addressing RAM.
The memory unit attached to the CPU is called the computer's *main memory*. It is also sometimes referred to as the *RAM*, or *random access memory*, although this is really a more general descriptive term for any memory made up of addressable locations. The main memory consists of a large number of locations, each holding a binary number. These locations can be "accessed randomly." That is, you can get at the contents of any randomly picked location at any time. The locations are numbered: location 0, location 1, location 2, and so on. The number of a location is called its *address*. To store or read data in a location, you need to know the location's address.

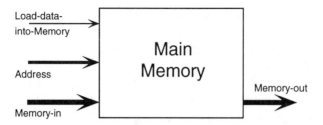

Figure 3.1. *The main memory of the xComputer. In this figure, as in all the figures in this chapter, the thinnest lines represent a single wire, while thicker lines represent bundles of several wires. Here, there are sixteen* Memory-in *wires, sixteen* Memory-out *wires, ten* Address *wires, and a single* Load-data-into-memory *wire. All these are connected to the CPU.*

In xComputer, the address will be a ten-bit binary number. This means that there will be 2^{10}, or 1024, different locations, numbered from zero to 1023. Each of these locations will hold a sixteen-bit binary number. The wires that connect the memory to the outside world are as follows: It has a sixteen-bit input, which is used to specify a number to be stored in memory, and a sixteen-bit output, which can be used to read a stored value. There is also a ten-bit input which is used to specify the address of the location that is to be accessed. (There are 1024 different locations for storing numbers, but at any given time only one of these locations is accessible, namely the one whose ten-bit address is on the Address wires.) Finally, there is a control wire which is used to tell the memory unit to load the sixteen-bit number on the data input wires into the location specified by the Address wires. A diagram of the memory unit is shown in Figure 3.1.

There are only two different things that you can do with main memory: You can store a number in a specified location, or you can read the number that is currently stored in a specified location. If you know how to do these two things, then you understand the memory completely from an external, "black box" point of view.

The procedure for reading a number is simply to put the address of the location that contains it on the memory's Address wires; the stored value can then be read on its output wires.

Storing a number involves a few more steps: The value to be stored must be put on the memory's input wires, and the address of the location where it is to be stored must be put on the Address wires. Then, the Load-

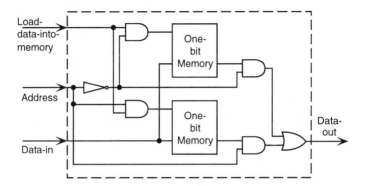

Figure 3.2. *The first step in designing addressable memory. This circuit uses a one-bit address to choose between two one-bit memories at "location 0" and "location 1." When the address wire is* off, *data can be stored into or read from location 0; when it is* on, *location 1 is in use instead.*

data-into-memory control wire is turned on briefly and then off again; this causes the value to be stored.[3] Note that this is the only time that Load-data-into-memory is ever used: Turning it on will load whatever value is on the Memory-in wires into whatever location is specified by the Address wires, replacing whatever number was stored there previously.

A black box understanding of main memory is sufficient for understanding the role it plays in xComputer, but it is interesting to see how an addressable memory can be built. To simplify the discussion, we will imagine that each location stores only a single bit, instead of sixteen. The real memory will consist essentially of sixteen copies of the circuit described here.

Each location is really just a one-bit memory of the type introduced in Section 2.3, with its own Data-in, Data-out, and Load-data wires. The difficulty is to arrange for the Address wires to pick out one location from all those available. The simplest case would be when there are only two

---

[3] As always, it takes some time for these procedures to do their work. When you put an address on the Address wires, the contents of the specified location are not *immediately* available on the output wires. You have to wait some minimum time to allow the effect of changing the address inputs to filter through the circuit. This minimum time must be less than the time between ticks of the clock. In a real computer, the time required would be some fraction of a millionth of a second.

locations, location 0 and location 1. In this case, only one Address wire is needed. This single Address wire is turned off to choose location 0 and on to choose location 1. A two-location memory of this type is shown in Figure 3.2.

Let's see how the single Address wire picks out one of the two locations. Each of the locations constantly outputs the value stored in it. Only one of these values should get through to the output wire of the circuit, depending on the value on the Address wire. The idea is that when this wire is off, certain data pathways in the circuit are open while others are closed. Turing it on will reverse the state of each pathway. If the Address wire is off, then the data from location 0 should get through to the output, while data from location 1 is blocked. If the address wire is on, the opposite should happen. You can easily verify that the circuit in Figure 3.2 works in this way. (The outputs from the two locations are combined through a subcircuit called a *multiplexer*. Multiplexers were introduced in Question 6 at the end of Chapter 2; the Address wire plays the role of the Select wire of the multiplexer.)

Turning now to storing values, the Data-in wire of the two-bit memory is connected directly to the Data-in wire of each of the two one-bit memories it contains. A one-bit memory does not actually store the value on its Data-in wire until its Load-data wire is turned on and off. The two-bit memory's Address wire is used to open up a pathway from its Load-data-into-memory input to the Load-data wire of one or the other one-bit memory. As shown in Figure 3.2, Load-data-into-memory is connected to the Load-data wire of each one-bit memory through an AND gate. The second input to that AND gate will control whether or not a signal on Load-data-from-memory will get through to the one-bit-memory. As you can see, this second input is controlled by the Address wire in such a way that if the Address wire is off, the signal gets through to location 0, while if it is on, it gets through to location 1. If Address is off, then turning Load-data-into-memory on and off will turn the Load-data for location 0 on and off, and the value on the Data-in input wire will be loaded into location 0. If Address is on, it is loaded into location 1.

Thus, the circuit as shown works correctly for both storing and reading data.

Now, the circuit that we really want to build has 1024 locations, not two. It might seem at first that that circuit would have to be about 512 times harder to build than the one we have just designed. In fact, though, it can be built by repeatedly applying exactly the same technique used to build the two-location memory. Each time it is applied, another address

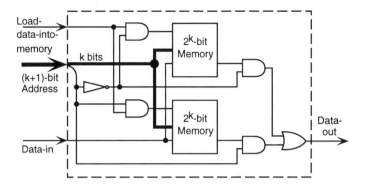

Figure 3.3. *The step from k to $k + 1$ address wires. This memory circuit has 2^{k+1} locations, and is made from two smaller circuits with 2^k locations each. One bit of the $(k + 1)$-bit address is used to distinguish between the two smaller memories; the other k bits are used to pick out locations within those memories. Aside from the extra k address wires, the logic of this circuit is the same as the logic of the two-location memory in the previous figure.*

wire is added and the number of locations is doubled. A memory circuit with $k + 1$ address wires can be built from two circuits with k address wires, as shown in Figure 3.3. We go from two locations, to four, then to eight and so forth, reaching the required 1024 after just nine steps.

This is another example of our general method of building a complex circuit by combining simpler circuits that we have already built, but there is an interesting twist. Except for having one fewer address wire, the smaller component circuits are essentially the same as the bigger circuit of which they are a part. We could almost say, "To make a memory circuit, start with two memory circuits and wire them together with a few extra logic gates." This statement if taken literally is paradoxical, since it says that a memory circuit contains two copies of itself. It must be read, of course, as, "To make a memory circuit [with $(k + 1)$-bit addresses], start with two memory circuits [with k-bit addresses]." This is our first example of a phenomenon called **recursion**, which occurs when a problem can be broken down into subproblems that are of the same type as the original problem. We will encounter recursion again in Chapter 7, where it is used as a technique in computer programming.

3.1.2. Registers. The main memory is not the only memory used by our computer. The CPU itself contains registers, which are memory circuits capable of holding some small number of bits. Each register has output wires on which the value that is currently stored in the register can be read at any time; when we build the CPU, these wires will be connected to input wires of other components in the CPU that need to use the value stored in the register.

Registers play an important role in organizing each computation that takes place in the CPU into a sequence of fairly simple steps. Consider, for example, the process of using the ALU to perform an addition. The two numbers to be added must be put on the two sixteen-bit inputs of the ALU, and the Select-add wire must be turned on. These values on all the input wires must be maintained while the answer is read from the ALU's output wires. In general, at each stage in every computation, we have to make sure that *all* the inputs to *all* the circuits are set to the correct values. With so many wires to worry about, this could be a very difficult task.

Suppose, however, that we connect some of the input wires of a circuit to the output wires from a register. Then, the circuit's input will always be equal to whatever value happens to be stored in the register. This value can only change when a new value is explicitly stored by turning the register's Load-data wire on and off. This means we can set up whatever input the circuit needs by dumping a number into the register; once that is done, we can stop worrying about that input, as long as we make sure to leave the Load-data wire of the register alone.

To apply this strategy to the ALU, we attach two sixteen-bit registers to its two data inputs. We will call these registers X and Y. In addition, we attach the sixteen-bit output of the ALU to the data input of another register called the accumulator, or AC. (You might recall from Chapter 1 that the accumulator is a register that holds the results of computations.) Figure 3.4 shows the ALU with all the registers that are attached to it. The procedure for adding two numbers then becomes a sequence of simple, independent steps:

1. Put the first number to be added on the input wires of register X, and turn that register's Load-data wire on and off. (Then forget about register X and its inputs.)

2. Put the second number to be added on the input wires of register Y, and turn that register's Load-data wire on and off. (Then forget about register Y and its inputs.)

3. Turn on the Select-add wire and, while it is on, turn the Load-data wire for the accumulator on and off.

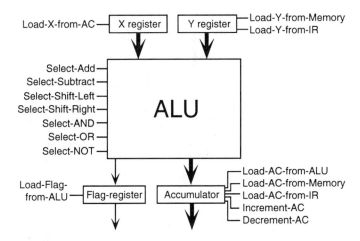

Figure 3.4. *The ALU and the four registers attached to it. X, Y, and AC are sixteen-bit registers. (AC is an abbreviation for "accumulator.") FLAG is a one-bit register. X and Y hold the numbers to be used as input for the ALU's computation. The result of that computation can be loaded into AC. The* Flag *output from the ALU, which can hold extra information about the result of the computation, can be loaded into the Flag register.*

After step 3, the sum of the two numbers is stored in the accumulator, and that sum can be read from its output wires at any convenient time, at least until the accumulator is explicitly loaded with a new value.

This three-step procedure could be used to add numbers with the ALU by hand, but of course our problem is more difficult than this. We have to design a Control circuit that will carry out this procedure, along with all the other procedures necessary to execute a machine-language program, without any intervention from us. Obviously, before we attempt to design such a circuit, we need a complete understanding of what those procedures should be. The three steps listed above are not complete enough.

In particular, in steps 1 and 2, we still have the problem of making sure that the *right* data for the operation gets onto the input wires of the X and Y registers. Since we will not be around while the program is running to set up the data inputs, they have to come from the outputs of other components in the computer. Figuring out exactly where they should come from requires a detailed knowledge of machine-language instructions and the steps involved in executing them. The machine lan-

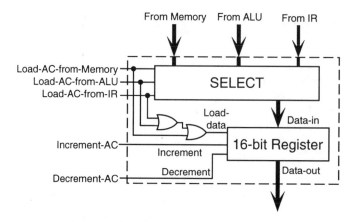

Figure 3.5. *Some of the internal structure of the accumulator, showing how it can load data from three different sources. The Select circuit is used to determine which of the three inputs to the accumulator gets through to the register that actually holds the stored number.*

guage of xComputer will not be covered in detail until the next section, but that discussion will make a lot more sense if you already have some idea of the general operation of the computer. I will explain some aspects of that operation in this section, but you should understand that some of the details discussed here are required for the execution of specific machine-language instructions that you don't know about yet.

Let's consider the X register first. As it happens, every machine-language instruction that uses the ALU requires X to be loaded with the current contents of the accumulator.[4] So, wiring X is easy: Its input is connected to the output wires from the accumulator. Turning on X's Load-data wire will load a copy of the number stored in the accumulator into X. To keep things straight, I would like to give a different name to every control wire in xComputer, so we will call the Load-data wire for the X register Load-X-from-AC.

If we turn to the accumulator, we find a more complicated situation. First of all, there are machine-language instructions for adding one to

---

[4] For example, one such instruction says to subtract a number in memory from the value in the accumulator. For this instruction, X is loaded from the accumulator and Y is loaded with the number from memory. The answer produced when Y is subtracted from X is loaded back into the accumulator, replacing the value that was there previously.

the accumulator and for subtracting one from it. The accumulator needs
Increment and Decrement control wires to implement these instructions.
(Increment and Decrement were discussed in Section 2.3.)

The input source for the accumulator also presents some problems.
When the accumulator is used to store the results of a computation, it
is loaded with the output from the ALU. However, there are machine-
language instructions that require the accumulator to be loaded from
other sources. To handle this, we provide the accumulator with three
separate data inputs—one from the ALU, one from main memory, and
one from another register called the IR. We provide a separate control
wire to load data from each of these sources into the accumulator. Registers with several different input sources are something new for us. Figure 3.5 shows how such a register can be constructed from an ordinary,
single-input register. The Select circuit in this figure is essentially the
same as the circuit we built in Subsection 2.2.6 to compute the output
of the ALU.

This should give you the general idea of how registers are designed
and what they are used for. All of the eight registers used in xComputer
are shown in Figures 3.4 and 3.6. Except for ADDR and COUNT, all
of the registers have already been mentioned. A full understanding of
these components will have to wait until the next section, but here is a
summary description (with some new hints about the overall operation
of the CPU):

• ADDR, the *address register*. A ten-bit register whose outputs are
connected to the Address wires of the main memory. ADDR is used to
control access to the 1024 locations in the memory. Recall that the value
on the memory's Address wires specifies which location in memory is to
be used when data is stored in memory or when a stored value is read.
Loading a number into ADDR selects a memory location. Any time
main memory is used—for reading or storing data or machine-language
instructions—that use is preceded by dumping the address of the desired
memory location into the ADDR register.

• IR, the *instruction register*. A program to be executed by the CPU is
stored in memory as a sequence of machine-language instructions. Each
instruction is coded as a sixteen-bit binary number. Recall that the program is executed by repeatedly fetching an instruction from memory and
then executing that instruction. Fetching the instruction will just mean
loading it into the IR. Once it has been loaded, any other component in
the CPU that needs to know what the current instruction is can read
that instruction from the output wires of the IR.

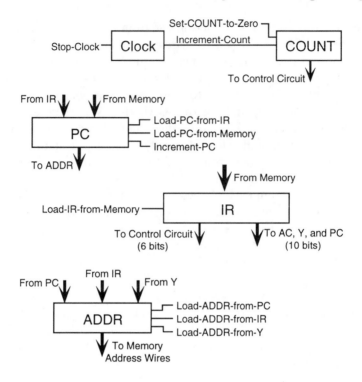

Figure 3.6. *The remaining four registers that are used in xComputer, together with the clock. COUNT is a four-bit register, and IR has sixteen bits. ADDR and PC each hold ten bits. Note that the output from IR is divided into two parts: the six leftmost bits, which feed into the Control circuit, and the remaining ten bits, which connect to the Y register, the program counter, and the accumulator. Except for the Control circuit, all the components of xComputer appear in this figure or in Figure 3.1 or Figure 3.4.*

• PC, the *program counter.* The PC was discussed in Chapter 1. It holds the location in memory of the program instruction that is next in line to be executed. At the beginning of each fetch-and-execute cycle, the CPU needs to load the next instruction into the IR. The PC holds the *address* of that instruction.

• COUNT, the *step counter.* This is a four-bit register which is unusual in that it has no data-input wires. It has two control wires, Set-COUNT-to-zero and Increment-COUNT. The second of these is attached to the output wire from the clock. As the clock ticks, this wire is turned on and off, and the value in COUNT is incremented. In fact, this is the only direct influence of the clock on the computer.[5] Each machine-language instruction is executed in a sequence of small, simple steps. COUNT is used to "count off" the steps in the execution of each *single* machine-language instruction. (This is not the same as counting off the machine-language instructions that make up a program; that counting is done in the program counter register.) At the beginning of the fetch-and-execute-cycle, COUNT contains the four-bit number 0000_2. As the clock ticks, the contents are incremented to 0001_2, then 0010_2, and so on. Each time the value changes, a new step is initiated.

• X, the *first operand register.* Represents one of the numbers to be used as input for a calculation by the ALU.

• Y, the *second operand register.* The second input to the ALU. (For those operations that require only one input—that is, for the operations NOT, shift-left, and shift-right—the value stored in Y is ignored.)

• FLAG, the *flag-bit.* This one-bit register will be loaded with the Flag output from the most recent calculation done by the ALU. For example, after an addition operation has been performed, FLAG will hold the carry-out from the left-most column. For shift operations, it will hold the bit that was "shifted off the end" of the number in the accumulator.

• AC, the *accumulator.* Grand Central Station for most of the data that flows through the CPU. When data values are loaded from memory, this is where they are stored. When a computation is performed by the ALU, this is where the result goes. Any number that is to be stored in main memory must be first loaded into the AC and then moved to memory from there.

Altogether, these eight registers have a total of eighteen control wires. There are nine other control wires in the computer: the seven controls of the ALU, main memory's Load-data-into-memory wire, and the clock's Stop-clock wire. Everything done by the CPU is accomplished by turning these control wires on and off. The COUNT register's Increment-COUNT wire is continually turned on and off by the clock. All the other control wires are connected to the Control circuit, which is responsible for turning them on in the correct sequence.

Recall that the CPU works by repeatedly carrying out a fetch-and-execute cycle. Each cycle has two parts: fetching a machine-language

---

[5] In real computers, the clock output is fed directly to a large number of components. A great deal of circuitry is devoted to making sure that the signal from the clock gets to each component at the proper time.

instruction from memory and then executing that instruction. The first of these two parts will be the same in every cycle; the second part depends on what instruction is being executed.

A fetch-and-execute cycle will be carried out in a sequence of steps. Step 1 is done when the value in the COUNT register is 0001_2, step 2 when that value is 0010_2, and so on. As the last step in each cycle, the value in COUNT will be reset to zero, and the next cycle will begin when COUNT is automatically incremented to 0001_2 at the next tick of the clock. Each step is completely defined by the control wires that are turned on during that step. Our job, as we try to construct a design for xComputer, is to specify both the sequence of steps necessary to carry out each possible machine-language instruction and which control wires need to be turned on during each step.

We can deal with the fetch part of the fetch-and-execute cycle without knowing anything about how to execute specific instructions, since the first three steps in each cycle will always be the same. Fetching an instruction means loading it from memory into the instruction register (IR). Now, before *anything* can be read from memory, its address must be loaded into the address register (ADDR). So, as the first step of the fetch-and-execute cycle, the CPU must load the address of the next instruction to be executed into ADDR. Since the required address is in the PC, this step can be accomplished simply by turning the Load-ADDR-from-PC control wire on and off.[6]

Once the correct address has been loaded into ADDR, the instruction we want will be available on the main memory's output wires. In the second step of the fetch-and-execute cycle, this instruction is loaded into IR by turning the Load-IR-from-memory control wire on and off. In the third step, the value in the PC is set up to get ready for the next instruction. We do this by turning the Increment-PC control wire on and off, in order to add 1 to the value in the PC. So, no matter what instruction is to be executed, the first three steps in the fetch-and-execute cycle will always be:

Step 1: Turn on Load-ADDR-from-PC.

Step 2: Turn on Load-IR-from-memory.

Step 3: Turn on Increment-PC.

---

[6] This is another example of the general process of reducing some "action" that the computer needs to perform to manipulation of control wires. Once again, I emphasize that this sort of thing is the key that makes it practical to build working computers.

For each step, I have listed the wire that is to be turned on during that step. In some of the later steps for executing certain instructions, several wires can be turned on at the same time. As each new step begins, any wire that was turned on for the previous step is to be turned off unless it is specifically listed for the new step.

The three steps listed here are done when the value in the COUNT register is, respectively, 0001_2, 0010_2, and 0011_2. For example, we must design our Control circuit so that when the value in COUNT is 0001_2, the Load-ADDR-from-PC wire, and only that wire, will be on. When the value in COUNT changes to 0010_2 at the next tick of the clock, the Load-ADDR-from-PC wire goes off, and Load-IR-from-memory comes on.

The steps that come after the first three depend on what instruction is being executed. (Of course, this depends in turn on the program stored in main memory, since the instruction was loaded from some location in memory.) We can't go any further in our analysis until we know exactly what instructions are available and how they are represented.

3.1.3. Input/Output. But before we do the hard work of getting xComputer to execute machine-language programs, we should make sure that we will be able to use the computer we design. Our computer will be perfectly useless if we have no way of getting a program into memory, no way of telling the CPU to start executing it, and no way of finding out the result of that execution. We need some way of getting data into and out of the computer. The process of moving data from the outside world into a computer is called *input*; data flowing in the opposite direction is called *output*. Collectively, input and output are usually referred to by the abbreviation I/O.

Real computers have sophisticated I/O capabilities, but in this chapter I am interested only in showing that I/O is possible in principle. How can we add enough I/O capability to make xComputer minimally usable?

We already know how to load numbers into main memory by hand. It's a simple matter of setting the values of the memory's input and address wires and then turning Load-data-into-memory on and off. When we put the computer together, all these wires will be connected to the CPU, but there is nothing to stop us from providing additional connections to a bank of switches that can be used to manually turn the wires on and off.

In order to load a program into memory, we need switches connected to its input, address, and control wires. In order to tell the CPU to execute that program, we must load the program counter with the address of the first instruction in the program. To do this, we need switches connected to the program counter's input wires and to its **Load-data** wire. Finally, we will need a switch connected to the **Stop-clock** wire. This switch can be on while we load the memory and PC. Once everything is set up, turning **Stop-clock** off will start the computer running.

We also need some way to determine the result of executing a program. This means that we must be able to inspect the contents of memory after the program ends. This is also easy. We can use the switches we have already attached to the address wires to pick out any location in memory whose value we want to check. Once we have done so, the number in that location can be read from the memory's output wires—we might attach a small light bulb to each of these wires to indicate whether that wire is off or on.[7] This simple I/O capability is enough to let us load programs, tell the CPU to execute them, and check the results.

3.2. Fetching and Executing

Each machine-language instruction to be executed by xComputer must be encoded as a sixteen-bit binary number. Most instructions specify two things: an operation to be performed, and some data that is to be used in the operation. In most cases, the data is the address of a location in memory. This address uses up ten bits of the instruction out of the sixteen available. This leaves the other six bits to use as an *instruction code*, which specifies the operation. Let's say that the six leftmost bits of an instruction will be used to encode the operation, and the rightmost ten bits the data. It will be useful to have names for each of the six bits of the instruction code; we will call them I_5, I_4, I_3, I_2, I_1, and I_0 (numbered from right to left, corresponding to the powers of two represented by the bits of a binary number). The format of an instruction then looks like this:

I_5	I_4	I_3	I_2	I_1	I_0	10 data bits

With six bits for an instruction code, we can encode up to 2^6, or sixty-four, different instructions. In fact, we will only have thirty-one,

---

[7] All this is not, by the way, as silly as it might seem. When the very first "personal computer," the Altair, was introduced in 1976, its I/O facilities were essentially the same as those described here. See [Levy, *Hackers*].

Instruction Code (binary)	Instruction Code (decimal)	Short Name	Long Name
000000_2	0	ADD	Add-to-AC
000001_2	1	SUB	Subtract-from-AC
000010_2	2	AND	Logical-AND-with-AC
000011_2	3	OR	Logical-OR-with-AC
000100_2	4	NOT	Logical-NOT-of-AC
000101_2	5	SHL	Shift-AC-left
000110_2	6	SHR	Shift-AC-right
000111_2	7	INC	Increment-AC
001000_2	8	DEC	Decrement-AC
001001_2	9	LOD	Load-AC-from-memory
001010_2	10	STO	Store-AC-in-memory
001011_2	11	HLT	Halt
001100_2	12	JMP	Jump
001101_2	13	JMZ	Jump-if-AC-is-zero
001110_2	14	JMN	Jump-if-AC-is-negative
001111_2	15	JMF	Jump-if-FLAG-is-set

Figure 3.7. *The sixteen basic instructions for xComputer, with instruction codes zero through fifteen. Each instruction has a long name, which says pretty much what it does, and a two- or three-letter abbreviation. For the instructions HLT, NOT, SHL, SHR, INC, and DEC, the data bits of the instruction are ignored. For the other instructions in this table, the data bits give the address of a location in main memory.*

and for the moment we will limit ourselves to the sixteen instruction codes shown in Figure 3.7. The remaining instructions will be modified versions of some of the instructions in this list.[8] The instructions shown in the figure have instruction code numbers between zero and fifteen. They also have names, and we will almost always refer to the instructions by name rather by number. (Remember, though, that the computer can only deal directly with the binary numbers.)

We are now faced with a double task: to understand the purpose of each of these instructions, and, more important, to determine a sequence

---

[8] In fact, the sixteen instructions in Figure 3.7 would be sufficient to build a general-purpose computer. The other instructions merely make the computer easier to program.

of steps that will execute the instruction. Once that is done, we will be ready in the next section to design a Control circuit to carry out those steps.

3.2.1. Stopping the computer.   Let's start with the simplest instruction, Halt. The purpose of the Halt, or HLT, instruction is to stop all further activity in the computer (that is, until it is manually restarted). We have arranged things so that this can be done simply by turning on the clock's Stop-clock control wire. Once that is done, the COUNT register will stop counting and no further steps will take place. There is only one step for executing HLT, beyond the three steps introduced in the previous section that are the same for all instructions.

Step 4 (HLT). Turn on Stop-clock.

A program will generally end with a HLT instruction, unless the program is really intended to execute forever (that is, until the computer is physically turned off or unplugged—which is the way most real computers actually work).

Note that the ten data bits of a HLT instruction are ignored. That is, it doesn't matter what value they have; the effect of the instruction will be the same. The same is true for the other instructions that do not require any data: NOT, SHL, SHR, INC, and DEC.

3.2.2. Moving Data.   The next two instructions we consider, Load-AC-from-memory and Store-AC-in-memory, are used to move data back and forth between the CPU and memory. The ten data bits for these instructions specify the location in memory that is to be used. When LOD is executed, a copy of the value in the specified location is loaded into the accumulator, erasing and replacing whatever was there before. For example, 0010010000011101, or "LOD 29," specifies that the number stored in memory location 29 is to be copied into the accumulator. STO moves data in the opposite direction, from the accumulator to the memory location; again, the previous contents of the memory location are erased and replaced.

These instructions are easy to execute. As always, before loading or storing anything in memory, we first load ADDR with the address of the memory location we want to use. When we are executing a LOD or STO instruction, this address is given by the ten data bits of the instruction in the instruction register. To get the address into ADDR, it is only necessary to turn the Load-ADDR-from-IR control wire on and off. Once that is done, the data can be moved using the appropriate control wire. The steps for executing LOD and STO are shown in Figure 3.8. Note

> ## To execute Load-AC-from-memory (LOD):
>
> Step 4 (LOD). Turn on Load-ADDR-from-IR.
>
> Step 5 (LOD). Turn on Load-AC-from-memory.
>
> Step 6 (LOD). Turn on Set-COUNT-to-zero.
>
> ## To execute Store-AC-in-memory (STO):
>
> Step 4 (STO). Turn on Load-ADDR-from-IR.
>
> Step 5 (STO). Turn on Load-data-into-memory.
>
> Step 6 (STO). Turn on Set-COUNT-to-zero.

Figure 3.8. *Steps for executing LOD and STO instructions. For each step, the control wire to be turned on during that step is specified.*

that the last step in each case is to reset the counter to zero. This is done at the end of each instruction to get ready for the next fetch-and-execute cycle, which will begin as the counter is next incremented to 1.

3.2.3. Two-operand Computational Instructions.

The first four instructions in Figure 3.7 perform arithmetic or logical computations that combine two numbers to give a result. Each of the instructions Add-to-AC, Subtract-from-AC, Logical-AND-with-AC, and Logical-OR-with-AC uses the value in the accumulator as one input or "operand" in the computation. The second operand is taken from some location in memory. The ten data bits of the instruction give the address of the location in memory that holds this second operand. The result of the computation is put back into the accumulator.

To execute one of these instructions, we first load ADDR with the address of the second operand. Then that number is copied into the Y register while the number in the accumulator is copied into the X register. At this point, one of the ALU's control wires is turned on to tell it which operation to perform. For an ADD instruction, we turn on Select-Add; for SUB, Select-Subtract; for AND, Select-AND; and for OR, Select-OR. While this control wire is turned on, we load the answer into the accumulator by turning Load-AC-from-ALU on and off. (In the case of ADD and SUB, we also load the Flag output of the ALU into the FLAG register.) The steps for executing an ADD instruction are shown in Figure 3.9.

3.2.4. One-operand Computational Instructions.

The remaining five computational instructions, Logical-NOT-of-AC, Shift-AC-

---

To execute Add-to-AC (ADD):

Step 4 (ADD). Turn on Load-ADDR-from-IR.

Step 5 (ADD). Turn on Load-X-from-AC
and Load-Y-from-memory.

Step 6 (ADD). Turn on Select-Add, Load-AC-from-ALU,
and Load-FLAG-from-ALU.

Step 7 (ADD). Turn on Select-Add.

Step 8 (ADD). Turn on Set-COUNT-to-Zero.

Figure 3.9. *The steps for executing an ADD instruction. The steps for SUB, AND, and OR are similar, except that a different control wire replaces* Select-ADD. *Also, for AND and OR, the FLAG register is not involved. There is one subtle point: The ALU must continue to output the result of the computation while* Load-AC-from-ALU *is turned on and off. If* Select-ADD *were turned off too soon, the output of the ALU might change before the process of loading the answer into the accumulator were complete. For this reason,* Select-ADD *remains on throughout Steps 6 and 7, while* Load-AC-from-ALU *is turned off at the end of Step 6.*

left, Shift-AC-right, Increment-AC, and Decrement-AC, perform computations that involve a single operand. The first three of these use the ALU to perform the computation and are very similar to the instructions discussed in the previous subsection. As an example, the steps for executing Shift-AC-right are shown in Figure 3.10.

When we come to INC and DEC, the situation is a bit different. These instructions change the value stored in AC but do not use the ALU. Incrementing or decrementing the value in the accumulator can be accomplished simply by turning a control wire of the accumulator on and off. This can be done in a single step. Here, for example, are the steps for executing INC:

Step 4 (INC). Turn on Increment-AC.

Step 5 (INC). Turn on Set-COUNT-to-zero.

3.2.5. Jumps. We come finally to the Jump instruction and the three conditional jump instructions Jump-if-AC-is-zero, Jump-if-AC-is-negative, and Jump-if-FLAG-is-set. Instructions of this type were discussed in Section 1.3. They are required to produce loops and to allow programs to make decisions between alternative courses of action.

To execute Shift-AC-right (SHR):

Step 4 (SHR). Turn on Load-X-from-AC.

Step 5 (SHR). Turn on Select-Shift-Right, Load-AC-from-ALU, and Load-FLAG-from-ALU.

Step 6 (SHR). Turn on Select-Shift-Right.

Step 7 (SHR). Turn on Set-COUNT-to-zero.

Figure 3.10. *The steps for executing a SHR instruction. The steps for SHL and NOT are essentially the same, except that NOT does not involve the FLAG register. The steps here are similar to those for the ADD instruction. However, since SHR has only one operand, there is no need to load a second operand from memory into the Y register.*

To execute a Jump (JMP):

Step 4 (JMP). Turn on Load-PC-from-IR.

Step 5 (JMP). Turn on Set-COUNT-to-zero.

To execute a Jump-if-Zero (JMZ):

Step 4 (JMZ). If AC is zero, turn on Load-PC-from-IR.

Step 5 (JMZ). Turn on Set-COUNT-to-zero.

Figure 3.11. *The steps for executing JMP and JMZ instructions. For JMZ, a control wire is turned on in step 4 only if the value currently stored in the accumulator is zero; if it is nonzero, no wire is turned on, the value in the PC is unchanged, and the instruction has no effect. JMF and JMN are similar to JMZ, except that a different condition is checked in step 4.*

When a JMP instruction is executed, it changes the value stored in the program counter. Since the PC holds the address of the instruction to be executed during the next fetch-and-execute cycle, this makes the CPU "jump" to a new location in the program instead of simply going on to the next instruction in sequence. The new value for the PC—that is, the address of the location to which the CPU will jump—is taken from the ten data bits of the JMP instruction. All that is necessary to execute a JMP instruction is to copy the data bits of the instruction from the instruction register to the PC.

In a conditional jump instruction, the value of the PC might or might not change, depending on whether or not some condition holds. If the condition holds, the PC is changed and the CPU jumps to the new location. Otherwise, the CPU will continue on with the next instruction in sequence just as if the conditional jump instruction had not been executed at all.

Our machine language includes three conditional jump instructions, which test three different conditions. JMZ will cause a jump to a new location in the program if the value in the accumulator is zero; if it is nonzero, the JMZ instruction will have no effect. JMN tests whether the value in AC is negative; because of the way we are representing negative numbers, this just amounts to testing whether the leftmost bit is one. And JMF tests whether the single bit stored in the FLAG register is one or zero; it produces a jump when this value is one.[9] The steps for executing jump instructions are shown in Figure 3.11.

3.2.6. Addressing Modes.   The machine language-instructions we have covered so far have six-bit instruction codes that begin with 00. The machine language for xComputer has fifteen additional instructions that begin with 10 or with 01. The new instructions are shown in Figure 3.12. The only difference between these instructions and those we have already covered is the interpretation of the ten data bits.

Consider, for example, an ADD instruction. Its data bits specify the address of a location in memory. That location holds the actual number that will be added to the accumulator when the instruction is executed. Suppose you wanted to add 37 to the accumulator. You would have to store the 37 in some memory location. Let's say you put it in memory location 1023 (1111111111_2 in binary). The instruction you would need to perform the addition would be "ADD 1023," or in machine language

$$0000001111111111.$$

The first six bits here, 000000, say that this is an ADD instruction. The remaining bits tell where the number 37 is to be found. It would be more convenient in this case to have an instruction whose data bits give the actual number to be added, rather than the location of that number in memory. That's what the instruction ADD-C is for: The ten data bits of ADD-C, interpreted as a binary number, are added to the

---

[9] JMF could be used, for example, to test whether a previous ADD instruction produced a carry form the leftmost column; this might represent an answer too big for the computer to handle. The JMF could jump to a section of the program written to handle such an error.

Instruction Code (binary)	Instruction Code (decimal)	Short Name	Long Name
010000_2	$0+16$	ADD-C	Add-Constant-to-AC
010001_2	$1+16$	SUB-C	Subtract-Constant-from-AC
010010_2	$2+16$	AND-C	Logical-AND-Constant-with-AC
010011_2	$3+16$	OR-C	Logical-OR-Constant-with-AC
011001_2	$9+16$	LOD-C	Load-AC-with-Constant
100000_2	$0+32$	ADD-I	Add-Indirect-to-AC
100001_2	$1+32$	SUB-I	Subtract-Indirect-from-AC
100010_2	$2+32$	AND-I	Logical-AND-Indirect-with-AC
100011_2	$3+32$	OR-I	Logical-OR-Indirect-with-AC
101001_2	$9+32$	LOD-I	Load-AC-Indirect-from-memory
101010_2	$10+32$	STO-I	Store-AC-Indirect-in-memory
101100_2	$12+32$	JMP-I	Jump-Indirect
101101_2	$13+32$	JMZ-I	Jump-Indirect-if-AC-is-zero
101110_2	$14+32$	JMN-I	Jump-Indirect-if-AC-is-negative
101111_2	$15+32$	JMF-I	Jump-Indirect-if-FLAG-is-set

Figure 3.12. *The remaining fifteen instructions in our machine language. The instructions in Figure 3.7 use "direct addressing." Each instruction listed here is a modified version of an instruction from Figure 3.7 that uses one of the other addressing modes, constant addressing or indirect addressing. The instruction code for a modified instruction is obtained from the instruction code of the original instruction by changing one of the two leftmost bits to one. This corresponds to adding 16 or 32 to the original code number.*

accumulator. There is no need to store the number elsewhere in memory. The instruction code for ADD-C is 010000_2, and 37 written in binary is 0000100101_2, so you could add 37 to the accumulator with the machine language instruction 0100000000100101, or "ADD-C 37."

When an ADD-C instruction is executed, there is no need to go to memory to find the data to be added. That data is already in the instruction register. Because of this, ADD-C takes one fewer step than ADD. The exact steps needed are left as an exercise.

We consider ADD and ADD-C to be the same instruction, using different **addressing modes**. The addressing mode refers to the interpretation of the data bits in an instruction. The regular addressing mode, used in ADD, is called **direct addressing**, whereas ADD-C uses

---

To execute Add-Indirect-to-AC (ADD-I):

Step 4 (ADD-I). Turn on Load-ADDR-from-IR.

Step 5 (ADD-I). Turn on Load-Y-from-memory.

Step 6 (ADD-I). Turn on Load ADDR-from-Y.

Step 7 (ADD-I). Turn on Load-X-from-AC
and Load-Y-from-memory.

Step 8 (ADD-I). Turn on Select-Add, Load-AC-from-ALU,
and Load-FLAG-from-ALU.

Step 9 (ADD-I). Turn on Select-Add.

Step 10 (ADD-I). Turn on Set-COUNT-to-zero.

Figure 3.13. *The steps for executing ADD-I. This is similar to the execution of an ADD instruction, but the number loaded into Y in step 5 is not the number we want to add to the accumulator. Instead, it is the* address *of that number. So, we must load this address into ADDR before we can load the actual number into Y in Step 7.*

a mode that we will call ***constant addressing***. Our machine language also includes constant addressing versions of SUB, AND, OR, and LOD.

Real computers can have many different addressing modes. This is a source of much of the complexity in machine languages. Constant addressing is particularly useful. I have included one other addressing mode in the machine language for xComputer, mainly to give you an idea of what other modes are possible. In ***indirect addressing***, the ten data bits of the instruction give the address of a location in memory. However, that location does not contain the data to be used in the instruction. Instead, it contains the address of *another* memory location that does contain the data. Admittedly, this is rather confusing. Looking, for example, at the steps for executing ADD-I, the indirect addressing version of ADD, might help. These steps are given in Figure 3.13.

There are indirect addressing versions of SUB, AND, OR, LOD, STO, JMP, JMZ, JMN, and JMF. For the jump instructions, the data bits give the address of a location in memory, and that location contains the number that is to be loaded into the PC.

The machine language for a real computer can be very complex, including hundreds of different instructions. As you should expect, this complexity must have some structure if it is to be managed. Addressing modes can help provide such structure. Instructions that perform the same operation but use different addressing modes can be conceptually grouped together. This structure is apparent even in our simple language. For example, the three addition instructions ADD, ADD-C, and ADD-I form such a group.

This structure is reflected in the six-bit codes we use for machine language instructions. The first two bits of the code indicate the addressing mode: 00 for direct, 01 for constant, and 10 for indirect. The remaining four bits indicate the operation: addition, load, jump, and so forth. If you inspect the construction of the Control circuit in the next section, you will see that its design is simplified by this division of the instruction code into addressing mode plus operation.

3.3. Self-control

We have now seen how the machine-language instructions for xComputer can be executed in the CPU. As I promised, the execution of a machine-language program is accomplished by nothing more than turning control wires on and off in the right sequence.

In order to determine which wires should be turned on, you need to know only a few things. First, you need to know which step of the fetch-and-execute cycle is currently being executed; this can be determined by looking at the four-bit number stored in the COUNT register. Second, when the step number in COUNT is greater than three, you need the six-bit instruction code of the instruction that is being executed. This code is stored in the leftmost six bits of the instruction register. Finally, for the case of the conditional jump instructions, you will need to know the numbers stored in the accumulator and in the FLAG register.

With just this information—the outputs of the COUNT, accumulator, and FLAG registers and the leftmost six bits of the output from the instruction register—you could execute the program by hand, turning on the necessary wires for each step.

Of course, the problem is that you aren't around to work the control wires while the program is being executed. It all has to be done by the CPU. Somehow, the computer has to control *itself*. This is what the Control circuit is supposed to do. Earlier in the chapter, I promised that when the time came to design the Control circuit, it would be simple. Perhaps you have already seen why that is so.

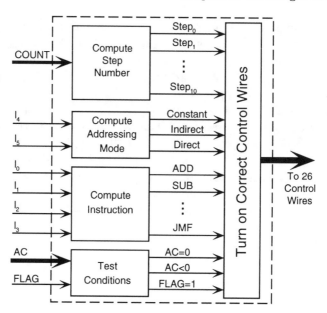

Figure 3.14. *A design for the Control circuit. The decoder circuits on the left convert the inputs to the Control circuit into a more useful set of signals. The circuit on the right uses these signals to decide which control wires to turn on.*

The Control circuit will have twenty-six output wires, which are connected to each of the computer's control wires (except for Increment-COUNT, which is connected to the output of the clock). It has twenty-seven input wires, which are connected to the four outputs from COUNT, the leftmost six outputs from IR, the sixteen outputs from the accumulator, and the single output from FLAG. For any combination of input values, we know which control wires should be turned on; thus, we know what the outputs should be. We could make a table containing this information. But wait! An input/output table of this sort is all that is needed to design a circuit, as we saw in Chapter 2. That chapter showed how to use Boolean algebra to build a circuit from a table of input/output values. So, without any work at all, we already know that the Control circuit can be built in principle.

In practice, the design of the Control circuit can be greatly simplified if its outputs are computed in two stages, as shown in Figure 3.14. The inputs to the Control circuit are fed through several "decoder" circuits.

The decoders translate these inputs into a more useful form for deciding which control wires should be turned on. The design of the decoder circuits is easy, since their outputs are given by simple Boolean expressions of their inputs. These outputs are:

- Step$_1$,..., Step$_{10}$. Exactly one of these wires will be on, depending on the value of COUNT. These can be used to test which step of the fetch-and-execute cycle is being currently executed. (None of the machine language-instructions requires more than ten steps, which is why we don't go up to Step$_{15}$.)
- Constant. This is turned on if the current instruction uses the constant addressing mode. In fact, this is just bit I_4 of the instruction register.
- Indirect. Indicates indirect addressing mode. This is bit I_5 of the instruction register.
- Direct. Indicates direct addressing mode. Its value is given by NOT Constant AND NOT Indirect.
- ADD, SUB, ..., JMF. Exactly one of these wires will be on, indicating the current instruction. Which wire is on depends only on bits I_0, I_1, I_2, and I_3 of the instruction register. Note that ADD is turned on for the instructions ADD-C and ADD-I, as well as for ADD itself. These three instructions are distinguished by the addressing mode wires.
- AC=0, AC<0, and FLAG=1. These outputs are used only in the conditional jump instructions, JMZ, JMN, and JMF. AC=0 is on whenever the number in the accumulator is zero; AC<0 is on if that number is negative; and FLAG=1 is on if the bit stored in the FLAG register is one.

It is straightforward to write a Boolean expression for each control wire in terms of the outputs from the decoder circuit. Some of them are very easy. For example, Increment-PC is turned on during Step 2 of every instruction cycle and at no other time. It follows that

$$\text{Increment-PC} = \text{Step}_2.$$

That is, Increment-PC can be connected directly to Step$_2$. Most wires, however, require nontrivial Boolean expressions that can be constructed by inspecting the list of steps for executing each of the thirty-one possible instructions. For example, the Select-ADD control wire of the ALU is used only in the execution of ADD, ADD-I, and ADD-C. After checking the list of steps for those instructions to see when Select-ADD should be on, we can write

Select-ADD = (ADD AND Direct AND (Step$_6$ OR Step$_7$))
$\qquad$ OR (ADD AND Indirect AND (Step$_8$ OR Step$_9$))
$\qquad$ OR (ADD AND Constant AND (Step$_5$ OR Step$_6$)).

This expression is **true** for exactly those steps of exactly those instructions when Select-ADD must be turned on. All we need to do is build the circuit specified by the expression and connect its output to Select-ADD.

We don't need to go through expressions for all twenty-six control wires here. It is easy, if a bit tedious, to write them down. The point is that with these expressions in hand, we can use them as a blueprint for a Control circuit that will turn control wires on and off in exactly the right sequence to execute any machine-language program. This gives us the last piece we need to complete a working CPU.

3.3.1. Black Boxes. And that's it! Our design for a working computer is now complete. We have what we set out to find: a machine that stores and executes programs.

It is worth stepping back for a minute and admiring the design, because it's an impressive piece of work. We started out with very simple tools: three types of logic gates and a mathematical theory of how to put them together to perform simple operations on individual bits. From there we built an ALU to perform more complex operations on binary numbers. We also constructed a main memory with a large number of individually addressable storage locations. This provided us with a place to store a program and a way of fetching its instructions one by one. The last step—getting the computer to do all the work of executing a program *on its own*—might have looked impossible. But by cleverly arranging the CPU so that the fetch-and-execute cycle could be done in a sequence of simple steps, we reduced the problem of building the Control circuit to an elementary problem in logic-circuit design.

The result is a complex machine, but one that can be understood. This understanding is possible because of the way we built up the structure step by step, one level at a time. It is not all that difficult to put logic gates together into one-bit adders. From there, we can easily put sixteen one-bit adders together, and suddenly our circuits can work with binary numbers, not just individual bits. Once we have circuits to do various operations on binary numbers, we can combine them into an ALU—a general-purpose calculating circuit that does a major part of the work in the computer.

On each level, we assemble a small number of components that we already understand. These components can be used as **black boxes**.

That is, we don't have to think about what's inside them. All we need to remember is what they can do and how to get them to do it. This is called the *interface* of the black box. The interface specifies its behavior. What's inside, the stuff that makes it behave the way it does, is called the *implementation*. The idea is that once you have built the black box—or bought it off the shelf—the implementation is not important. All you need to know in order to use it is the interface.

The idea of keeping implementation separate from interface is sometimes called the *Black Box Principle*. One aspect of this principle is that in order to use something you need to know "how to work it," but you don't need to know "how it works." This, however, is only one side of things—the view from outside the box. Viewed from the inside, the Black Box Principle says that in order to *design* something, you need to know what it's supposed to do, but you don't need to know the exact use to which it will be put. For example, when we designed our addition circuit, our goal was to create a circuit that would add two binary numbers. At the time, you didn't know (or care) how it would be incorporated into a computer.

The Black Box Principle is really just another, more concrete way of formulating the idea of structured complexity that we first encountered in Chapter 1. It is a way of limiting the amount of detail you have to deal with at one time by keeping the various components and the various levels of a complex system separate. I hope you will agree that our success in designing a working computer shows the power and usefulness of this idea.

3.4. Postscript: Assembly Language

This chapter has dealt extensively with individual machine-language instructions. But such instructions are only really useful when combined into a program that does something interesting. It is only fair before leaving the chapter that I give you some idea what such programs look like.

Consider a simple program that adds the two numbers in locations 200 and 201 and puts the result back into location 200. In the machine language of xComputer, such a program would read

```
0010010011001000
0000000011001001
0010100011001000
```

Obviously, programs that look like this are not meant to be read, or written, by humans. As a first step, instead of writing six-bit instruction codes, we can write the name of the instruction. And instead of writing the ten-bit data part of the instruction in binary, we can write it in base ten. With these changes, the program becomes

LOD   200

ADD   201

STO   200

Written in this way, the program is much more readable, and it is easy to translate it into machine language—so easy, in fact, that a computer program can be written to do the translation. A program that is written using instruction names instead of binary instruction codes is called an *assembly-language program*, and a program that translates assembly language into machine language is called an *assembler*. It assembles a "real" machine-language program out of the merely convenient assembly language form.

Before turning to a more interesting example, it will be useful to make our assembly language even more flexable. We already allow names to be used in place of instruction code numbers. Names are easier than numbers for humans to deal with. It would be nice if we could use names for memory locations as well. Names used in this way—as names for memory locations—are called *labels*. A label can refer to a memory location that contains data, or it can refer to a position within the program itself. Labels of the first type could be used in ADD, LOD, and STO instructions; labels of the second type could be used in jump instructions. For example, if an assembly-language program uses the label "sum" for memory location number 200, then that program could say "LOD sum" instead of "LOD 200."

The idea of using labels is a powerful one. A programmer can create and use a label without even knowing what location in memory that label refers to. The assembler can do all the work of figuring out where the data is actually stored, or which location a jump instruction is supposed to jump to. All the programmer needs to know is that the location exists. The example in Figure 3.15 shows how labels can be assigned to specific memory locations and used in a program. The labels in this example, *Loop*, *Done*, *Num*, and *Ans*, are meaningful names chosen by some programmer. It is much more natural to use such names instead of meaningless, arbitrary-looking numbers.

Neither program in Figure 3.15 could be executed as-is by a computer. An assembler would have to be applied to either program to convert it

Location	Instruction		Label	Instruction	
0	LOD-C	100		LOD-C	100
1	STO	13		STO	Num
2	LOD-C	0		LOD-C	0
3	STO	14		STO	Ans
4	LOD	14	Loop:	LOD	Ans
5	ADD	13		ADD	Num
6	STO	14		STO	Ans
7	LOD	13		LOD	Num
8	DEC			DEC	
9	JMZ	12		JMZ	Done
10	STO	13		STO	Num
11	JMP	4		JMP	Loop
12	HLT		Done:	HLT	
			Num:	data	
			Ans:	data	

Figure 3.15. *Two programs for adding up the numbers 100, 99, 98, ..., down to 1. The program on the right uses labels, or names, for memory locations. Note that the program on the left must be stored in memory starting at location 0; otherwise, the JMP command will not jump to the correct instruction. The program on the right can be assembled to start at any memory location. The assembler will determine the correct location number to use in the JMP instruction. The "data" instruction used on the last two lines of this program does not represent a machine-language instruction; instead, it is a place-holder that tells the assembler to reserve a memory location for some data.*

into a machine-language program consisting entirely of zeros and ones. In the machine-language program, any labels in the program will be replaced by the binary numbers they represent. Fortunately, the tedious task of "counting off" the instructions in the program to determine what number each label represents is easy enough to leave to the assembler program.

The sample program in Figure 3.15 actually performs a nontrivial computation: It adds up the numbers from 1 to 100. To do this the program must do 100 additions. The idea is to start with zero and then add in each of the numbers, one at a time. Although we could do this with 100 separate instructions, it makes more sense to use a loop. Each time through the loop, we add one number. The heart of the loop, then, consists of adding the next number to the sum we have computed so far. This part is essentially the same as the three-instruction program given at the start of this section. That much is easy, but there are a lot of details to work out. We have to use a memory location to store the sum we are computing, we need another location to keep track of which numbers have been added to the sum so far, and we have to exit from the loop when all the numbers have been added. It is a little easier to add the numbers in reverse order, starting with 100. That way, we can use a JMZ instruction to exit from the loop when the number being added gets down to zero.

The program uses two memory locations for storing data. These locations are referred to as *Ans* and *Num* in the second version of the program. *Ans* is used to store the sum computed so far. When the program ends, this location will contain the sum of all 100 numbers. *Num* is used to store the next number that still has to be added to the sum. The first four instructions set things up so that the sum starts out at zero and the first number to be added will be 100.

The loop starts with the location labeled *Loop*. The first three instructions in the loop add *Num* to *Ans*. The next two instructions subtract one from *Num*. If the result is zero, then all the numbers have been added; the JMZ instruction will jump out of the loop to the halt instruction at the end of the program. Otherwise, the result, which is the next number that still has to be added, is put back into *Num*, and the JMP instruction jumps back to the beginning of the loop.

This example should convince you of two things: First, that machine-language programs can do nontrivial things, and second, that it is not necessarily easy to write those programs. In the early history of computing, most programming was done in assembly language. Even after compilers became available that could translate more sophisticated high-level languages into machine language, many programmers preferred to write in assembly language because by working in the "native language" of the computer, they could write faster, smaller programs. As computers have become faster, memory cheaper, and compilers better, the use of assembly language has become rare, but it is used even today when the speed or size of the program is especially critical. However, high-level languages are easier to use, and I will postpone serious consideration of programming until I introduce a high-level language in Chapter 6.

Chapter Summary

A computer is a *machine*. Although it does not consist of levers and gears, it is mechanical in that its operation consists of a sequence of steps, each of which directly and inevitably causes the next. Ultimately, this process is driven by a *clock*, which emits a regular sequence of on/off pulses as it ticks. At each tick of the clock, one small step in a computation is performed. What that step will be depends entirely on the contents of the CPU's *registers*. Since some of these registers are connected to the computer's main memory, the course of the computation is affected, in a purely mechanical and predictable way, by the contents of that memory. Of course, looked at from the right point of view—the human point of view that sees a world of meaning—all this mechanical activity can add up to the execution of a complex, meaningful, and perhaps infinitely surprising program.

By exhibiting the detailed design of a working model computer, this chapter has shown how the execution of a computer program can be reduced to a sequence of very simple, mechanical steps that can be carried out by circuits of the type introduced in Chapter 2. Each individual step is performed by turning on control wires attached to such circuits. The control wires that need to be turned on are determined entirely by just a few bits of information, namely (in our model computer) by the contents of the COUNT register, the accumulator, the flag register, and part of the instruction register. This information is fed into a logic circuit called the *Control circuit*, which turns control wires on and off in a pattern completely determined by its inputs.

The computation performed by our model computer is made up of a sequence of *fetch-and-execute cycles*. During each cycle, one *machine-language instruction* is fetched from memory and executed. An individual machine-language instruction doesn't accomplish very much. Certain instructions perform simple computations (such as ADD, SHL, and INC). Others—LOD and STO—move individual pieces of data between the CPU and the main memory. Still others—the jump instructions—control the order of execution of program instructions by changing the value of the *program counter*. Beyond this, there is really not very much, even in computers much more complicated than our model, but some flexibility is provided by the existence of various *addressing modes*.

The construction of complex programs from such simple instructions is aided by the existence of *assemblers*. These are programs that manipulate other programs. They can take programs written in *assembly language* and translate them into the zeros and ones of machine language. Assembly language uses *names* instead of binary numbers for instructions and memory locations. The important role of names carries over into *high-level programming languages*, which are covered in later chapters.

Questions

1. Since the X register is always loaded from the accumulator, why can't we just eliminate X and connect the output of the accumulator directly to the ALU's input?

2. Make a drawing of xComputer showing how all of its components are interconnected. (Use a large piece of paper!) Using this diagram, follow in detail the flow of data within the computer as several different machine-language instructions are executed. Try to understand how each connection is used and why it is necessary. That is, what machine-language instructions require the connection, and what data flow along it.

3. Our machine-language instructions are coded as six-bit instruction codes. There are 64 different codes, but we have only 31 different instructions. More than half of the instruction codes are meaningless. Suppose one of these meaningless codes is loaded into the instruction register. How should the CPU react? One possibility is to ignore the code and do nothing during the execute part of the fetch-and-execute cycle. Another would be to be to assume that the bad code is an error and halt the computer. You might be able to come up with other possibilities. After deciding what you would do, explain how you would implement it. What specific changes would be required in xComputer's Control circuit? Try to figure out what xComputer will do with bad instruction codes if you build the Control circuit exactly as described in this chapter.

4. Perhaps the control wires that contribute the most to the "intelligence" of xComputer are Load-PC-from-IR and Load-PC-from-memory. These wires are used in the jump and conditional jump instructions to change the value of the program counter. Without them, the CPU would be doomed to following a sequence of instructions from beginning to end with no loops or decisions. Only very dull programs could be written. Design the part of the Control circuit that controls these wires. You will need to consider the sequence of steps for executing each of the eight jump instructions (using both direct and indirect addressing).

5. What changes would be necessary in xComputer to allow it to use more memory locations? To allow it to work with binary numbers with more bits? (These two questions are interdependent. Why?)

6. This chapter ignored the fact that much of the data manipulated by computers represents characters rather than numbers. This question shows that the machine-language instructions that are available in xComputer can perform some useful operations on character data. Recall that a character is represented as an eight-bit ASCII code. Each location in memory holds sixteen bits. If we want to save space, we can store characters in a "packed" format, two characters per location. But it is generally more convenient to store characters in an "unpacked" format, with one character per location. In unpacked format, the eight leftmost bits are set to zero. Write two small assembly-language programs to convert between packed and unpacked character representations. One program should take two characters stored in packed format in a single location, and it should separate those characters into two locations in unpacked format. The second program should do the reverse. (Hint: What happens when you AND a number with 0000000011111111_2?)

7. Recall from Chapter 1 that a subroutine is a sequence of instructions that can be jumped to from another part of a program. After the subroutine ends, the computer should pick up where it was when the jump to the subroutine occurred. The machine language for xComputer does not directly support subroutines. Nevertheless, you can use subroutines if you handle their implementation "by hand." The subroutine must end with a jump back to the correct memory location. Before the jump to subroutine occurs, the program must stash this location in a place where the subroutine can find it when it needs it. Work out this implementation in detail.

8. If you would like a real challenge, you might try to write an assembly-language program that multiplies two numbers. Assume that the product of the two numbers is small enough to be represented with sixteen or fewer bits. (In all honesty, this is much too hard a problem for me to ask you to do at this time. Remember that the answer is in the back of the book.)

Chapter 4

Theoretical Computers

IN THE MID 1930s, it was discovered that there are certain surprising limitations on what can be accomplished by computers, even given unlimited time and memory. This was all the more remarkable, given that no computer even existed at the time.

The mathematicians who made these discoveries were faced, first of all, with defining exactly what it means to compute something. Several very different-looking definitions were invented. Using any of these definitions, it was found that certain things are "uncomputable." It might seem that the best course would have been to look for better definitions. But another surprise lay in store.

As people began comparing definitions, it was realized that even though they seemed quite different, in fact, the very same things would turn out to be computable no matter which was used. All the definitions that had been put forward were fundamentally equivalent. And since then, no one has come up with anything better. Any proposed definition of computability has been proved to be either equivalent to those invented in the 1930s or strictly more limited than them.

In a sense, any computer that is built can be thought of as a definition of what it means to compute. We could simply say "computation is what *this* computer does." Now, there are obvious limitations to what any real computer can do. It might run into problems that it can't solve only because it doesn't have enough memory, or because you aren't willing to give it enough time—say, several million years—to find a solution. But we can imagine giving the computer as much memory as it needs and letting it run for as long as necessary, and we can ask what it can do given such unlimited resources. We then find that the answer doesn't depend on the computer at all. Ignoring limitations imposed by lack of memory and time, all computers are equivalent in what they can compute. And they are all equivalent to the theoretical computers developed in the 1930s. In particular, they are all subject to fundamental limits that apply even given unlimited time and memory.

In this chapter, I will explain how we know that all computers are equivalent. Then, I will discuss Turing machines, a particularly simple type of theoretical computer introduced by Alan Turing in 1936. The advantage of using Turing machines to define computability is their simplicity, which makes it easier to analyze them than it is to analyze real computers. We will take advantage of this simplicity to show that there are interesting problems that can't be solved by Turing machines, nor therefore by any computer.

4.1. Simulation and Universality

Over the course of the last two chapters, we developed a design for a simple working computer, which we called "xComputer." But it might have seemed to you that xComputer could not be capable of very much. It can execute thirty-one different machine-language instructions, but each instruction does very little. The things the instructions do are variations of only a few types of operations: moving data around, performing arithmetic and logical operations, and changing the value of the program counter. Yet I am claiming that any computation that can be done by any computer can be done by a program written using only these thirty-one simple instructions.

Note that I am not claiming that xComputer can necessarily run that program. We gave our computer an extremely limited memory, which is simply not big enough to hold any but the most simple programs. But we could easily redesign it with as large a memory as necessary to run any given program, without changing the instructions that it can execute. I am really interested in a theoretical version of xComputer, with a memory "as large as necessary." (How large will depend on the program we want to run, so I cannot fix a size once and for all.) In the rest of this chapter, when I talk about xComputer, I will be referring to this imaginary, theoretical version.

Note also that my claim has nothing to do with input/output. When you use a real computer, you probably engage in a kind of dialog with it, in which you give it a command or enter some data and wait for it to respond. This interaction is not itself computation—merely a way of telling the computer what to compute. It's what the computer does internally, while you are waiting, that I am calling "computation." Obviously, xComputer cannot imitate the sophisticated interaction that you can engage in with real computers; it lacks a mouse, monitor, and keyboard, for one thing. What I am claiming is that xComputer can perform any computation that any other computer can do, once that computer has been set up to compute something—with data and programs already loaded into memory.[1]

Finally, I am not claiming that xComputer can directly run a program written for another computer. Each computer is built to execute its own machine language. Different languages can provide different instructions, and they probably use very different encodings even for instructions with the same meaning. If you load a machine-language program written for another computer into xComputer's memory and try to run it, xComputer's circuits will react to the bit patterns in the program in ways that have nothing to do with their intended meanings. The result will look completely random.

So what do I mean when I say that xComputer can perform any computation that can be done by any other computer? First of all, I mean that if you give me any program written for any computer, I can write a program for xComputer that will always produce the same result as your program, given the same data. Here, "giving the program data" just means loading that data into memory with the program. As the program runs, it can read the data, make changes to it, and write new

---

[1] Actually, real computers *do* get extra computational power from their input/output capabilities, but this is only because they have main memories of a fixed, limited size. If the computer can do input and output between main memory and the outside world, it can use more data and program instructions than can fit into its memory at one time. The outside world here can refer to so-called "external memory" such as disk drives and magnetic tape drives—or to a human who can type in data as needed. Note that if the computer's main memory is "as large as necessary," then the ability to do I/O becomes irrelevant, since we can load a program and all its data into memory and also leave room for any "scratch work" that the computer might need to do during the course of the computation.

data. By the "result" of running the program with that data, I just mean the contents of memory after the program halts. Note that I am required to produce a *single* program that will give the same result as your program for *any* possible data. This requirement is important; if I were permitted use different programs for different data, I could cheat by producing programs that simply write the desired result to memory without doing any computation at all!

What I will actually show is that xComputer can **simulate** any other computer. Simulation means something stronger than just giving the same result: xComputer will get the results by following the same steps as the other computer, on some level. Because xComputer is relatively simple as computers go, it might take it many steps to accomplish what can be done by one instruction on other computers. But there will be a sequence of stages in xComputer's computation that will correspond to the steps taken by the other computer. While step-by-step simulation is not in itself my goal, it provides an effective way of proving that one machine can do any computation that can be done by another.

4.1.1. Translation.   Given a program written in any other language, the most natural approach is to try to **translate** it into a program in xComputer's machine language. This will provide the fastest possible simulation, but it will be easy only if the original language is almost the same as xComputer's in the first place.

For example, if the original program contains an instruction that adds a value from some location to the accumulator, it can be translated directly into an ADD instruction for xComputer. However, if the original program contains a multiplication instruction, it will have to be translated into a sequence of many instructions, since xComputer does not have a single instruction that does multiplication.

The problems can be much worse than this. The original program might use subroutines. It might include addressing modes that are not available for xComputer. It might use "real numbers" (with decimal points), not just integers. All of these things can in fact be translated into the machine language of xComputer, but it's not easy, and I won't convince you just by saying so. Simply talking about translation is not going to convince you of xComputer's power.[2]

---

[2] Nevertheless, translation is very important. It can be applied to any language—even if it's not the machine language of any existing computer. This is the case for two types of translators that have already been mentioned, assemblers and compilers. These translate, respectively, assembly languages and

4.1.2. Interpretation. Closely related to translation is another form of simulation called *interpretation*. Instead of translating the program all at once, we let xComputer inspect the instructions in the program and perform the actions encoded by each instruction, one at a time.

Of course, when I say that xComputer will do this, I mean that it will run a program to do it. That program is called an *interpreter*. The original program and its data are loaded into part of xComputer's memory. The interpreter, which is written in xComputer's machine language, is loaded into another part of xComputer's memory. When it is run, it will read the instructions in the original program and carry them out one by one; we say that it *interprets* that program.

As the interpreter interprets another program, it is in effect playing the role of the CPU of the simulated computer, imitating the exact sequence of fetch-and-execute cycles that that CPU would go through. Important data that the CPU would keep in its registers are kept instead in xComputer's memory. For example, one memory location would be a "simulated program counter," which the interpreter uses to keep track of which instruction is next in line to be executed in the program it is interpreting. Another memory location might hold the equivalent of the simulated CPU's accumulator.

The basic structure of an interpreter program is fairly simple. It consists of a loop that imitates the fetch-and-execute cycle of the simulated computer. That is, the loop finds the next instruction to be executed and simulates its execution, and then it repeats this process over and over until the program halts. The part of the loop that simulates the execution of one instruction is just a decision among a number of alternatives, one for each possible instruction code used by the simulated computer. Given an instruction to be simulated, the interpreter compares its instruction code to each possible code and then jumps to a segment of the interpreter program designed to simulate that particular instruction.

---

high-level languages into machine language. Programmers who write in a high-level language such as Pascal or BASIC tend to think as if there were a computer that could run their programs directly. Such an imaginary computer is called a *virtual machine*. When a high-level language program is translated into machine language, this virtual machine is being simulated by a real computer. In theory, it would be possible to build a real computer that executes high-level language programs directly, but its circuitry would be extremely complex. Translation allows the programs to be run on much simpler machines.

When it comes to simulating these individual instructions, however, we run into the same sort of problem we had with translation: Simple instructions are easy to simulate, but it is not obvious that we will be able to handle all the complex types of instructions that we might encounter.[3]

However, we can make things easier for ourselves by dropping down one level of complexity. Recall that when the CPU executes an instruction, it does so in a sequence of steps. A single step might, for example, move a number from one place to another, increment the value in a register, or load a register with the output value from a complex circuit like the ALU. Instead of trying to simulate an instruction all at once, suppose we simulate each of the small, simple steps needed to execute that instruction.

Simulation on this level will allow many of the details to take care of themselves. For example, simulating a jump-to-subroutine instruction might seem pretty complex for xComputer, which does not implement subroutines directly in its machine language. However, the simulated computer must execute such an instruction in a series of simple steps such as storing a value in memory and changing the value of the program counter. By simulating those steps, xComputer will simulate a jump-to-subroutine without ever "knowing" that it is doing so.

This whole discussion still assumes that the simulated computer is very similar in design to xComputer. And it still leaves us with the problem of simulating complex operations such as multiplication. So I still can't claim to have convinced you that xComputer can simulate any other computer. But maybe you can see what the final step is: If simulation at a lower level makes things easier, maybe we should work on the lowest possible level.

4.1.3. Low-level Simulation.   From a low-level point of view, computers are constructed from extremely simple components, which are easy to simulate. I will assume in my discussion that those components are AND, OR, and NOT gates (and a clock), but the discussion will clearly apply to any computer that is built of components that take a small

---

[3] Still, interpreters, like translators, are important programs. I can buy a program for my Macintosh SE/30 computer that will allow it to run machine-language programs written for the IBM PC. The PC programs cannot be executed directly by the Macintosh's CPU. Instead, they are interpreted in just the manner described here. In addition, interpretation can be applied to high-level languages as well as to machine languages. At least one such language, LISP, is usually interpreted rather than compiled.

number of one-bit inputs and produce a one-bit output according to some simple rule.[4]

Suppose that we want to simulate some computer. To prepare for the simulation, we load xComputer's memory with a complete representation of that computer on the logic-gate level. Each logic gate is represented by a block of several memory locations. One of these locations holds a code indicating what sort of gate is being represented; we use a code of 0 for a NOT gate, 1 for an AND gate, and 2 for an OR gate. A second location holds the value—0 or 1—on the gate's output wire.

For each of the gate's input wires, we use *two* memory locations. One of these just holds the value of the input. The other is used to encode information about how wires are connected in the computer. A computer is not just a bunch of gates; it is a bunch of gates intricately connected in a very specific pattern. Each input wire of each gate is connected to the output wire from some other gate. The identity of that output wire is the second piece of information we must store for each input wire. We encode that identity simply by storing the address of the memory location that holds the value on that output wire.

Finally, we need one memory location to store the value on the clock's output wire. We use memory location number one for this purpose and reserve memory location zero for "scratch work" during the course of the simulation. Figure 4.1 shows how a very simple logic circuit would be represented in xComputer's memory.

When the simulated computer is in a steady state—that is, when the values on wires are not changing as they do during the course of

---

[4] In this text, I am following the common practice of using the term "computer" to refer to what is more properly called a "digital computer." The components that make up a digital computer have inputs and outputs that can take on only the two values zero and one (or possibly some other small set of values such as the decimal digits from zero to nine). An *analog computer*, on the other hand, includes components whose inputs or outputs can vary over a continuous range of values. For example, instead of just being on or off, the voltage on an input wire might be any of the infinitely many numbers between 0 and 1. However, since voltages on a wire can never be measured with complete accuracy, there is an inherent degree of error in analog computations. In fact, the activity in an analog computer can be simulated in a digital computer—with even more accuracy than is physically possible in the analog computer itself. This would seem to imply that digital computers can do anything that analog computers can do, and analog computers have mostly fallen out of use. However, there is increasing interest is a certain type of analog computer called a "neural net." Neural nets are used in artificial intelligence research, and we will meet them again in Chapter 12.

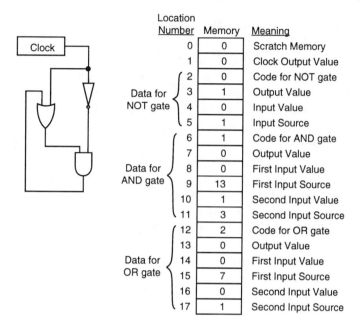

Figure 4.1. *Here's how we could simulate a small (and perfectly useless) logic circuit in xComputer's memory. Each gate in the circuit on the left is represented by a block of memory locations. Those locations store information about what type of gate it is, where its inputs are connected, and what the values are on its input and output wires. Location 1 stores the value on the clock's output wire. If this value is changed, it is easy to simulate the resulting changes in the circuit. Simulating a whole computer is just a larger version of this example.*

a computation—the value on each input wire must be the same as the value on the output wire to which it is connected. However, whenever the value on some output wire changes during the course of a simulated computation, the value on any input wire connected to that output also changes. Then, of course, it is possible that the output from the gate to which that input is connected will change. This can cause further changes down the line. This cascade of changing values is, in fact, the substance of a computation, and it is such sequences of changes that we have to simulate.

Recall what the activity inside a computer looks like on this level: The computer is in a steady state. Then the clock ticks; that is, the value on the clock's output wire changes. This sets off a ripple of activity in the computer's circuits that can change the values on many gates. Eventually, the activity stops with the computer in a new steady state, which lasts until the clock ticks again. We have everything we need to simulate the activity of the computer on this level.

Before running the simulation, we must set up the contents of xComputer's memory to represent the state of the other computer at the moment before it starts executing a program, including the contents of its main memory. But recall how bits are stored in memory: Each bit is stored in a one-bit memory circuit and is represented by the value on the output wire from one of the gates in that circuit. So, if we store all the information about the state of each gate in the computer, we have *already* represented the contents of its memory along with everything else! (You might object that this does not really represent the contents of the computer's memory, but in fact every bit in that memory is represented by some bit in xComputer's memory. You can inspect the values of these bits after a computation has been simulated, to determine the result of that computation. It's true that those bits are scattered through xComputer's memory, and it might take some work to pick them out, but obviously it is not the point of this discussion to make things convenient.)

Once all this is set up in memory, we need only a fairly short xComputer program to do the actual simulation. The program uses memory location 0 to determine when activity in the simulated computer dies down between ticks of the clock. I leave it to you to convince yourself that this program can be written in xComputer's machine language.

Step 1. Change the value in location 1 (from 1 to 0, or from 0 to 1). This represents a tick of the simulated computer's clock.

Step 2. Store a 0 in location 0. (This will be changed to a 1 in step 4 unless the cascade of changes set off by the tick of the clock has ended.)

Step 3. Loop through each of the gates of the simulated computer. For each input wire, check whether the value recorded for that input matches the value recorded for the output wire to which it is attached. (Recall that we have carefully put the address of this output value where xComputer can find it.) If not, change the value recorded for the input wire.

Step 4. Loop through each of the gates of the simulated computer. For each gate, check its inputs and compute what the corresponding output should be. (This involves checking the type of gate, as well as the input values.) If the output recorded for the gate does not agree with the correct output, change the recorded output value *and store a 1 in location 0.*

Step 5. Check the value in location 0. If it is 1, then jump back to step 2. (A 1 in location 0 means that some output wire has changed value, and therefore the activity in the simulated computer has not yet died down. Steps 2 through 5 will repeat until no further changes occur.)

Step 6. Check the value in whatever memory location represents the Stop-clock wire. If it is one, then Halt; the simulated computation has finished. Otherwise, go back to step 1 to begin simulation of the next tick of the clock. (The simulated computer might have some other method of indicating that a computation is finished. This step should make the appropriate test. The computer must have some simple way of indicating that the computation is finished—turning some wire on or off, loading a certain value into some register or some memory location, or executing a jump to some specific location. These are all things that can be tested, with more or less difficulty.)

Running this program will simulate every detail of the activity inside the simulated computer as it performs its computation. It follows that the result of the simulated computation must be the same as the result when the computation is performed by the real computer. This shows that xComputer is capable of doing any computation that that computer can do.

The simulated computation will, of course, take an outlandishly long time. For each tick of the simulated clock, xComputer will have to loop through all the simulated gates, perhaps many times. It will execute literally millions of instructions (from its own machine language) to simulate a single step of the computation. If you want a practical simulation, you will have to use translation or interpretation. But remember that we are trying to determine what computers can do in theory, ignoring limitations imposed by time and memory restrictions.

The advantage of very low-level simulation is the *simplicity* and the *generality* of the approach. It is simple enough to be implemented on xComputer, or even on a much simpler machine. And it is general enough to allow simulation of any computer. Thus, it provides what I hope is a convincing demonstration that any computation that can be done by any computer can be done—perhaps much more slowly—by xComputer.

4.1.4. Computational Universality. Everything I have been saying about xComputer is true about any computer with a reasonable set of machine-language instructions. It should be clear that I have been talking about "xComputer" only so that I could keep straight the difference between the computer doing the simulation and the computer being simulated. In fact, apart from limitations imposed by time and memory, any computer that has some minimal level of computational capability can simulate any calculation that can be done by any other computer. If we compare two computers, again ignoring limitations of time and memory, we will find that each can simulate the other, and therefore neither is in theory more powerful than the other. In this sense, all computers—at least, all computers worthy of the name—are equivalent.

Let's put it another way: We can divide all possible problems into two classes: those that can be solved by a computer given enough time and memory, and those that cannot. When we make this division, it doesn't matter what computer we are thinking of. *Any* computer can solve *all* the problems in the first class, but it will be foiled by any problem in the second class. We say that any given computer is ***computationally universal***. This just means that it can be universally applied to all problems that can be solved by computer.

I will show later in this chapter that there are, in fact, problems that cannot be solved by any computer. Note, however, that this does not settle the issue of whether there are problems that *cannot* be solved by computer but that *can* be solved by some other method that we would be willing to call computation. The hypothesis that there are *no* such problems is called the ***Church-Turing Thesis*** (named after Alonzo Church and Alan Turing who independently proposed the thesis in the 1930s). The Church-Turing Thesis asserts that anything that can reasonably be called computation can be done by a computer. This thesis is generally believed to be true, but it is not something that can be proved since its truth depends to some extent on what people are willing to call computation.

We have seen that a computer does not have to be very complicated to be computationally universal. In the next section we shall see that a very simple machine indeed can display this surprising property. How can it be that the complex computations of sophisticated computers can be simulated with such meager resources? In fact, the answer was already implicit in the discussion of structured complexity in Chapter 1.

Considered at a low enough level, computers are made from very simple parts which interact with each other in very simple ways. Complexity arises from the large number of parts used and from the way those parts are connected together. But the interconnections among the parts can be treated as passive data—just a list of facts—that can be stored in another machine's memory. Once this is done, that machine can run a simulation using very few computational resources. The complexity is still there, but it is in the machine's memory rather than in its circuitry. And, if we get tired of simulating one computer, we can always load a description of a different computer into memory and simulate that one instead. The same simple machine can still do the job.

4.2. Turing Machines

One of the theoretical models of computation developed in the 1930s was based on abstract machines that we would recognize today as simple computers with infinite memory. These machines are now called **Turing machines**, after their creator, Alan Turing. Turing machines are abstract in that they cannot really be constructed, because of the requirement of infinite memory. Indeed, they were never meant to be constructed. Turing was interested in studying the theory of computation. He needed a definition that would be easy to analyze rather than practical. He was able to use his imaginary machines to prove many fundamental results, and his definition of computation is still the one most commonly used in the abstract study of the theory of computation.

A Turing machine has two parts, analogous to the CPU and main memory of a computer. Its processing unit is much simpler than the CPU of any computer, which is what makes Turing machines easy to analyze. On the other hand, it has an infinite memory in which data structures of any degree of complexity can be stored.

The memory of a Turing machine is called its **tape**. It can be visualized as a strip of paper, stretched out to infinity in both directions. The tape is divided into **cells**, which correspond to the memory locations in a computer. Each cell either can be **blank** or can hold a single symbol. The only symbols I will use in this chapter are the digits 0 and 1 and the letters x, y, and z.[5] A Turing machine tape, then, might look like this:

---

[5] The details of the definition of a Turing machine can be varied in many ways. For example, its tape might be infinite in only one direction, or it might be limited to using only the symbols 0 and 1. The variations don't matter in the end, for a reason that should not surprise you: Each type of Turing machine can be *simulated* by any other type, so that no type has more computational power than any other.

	1	1	0	x		0	0	z	1	1			

$\cdots$ ... $\cdots$

Sometimes, I will need to write a blank so that you can see it; in that case, I will write it as a sharp sign ($\#$).

The Turing machine's processing unit is a small device that moves back and forth along the tape, reading, writing, and erasing symbols. Its activity is very simple. It can work on only one cell on the tape at a time. It reads the contents of that cell. It might or might not change those contents. Then, it moves one cell over, either to the left or right. And it repeats this process continually until it halts.[6]

Like a CPU, the processing unit of the Turing machine has some internal memory, but that memory holds only one piece of data, the current *state* of the Turing machine. There is one special state called the *halt state*, which we will denote by h. A Turing machine enters the halt state when it finishes a computation. The other states are represented by numbers between zero and some maximum value. Different Turing machines can have different numbers of states, but any particular machine has a fixed, finite number of possible states. When we say that a Turing machine is "in state number N," we just mean that the number N is stored in its memory. As a Turing machine computes, moving from cell to cell on the tape, it can also change from one state to another.

To perform a calculation with a Turing machine, we will write some data for the calculation into some cells on its tape. Then we set the machine down on some cell and start it up in state number zero. At each step in the calculation, it reads the contents of the current cell—x, y, z, 0, 1, or blank. It then takes some action, based *only* on the contents of the cell and on its current state. The action it takes will have three steps:

1. It *writes* a symbol or a blank on the cell it is currently occupying, replacing the previous contents of that cell. (It doesn't necessarily change the contents of that cell; the value it writes might be the same as the

---

[6] Note that the tape of a Turing machine differs from the memory of a computer in one essential aspect. A computer's memory is random access; that is, the computer is able to read any location at any time just by specifying its address. A Turing machine, on the other hand is capable only of *sequential access*. At any given time, the Turing machine is positioned at some particular cell on the tape. To move to a different cell, it must pass sequentially over all the cells between its old position and its new position. In fact, the cells do not even have addresses. There is nothing to distinguish one cell from another, and the Turing machine doesn't "know" which cell it is currently reading.

Current State	Current Cell Contents	New Cell Contents	Direction of Motion	New State
0	0	1	R	1
0	1	0	L	0
0	#	1	R	1
1	0	0	R	1
1	1	1	R	1
1	#	#	L	h

Figure 4.2. *The specification of a simple Turing machine. Each line in the table specifies the action that will be taken by the machine when it is in a certain state, and the cell it is scanning contains a certain character. The action will consist of (possibly) changing the contents of the cell, moving to the next cell either to the right or to the left on the tape, and (possibly) changing to a new state. In the last line of the table, the new state is the halt state, h. If the Turing machine ever enters this state, it will halt. This table is actually incomplete. It does not specify what the Turing machine will do if it encounters a x, y, or z. To complete the table, we specify that if it encounters one of these symbols, it will move right and halt.*

old value.) We specify this part of the action by stating what value the machine writes. This can be x, y, z, 0, 1, or #.

2. It then *moves* on the tape either one cell to the left or one cell to the right. We specify this part of the action with one of the letters L or R.

3. It then *changes state*. (It is allowed to "change" to the same state that it is currently in.) The new state is specified by h, for the halt state, or by the number of the new state. If the new state is the halt state h, then the computation is finished; otherwise, the machine begins another step in the calculation.

A Turing machine can be completely specified by a table that gives the action that it will take for each possible combination of current state and current cell contents. In practice, we do not require that each possible combination actually appears in the table; we assume that for any combination of state and cell contents not listed in the table, the action taken by the Turing machine is to move right and halt. (In most cases, the omitted lines of the table are irrelevant to the intended use of the machine.) Figure 4.2 shows a specification of this type for a simple Turing machine.

You can imagine a Turing machine's processing unit as containing a Control circuit which controls the activity of the machine. The inputs to this circuit are the current state number and the contents of the current tape cell. The outputs of the circuit determine the action to be taken by the machine. A table like that in Figure 4.2 can be thought of as a specification for this Control circuit. Sometimes this type of table is referred to as a "program" for a Turing machine, but that can be misleading because, unlike a program, the information in the table is *hard-wired* into the machine. When we do finally encounter something more like programs for Turing machines, those programs will be placed on the Turing machine's tape, just as programs for a computer are placed in its memory. And it will only be very special Turing machines that can run such programs.

4.2.1. Useful Machines. When you look at the table in Figure 4.2, it probably seems pretty random, and if you were to start up the machine it specifies, its activity might seem random as well. Of course, that activity is completely determined by the table and by the contents of the tape, and we can trace by hand the exact steps that the Turing machine will take.

Suppose, for example, that the tape contains 1011 in four consecutive cells and that the rest of the tape is blank, and suppose we start the machine running on the rightmost 1. Remember that a Turing machine always starts in state 0. According to the table, since it is in state 0 and reading a 1, it should write a 0, move left, and remain in state 0. The tape now reads 1010, and the Turing machine is on the second digit from the right, in state 0. In the second step of the computation, the same rule applies, so the machine again writes a 0, moves left, and stays in state 0. This time, the cell contains a 0. In state 0, reading a 0, the Turing machine writes a 1, moves right, and changes to state 1. The tape now reads 1100.

If you continue to trace its activity, you will see that the Turing machine moves right twice, without changing the tape or changing state. In the final step of the computation, it encounters a blank, moves left and changes to the halt state h. This ends the computation. So in the end, the tape contains 1100 and is otherwise blank. The Turing machine is positioned on the rightmost zero.

Nothing that Turing machines do is more complicated than this, except that the tables that dictate their actions can be longer. Yet we have seen that complex calculations can be performed as a sequence of very simple steps, and the question is, can the simple steps taken by a Turing machine add up to something interesting? In fact, it can be shown that Turing machines can perform any calculation that can be done by any computer.[7]

In fact, even the simple Turing machine of Figure 4.2 does something interesting: It adds one to a binary number. If you write the number n in binary on a tape and start up the machine on the rightmost digit, then when it halts, the tape will contain the binary number $n + 1$. For example, $1011_2 + 1_2 = 1100_2$, and when we traced the calculation of this Turing machine with input 1011, we saw that it eventually halted with 1100 on the tape. You should trace its calculation on other inputs, such as 100, 0, and 1111, to convince yourself that it works as advertised in all cases.

To deal more rigorously with the theory of Turing machines, we need a standard definition of what it means for a Turing machine to compute something. The definition formalizes the idea of giving the machine some input, letting it compute, and seeing what output it produces. Our definition does not represent the only way of using Turing machines, but it is a definition that is convenient for mathematical analysis.

The inputs and the output will be nonnegative integers $(0, 1, 2, \ldots)$, written on the tape as binary numbers.[8] We will always write a specified number of inputs on the tape, with one blank space between consecutive inputs. The rest of the tape will be blank. The Turing machine will be started, in state 0, on the rightmost digit of the last input. We will say that this computation produces the output n if the Turing machine

---

[7] This does not say that any Turing machine you happen to make up is computationally universal. You might need a different Turing machine for each different calculation. However, as we will see below, there *are* certain individual Turing machines that are computationally universal.

[8] Of course, as we saw in Chapter 1, any type of data can be *encoded* as binary numbers. Since the meaning of a calculation is always an interpretation, we can always interpret a Turing machine as working with other types of data if we like. For example, we could write a list of words in ASCII code on the tape and try to build a Turing machine whose output will be the same list of words sorted into alphabetical order. From one point of view, that machine takes a binary number as input and computes another binary number as output. From a lower level point of view, all it does is move back and forth on a tape, reading and writing symbols. But from the point of view of the user, it is performing the useful task of alphabetizing a list of words. In *any* of these cases, the computation in itself has no meaning. The meaning comes from the interpretation.

halts with the number n written in binary on an otherwise blank tape. There are two things that might go wrong: It is possible that the Turing machine might just keep running forever. Or, even if it does eventually halt, the tape might not contain a single binary number when it halts. In either of these case, we will say that the Turing machine produces *no output* for that input. We are mostly interested in machines that produce outputs for all possible inputs.

For example, if I say that a certain Turing machine adds pairs of binary numbers, I mean that if you take any two binary numbers whatsoever, write them on the tape separated by a blank and start up the Turing machine on the rightmost digit of the second number, then the machine will eventually halt with the sum of the two input numbers written on the tape. Furthermore, the tape will be blank except for this sum.

Suppose, more generally, that k is some fixed number, and that T is a Turing machine that produces an output for *any* set of k binary inputs. (That is, we are assuming that for any such inputs, T will halt with some single binary output number written on its tape.) We then say that T computes a ***function*** from $\mathbf{N}^k$ to $\mathbf{N}$. Here, following standard mathematical notation, $\mathbf{N}$ represents the set of all nonnegative integers, and $\mathbf{N}^k$ represents all possible sequences of k nonnegative integers. A function from $\mathbf{N}^k$ to $\mathbf{N}$ associates some single output integer to each possible set of k inputs. If f is the name of a function from $\mathbf{N}^k$ to $\mathbf{N}$, and $n_1, n_2, \ldots, n_k$ are any k integers, then the notation $f(n_1, n_2, \ldots, n_k)$ is a short-hand way of saying "the output of the function f when it is given the numbers $n_1, n_2, \ldots, n_k$ as input." For example, addition can be considered as a function with two inputs; in this case, $f(n_1, n_2)$ is given by $n_1 + n_2$.

Turing machines provide one way of defining functions, but it is *not* the case that *every* function from $\mathbf{N}^k$ to $\mathbf{N}$ can be computed by a Turing machine. Those special functions that can be are called ***Turing computable***.[9] To reiterate the definition: A function f from $\mathbf{N}^k$ to $\mathbf{N}$ is

---

[9] I mentioned at the beginning of the chapter that several definitions of computability were developed in the 1930s. Turing computability is one of those. You might be curious about what other sorts of definitions are possible that would be "very different" form this one. Well, Alonzo Church's definition bypasses the whole *process* of computation entirely! What Church did, more or less, was say, "Here are some very simple functions that are obviously computable, and here are some simple things we can do with functions to generate new functions. Let's say that all the functions that we can generate in this way

called Turing computable if there is some Turing machine T that computes f. And T is said to compute f if whenever T is started on a tape with k integers n_1, n_2, ..., n_k as input, it will eventually halt with output $f(n_1, n_2, \ldots, n_k)$.

4.2.2. Building Blocks. So far, we have seen only one example of a Turing machine, as given in Figure 4.2. This Turing machine computes the function $f(n) = n + 1$, which is not a completely trivial accomplishment but is still very far from the level of complexity of computations that can be done by computers. In order to be able to deal with such complexity effectively, we need some way of combining simpler Turing machines into more complex machines. The basic ideas for constructing new machines from old are simple: (1) When a machine halts, we might want to restart it in state number 0 to continue its calculation; (2) We might want one machine to take up where another leaves off; (3) When the first machine halts, we might want to start up one of several different possible machines, based on the status of the first machine when it halts.

These three constructions ought to look familiar. They are essentially the same as the three ways we can build complex programs: loops, sequences of instructions, and decisions among alternatives. Building complex Turing machines turns out to look very much like programming. I will not give the complete details of how each construction is done, since they are rather technical. However, I will give some examples.

Actually, we don't work with the machines themselves but with the tables that specify their behavior. As an example, let's consider the Turing machine of Figure 4.2. Suppose we modify the last line of the table in this figure by replacing the h in that line with a 0. The resulting table will define a new machine. When this machine encounters a # while in state 1, it will enter state 0, instead of state h. Where the first machine would have halted, the new machine will *loop back* to state 0 and continue computing. After adding 1 to its input, this machine will then go on to add 1 to the result, and it will continue adding 1 to the number on the tape forever. It is effectively counting in binary.

In general, a loop can be introduced into any Turing machine's calculation by changing the halt state h to some other state in one or more lines of the specification of that machine.

---

starting with the trivially computable functions are ***recursively computable***, and see what we can prove about them." In the end, as I mentioned, it turns out that the recursively computable functions and the Turing computable functions are the same.

Current State	Current Cell Contents	New Cell Contents	Direction of Motion	New State
0	0	1	R	1
0	1	0	L	0
0	#	1	R	1
1	0	0	R	1
1	1	1	R	1
1	#	#	L	2
2	0	1	R	3
2	1	0	L	2
2	#	1	R	3
3	0	0	R	3
3	1	1	R	3
3	#	#	L	h

Figure 4.3. *A specification for a Turing machine that adds 2 to its input. This table is made of two copies of the table from Figure 4.2. In order to avoid conflicts between state numbers, the second copy has been modified by adding two to each state number. The first copy has been modified so that instead of halting, it will enter the first state of the second machine. In states 0 and 1, this machine adds one to its input. Then in states 2 and 3, it adds one to the result. After doing the second addition, it halts.*

Next, suppose we want a machine that will add 2 to its input. We already have a machine that adds 1. I would like to take two copies of that machine and have the second one start when the first one halts. That is, in the case where the first machine would halt, I would like it instead to enter the starting state of the second machine. The table for the combined machine will consist of modified copies of the tables for each machine, as shown in Figure 4.3.

A similar construction can be used to sequence the calculations done by any two machines. It is a simple extension from this to allowing one machine to "decide" which of several possible machines to start up after it halts, provided there are several lines in the first machine's table in which that machine enters the halt state. We can modify each of those lines so that, instead of halting, it will enter the starting state of one of the other machines.

We can use a combination of methods to construct complex Turing machines. Consider for example the problem of adding two binary num-

Current State	Current Cell Contents	New Cell Contents	Direction of Motion	New State
0	0	0	L	1
0	1	1	L	2
1	#	#	R	h
1	0	0	R	h
1	1	1	R	h
2	#	#	R	h
2	0	0	R	h
2	1	1	R	h

Figure 4.4. *A Turing machine that checks whether a number is zero. This machine must be started on the rightmost digit of the number, and the number must be preceded by a blank on the tape. The calculation performed by this machine consists of just two steps. It moves left on the first step and right on the second. It does not change its tape, and it halts in the same position in which it was started. However, it halts with "knowledge" of whether or not the number on the tape is zero. If that number is zero, the machine will see a zero on its first step and a blank on its second step. The second step it takes is the one indicated by the third line in the table. If we change the h in the third line of the table to the start state of a second machine, then that machine will be run provided the number on the tape is zero. If there is another machine that we want to run when the number on the tape is nonzero, we just have to change the h in each of the other lines of the table to the start state of that machine.*

bers placed as input on a tape. One way of doing this is to subtract one from the second number and add one to the first number, and repeat this until the second number is zero. If that zero is then erased, the number remaining on the tape is the sum of the two input numbers.

A Turing machine to do this can be constructed from separate machines that add one to a number, subtract one from a number, check if a number is zero, erase a number, and move left or right from the rightmost digit of one number to the rightmost digit of the number next to it on the tape. Each of these machines is easy to construct. The one obscure point is what it might mean for a machine to "check if a number is zero." This is explained in Figure 4.4.

From these small machines, we first construct a single machine that subtracts 1 from a number, then moves left to the neighboring number on the tape, adds 1 to that number, then moves back to the number on the right, and halts. Let's call this Turing machine T_1. Next, we build a machine that checks if its input is zero. If so, it starts up a machine that erases the zero; otherwise, it starts up the machine T_1. Let's call this Turing machine T_2. Finally, we introduce a loop into T_2 by modifying it so that after its submachine T_1 finishes its calculation, T_2 will loop back to its start state instead of halting. This modified machine, T_3, is a Turing machine for adding binary numbers.

4.2.3. Universal Turing Machines.

It is possible to build very complex Turing machines, but can Turing machines really do any computation that can be done by computer? One way to prove that they can is to build a Turing machine that can *simulate* the computations done by computers. Such a machine would be computationally universal.

In fact, it is possible to build a Turing machine that can perform low-level simulations of computers similar to the type of simulation discussed in Subsection 4.1.3. When a suitably encoded description of the computer is written on its tape, this Turing machine will simulate the computation of that computer using the six-step procedure outlined in Subsection 4.1.3. I will not try to give the details of the construction of such a machine, but I hope that the hints I give will convince you that it can in fact be built.

When we used xComputer to simulate another computer, we used xComputer's memory to store information about each logic gate in the machine being simulated. We could instead write all this information onto a Turing machine's tape, with the numbers from consecutive memory locations separated on the tape by a blank cell. In steps 3 and 4 of the simulation, where xComputer "loops through each of the gates of the simulated computer," the Turing machine will move along its tape and perform the equivalent actions.

Consider step 4 first. It is easy enough to design a Turing machine that will look at the inputs to each simulated gate, decide what the output should be, and check whether the output recorded for that gate is correct. If it is not correct, though, the Turing machine is supposed to store a 1 in location 0. In order to do this, the Turing machine will have to move all the way back to beginning of the data on the tape, where the number in location 0 is written.

There is no problem with doing this, but then the Turing machine will have to return to the location on the tape where it discovered the incorrect output value, so that it can continue on to process the next gate. The solution is for the machine to write a y at the spot where it is

Current State	Current Cell Contents	New Cell Contents	Direction of Motion	New State
0	#	y	L	1
1	0	0	L	1
1	1	1	L	1
1	#	#	L	2
2	0	0	L	1
2	1	1	L	1
2	#	#	R	3
3	#	#	R	4
4	0	1	R	5
4	1	1	R	5
5	0	0	R	5
5	1	1	R	5
5	#	#	R	5
5	y	#	R	h

Figure 4.5. *The specification of one of the submachines used in constructing a Turing machine that simulates computers on the logic-gate level. If this machine is started on a blank cell, it will change that blank to a y [in state 0] and then move left [in states 1 and 2] until it encounters two consecutive blanks. (This is how it recognizes the beginning of the data on the tape.) It then moves right two cells [in states 2 and 3] to a cell that must contain a 0 or a 1. If it contains a 0, the machine writes a 1 into the cell [in state 4]. It then moves right [in state 5] until it encounters the y it left to mark its place, changes the y back to a blank, and halts.*

working before it moves. Then, it will be able to return to that spot by searching for the y.[10] Figure 4.5 gives a specification for a submachine that carries out the task equivalent to storing a 1 in location 0.

Step 3 of the simulation is somewhat harder, since it involves looking up values at specified addresses in memory, but Turing machines have no built-in way of addressing memory. Here is one way we can make a Turing machine simulate addressing. Suppose that the Turing machine is currently located at the beginning of a number written on its tape and that the number specifies some address in the memory of xComputer. We want the machine to move to the position on the tape corresponding

---

[10] I'll bet you were wondering what I was going to do with the symbols x, y, and z.

to that address. After reading the value stored at that address, the machine must return to its original position.

The Turing machine should start by marking its current location with a y. Then, it should copy the address to the beginning of the data on the tape and mark the beginning of the data with an x. It is also convenient to mark the end of the address with a z. At this point, the tape might look like this:

| $\cdots$ | | | 1 | 0 | 0 | z | x | 1 | | 0 | | 1 | 1 | 0 | | 1 | 0 | | $\cdots$ |

Here, the address is the number, 100_2, to the left of the z. The cell to the right of the x corresponds to memory location 0. Next, the machine enters a loop in which it repeatedly subtracts 1 from the address and then moves the x from its current location to the next blank cell to the right of that location. Since the contents of xComputer's memory locations are stored sequentially on the tape, this corresponds to moving the x from one location to the next. When the address is reduced to zero, the x will be marking the cell on the tape corresponding to the original value of the address. The Turing machine can read the value stored at that address, erase the x, and return to the y that marks its starting position. In the example, where the address is 4, the x will be moved right 4 times and will therefore mark the data on the tape that represent the contents of memory location 4.

This is complicated by the fact that there will be a y somewhere on the tape that must be counted like a blank but must not be lost or moved. Copying an address from somewhere on the tape to the beginning of the data is also nontrivial. I leave you to work out these and other details if you like. See Question 4 at the end of the chapter. In any case, I hope you have seen enough to believe that it is possible to complete the construction of a computationally universal Turing machine. The existence of such a machine shows that what we call computation can be done by a very simple machine indeed, although we might have to give that machine very complex data to work with, and we might have to wait a very, very long time for it to get anything interesting done.

When we are interested in the mathematical analysis of Turing machines, the type of universal machine we need is one that can simulate other Turing machines, rather than computers. A ***universal Turing machine*** is a Turing machine that can simulate the computation of any other Turing machine on any input data. Since Turing machines can do anything computers can, a universal Turing machine is computationally universal in the usual sense.

To use a universal Turing machine, we will write on its tape an encoding of the Turing machine to be simulated, along with its input data. We need to agree on some method of encoding. Everything there is to know about a Turing machine is contained in the table that specifies its behavior, so we can simply encode that table as a long binary number. This is just an exercise in constructing a complex data representation: The encoding for a complete table is obtained by stringing together encodings for each line in the table. An individual line, which has five entries, is obtained by stringing together representations for each of the five entries. Since we have not put a limit on the number of states a machine might have, we cannot simply use a fixed number of bits to encode the possible individual table entries, so we have to be careful here. We will encode the value of an entry in the table as a string of ones followed by a single zero.

Specifically we encode L and R as 10 and 110. We encode the symbols #, 0, 1, x, y, and z as 10, 110, 1110, 11110, 111110, and 11111110. And as for states, we encode h as 10, state number zero as 110, state number one as 1110, and so forth. The details are not important, as long as we pick a representation and stick to it.

For example, consider a simple Turing machine described by the two-line table:

$$
\begin{array}{ccccc}
0 & 0 & 1 & L & 1 \\
1 & 0 & y & R & h
\end{array}
$$

Since the code for 0 (state or symbol) is 110, for 1 is 1110, and for L is 10, the binary code for the first line of this table is 1101101110101110. When we string this together with the code for the second line, we find that the binary number that encodes this Turing machine is

$$110110111010111011010101111011010.$$

Note that if a binary number contains two consecutive zeros or if the number of zeros is not a multiple of five, then that binary number cannot be the code of any Turing machine. But it is easy to check whether a given number is the code for some machine. In fact, we could even have the universal Turing machine do the checking for us.[11]

---

[11] I should point out that once each Turing machine has a code number, it becomes easy to show that there are functions $f: \mathbf{N} \to \mathbf{N}$ which cannot be computed by any Turing machine. The trick is to write down a function that behaves differently from every possible Turing machine on at least one input. To define such a function, f, we define $f(n)$ for each input number n as follows: If n is not a code number for some Turing machine, let $f(n) = 0$. (In fact, it

Let's consider a universal Turing machine, U, in more detail. With an encoding scheme in place, we can be more specific about what U must do. Given two binary numbers n and m as input, it will first check whether n is a legal code number for some Turing machine. If not, U will just halt immediately. (I really don't care what it does in this case.) If n is the code number for the Turing machine T, then U should simulate the calculation that T would perform when given input m. The details of the simulation don't matter as long as the end result is the same: If T never halts after being started with input m, then U must fail to halt when started with n and m as inputs; if T does halt on input m, then U must halt when given n and m as input, and the resulting tape must be identical to the tape produced by T on input m.

Since we already know that a computationally universal Turing machine exists, I will ask you to take the existence of U on faith. (To stretch a point—possibly beyond breaking—you could always have U simulate a computer running a simulation of a Turing machine!) The rest of this chapter does not use the universal Turing machine, but it does depend essentially on the existence of a coding scheme for Turing machines. Such a scheme makes it possible for one machine to use a representation of another machine as data on its tape.

4.3. Unsolvable Problems

Suppose that we start up a Turing machine T after writing some input on its tape. We wait eagerly for it to halt to see what output it produces. After some time—a few years perhaps—it dawns on us that perhaps it

---

makes no difference how we define f in this case.) If n is the code number of a Turing machine T, then we consider what happens when T is run with input n. Note that we are giving T its own binary code number as input. If T does not produce an output when given input n, because it fails to halt or halts with illegal stuff on its tape, then we define $f(n) = 0$. Note that such a T certainly doesn't compute f because f gives output 0 on input n, while T fails to give any output at all. Finally, if T produces output m, then we define $f(n) = m + 1$. Again in this case, T does not compute f because f and T give different outputs on input n. Since every Turing machine has a code number and since we have set up f so that no machine with a code number computes f, it follows that no machine at all computes f. At the beginning of the chapter, I promised that we would find some *interesting* uncomputable functions. f is uncomputable but not really interesting. In the next section, I will show you some more interesting examples.

is never going to halt at all. Should we stop it, or should we let it go for another few years to see what will happen? Perhaps if we wait just a little longer, it will halt. But if, in fact, it is destined to run forever, we will never find that out by just standing around watching it compute. How can we tell, without waiting around literally forever, that the Turing machine is never going to halt?

Now, there are certainly cases where, just by looking at the machine's specification, we can tell that a machine is never going to halt. Suppose that in state 0, reading any input at all, the machine will write a 1 on the tape, move right, and stay in state 0. No matter what input this machine is given, it will just travel forever to the right, writing an infinite string of ones. This is a trivial example, but whenever we can tell just by looking at the specification table of a machine that it will enter an infinite loop with no way of breaking out of it, then we can tell that the machine will run forever—and we can do this without actually running it. Perhaps if we are clever enough we can always decide in advance whether or not a given Turing machine will ever halt when run with a given input.

Now as for myself, I have often written computer programs that turned out to contain infinite loops that I would have sworn were not there. So I am not satisfied to rely on my "cleverness" to determine whether or not a Turing machine will run forever. What I would like is a foolproof computer program that would answer the question for me. Or, since Turing machines can do anything computers can, I would like a Turing machine which could look at the specification for any Turing machine and the input I intend to give to that machine and tell me whether or not that machine will ever halt after being started with that input. A Turing machine that could do this would be said to solve the *Halting Problem*.

Alas, it's not going to happen. The Halting Problem is unsolvable. That is to say, there is no Turing machine that solves it. It is surprisingly easy to give a proof of this fact.

4.3.1. The Halting Problem.   To be more definite, let H be a Turing machine. We say that H solves the Halting Problem if when run with binary numbers n and m as input, it will halt and give an output of either 0 or 1; it will produce output 1 if n is a valid code number for some Turing machine and if that machine will halt when run on input m; in any other case, H will produce output 0.

Let H be any Turing machine whatsoever. I will show you that this H does not solve the Halting Problem. Since my proof works for *any*

Turing machine H, it will follow that there is *no* Turing machine that solves the halting problem.

All I have to do is produce one case of a Turing machine and an input number for which H does not work.[12] Let's call the Turing machine I am going to build K. K will use H itself as an essential submachine, and in a sense what I will show is that no Turing machine can be powerful enough to analyze itself.

K is made by stringing three machines together. When K is started with an input number m, the first of these machines will make a copy of m. There will then be two identical numbers on the tape. The second submachine of K is H, which will therefore run with two copies of m as input. If and when H halts, the third machine is started up. This machine will check whether the tape contains an output value of 0. If so, it will halt immediately; if not it will go into an infinite loop in which it moves forever to the right.

To make this clearer: Suppose that m is the binary code number of a Turing machine, T. When we run K with input m, K will start by running H with input m,m. If H were a solution to the halting problem, running it with input m,m would test whether or not T will ever halt when given its own code number, m, as input. Now there are three possible outcomes. First of all, H might not produce any output at all when run with input m,m. In that case, we *already* know that H does not solve the halting problem, since if it did, it would give an output of 0 or 1 in all cases. If H does produce an output of 0 or 1, thereby making a prediction about whether T will halt on input m, then K looks at this prediction and behaves in the opposite way. Thus, K halts on input m if and only if H predicts that T will *not* halt on input m, where m is the binary code number for T.

It doesn't seem as though this proves anything, but the payoff comes when we give K its own binary code number as input. Let k be this code number. When K is run with input k, it will first run H with input k,k. Since the Turing machine encoded by the number k is K itself, H is being asked to make a prediction about whether K will ever halt on input k. But H is actually being run as part of the computation that K performs on input k! H is being asked to predict whether this ongoing

---

[12] Of course, there will be many machines on which H will fail, but finding just one is enough to show that H doesn't solve the halting problem. You might object that you could always fix H so that it works for the particular case I find, but this won't get you very far—the new machine you produce will fail for some other case.

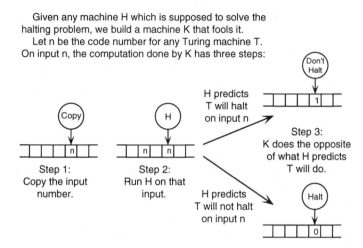

Given any machine H which is supposed to solve the
halting problem, we build a machine K that fools it.
Let n be the code number for any Turing machine T.
On input n, the computation done by K has three steps:

But if T is K itself, then K does the
opposite of what H predicts K will do.
So, H was wrong!

Figure 4.6. *Given any Turing machine H that is supposed to solve the
halting problem, it is possible to find a case where it fails, either because
it gives no answer or because it gives the wrong answer. The machine
for which H fails includes H itself as a submachine. (In this picture,
where "n" is shown on a tape, it is actually the binary expansion of the
number n that should be shown, probably filling many cells.)*

computation will ever end. Can H possibly get this right? If H makes no
prediction, it has already failed. But if it ventures a prediction that the
computation halts, as soon as K sees this prediction it sends the computation into an infinite loop, thereby retroactively making the prediction
incorrect. On the other hand, if H predicts that the computation will go
on forever, then K will react by halting, so that H's prediction is wrong
in this case as well. So, no matter what H does, it cannot possibly give
the correct answer.

You can imagine H's predicament. If it could think, it might say
to itself, "Let's see.... If I say that this computation will halt, then it
won't halt, and if I say it won't, then it will. I'm in trouble." Of course,
H doesn't think. It merely follows rules. The point is that whatever
rules it uses to make predictions, *they do not work in all cases.* H does
not solve the halting problem.

It is important to understand what has been proved here and what has not been proved. When we say that the halting problem is unsolvable, we mean that no Turing machine correctly predicts the halting behavior of all Turing machines for all inputs. But you might find a machine that makes correct predictions in a great many cases, perhaps even for all the cases that you are really interested in. In fact, if you are designing Turing machines, or writing programs, there is nothing to stop you from consciously trying to produce machines or programs whose behavior can be analyzed. The lesson that a programmer should learn from the unsolvability of the halting problem is not that it is impossible to write good programs, but rather that good programs don't happen automatically. I will have more to say in Chapters 6 and 7 about techniques for writing good programs.

Furthermore, our proof says nothing, one way or the other, about whether *people* can solve the halting problem. It is still conceivable that, given any Turing machine and input, you might eventually be able to decide whether or not that machine will halt on that input. However, you will not be able to write down a fixed set of rules that can be used to make the decision in all cases, since once you had done so, you could build a Turing machine that solves the halting problem by following those rules. (Though how you could ever be *sure* that you would get the right answer in all cases without writing down a set of rules, I have no idea!)

4.3.2. Other Problems. The halting problem is only the first of many unsolvable problems. There are many natural questions that can be asked about computers and Turing machines that cannot be answered—not, at least, by a Turing machine or a computer program. Here is a sampling of such problems. In each case, saying that the problem is unsolvable means that there is no Turing machine that can correctly answer the problem in *all* cases:

• Given any Turing machine T, determine whether T will ever halt after being started on an empty tape.

• Given a Turing machine T, determine whether there is *any* number n such that T will halt when started on input n.

• Given a Turing machine T, determine whether it computes a function from $\mathbf{N}$ to $\mathbf{N}$. That is, given any binary number n as input, will T always halt with a binary number as output on its tape?

• Given two Turing machines, T_1 and T_2, decide whether T_1 and T_2 compute the same functions. That is, will they always give the same output when started on the same input?

• Given any computer running any program, determine whether or not the computer will run out of memory before the program halts.

• Given any computer running any program, determine how long to wait before concluding that the program is never going to halt.

Each of these problems can be shown to be unsolvable by showing that if there were a Turing machine that solved that problem, it could be used as a basis for building a machine that solves the halting problem.

Consider, for example, the first problem in the above list. Suppose that you have a Turing machine E that solves this problem. That is, when given the code number for a Turing machine T as input on its tape, E performs some calculation that determines whether or not T will ever halt when started on an empty tape. If E actually worked as advertised, then it could be used as a basis for building a machine H that would solve the halting problem. (Then, since no such H exists, we know that no such E can really exist either.)

How can we build H from E? Here is an informal description of how H would work: Suppose that H is given the numbers n and m as input, where n is the code number of a Turing machine T. H is supposed to determine whether T will ever halt when given input m. The trick is to have H make up a new machine M that does the following: When M is started on a blank tape, first it will write out the number m on that tape and then it will run the machine T on that input. Thus, running M on a blank tape is equivalent to running T with input m. In particular, M will halt when started on a blank tape if and only if T will halt when given input m. Now, our machine H just has to use the given machine E to check whether or not M will in fact halt on an empty tape. By doing this, it is also solving the equivalent problem of whether T will halt on input m. That is, it is solving the halting problem (which we know is impossible)!

It is not easy to fill in the details in this informal description. What, for example, does it mean for the Turing machine H to "make up" a machine M? It can only mean writing out the code number for M on its tape. We have to check that it is possible to design a machine H that can do this. I will have to ask you to take this on faith, keeping in mind that M is defined in a straightforward way from the inputs n and m that H has to work with.

If you want to learn more about Turing machines and unsolvable problems, they are usually covered extensively in textbooks on "automata theory" or "formal language theory," such as [Lewis and Papadimitriou].

Chapter Summary

All computers are equivalent, at least if we ignore limitations on memory and time. In this sense, every computer is *computationally universal*, since all computers can solve the same set of problems, at least if they are given as much time and memory as they need. We know this because it is possible for one machine—even one with very limited computational capabilities—to *simulate* another. *Translation* and *interpretation* are two efficient methods of simulation, but it is *low-level simulation* that offers the strongest evidence for the equivalence of all computers.

This equivalence of many different types of machines is part of the evidence for the *Church-Turing Thesis*, which is the claim that anything that can reasonably be called computation can in fact be done by a computer.

In reality, only a machine with infinite memory can truly be computationaly universal. A finite memory is a real limitation, since given a fixed, finite memory, there will be complex computations that require more memory than is available. A *Turing machine* is an abstract computer with an infinite amount of memory. Its memory consists of an infinitely long *tape*. The Turing machine moves back and forth along its tape, reading and writing symbols. The machine has an internal *state*, and the action it takes at any given time is completely determined by its state and by the symbol written at its current position on the tape. Although Turing machines are very simple, there are *universal Turing machines* that can solve any problem that can be solved by any computer.

However, not every problem can be solved by computer. In particular, the *Halting Problem* is unsolvable. There is no Turing machine (or computer program) that can tell, in advance and in all cases, whether or not a given Turing machine will ever halt when it is run with a given input.

This chapter seems to have two contradictory messages. The first is that computation is simple. Any computation that can be done by even the most sophisticated computer can also be done by much simpler machines—even by something with the very limited computational resources of a Turing machine. On the other hand, computation is complex. We can't give any definite rules for answering even the most natural question: Will a given computation ever end?

Perhaps the real message is that even though computations are made up of very simple individual steps, *computation can surprise you*. If you have a computer program sitting in front of you, and you want to know what it does, the only general way of finding out for sure is to run it. Using the method of simulation, you can run it on any machine you like—you might get your answer faster by running it on a fast, complex machine, but even a very simple machine will do. But no method of analysis will allow you to predict in advance what *all* programs will do when they are run.

Questions

1. Figure 4.1 shows a logic circuit represented in xComputer's memory in a way that will allow it to be simulated using the six-step procedure outlined in Subsection 4.1.3. Follow this procedure *by hand* to trace the effect of several ticks of the clock on the circuit in this figure. Do you believe that this procedure can be used to simulate any circuit, including a complete computer?

2. After each step in its calculation, a Turing machine must move either one cell to the left or one cell to the right on its tape. Why don't we also allow the possibility that it can stay in the same cell? Would it make any difference if this were allowed? Explain.

3. Give a complete specification for a Turing machine that subtracts one from a binary number, provided that number is greater than zero. You should probably start by figuring out how to do such subtractions by hand. Trace the calculation performed by your machine for several different inputs. What does your machine do if you ask it to subtract one from zero? Once you have a machine to subtract one, you might want to try to build a Turing machine to add any two binary numbers, as described in Section 4.2.2.

4. Fill in as many details in the construction of the computer-simulating Turing machine described in Section 4.2.3 as necessary to convince yourself that it exists. You might want to work on the method of dealing with addresses that was discussed in that section. You might also try designing a machine that copies a binary number from one place to another on a tape. Assume that the number to be copied is marked by a y at the right end of the number. Also assume that beyond the left end of the data on the tape, there is a z that marks the place where the number is to be copied. All the cells between the z and the y contain 0, 1 or #. For example, you would want to transform the tape:

				z		1	0		1	0	1	y		

to

	1	0	1	z		1	0	y	1	0	1			

Your machine will have to copy one digit at a time. To remember which digit it is "carrying," it will have to use different states when it is carrying a 1 and when it is carrying a 0. I suggest that your machine move the y to the left as it copies the number, leaving it on the square to the left of the number as shown. During the calculation, the y marks the original position of the digit that is currently being copied.

5. At the end of this chapter, after showing that no Turing machine can solve the halting problem, I made the leap to the assertion that, "We can't give any definite rules for answering the question: Will a given computation ever end?" Is this leap justified? What does this have to do with the Church-Turing Thesis? (See Subsection 4.1.3.)

6. Imagine a scene from *Star Trek* in which Dr. McCoy and Mr. Spock are walking beside a lake arguing about the usefulness of logic. Dr. McCoy picks up a rock and says, "All right, Mr. Spock give me a demonstration of your famous logical ability. Make me a prediction: Will I throw this rock into the lake or not?" What can Spock do? Compare his predicament to that of H in our proof of the unsolvability of the halting problem. What does this question show about the limitations of logic?

Chapter 5

Real Computers

CYBERSPACE IS HERE, though perhaps not everyone has gotten the news. The term *Cyberspace*, apparently invented by William Gibson in his science fiction novel *Neuromancer*, refers to the developing global network of interconnected, intercommunicating computers. In the minds of many who visit it whenever they use one of those computers, Cyberspace is a real place, a sort of alternative reality, where you can make friends, do your shopping, play games, discuss the things you care about, and perhaps earn a living. All this is here now, even while Cyberspace is still in the process of being born.

Computer science had its beginnings in mathematics, and many of the early workers in the field were mathematicians. But there are no Turing machines in Cyberspace (although I might argue that they provide its fundamental mathematical substance). The real computers that make up Cyberspace are incredibly fast, with large memories and sophisticated input/output capabilities. They communicate over high-speed data links that make it possible for someone like me, sitting in front of my computer in my home, to use computers all over the world in real time. They exist because of the efforts and dedication of many thousands of people in many different professions—programmers, engineers, computer scientists, and others. And their influence extends beyond this technical community to all the people who use computers directly, or whose lives are affected by them.

We are told that we are living at the beginning of the Information Age, a post-industrial society in which information will be the most important commodity, and the material needs of the population will be met by a small part of the workforce overseeing sophisticated, perhaps intelligent, machines. The defining technology, and most important symbol, of this new age will be the computer. Many social theorists who speak of the Information Age imagine a utopia in which people, freed from the drudgery that many workers face in today's jobs, will develop their full human potential in creative employment and increased leisure. Others see at least as many dangers as opportunities. They warn of a world in which the commodification of information makes personal privacy obsolete, and in which computers are an instrument of social control rather than individual empowerment. It is worth noting that Gibson's *Neuromancer* presents a gloomy view of a post-industrial society in which many of these fears have been realized.

My own opinion is that the transformation of society will not be as far-reaching or as quick as some writers have predicted, but that the new information technology does present us with both great opportunity and great danger. What is certain is that we, as a society, need to be informed about the technology and about its potential impact if we are to decide wisely about how it will be used. This entire book is, of course, meant to provide a basic overview of computers and computer science, but in this chapter on "real computers," in addition to explaining how real computers differ from the model computers introduced previously, I will be more explicit about dealing with the technology in a historical and social context.

Computers have come a long way in the half-century since the first of their kind were invented. They have penetrated into all aspects of daily life, in many cases to the extent that they have become effectively invisible. It is unlikely that any reader of this book needs a description from me of what a standard computer looks like, or what a keyboard or mouse is for. However, for most people a computer is a "black box." That is, they know something about how a computer is used and what it can be used for, but they have very little idea about what goes on inside.

The first few chapters of this book have opened that box up to some extent. What you learned there does apply to real machines, but it is only a part of their story. The rest of this book carries on the process of opening the black box by looking at real computers and real computer programs. We start in this chapter with a historical look at how real computers came to be invented, followed by a survey of some fundamental aspects of the design of real computers. The final section of the chapter deals with their actual and potential impact on society. Then, the next three chapters will cover the basic concepts of computer programming and programming languages. The four final chapters of the text deal with computer applications; Chapter 9 surveys several basic applications, and Chapters 10, 11, and 12 deal with three of the most exciting and active areas in computer science today: networks and parallel processing, computer graphics, and artificial intelligence.

5.1. A Brief History

The use of calculating devices is probably at least as old as the abstract idea of number.[1] The prehistoric herder who kept track of the number of sheep in a herd by making notches in a piece of wood was engaging in an activity not so much different from the modern accountant who enters sales figures in a computer. The abacus, which has been in use for thousands of years, allows calculation at a speed that rivals that of anything else available before the introduction of computers.

The first machine that we would recognize as a calculator in the modern sense was invented by a German professor, Wilhelm Schickard, in 1623, but his work was forgotten after his death in 1635 and remained unknown until 1935. More influential were the devices created by the philosophers Blaise Pascal and Gottfried Leibnitz later in the seventeenth century. Pascal's calculator could add and subtract using a system of geared wheels similar to the mechanism in a car's odometer. Each wheel had ten positions, representing the digits from 0 to 9, and the wheels were connected so that as one wheel advanced from 9 to 0, the wheel to the left would be advanced one position. This is the same basic mechanism used in more modern mechanical calculators. Leibnitz, building on Pascal's work, designed a more complex machine that could do multiplication and division. The method used for these computations involved repeated additions, subtractions, and shift operations. Essentially the same procedure is used in computers today.

---

[1] It is impossible in this short section to give more than a sketch of the complex history of computing devices and computers. Most of the material in this section can be found in more detail in any history of computers. My discussion here is based on material from [Augarten], [Goldstine], [Hodges], and [Kurzweil].

But being able to do individual arithmetic operations does not make a machine a computer. One thing that makes a computer different from a mere calculator is its programmability. Now, the idea of a mechanism that can perform complex, programmed actions without human intervention is also not new. Devices called *automata*, or "self-movers," which could imitate complex movements of living animals or people, have been constructed at least since the time of ancient Greece. And mechanical clocks, which have existed since the fourteenth century, were among the most complex and accurate machines of their time. They provided the Newtonian revolution of the seventeenth century with its image of a "clockwork universe" whose complexity could be explained in terms of mechanism—that is, in terms of fundamentally simple parts moving in complex patterns but completely controlled by a small number of physical laws.

But these early automata and clocks were not computers. What makes computers unique among machines is their universality, as discussed in the preceding chapter. It's not just that computers can carry out complex computations autonomously. It's that the same computer can be programed to carry out any computation. To be a true computer, a device must operate under the direction of a program that can be *changed*, and the range of programs that it can execute must include all possible computations.[2] The first devices that met these criteria were constructed in the 1940s, during and just after World War II, but there was an interesting near-miss a century earlier, when Charles Babbage conceived and designed a computer he called the Analytical Engine. The inspiration for this programmable machine came not from lifelike automata or clocks, but from the mechanical loom.

5.1.1. Weaving Algebra.   Ada Lovelace, a supporter and colleague of Babbage who is often called the world's first computer programmer because of her work developing programs to run on the Analytical Engine, wrote that, "We may say most aptly that the Analytical Engine weaves algebraic patterns just as the Jacquard loom weaves flowers and leaves."

---

[2] Of course, this is literally impossible since any finite machine will in some cases run out of resources such as memory. The point is that the individual operations that it can perform, and the methods provided for combining them into complex computations, must be sufficient to express any possible computation, although the computer might lack sufficient time, memory or some similar resource to actually complete the calculation.

The Jacquard loom, invented by Joseph-Marie Jacquard in 1801, is a programmable device that can weave cloths with very complex patterns. Cloth can be woven from two sets of threads running perpendicularly to each other. These two sets of threads are referred to as the **warp** and the **weft**. Think of one set running east/west and the other north/south. When cloth is woven on a loom, the warp threads are strung on the loom and then the weft threads are added one at a time. Some of the warp threads are lifted to lie above a given weft thread while the others lie below, holding it in place. The set of threads that lie above is changed after each weft thread is added. The pattern in which the warp threads on the loom are raised and lowered as the cloth is woven determines the pattern in the cloth. A complex pattern requires threads of several different colors to be raised and lowered in just the right sequence. Controlling the threads by hand is time-consuming and error-prone.

In a Jacquard loom, the warp threads are controlled by programs consisting of holes punched in cards.[3] Each card corresponds to one weft thread; each hole in the card allows some particular warp thread to be raised as that weft thread is added to the cloth. The pattern of holes on all the cards determines the pattern woven into the cloth. The cards are physically connected into something like a ribbon, and after a given card is used, the ribbon is advanced so that the next card takes its place. The two ends of the ribbon can be connected to form a loop. In that case, the pattern will be automatically repeated over and over.

This should sound familiar. The loom's cards correspond to machine-language instructions in a computer that are executed automatically one after the other, and the loom shares with the computer the ability to repeat a loop of instructions. However, the Jacquard loom does not perform computations as such, and in particular, it has no way of testing conditions and making decisions between alternatives. But the basic idea is there of how a single machine can be made to perform a wide variety of tasks, simply by giving it different programs to execute. Clearly, Ada Lovelace's comparison of the Analytical Engine with the loom was more than just poetic imagery.

Today, in a time when trigonometric and logarithmic functions can be computed on demand by a ten-dollar calculator, it is difficult to imagine

---

[3] Note that a program here means a physical deck of cards. The idea of a program as *information* that can be stored in a computer's memory came much later, as we will see below, and was an essential step in the development of the modern computer.

that in the not-too-distant past people depended on printed tables of the values of such functions. The production of these tables demanded a vast amount of time and effort from people known as "computers," aided at most by mechanical calculators to do the basic arithmetic operations. Charles Babbage was inspired to begin work on his calculating engines by a vision that such tables might be computed and printed by machine, automatically and without error.

Babbage's first design was for a machine called the Difference Engine, which was to compute such tables using a mathematical process called the "method of constant differences." The Difference Engine was designed as a special-purpose device, implementing just this one procedure, but it would have been a mechanical calculator on a grander scale than anything that had been seen before. A small demonstration device was built in 1822, and Babbage obtained government support to continue the project. A decade later, a section of the complete machine was constructed, containing 2000 out of a projected 25,000 parts. But the project never advanced beyond this stage, partly because of disputes between Babbage and the government and his chief engineer, and partly because Babbage realized in 1834 that the methods employed in the Difference Engine could be used to produce an altogether superior machine: the Analytical Engine.

The great originality of the Analytical Engine lay in the fact that it was to be a general-purpose, programmable calculating machine. Its programs were to be coded as punched cards strung together into ribbons, similar to those used in the Jacquard loom. The instructions on the cards were not loaded into the Engine's memory; instead, the cards themselves directly controlled its operation.

Aside from the fact that it was controlled by punched cards rather than by a program stored in its memory, the Analytical Engine was strikingly similar to a modern computer. It had a processing unit, which Babbage called the *mill*, and a memory unit for data, which was known as the *store*. It was not limited, like the Jacquard loom, to following a sequence of instructions from beginning to end. Like a modern computer, it was designed to perform loops, conditional jumps and subroutines. These were executed by physically moving the ribbon of cards back and forth through the card reading mechanism, under the control of the program instructions. Because of these abilities, Babbage's Engine was the first computationally universal machine ever conceived.

The Analytical Engine was never built, and it has sometimes been claimed that the complexity and precision of engineering it would have required were simply not available at the time. But in 1991, a team of engineers at the London Science Museum completed a working model of Babbage's Difference Engine No. 2, a more advanced version of his first Difference Engine. Its 4,000 parts were made using some modern methods, but were machined only to the same precision that Babbage achieved on the parts he did construct. The builders of Difference Engine No. 2 believe that the Analytical Engine could have been built in the nineteenth century [Swade].[4]

5.1.2. Beginnings. Although it was not until the late 1940s that devices as versatile as the Analytical Engine were actually produced, mechanical calculating devices of increasing sophistication and practicality continued to appear. A watershed in their development occurred in 1890, when the results of the U.S. census were tabulated by machine for the first time. The machines used for that census were invented by Herman Hollerith, whose company later, after a merger, became the heart of the International Business Machines Corporation (IBM). The keyboard calculator, a mechanical desktop calculator in which numbers are entered by pressing keys, was introduced at about the same time. Soon, mechanical computing devices were in common use in business and science.

In the meantime, technologies not obviously related to computing had produced the switching elements that were to be crucial in the design of early computers. Three types of switches have been used in computers: relays, vacuum tubes, and transistors. In all of these, the connection between an input wire and an output wire is switched on and off by current on a control wire. Transistors were not invented until 1947, but by the 30s, relays were in common use in telephone networks, and vacuum tubes were used in radio. The relay, a mechanical device thousands of times slower than the vacuum tube, was used in some early computers. Most computers, however, have been **electronic**, based at first on vacuum tubes and later on transistors.

By the late 1930s, then, the time for general-purpose computers seems to have arrived. By that time, several independent projects were underway in three countries: Germany, Great Britain, and the United States. The development of the computer can be traced through the entire decade of the 1940s. It is a twisted history, involving many individuals

---

[4] It is interesting to imagine a world in which the Industrial Revolution brought with it the introduction of steam-powered, mechanical computers. This possibility provides the background for at least one science-fiction novel [Gibson and Sterling].

working on a number of mostly independent projects. The history is complicated by the fact that much important work was done during World War II, on classified projects. It was not until 1948 and 1949 that several machines appeared with all the characteristics of a modern computer. These were the first *general-purpose, electronic, stored-program* computers. The first of these machines, a fairly small prototype, was the Mark I which ran its first program at Manchester University in England on June 21, 1948. A year later, the first such full-scale computer, the EDSAC, became operational at Cambridge University. It had taken about twelve years for all these ideas to come together in one machine.

The first programmable computing machine was the Z3, built in 1941 by a German engineer, Konrad Zuse, who was inspired to work on the problem of automatic computation by the drudgery of computing solutions to differential equations by hand. The Z3 was the third in a series of machines built by Zuse, starting in 1938. It was made from 2600 relays and used the binary number system. The Z3 was programmable in the sense that it could automatically execute a program encoded as holes punched in a paper tape. However, it could only carry out those instructions from beginning to end. It had no way of making decisions, so although it was "general-purpose" in that it could carry out any *sequence* of operations automatically, it was not computationally universal. Many of the early machines that are called computers share this limitation and therefore are not quite computers in the modern sense of the term. The Z3 saw some use in the German missile program during World War II, but for the most part, Zuse received little support for his machines from the German government.

The German military effort did, however, depend on another machine known as the Enigma. This was a device for encoding and decoding messages which was used by the German military throughout the war. The breaking of the Enigma code was the target of the major wartime computing effort in Britain. This 10,000-person secret project, codenamed Ultra, was able to successfully decode German communications throughout the war and is considered to be one of the major factors in the Allied victory. One of the significant players in this project was Alan Turing, who had already made a major contribution to computer science with his invention of Turing machines.

The Ultra project produced two series of code-breaking computers, Robinson and Colossus, of increasing sophistication. The Colossus computers were electronic, with thousands of vacuum tubes. They were special-purpose machines, but they were programmable to a limited extent. In particular, they could make decisions about what to do next based on the result of a previous computation. Perhaps more important for the history of computers than the machines themselves was the pool of expertise produced by the project, which made possible the great post-war achievements in British computing.

In the United States, several projects produced computing machines during the war years. The Mark I, begun in 1937 by Howard Aiken at Harvard University and completed in 1943 with the support of IBM, was the first computer to become widely known to the public. It was based on decimal numbers and used rotating wheels as well as relays. It could execute sequences of instructions punched on paper tape. In some sort of unintentional tribute to Babbage's vision of the Difference Engine, it was to spend most of the next sixteen years calculating mathematical tables. However, with regard to the future development of computers, it was a dead end.

More important was the ENIAC, which was the first electronic, programmable computer. Conceived in 1943 by John W. Mauchly and J. Presper Eckert, it was built in secrecy with military support at the University of Pennsylvania. It was completed in 1945, three months after the end of World War II.[5] Although it was designed for a specific task—computing tables to be used in artillery targeting—the ENIAC was universal in the sense that it could be used to perform any computation. Programming the ENIAC, however, involved a physical modification of the machine: Connections between different components had to be rewired by plugging and unplugging connecting cords, and a bank of 6000 switches had to be set. As a result, it took several days to set up a program. If the definition of a universal machine is that an *unmodified* machine must be able to perform different computations when given different programs, then the ENIAC does not meet this standard.

But even before the the the construction of the ENIAC was begun, Eckert and Mauchly had the crucial insight that would make possible the first truly universal machines[6]: that a program could be treated as a type of

---

[5] Neither Colossus nor ENIAC was the first electronic calculating device. That honor belongs to the ABC computer, built in 1940 by John V. Atanasoff at Iowa State University. However, the ABC was a fairly small, nonprogrammable device. Mauchly was aware of Atanasoff's work and had visited his lab.

[6] Although in hindsight we might look on the creation of a universal computer as the culmination of all the work that came before, there was no research program whose goal was to produce a universal machine as such. I am not sure when it became clear to the researchers involved that such a thing was possible

data and stored in a computer's memory. The result of this insight was a
proposal to build the EDVAC, which was the first truly modern computer
to be conceived. A draft report on the design of the EDVAC was written
by one of Eckert and Mauchly's colleagues, the well-known mathematician John von Neumann, who contributed many of his own ideas. This
report outlined the design of the modern computer in all its essential
details: a central processing unit based on Boolean algebra and using binary arithmetic, with a random-access memory containing both data and
programs. Because of his association with this report, computers of this
general design have come to be known as *von Neumann machines*.

The first von Neumann machines to be completed were the two
British computers, the Manchester Mark I and the EDSAC, mentioned
above. Their builders learned about the idea of a stored-program computer from von Neumann's report on the EDVAC and from a series of
lectures given by Eckert and Mauchly at the University of Pennsylvania in the summer of 1946. The EDVAC itself was not completed until
1952. By that time, Eckert and Mauchly had left the University of
Pennsylvania and started a computer company, where they completed a
stored-program computer known as the BINAC in late 1949.[7]

5.1.3. Generations. With the development of the von Neumann
machine, the history of computers entered a new stage. From a theoretical point of view, computers already had all the computational ability that they would ever attain, and future development would merely
make them smaller, faster, cheaper, and easier to use. But the extent of
these "merely" practical improvements has been truly astonishing and
has made possible a world not only in which computers themselves are
household appliances, but in which an appliance as mundane as a microwave oven might be controlled by a microchip with more circuitry
than was to be found in the ENIAC.

Computers have decreased in size and increased in speed and complexity more or less continuously since their invention. But there have

---

or even desirable, but the credit should most likely go to John von Neumann,
who was familiar with Turing's work.

[7] One unusual feature of several early computers, including the EDVAC and
the EDSAC, was the type of memory they used. Their memory units consisted
of tubes of mercury, which stored data in the form of sound waves! The sound
waves traveled from one end of the tube to the other, where they were detected,
amplified, and fed back into the first end. Numbers could be read from memory
only as they completed their trip through the tube. New numbers could be
stored by changing the value fed back into the tube [Goldstine, p. 188–191].

been several changes in computer technology whose impact was so great that each can be considered to mark the beginning of a new generation of computers. The first generation, including most of the machines mentioned above, used vacuum tubes as switching elements. Although transistors were invented in 1947, techniques for manufacturing them in quantity and at reasonable cost did not exist until the mid-1950s, and it was 1957 before the first computer of the second generation—using transistors as switching elements—was introduced. Besides being smaller, cheaper, and faster than vacuum tubes, transistors were much more reliable. (Many engineers believed that the ENIAC, with 17,000 tubes, would be so plagued with burned-out tubes as to be almost useless.) By the early 60s, most new computers were transistorized.

The invention that led to the third generation of computers was the *integrated circuit*. An integrated circuit replaces a number of separate transistors, along with interconnecting wires and other electrical components, with a single "chip." A chip is a small, thin piece of silicon, or other semiconducting material, which contains the equivalent of a complete electronic circuit.[8] The result was a new level of miniaturization, together with another increase in reliability resulting from the smaller number of individual parts and interconnections. The transition to computers based entirely on integrated circuits took place from the mid 1960s to the early 70s.

The first integrated circuits contained only a few transistors. For example, a complete AND gate could be fabricated on a chip. The first integrated circuits containing a large number of components were memory units, which are relatively easy to design and manufacture because of the orderly, repetitive structure of computer memory. In 1968, a random-access-memory chip holding 256 bits of storage was introduced, and it took only a few months to raise that to 1,024—that is, 2^{10}—bits. This rate of progress has continued. As I write this in March 1993, the current issue of *Byte* magazine includes a short news item on the introduction of the first memory chips with a capacity of 2^{26} bits, more than 64 million! This represents a doubling of capacity each year over the course of fifteen years.

As the number of components in an integrated circuit increased, it was inevitable that someone would have the idea of putting an entire

---

[8] The manufacture of integrated circuit chips is an impressive technology which involves diffusing other elements into the silicon, layering materials onto it, and etching parts of those layers away—all on a microscopic scale of detail.

central processing unit on a single chip. The first such CPU-on-a-chip, or *microprocessor*, was invented in 1971. This can be seen as the beginning of the fourth generation of computers, based on *very large scale integration*, or VLSI. By the end of the decade, microcomputers, built around microprocessors, could be purchased for home use, and general-purpose microprocessors with special-purpose programs permanently burned into their memories were being developed for use in printers, compact disc players, cars—and microwave ovens.

Microprocessors can contain millions of transistors on a fingernail-sized chip. Circuitry equivalent to the entire, room-sized ENIAC computer would be a barely visible dot on that chip. Its cost, as a proportional part of the cost of the entire chip, would be on the order of a few dollars.

What is the fifth generation of computer hardware? The term is generally used to refer to *multiprocessing computers*, which use a number of processing units working together to solve a problem. I will discuss multiprocessing in Chapter 10. There might even be a sixth generation of computers on the horizon, consisting of devices that use light rather than electricity to store programs and to process information. Such devices are still in the early stages of research, but as integrated circuits near the limits imposed by basic physical law, light-based computers hold the possibility of continuing the progress of computers to new levels of speed and miniaturization.

5.2. Usable Computers

The first commercial computers were used by universities, government, and large corporations, and they required highly trained staffs of programmers and technicians to keep them operating. Computers have become smaller and more affordable, but this in itself would not have put computers in homes, small businesses, and elementary school classrooms if computers had not also become more and more easy to use. Today's computers can be used with no special training at all. And although programming a computer might never be truly easy, the payoff for a given amount of programming effort has certainly increased with time. The increased usability of computers is not due simply to faster CPUs and larger main memories. To be usable at all, a CPU and memory must be part of a computer *system*, which also includes other hardware, such as a keyboard, monitor, and disk drive, as well as software for the computer to run.[9]

5.2.1. From Input/Output to Dialog.

The way people interact with computers has been fundamentally transformed since the introduction of the first commercial computers. In the beginning, computers were machines for processing input into output. Programs and data were laboriously prepared on punched cards, or in some other machine-readable form. The cards were loaded into a mechanical card reader which would translate the pattern of holes on each card into the electrical signals that would load the input into the computer's memory. Then, as the program ran, any output it produced could be printed, punched onto cards, or rendered in some other form that could be used, however inconveniently, by humans.

Most computer users never even got close enough to the machine to observe this interaction, such as it was, first-hand. The user would prepare a deck of punched cards on a typewriter-like machine and then submit that deck to a technician. The technician would bundle the deck together with decks submitted by other users into a *batch* to be loaded into the card reader. Eventually—and that might mean hours—the input deck would be returned to the user, along with any output produced. Pity the poor programmer who might get back as output only the single line, "Error found on line 357 of program"!

This mode of using a computer, in which a program is submitted to be processed by the computer without further interaction, is still called *batch processing*, even though the programs are no longer processed as batches of punched cards. Most computer systems still allow some type of batch processing, since it is appropriate for programs that take a long time to run and that require no interaction with a user while they are running.

---

[9] The term *hardware* refers to any physical part of a computer system, while *software* refers to programs that are executed by the hardware. While software has to be carried around on a piece of hardware, such as a computer disk, the software itself is *information*, which has an abstract rather than a physical sort of existence. It's like "the short stories of Edgar Allen Poe." If you want to read the stories, you need a book in which they are printed. But the stories are not the book or the paper or the ink, but rather the information that is conveyed by the arrangement of dots of ink to anyone who knows how to read English. This analogy highlights another aspect of software: It is only useful to a computer that "understands" it, so that programs written for one type of computer system will not necessarily work on another.

It was clear that computers could be used more productively if users could get faster and more immediate feedback. But computers were large and very expensive machines, and it was very unusual for a computer to be devoted to a single user. By the early 1960s, a solution to this dilemma had been developed by researchers at MIT [Augarten, p. 255]. The solution, known as *timesharing*, allowed a large number of users to interact with the same machine at the same time. Each user could engage in a kind of dialog with the computer, typing in a line of input and receiving an almost immediate response. The great speed of the computer enabled it to rapidly shift its attention from user to user, giving each user the illusion of having the machine's undivided attention.

Timesharing made it possible for large numbers of users to experience the direct interaction with a computer that had previously been available only to a few researchers.[10] It became possible for programmers to find and correct errors in a program in a few minutes rather than hours, for businesses to make their records instantly accessible on a computer screen, and for everyone to play interactive computer games.

The style of human/machine interaction used on early timesharing systems—in which the user types some input and the computer types back a response—is called a *command-line interface*. Although it is a big improvement over batch processing, a command-line interface still requires the user to learn a cryptic and unnatural command language. When personal computers were introduced, they used a similar interface. People with the time and inclination to become expert with the system could achieve a sense of having an easy and natural dialog with the machine. For most people, however, the interface was a barrier.

This situation changed with the introduction of the *graphical user interface*, or GUI. In a GUI, cryptic commands are replaced by manipulation of graphical representations of objects and by choosing commands from menus. Instead of typing "rm mydoc.txt," the user can drag a picture, or *icon*, representing mydoc.txt to a picture of a trash can. Instead of remembering the command "mkdir," the user can select "New Folder" from a menu.

The graphical user interface brought the experience of communicating with a machine to many people who would never be comfortable memorizing long lists of commands. Although at the heart of the computer there is still a CPU mechanically processing input into output, the

---

[10] And to a few computer "hackers" at MIT. These hackers were among the first people to understand the full potential of computers. See [Levy, *Hackers*].

computer as experienced by the user has become something else entirely: an independent, responsive entity that can be an active participant in a dialog. We will return to the implications of this view of computers at the end of this chapter. But first, we should try to understand some of the technology that lies behind these modern, interactive computers.

5.2.2. Multiple Devices. It is easy to imagine how a punched-card reader might be used to load a program into a computer's memory: Small metal probes pass through the holes, closing electrical circuits that directly load the number encoded on the card into memory. It is not much harder to imagine output values from the computer's memory being used to directly control some sort of output device. But in modern computer systems, the CPU and main memory are only two devices among many, and the relationships among all these devices are not always so simple. We will take a look at some of these devices and how they can communicate with the CPU.

Fundamentally, there is only one way for components to communicate: One component turns one or more wires on or off, and another component connected to those wires reads the values they carry. This can be modified by using a memory location or a register accessible to both devices as an intermediary in the communication. One component can load a value into the shared memory, and the other can read that value at its convenience. In general, whichever method is used, the two devices will need some way to control the flow of information between them. For example, one device might need to signal the other that it has data ready to send, or that it is ready to receive data. It is easy enough to reserve some of the connecting wires or memory bits for such control messages, while the remaining wires or bits are used to transmit data.

Let's consider the two most basic input/output devices first: the monitor and the keyboard. We will look at some of the ways that these might work before discussing how a complex system with many devices can be constructed.[11]

The most common method of managing communication between the CPU and a video display monitor was already mentioned in Chapter 1. The image displayed on the monitor is simply a reflection of data stored in video memory, a region of the computer's memory reserved for this

---

[11] My discussion is written to apply to a personal computer system, since that is what most people are familiar with, but large multiuser computers are not essentially different.

purpose. On a black and white screen, each pixel on the screen corresponds to one bit in memory. The pixel is off if that bit is zero and is on if the bit is one. Color and grayscale monitors use several bits to specify the color of each pixel. This color information is read approximately sixty times per second by a special-purpose video controller chip, which repeatedly draws and redraws the image on the screen based on the information it finds. The CPU changes the image on the screen simply by changing the data stored in video memory. This method of communication, using locations in main memory accessible to both devices, is known as *memory-mapped I/O*.

Now, this explanation of the way a monitor works is incomplete in at least two ways. First, it is easy enough to say that the video controller chip and the CPU both have access to the video memory. But memory is constructed in such a way that only one location can be accessed at a time—the location indicated by the value on its Address wires. If two devices actually tried to set up different addresses at the same time, the result would be chaos. There has to be some method of controlling access to memory by the CPU, the video controller chip, and any other devices that need it.

The second remark has to do with a difference between the picture I have given you of memory and the actual memory in a computer. It is convenient to picture memory as a tall stack of numbered locations, each holding a certain number of bits. This is a "logical" picture of the structure of memory—the picture you should have of it in your mind, that tells you how it works. But there is no reason for the physical structure of memory to be anything like this. For example, two bits that are logically part of the same location might be physically on two altogether separate memory chips. More to the point, there is no need for the video memory to be physically anywhere near the rest of memory. All that matters is that when the Address wires are set to a certain value, the corresponding location in memory, wherever it is physically, becomes accessible for reading or storing data. The video memory, for example, can be physically a part of the circuitry that controls the display. We will see that a computer system might contain many devices, each with its own chunk of memory.

We find an even more complicated situation when we look at the keyboard, which is used to input characters into the computer. The quantity of data from a keyboard is really very small, but that data can come at any time, at the whim of the user.

Although it is not likely to be literally true in a real system, let's imagine first that there are several wires connecting the keyboard directly to the CPU. The binary number carried by these wires encodes the key currently being pressed (along with any modifiers such as the shift or control key). If no key is pressed, the value on the wires is zero. In the simplest case, the CPU could simply execute a loop in which it reads the value on the keyboard wires over and over. When the value changes, indicating that the user has pressed a key, the CPU can process the character that was typed and then return to the loop to wait for the next input. The CPU, or rather the program it is running, will have to be smart enough not to process the same input twice, unless the user holds down a key long enough so that it should "auto-repeat."

This method of sitting in a loop, watching for some input to occur, is called *polling*. Polling has several disadvantages. First of all, the CPU wastes much of its time just waiting for input to occur. Even worse is the possibility that the CPU might take so long processing one input that it misses other inputs that come along while it is not watching for them.

As an alternative to polling, we can imagine a two-way flow of communication between the keyboard and the CPU. In addition to the actual data flowing from the keyboard to the CPU, there will be control signals sent by each device to the other to regulate the flow of data between them. Of course, this requires that the keyboard be more than a "dumb" mechanical device. Some of the processing that we have imagined being done by the CPU must be done instead by a "keyboard controller circuit," which acts as an intermediary between the mechanical keyboard itself and the CPU. This circuit will detect the input coming from the keyboard and do some preliminary processing of that input. It will engage in a sort of two-way conversation with the CPU to transmit the input data to it in an orderly way.

In general, the devices in a computer system are "smart" in this sense. They include their own processing circuitry, which might be very sophisticated, even to the extent of including a full-powered microprocessor. These devices should be thought of as participants in two-way communication with the CPU, rather than as passive sources or recipients of data.

There are several ways of controlling the flow of data between two devices. One simple type of control called *handshaking* can be used to make sure that no data is sent until the recipient is ready to receive it. The recipient sends a signal when it is willing to receive data; it might do this, for example, by turning on a wire dedicated to the purpose.

Another style of communication uses *interrupts*, an idea with far-reaching implications. The idea here is that a device can interrupt the CPU, which will put aside whatever it is doing to process the communication from that device. Although this is one aspect of the CPU that I have not mentioned previously, the fact is that every real CPU is designed with the ability to handle interrupts. A device "signals" an interrupt by turning on a wire connected to the CPU; the CPU "acknowledges" the interrupt by turning on another wire leading back to the device. Generally, a CPU can handle several different types of interrupts, corresponding to different kinds of events that it must be able to handle.

An interrupt is similar to a subroutine. When an interrupt occurs, the CPU executes an *interrupt handler*, a sequence of machine-language instructions designed to respond to whatever condition caused the interrupt. After the interrupt handler finishes, the CPU must return to whatever it was doing when the interrupt occurred. Before jumping to the start of the interrupt handler code, it must stash away enough information to enable it to pick up where it left off. This information will certainly include the current value of the program counter and may include the contents of other registers.

Some CPUs are hard-wired to jump to a specific location in memory when an interrupt occurs; the interrupt handler must be loaded at that location. In other CPUs, the location of the interrupt handler can be specified by a program. But in any case, the processing that is done in response to an interrupt will depend only on the machine-language instructions that the CPU finds at the location of the interrupt handler. Thus, although an interrupt is a hardware event, the computer can be programmed to respond in any desired way to the interrupt.

As an example of how interrupts can be used to control communication, a keyboard might be designed to signal an interrupt each time the user presses a key. The interrupt handler can process the keystroke immediately or, more likely, store the character where it can be found when the program that is running is ready to process it.[12] You can see

---

[12] Typed characters are stored in a "queue" or "buffer" which can hold a number of characters. You probably have had the experience of typing characters that do not immediately appear on the screen because the computer is busy with something else. Those characters have in fact been dumped into the queue by an interrupt handler, where they will stay until some program removes them for processing at its convenience. It is that program that will later write them onto the screen, if appropriate.

that interrupts provide a convenient way for the CPU to handle communication with a large number of devices without having to monitor all of them continually. In practice, communication in a large computer system might involve a complex combination of memory-mapped I/O, polling, handshaking, and interrupts.

5.2.3. On the Bus.

We seem to have created a new chaos of devices, interconnections, and methods of communication. Somehow all this has to be coordinated into a working computer system. Fortunately, there is a clever and effective way of bringing order to this chaos: the *bus*.

A bus is simply a set of wires that can be used for communication among devices. What is special about a bus is the fact that many devices can connect to it. Any of these devices can send signals along the bus and read signals sent by other devices. Since only one device at a time can send a signal over the bus, its design must include some way of regulating when the devices are permitted to send signals.

A typical system might have three busses, a *data bus*, an *address bus*, and a *control bus*, each devoted to carrying a different type of signal. (A real system might well have more than three busses and might include devices that communicate directly rather than over a bus. But for the sake of simplicity, I will ignore such possibilities in this discussion.) The control bus includes a number of wires used for sending control signals, such as those used in handshaking and interrupts. These signals are used to initiate or regulate the exchange of data between two devices. The data itself is always transmitted over the data bus. When data is being read from memory or loaded into memory, the address bus is used to specify the memory location involved in the data transfer.

Data transfer using the data and address busses is actually more general that it first sounds, since it can be used for arbitrary communication between devices via memory-mapped I/O operations. Furthermore, as I noted above when discussing video memory, the computer's memory does not have to be physically all in one place—it can be scattered in pieces among various devices, with each device being assigned some subset of all the available memory locations. A video memory that is physically part of the video controller is one example of this. As another, the keyboard controller might include a memory location that contains a code for the key currently begin pressed; the CPU can simply read that location, as it would read data from any memory location, to find out what key has been pressed.

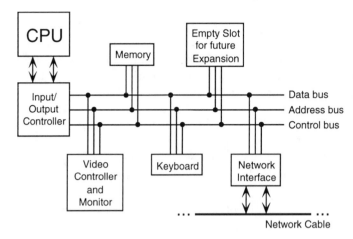

Figure 5.1. *A computer system with three busses: one for transmitting data, one for specifying a memory address, and one for control signals such as handshaking and interrupts. Busses provide a uniform and conceptually simple way for all the devices in a complex system to communicate. Furthermore, it is easy to add new devices by attaching them to the bus. Most computers have "expansion slots" that are used to plug devices into the bus. Here, the CPU is shown interfacing to the bus via an input/output controller, which might actually be a physical part of a CPU chip.*

And as a final example, a sound device might include a memory location whose contents determine what note it is playing. The CPU could play a song simply by writing the appropriate sequence of numbers to that location. As far as the CPU is concerned, it would simply be using Store instructions to load numbers into memory. The fact that doing so causes a song to be played is due to the way the computer system as a whole, hardware and software, is constructed.

Computer systems are designed so that it is easy to connect new devices into the system. These connections are made through **ports** and **expansion slots**. An expansion slot provides a direct connection to the bus; a card, known as an expansion card, containing all the circuitry necessary to support a device, is simply plugged into the slot. In many cases, the expansion card provides only an interface between the device itself and the system. For example, to add a monitor to a system you need a video expansion card, in addition to the monitor itself. The card contains the video memory, the video controller circuitry, and a socket—

Disk drives. These so-called "secondary memory devices" can store large amounts of data and programs, which must be loaded into main memory before they can be used by the CPU. There are many different types of disk drives, using various methods of data storage.

Modems. A modem can convert a stream of bits coming out of a computer into a signal that can be sent over an ordinary telephone line. It can also perform the reverse conversion. Two computers can communicate over a phone line if each is equipped with a modem.

Digital Signal Processing (DSP) chips. A DSP chip can quickly perform complex operations used in processing audio and video signals. The CPU itself could do such operations, but much more slowly. DSP chips are just one example of special-purpose processors that can be added to a system to speed up a particular type of calculation.

Optical scanners. An optical scanner digitizes an image so that it can be displayed on a computer screen. It works much like a photocopier, except that instead of duplicating the image, it converts it into a stream of bits that are transmitted to the computer.

Voice recognition. A voice recognition device analyzes the signal produced when the user speaks into a microphone, and tries to determine what words the user is speaking.

Network connectivity. Networks provide a way of connecting a number of computers so that they can communicate with each other and share resources such as printers. A network interface device in each computer handles communication between that computer and the network.

Figure 5.2. *A brief beastiary of devices. This short list gives some indication of the range of devices that might be found in a computer system.*

which sticks out the back of the computer—where the monitor is to be connected.

A port also allows an external device to be plugged into the system. It is similar to a socket on an expansion card—and in many cases may be exactly that. That is, a port consists of a socket and circuitry to interface it to the bus (or perhaps directly to the CPU). The port provides a specific type of physical connection and style of communication. Any device that physically fits the socket and uses that style of communication can be plugged into the port. Most computers have both a serial port, through which data is transmitted as a series of single bits, and a parallel port, which allows eight or more bits to be transmitted simultaneously over a set of "parallel" wires. A SCSI, or Small Computer System Interface, port allows not just a single device but a chain of different types of devices to be attached to the computer, with each device plugging into the preceding device on the chain.

Expansion slots and ports allow a great number and variety of devices to be added to a computer system, limited only by the imagination of the people who design such devices. How can the CPU cope with such a large and potentially expanding variety? All that the CPU ever does is execute machine-language instructions. When a new type of device is added to the system, software must also be added to enable the CPU to communicate with and control that device. More generally, we say that the system must be *configured* to use the new device. Besides the loading of appropriate software, configuration can include making physical changes, such as setting switches, when the device is installed. And in the case of devices that include memory to be used for memory-mapped I/O, it can include assigning the range of memory addresses to be used by the device. Some parts of the configuration, such as loading software, must be done every time the computer is started up. Before discussing this in more detail, we need to consider the general question of system software.

5.2.4. The Operating System. Every computer system includes some software that is considered part of the system itself, rather than merely a program to be loaded by the user when it is needed and thrown away when it is not. This system software is called the *operating system*. It is the operating system that gives the computer its "personality." Systems with identical hardware but running different operating systems can appear completely different to the user. Programs which are not part of the operating system are called *application programs*. Such programs are loaded at the user's request to perform specific tasks such as painting and drawing, word processing, and database management.

The computer's CPU can perform only simple operations such as adding or multiplying two numbers, or copying a number from one place to another. A usable computer system must perform more complex tasks, such as displaying a character on a monitor, detecting when a button is clicked on a mouse, sending output to a printer, or reading a program from a disk and setting up the CPU to execute it. Such things are made possible by the operating system. Fundamentally, the operating system is a collection of subroutines and interrupt handlers for performing such complex tasks.

System software also includes a program that runs when no application program is running, accepting commands from the user and carrying them out by calling operating system subroutines. This program goes by different names in different systems, but I will refer to it generically as the *command shell*. Note that while the command shell is usually considered to be part of the operating system, it is possible to change the command shell without changing the operating system in a fundamental way. The only thing that will be changed is the way that the user interacts with the system.

Operating system subroutines can also be called directly by application programs. Of course, this greatly simplifies life for the programmers who write such programs, since they can simply use the operating system subroutines as black boxes, without recreating them every time they are needed and without understanding the details of how they work. The rules for calling operating system subroutines from application programs form what is called an *application programming interface*, or API.

At the moment when a computer is turned on it is, relatively speaking, brain-dead—or more precisely, suffering from amnesia. The main memory of most computers consists largely of *dynamic random access memory*, or dRAM, which requires continuous power to retain the data stored in it. This type of memory is erased whenever the computer is turned off, so that any data and programs it contained are forgotten. Among the things forgotten are all the programs that the CPU needs to make it possible to communicate with other devices in the system! So even though all the information it needs is still somewhere in the system—stored in disk drives, for example—the CPU on its own doesn't know how to access that information.

The solution is to allow the CPU to keep some part of its memory even when the power is off. This is done by building a portion of main memory from ROM, or *Read-Only Memory*, instead of from dRAM. ROM is a type of memory that retains its data permanently, even when the power is off. The computer can read the contents of ROM but cannot change the information that is stored there. The ROM might contain

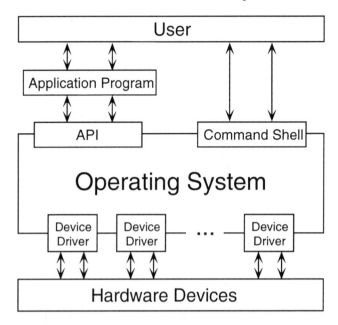

Figure 5.3. *The operating system provides subroutines to perform many common tasks, especially those that involve all the different hardware components that can be part of a computer system. When a new device is added to the system, the software necessary to control it and communicate with it is added to the operating system. These software components are called device drivers. Operating system routines are made available to programs through an API (application programming interface). They can also be used through a command shell that accepts commands from the user and carries them out.*

some basic parts of the operating system, but more important for the present discussion, it contains a ***start-up program*** that is automatically executed by the CPU when the computer is turned on. The CPU is constructed in such a way that when the power is turned on, the address of the start-up program in ROM is automatically loaded into the program counter. The CPU starts executing instructions at that address, and it never stops executing instructions until the power is turned off.

Executing the start-up program transforms the computer from a heap of components into a complex, coordinated system. It does that by loading essential parts of the operating system into main memory, doing any necessary configuration of the system, and starting up the command shell so that the user will have a way of interacting with and controlling the

DOS. The single most common operating system, used on the IBM PC and similar computers. The basic line-oriented command shell is a program called COMMAND.COM, although newer, menu-based shells are also used. System configuration at startup time is controlled by a file called CONFIG.SYS, which must be maintained by the user to handle all the devices included in the system.

Windows. Not quite an operating system itself, Windows adds many system routines, a new API, and a graphically oriented command shell to DOS. Windows-NT, a new operating system, uses a similar command shell and API but is not based on DOS and is much more sophisticated than Windows.

The Macintosh OS. The Macintosh GUI is built right into the operating system, which provides a very large API, called the Toolbox, to support the GUI. The Toolbox allows all programs to have a similar look and feel. The command shell, a program called the Finder, uses the same interface. One nice feature of the Mac OS is that system configuration is done automatically, without burdening the user.

UNIX. UNIX is a multi-user, timesharing operating system originally designed to run on large computers. It was designed so that it could be implemented on many different computer systems, and it is now available on personal computers. The idea is to provide a single API for high-level languages that will work on any machine running UNIX, but the goal of compatibility has usually been met only approximately. There are several command-line oriented command shells for UNIX. The most basic one is called the C shell.

Figure 5.4. *A brief beastiary of operating systems, listing just a few of the commonly used systems.*

whole thing. Configuring the system means making any modifications or additions to the operating system that are necessary to adapt it to the particular hardware in the system and to the preferences of the user. For example, many hardware devices require special software, called *device drivers.* A device driver is a set of routines that the CPU executes in order to communicate with and control the device; without it, the device is useless. The start-up program must make sure that all the software needed to drive all the devices is available.

5.2.5. Multiple Processes. One aspect of the operating system that might seem mysterious is its ability to allow several programs to run "at the same time." This is most apparent in time-sharing systems, where there might be hundreds of people using the computer simultaneously. But even on personal computers, it is possible for the user to be interacting with one program while at the same time other programs are running in the background. For example, the user might be typing a document using a word-processing program while at the same time, another document is being printed, a spreadsheet program is performing a long calculation, and a clock program is displaying a continually changing time. Somehow, the CPU manages to divide its time among several users or several programs. How can it do this?[13]

The answer is easier to understand after the idea of a *process* has been introduced. As the computer executes a program, it passes through a sequence of *states*. A state consists of all the information relevant to the program being executed, such as the contents of the CPU's registers. A process is defined to be the sequence of states that the computer goes through as it executes a program. A process is dynamic, like a movie; it takes place over a period of time. The program itself is static; it just sits there like the script for the movie. The point is that the process can be interrupted at any time and restarted later, provided that the computer is restored to the exact state that the process was in before it was interrupted. If this is done, the process will continue on exactly as it would have if it had never been interrupted.

In a timesharing system, each user has a separate process. Only one of these processes is running at a given time. Every so often, many times per second, the current process is stopped, its state is saved, and

---

[13] I should mention that there are computers that have more than one CPU. On such a computer, each CPU can work on a different task. Such *multiprocessing computers* are discussed in Chapter 10. On a standard computer, the single CPU can only work on a single task at a time, but even a standard computer usually includes a few devices that can do some processing on their own. The obvious example is a video controller that can redraw the display screen without help from the CPU. Another example is a network interface chip that handles all the interaction with a network, communicating with the CPU only when there is incoming or outgoing data.

one of the waiting processes is restarted. This process-switching is actually done by an interrupt handler responding to interrupts that are generated by a system clock. Timesharing is an example of **preemptive multitasking**, in which the processes that are sharing the CPU have no control over when they will be interrupted or how long they will be allowed to run. Another type of multitasking, called **cooperative multitasking**, is used on some personal computers, such as the Macintosh. A process running under cooperative multitasking must explicitly give up the CPU before another process can take over. The disadvantage of this is that an "uncooperative" process might hog the CPU and prevent any other process from running.

This section has shown how a complex computer *system* can operate. But no matter how complex the system, the CPU just keeps doing what it always does, fetching simple instructions from memory and executing them one-by-one, occasionally responding to interrupts by executing some instructions out of their usual sequence. It is the programs—operating system, device drivers, application programs—that together produce the great complexity and variety of behavior that the computer displays. It seems that we have reached the point where we should turn from hardware considerations to an attempt to understand how these complex programs can be designed and written. Our serious study of programs will begin in the next chapter. But first, having gotten some idea of how real computers were invented and how they work, we consider the impact they have on the real world.

5.3. Computers and Society

It would seem irresponsible on my part not to include a section such as this one, on the impact of computers on society, in a book that claims to be a survey of computers and computing. However, I should warn you that I am dealing in a few pages with a topic that really requires a book of its own, or several books. Everyone agrees that computers have significantly changed the world,[14] and that their influence will increase,

---

[14] Inevitably, when discussing the impact of computer technology on society, we think first of the industrialized countries where such technology is widespread, and my discussion will be limited to this aspect of the issue. A truly global discussion would have to consider how computer and information technology can be applied in the developing world and how it might affect North-South relations.

but there is little agreement on the extent of their impact, on whether it will be positive or negative, or on whether it will be driven mainly by the technology itself or mainly by human choice.

It should be clear to any reader of this book that I consider the theory of computers and the machines themselves to be among the great creations of the human mind. It is tempting for me to believe, along with some social theorists, that computers will be a liberating and democratizing force. However, I am faced with the fact that computers were born as machines of war and much computer research continues to be directed towards their war-making capabilities; that computers can threaten jobs and in some cases make existing jobs less interesting and less fulfilling; and that their ability to manage large amounts of information can be used to invade people's privacy.

On the whole, I tend to believe that the technology itself is neutral and that human choices will determine whether its effects will be positive or negative. If this is true, it puts a burden on those who develop the technology and on those who will be affected by it—and in the case of the computer, that means essentially everyone—to become familiar with the issues involved and to be activist in the decision-making that will determine the technology's effects.

In this section, I try to give a brief survey of some of the issues that need to be considered. Inevitably, my own opinion plays a larger role in this section than it does in the rest of the book. Interested readers will find more subjects covered and greater depth of coverage in the survey by Richard S. Rosenberg and in the collections of articles edited by Tom Forester, all of which are listed in the bibliography.

5.3.1. Computers Everywhere.   One way to begin a discussion of the impact of computers on society would be with a list of all the different ways in which computers are used. But those uses are so many and so varied that such a list would surely fill a book. The obvious uses— with a person sitting in front of a terminal or microcomputer—are only the beginning of the story. Computers are so pervasive that they affect virtually every aspect of life.

People drive cars in which microprocessors increase performance and safety, acting on information from sensors that monitor things like engine temperature and fuel consumption. Some people fly jet fighters that would crash and burn if their computer systems failed, because an unaided human is simply not capable of reacting fast enough or with enough precision to keep such a plane in the air.

Most people trust their money to a banking system in which that money will become a piece of data in some computer's memory—or they pay it to the government in taxes that will be recorded in one of the largest computer systems in existence. If they happen to be criminals, they might be inspired to find novel ways of extracting other people's money from its electronic storage places.

Their telephone calls are routed to their destinations by computer. The stories they read in newspapers were written on computers, and are laid out with the aid of computer programs. The pictures in those papers are processed and enhanced by computer, and they might just as easily be falsified.

They can spend their leisure time playing games on computers. When they go on vacation, they book their airline flights and lodgings on nationwide computer reservation systems. If they stay home and watch an old movie on TV, it might well have been "colorized" by a computer process that can add color to black and white video.

But I will discuss many specific applications (at least the ones that have something interesting to teach us about computers) in the last four chapters of the book. Rather than try to give an exhaustive (and exhausting) list of computer applications, I will concentrate here on the potential of some aspects of computer technology to bring about real social change.

5.3.2. Computers and the Workplace. Some social theorists claim that we are seeing the emergence of a *post-industrial society* or *information society*, in which information will be the primary source of wealth and the majority of the workforce will be employed in producing, processing, and communicating information. Before the industrial revolution, a majority of people worked in agriculture. Today in the United States, the agricultural needs of the country are met by about three percent of the workforce. It is not that less food is produced but that the productivity of agricultural labor has greatly increased. Productivity refers to the output produced by a given quantity of human labor. If a worker driving a tractor can accomplish the same work as several manual laborers, productivity is increased severalfold. Computers have the potential to increase productivity in traditional goods and services industries, perhaps to the extent where they consume the labor of as small a proportion of the population as agriculture currently does.

When general levels of productivity in a society increase, the same goods and services can be produced with a smaller amount of labor. In the first analysis, it might seem that the necessary consequence of this decreased demand for human labor will be an increase in unemployment. But while unemployment in specific industries will tend to increase, the effect on society as a whole is not so clear and can be influenced by social policy.

When productivity in one industry increases because of the introduction of new technology, jobs that are eliminated in that industry are balanced to some extent by new jobs that support that technology. Tractor manufacturing might contribute to agricultural unemployment, but it also creates manufacturing jobs that were not there before. In the same way, robots working on assembly lines displace workers, but at the same time, new jobs are created for the people who design, build, program, and maintain those robots. In general though, new technology will not be introduced unless the *net* effect is a lowering of costs, and that will presumably translate to a net loss of jobs, even counting any new jobs created in supporting industries.

Looking at this loss of jobs in a positive way, as human labor and creativity now freed to be devoted to new purposes, we can ask how society will use this resource. In the worst case, it could be wasted, with high levels of unemployment driving down overall wage levels and impoverishing not just the unemployed but society as a whole. On the other hand, it could be used to raise the standard of living of the entire society and could support the creation of completely new industries based on the new technology. It could allow people to devote more of their time to creative work and to leisure. This is the vision of the Information Society. But the extent to which computer technology will change the workplace, and who will benefit from those changes, will be determined to some extent by social policy, even if that policy is to do nothing and allow the changes to be driven purely by economic forces.

Turning from theoretical considerations to actual applications, we can ask what changes computer technology brings to the workplace. In some cases, these changes mean complete automation of tasks previously performed by humans. Perhaps the most dramatic example here is the replacement of human workers on an assembly line by robots. The robots in this case, currently at least, are neither intelligent nor human-like. They are machines of size and shape appropriate to the task that simply repeat the same programmed sequence of actions over and over. Tasks that require a significant degree of flexibility are difficult or impossible to automate, but the design of more "intelligent" robots is an active area of research.

More commonly, though, computers are introduced as tools to be used by people. Examples in this category include the computers used in offices for word-processing, accounting, and storing and retrieving all the data necessary to run a business. Other computers running CAD (Computer-Aided Design) programs replace pencil and paper as design tools for engineers and draftsmen. Managers can use programs called spreadsheets to help forecast the results of various decisions by numericly modeling the effects they might have.

There are many success stories about the introduction of computer technology, but the results do not always live up to expectation. In particular, it seems to be generally agreed that massive investment in computer technology in the office has not had the promised impact on productivity. There are many reasons for this, but a principle reason seems to be that merely introducing technology, without analyzing and modifying procedures and personnel structures to take advantage of it, will not automatically lead to improved productivity.

When we consider computers in the workplace from the point of view of the affected worker, we must ask questions about how they will affect the *quality* of jobs, not just the quantity. One concern is the possibility of *de-skilling*. This refers to the replacement of well-paying, interesting, high-skill jobs with jobs that require fewer skills and offer fewer rewards. It has been proposed that computers, by allowing skill to be embedded in the *tools* used for a task, would decrease the level of skill needed by the worker. De-skilling is not unique to the computer age: Its primary symbol is the assembly line, where a sequence of workers each performing one small, repetitive, almost mindless task assemble a complex product that might otherwise have required the efforts of a team of skilled craftsmen. It seems possible that computers might allow the de-skilling of a whole new range of occupations. So far, though, computers have not brought about massive de-skilling. In fact, there is some evidence that computers lend themselves more easily and more effectively to "human-centered" systems which seek to take full advantage of human skill and flexibility [Forester, 1989, p. 13].

5.3.3. Computers and the Individual. One of the most disturbing aspects of computer technology is the threat it holds for individual rights, especially the right to privacy. The ability of computers to maintain large databases of easily accessible information means that an unprecedented amount of information about people is being collected and stored.

Any person living an ordinary life in an industrialized country constantly generates data that flows into computer databases, some of them public and some with access restricted to use for specific purposes. This data flow consists not just of major events such as birth, death, marriage, and property transfers. Transactions using checks or credit cards, subscriptions to magazines and newspapers, telephone calls (the number dialed and the length of the call), mail-order purchases—all are recorded electronically, along with educational records, tax and employment records, medical history, criminal record, credit reports, and so on. Much of this data has always been available, on paper in filing cabinets and storage boxes. But once it has been entered into a computer, it becomes almost instantaneously accessible. Furthermore, the speed and power of the computer makes it possible to gather and correlate large amounts of data from many sources. And once data about an individual has been collected, it can be bought and sold, usually without the permission or knowledge of that person.

Although a number of laws have been passed dealing with privacy issues and computer databases [Rosenberg, p. 203–209], questions about who should have access to the data and what it can legitimately be used for are far from being settled. In a few cases, such as the databases used to generate credit reports, people have the legal right to know what data about them is contained in a database and to demand correction of erroneous data. The privacy of some records is protected by law, but there is a tension between the individual's right to privacy and the public's right to know. For example, court proceedings are a matter of public record, but they can and have been used by employers to deny jobs to workers who have filed a worker's compensation claim against another employer and by doctors to deny treatment to patients who have in the past sued a doctor for malpractice [Rosenberg, p. 213].

Even more troubling, though, are potential abuses of government power that are made possible by the government's ability to gather huge amounts of data about people and their activities. The question here is whether information technology, which has the potential to be a democratizing and empowering force, will be used instead as an instrument of social control and oppression.

5.3.4. Electronic Mirror.   One other aspect of the impact of computer technology deserves to be mentioned. Computers are a new sort of thing in the world. They behave differently from other artifacts (which for the most part do not have any "behavior" at all). We can ask what impact this new type of machine has on people's views of themselves, of their human nature, and of their place in the order of things.

In her book, *The Second Self: Computers and the Human Spirit*, Sherry Turkle reports on her sociological studies of several components of the computer culture: children encountering computer toys, adolescents learning about computer programming in school, hackers who "love the machine for itself," personal computer users, and artificial intelligence researchers. She found a wide range of responses of people to computers and a wide variety of styles of using them (and she urges a "healthy skepticism toward any who propose simple scenarios about the impact of computers on society").

Turkle found that for many people the computer is an object that lies uncomfortably on the boundary—between living and nonliving, between psychological and mechanical, between mind and non-mind. It is easy to experience computers as responsive entities rather than as mechanical devices. They can display what looks like rationality and purpose. As objects on the boundary, computers raise questions. They invite a consideration of what it means to be human or to be a machine. A user who experiences a computer as a partner in a dialog and who sees it performing what seem to be difficult intellectual tasks might be led to ask, "If a machine can do so much, am I then (merely) a machine?" Or, alternatively, "Is it possible for a machine to be human?"

Of course, I don't plan to answer these questions, although we will return to them again at the very end of the book, as part of a discussion of artificial intelligence. I raise them now to point out how thoroughly the computer has infiltrated our consciousness, our metaphors, and our very self-conception.

Chapter Summary

This chapter has presented a kind of whirlwind tour of mechanical calculation, from its beginnings in the seventeenth century through the invention of the first computationally universal devices in the 1940s and on to the development of today's fast, powerful, and "user-friendly" desktop computers. These real computers are quite a bit different from the small model computer designed in Chapter 3 and from the Turing machines from Chapter 4. But the differences are more quantitative than qualitative. Ultimately, computation consists of a large number of very simple individual steps, and computing machines are built from a large number of simple parts. This chapter makes clear the extreme degree of complexity that can be achieved when such simple parts are assembled into complex systems.

Today's computers are *von Neumann machines* that store their programs as information in memory and do their calculations in a *central processing unit*. But a complete computer system includes many other types of *devices*. The interaction of the CPU with these devices and with the user is controlled by the *operating system*, which includes *device drivers* that the CPU executes to communicate with and control the other devices in the system. Communication among these devices often takes place over a *bus* which allows for the exchange of data as well as the transmission of control signals such as *interrupts*.

Mechanical calculating devices have brought the possibility of a fundamental transformation of society, perhaps as fundamental as the Industrial Revolution. We are in the process of moving from an industrial age into an *information age*. This transformation brings both opportunities and dangers, as we as a society decide whether to control the technology or to be controlled by it—or let the decision be made for us through inaction.

Questions

1. I say that the ENIAC was not really a computationally universal device because changing its program involved rewiring. Is this fair? Do you think the ENIAC deserves to be considered a computationally universal computer? How is unplugging and plugging a few wires any different from loading a new program into a computer's memory, or changing the deck of program cards in the Analytical Engine?

2. At one point in this chapter, I say that appliances like microwave ovens might contain general-purpose microprocessors with special purpose programs permanently burned into their memory. What does this mean? Why is the program permanently stored in memory? Why would anyone use a *general purpose* CPU for such a specific application, when its program will never be changed?

3. A *mouse* is a device that can be used to "point" at things on a display screen. As the user moves the mouse around on a desk, signals are sent from the mouse to the computer that cause a cursor or pointer to move on the screen. The mouse has one or more buttons that the user can press; these send other types of signals to the computer. Discuss how a mouse might work. What happens when a signal is sent to the computer? How does the cursor get moved? What happens to the part of the displayed image that is beneath the cursor? The object of this question is for you to figure out various ways a mouse might work, not to find out how a real mouse works.

4. Suppose I have two identical computers sitting side by side, running two different operating systems (say, UNIX and DOS). I would like to take a machine-language program from one of those machines and run it on the other, but I find that it doesn't work. Why not? If the CPUs in the machines are identical, shouldn't they be able to execute exactly the same machine-language programs? Are there any machine-language programs that *would* run on both machines?

5. In Mary Shelly's novel, *Frankenstein*, Dr. Frankenstein creates and gives life to a "monster." He recoils in horror from his creation and abandons it. In the end, of course, the monster has its revenge. It is generally thought that Dr. Frankenstein paid for trying to take on God-like powers by creating life. But perhaps his real crime lay in refusing to take responsibility for his creation. Comment on this (in the context of Section 5.3).

6. Make a list of all the computerized databases that might contain information about you. Use a large sheet of paper.

Chapter 6

Programming

THE NICE THING about computers is that they will do exactly what you tell them to do. Unfortunately, they will do it *exactly*, so you need to get your instructions exactly right.

Computers work by following programs which determine in excruciating detail every little step that they take. The process of creating those programs is called ***programming***. For most people, programming is an unnatural activity, in the literal sense that it is not something that they do naturally. In some sense, programming is similar to giving another person a set of instructions, or a recipe, for performing some task. But when you give instructions to people, you rely on their intelligence and their huge pool of background knowledge to fill in the details and to work out any ambiguities. A computer has no intelligence or background knowledge and absolutely no tolerance for ambiguity. To be correct, a program must specify the exact procedure to be followed, in full detail, taking all possible contingencies into account. And the programmer has only a small number of resources to work with—some basic instructions and a limited number of ways of combining them into more complex structures.

Writing programs for something as literal-minded and as simple-minded as a computer can be difficult and frustrating. But it can also be rewarding and fun. Writing such programs is a skill that seems to come more naturally to some people than to others, but it is a skill that

can be learned by anyone. Not that everyone needs to learn programming, any more than everyone needs to be an automobile mechanic—but
anyone who wants to claim a basic understanding of computers needs to
encounter at least the basics of how they can be made to carry out complex tasks. Such an understanding can be gained without becoming an
expert programmer, and you should not expect to become an expert
programmer just by reading this book. However, what you do learn here
will, I hope, deepen your understanding and appreciation of computers.
Furthermore, the techniques and skills that are used in programming
have more widespread application to dealing with complex systems and
to problem solving in general, so learning about them is useful for their
own sake.

Curiously, the techniques and skills that the typical programmer uses
to write very short programs are quite different from those needed to design the massive, complex programs on which professional programmers
spend most of their time. Short programs can be composed more or less
on the fly, from a design that exists nowhere but in the individual programmer's head. This seat-of-the-pants style of programming is called
hacking (one of several different meanings for this common term). Although hacking can be both exciting and satisfying, it is not necessarily
the best way to write even short programs. Sooner or later—usually
sooner than they would like to admit—all programmers run up against
problems too complex to solve without a more organized approach. The
alternative to hacking is known as *software engineering*. Like all engineering, software engineering deals in the systematic analysis of problems and in the careful design of correct solutions. You will find the
engineering theme of good design running throughout my discussion of
programming.

In this chapter and the next, I will discuss programming in my own
made-up high-level language, which I call *xTurtle*. The design of this
language puts it in the mainstream of programming languages, along
with such commonly used "real" languages as Pascal, C, and Ada. Programs written in these mainstream languages imitate machine-language
programs fairly closely, even though a single instruction in a high-level
language can correspond to many machine-language instructions. There
are other, very different types of programming languages, and I will discuss some of these in Chapter 8.

xTurtle includes a set of so-called *turtle graphics* routines. These
routines can be used for drawing pictures on the computer's screen.

Turtle graphics were introduced in the language Logo, developed by Seymour Papert at MIT. Logo was designed to be used in teaching children how to program. The original "turtle" was a small, motorized robot on wheels that would move around on a large piece of paper under the control of a Logo program. It carried a pen that traced out its path as it moved. Turtle graphics routines represent commands that would be appropriate for such a robot, such as telling it to move forward five units. Of course, in xTurtle, these commands draw on the computer screen instead of on a sheet of paper. Except for the basic graphics routines, though, xTurtle and Logo are not closely related languages.

I have chosen to include turtle graphics in my language in order to make the programs less abstract and easier to follow than programs that simply move numbers around inside the computer's memory. But keep in mind that the pictures are not the main point. The main point is the programming process: the analysis of a complex problem and the construction of a set of instructions that the computer can follow to solve that problem.

6.1. The Power of Names

In folk magic, names are believed to be a source of power. The name is an essential part in magical incantations and spells, so that knowing a person's true name can give you magical power over that person. Whatever the validity of this idea in the realm of magic, names really do play an important and powerful role in the "incantations and spells" that control computers.

Understanding the way names are used in computer programs is the essential first step in understanding how to program. Many different types of things in programs are referred to by name. To program effectively, you need to know the rules for assigning names to things and for using those names.

Now, when you are trying to learn a language, there are two different types of rule that you have to pay attention to: rules that tell you what something looks like, and rules that tell you what it means. More formally, the rules that specify appearance or structure are referred to as the *syntax* of the language, while those that determine meaning make up the *semantics* of the language. Every language, including English, has a syntax and a semantics, but for programming languages the syntax and semantics must be specified completely and unambiguously.

It is easy enough to deal with the syntax of names in our programming language, xTurtle, although even in this simple case a full specification can become rather painful. A name in xTurtle is a sequence of characters where each character is a letter, a digit ('0' through '9'), or an underscore ('_'); the first character must be a letter or an underscore; the name can contain no more than thirty-one characters; upper- and lowercase letters are considered to be the same, so that *Quack*, *quack*, and *qUaCK* are just different ways of writing the same name; a few words (which I won't bother to list) are reserved for special purposes in the language and so cannot be used as names.

Now, this sort of detail certainly alienates many people, and with some justice. Do you really need to remember all this? Well, yes and no. For the most part, in fact, you can get by with a general feel for what names are like. If I told you that names are things like *Rate*, *Num*, *x1*, *x2*, and *length_of_side*, you would already know enough about names to follow all the examples in this book and to use names correctly in programs of your own. In fact, because of your intelligence and huge pool of background knowledge, you would understand all sorts of things that are not at all apparent from reading the complete formal description. You would know that names are more or less like English words, except that underscores can be used to write multiword names such as *length_of_side*, while digits are clearly meant to be used in similar names for related things, such as *x1* and *x2*. And I think you would be pretty sure that *_3xW1_7* is not really meant to be used as a name, even though it is perfectly legal according to the rules. However, computers deal *only* in formal rules, and sometimes it is necessary to be familiar with exactly what those rules say. This is especially true when you are trying to figure out what is wrong with a program that contains a violation of the rules. The point is to avoid being scared off by the details. Concentrate on the examples, but remember that the details are there to look up if you need them.

When we turn from syntax of names to their semantics, we find that there is even more to understand. But here again, the basic idea is straightforward. A name refers to something. The meaning of a name is the thing it refers to. In xTurtle, there are really only three things that a name can refer to: a chunk of program code, an item of data, or a location in memory.

Names that refer to chunks of program code are called **subroutines**. We already encountered the basic idea of subroutines in Chapter 1: The instructions necessary to perform a certain task are chunked together into a unit that can then be used as a black box whenever that task needs to be performed. With subroutines, the analogy to a magic spell is not so farfetched. The name of a subroutine is a single word which can have a complex and far-reaching effect.

A name which refers to a location in memory—or to the data stored at that location—is called a *variable*. (This is a poor choice of terms, since it suggests a mathematical analogy which is not really correct and not very helpful, but unfortunately the term is too traditional to be avoided.) In general, the same variable name can be used with either meaning, depending on the context in which it is used. This duality of meaning can be a source of much confusion to novice programmers, but usually only because the distinction is not pointed out to them or because they do not pay attention to it.

6.1.1. Built-in Subroutines.
Our goal is to understand how complex programs can be constructed. The idea, of course, is that certain basic operations are available, along with methods for combining operations into more complex structures. The most basic operations are simple things like moving data from one place to another or performing simple arithmetic calculations. In xTurtle, as in most programming languages, the combination methods are loops, decisions, and subroutines. Loops and decisions will be covered in the next section; the methods for writing new subroutines are deferred until the next chapter.

It's a long way from data-shuffling and simple arithmetic to a complete, working program. Every high-level programming language provides some large, prefabricated pieces to help simplify the work. These pieces are the *built-in subroutines* of the language. A built-in subroutine is a true black box. The programmer who uses one knows what task it is supposed to perform but might well have no idea how it accomplishes that task. Every language includes some built-in subroutines for performing input and output. As we saw in the previous chapter, I/O operations involve complex coordination between the CPU and hardware I/O devices. All this complexity can be hidden inside subroutines, leaving the programmer free to imagine that input and output are simple, basic operations.

The built-in subroutines in xTurtle include the turtle graphics routines for drawing on the computer screen. These routines control a simulated "turtle" that moves around on the screen. The direction in which this turtle is facing is called its heading. Its position is given by two numbers, an x-coordinate for the horizontal position and a y-coordinate for

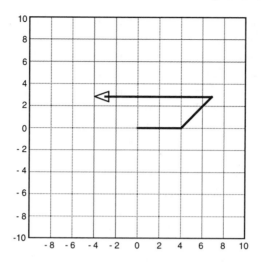

Figure 6.1. *In the examples in this text, the turtle moves around in a 20-by-20 square, in which its horizontal position is given by a number between − 10 and 10, and similarly for its vertical position. Grid lines are shown here for reference, but are not part of the picture that would be seen on the screen. The turtle always starts in the center of the square at the position (0,0), facing toward the right. Shown here is the path it would draw as it follows the sequence of commands: forward(4) turn(45) forward(4) turn(135) forward(10). The turtle itself is shown as a small triangle at the position and heading it would have at the end of this sequence of commands.*

the vertical. (See Figure 6.1.) The two most basic routines are *forward*, which causes the turtle to move, and *turn*, which causes it to change its heading. The imaginary turtle carries an imaginary pen which it can use to sketch its path on the screen as it moves. This pen can be either up or down; it only draws when it is down. Two routines, *PenUp* and *PenDown*, cause the turtle to raise and lower its pen; these routines are used to control whether or not the turtle draws as it moves.

An instruction in a program that tells the computer to execute a subroutine is called a **subroutine call statement**, and using such an instruction is known as "calling" the subroutine. A subroutine call statement for the routine *PenUp*, for example, consists simply of the name of the subroutine.

For the subroutines *forward* or *turn*, a call statement must include some extra information besides the name of the routine. An instruction to move forward must include the distance to move; an instruction to turn must specify how many degrees to turn. This extra information is listed in parentheses after the name of the subroutine. For example, the command

forward(5)

will cause the turtle to move five units forward in whatever direction it is currently facing, and

turn(90)

will cause the turtle to make a 90-degree left turn. (Angles are measured in degrees, with positive numbers specifying a counterclockwise rotation while negative numbers specify a clockwise rotation.)

The "5" and the "90" are called **parameters**.[1] Recall that a subroutine works like a black box. A parameter is like a "slot" in that box through which information is passed into or, as we see later, out of the box. It is possible for a subroutine to have zero, one, two, or more parameters. *PenUp* and *PenDown* are simple commands with no parameters. The command *moveTo*, which tells the turtle to move to a point with specified coordinates, has two parameters. For example, *moveTo*(3, −7) causes the turtle to move to the point with horizontal coordinate 3 and vertical coordinate −7. Notice that when there is more than one parameter, the parameters are listed in parentheses and separated by commas.

At this point, we already know enough to write simple programs. In fact, of course, a single command such as "*forward*(5)" is itself a program; executing this program draws a single line on the screen. We can create more complicated programs by stringing commands together. Here, for example, is a program for drawing a 7-by-4 rectangle:

forward(7)   turn(90)
forward(4)   turn(90)
forward(7)   turn(90)
forward(4)

Note that xTurtle has no official rules about how you have to arrange your program. For example, it doesn't require each command to be on a

---

[1] This odd use of the term parameter is based on the use of the term in mathematics. It refers to an input that can be set to different values to produce different behaviors. A subroutine with a parameter corresponds to an infinite number of different commands—for example, *forward*(3), *forward*(2.775), *forward*(−7), . . . —that differ only in the value of the parameter. (More magic!)

separate line. Of course, as a rule of good programming style, programs should always be laid out so that they are as easy as possible to read.[2]

In addition to *forward*, *turn*, *PenUp*, *PenDown*, and *moveTo*, there are only a few other turtle graphics routines that will be used in the examples in this book.

The command *back(x)*, where *x* is any parameter value, causes the turtle to back up *x* units, that is, to move *x* units in the direction *opposite* to its current heading. (In fact, negative numbers are allowed as parameters for both *forward* and *back*, and *back(x)* is provided only as a convenient shorthand for *forward(−x)*.)

The command *face(x)* makes the turtle turn to a heading of *x* degrees from heading zero. (With a heading of zero, the turtle is facing toward the right edge of the screen.) For example, *face(90)* points the turtle straight up, *face(−90)* points it straight down, and *face(180)* points it to the left. Note the distinction between *turn* and *face*: *turn* specifies a change in direction from the current heading, while *face* specifies a new heading without any reference to whatever the old direction might have been.

Finally, the command *move* is related to *moveTo* in the same way that *turn* is related to *face*. That is, while *moveTo(x,y)* says "move from the current location, whatever it is, to the point with coordinates *(x,y)*," *move(x,y)* says "move *x* units horizontally and *y* units vertically from the current location." Note that these commands do not depend upon or change the heading of the turtle. Either command will draw a line if the pen is down.

There are a few other, non-graphics subroutines that you need to know about. These are mentioned below.

6.1.2. Variables and Assignment Statements.
In almost all high-level languages, access to the basic data storage and manipulation abilities of the computer is provided through variables. Fundamentally, a variable is a named memory location. The name allows the programmer to refer to that memory location, or, indirectly, to the data stored at that location, without having to keep track of where in memory that location happens to be. The computer—or more exactly, the compiler

---

[2] By the way, I haven't said anything about the mechanics of creating and running programs. You should just assume that you have some way of typing in a program and then telling the computer to execute it. The details of how this is done are irrelevant.

or interpreter that translates the high-level-language program into machine language—sets aside the memory needed for any variables in the program and translates any use of a variable name into a reference to the corresponding memory location.

In an xTurtle program, before you can make any use of a variable, you must explicitly declare that you want to use it and give it a name. For example, the statement

declare x

tells the computer to set aside memory for a variable named x, while

declare *InterestRate, Amount*

declares two variables with a single statement.[3] When you declare a variable, the computer sets aside memory space for it, and remembers the name and the location it corresponds to. If you try to use a name that has not been declared, the computer will tell you that your program contains an error. Declaring variables might seem like an inconvenience, but in fact it makes writing correct programs easier in the long run. For example, you might think that your program uses the single variable *length*, whereas because of your poor typing it really contains two different names *length* and *lenght*. If the computer were not able to detect "*lenght*" as an error, the program would run but would probably give incorrect results—leaving you with the problem of figuring out what went wrong, or worse, not knowing that the answer is incorrect. (In general, the more errors the computer can detect automatically, the better. This principle is a major influence on the design of programming languages.)

Recall that a program is just a list of instructions—which for no good reason whatsoever are usually called "statements"—to be mechanically executed by the computer. So far we have seen subroutine statements and declaration statements. Obviously, a programming language must also include statements for getting data into the variables and for doing calculations with that data.

---

[3] Note that all variables in xTurtle are designed to hold ***real numbers***, that is, numbers that can contain an optional decimal point and a fractional part, such as 7.3 and -127.006. xTurtle is extraordinarily limited in this respect. Real numbers are just one possible type of data. Computers must deal with many types, including integers, strings of characters, dates, digitized pictures, and so forth. Most programming languages provide different "types" of variables to hold different types of data. In those languages, when you declare a variable, you must say what type of variable it is. This aspect of programming will be discussed in Chapter 8.

An *assignment statement* is used to store a value in a variable. The value to be stored can be a constant number, the value of another variable, or the result of a potentially very complicated calculation. Suppose that *Amount*, *Deposit*, and *InterestRate* are variable names in an xTurtle program.[4] Then that program could contain the following sample assignment statements:

$$InterestRate := 0.06$$
$$Amount := Deposit$$
$$Amount := Deposit*(1 + InterestRate)$$

The funny symbol ":=" is called the *assignment operator*. It would probably be best to read it as "gets the value," since its meaning is that the value on the right side of the operator is to be computed and stored in the variable on the left. Thus, the first statement tells the computer to store the number 0.06 in the memory location assigned to the variable named "InterestRate." The second tells it to store a copy of the value of the variable *Deposit* into the variable *Amount*. And the third tells it to perform a certain calculation and then to store the answer in *Amount*.

Note that a variable that appears on the left side of an assignment statement is being used in a very different way from one that appears on the right side. The name on the left refers to the memory location of the variable. The value in that location *before* the statement is executed is of no interest at all—it will be erased and replaced when the new value is stored there. For a name on the right, on the other hand, it is the value of the variable that is being used, not the location in which it is stored.

When an assignment statement is executed, the value on the right is computed. Then, in a separate operation, that value is stored into the variable on the left. This allows us to do something like this statement, in which the same variable is used on both sides:

$$x := x + 1$$

When the computer executes this statement, it first computes the value on the right. It does this by fetching the value currently stored in the variable x and adding 1 to that value. The result of this computation is then stored in the variable on the left of the assignment operator, which

---

[4] Since you can choose any name you like for variable names, it is a good idea to choose meaningful names that indicate how the names will be used in the program. This is not for the benefit of the computer (which, of course, couldn't care less), but for any human reader who might have to look at the program—including the person who wrote it!

just happens to be x. The effect of all this is to increase the value stored in x by one.

Finally, we should discuss in more detail exactly what is allowed on the right side of an assignment statement. Look at the formula

$$Deposit*(1 + InterestRate)$$

in the third example above. This formula represents the result of adding 1 to the value from the variable *InterestRate* and then multiplying the result by the value of *Deposit*. With a few exceptions, such as the use of an asterisk ($*$) to represent multiplication, the rules for writing formulas in xTurtle are the same as in ordinary mathematics, and I won't belabor them here. I will note that formulas can include certain mathematical functions, such as the trigonometric functions *sin* and *cos*. For example, if x, *radius*, and *angle* are variables, then

$$x := radius * \sin(angle)$$

would be a legal assignment statement. Certain common functions have uncommon names in xTurtle. For example, since there is no way to type something like $\sqrt{x}$, the square root function is named *sqrt*, as in "$sqrt(x)$." Note that a mathematical function is really a special kind of built-in subroutine. It is a black box that performs a complex computation, but it differs from an ordinary subroutine because its purpose is to compute a value, rather than to perform an action. Whereas "*forward*(5)" makes perfect sense standing on its own as an instruction in a program, "$sqrt(5)$" by itself is incomplete, because there is no indication what should be done with the value that is computed. It can only be used as part of a complete instruction such as "$x := sqrt(5)$."

While we are on the subject, take another look at the instruction *forward*(5). The value "5" tells the computer how far the turtle is to be moved. There is no reason why this distance should not be given as the value of a variable or as a formula, and in fact, xTurtle will accept instructions such as *forward*(*dist*) and *forward*(5*$sqrt$(*dist*)), where *dist* is a variable.

Note that the effect of the instruction *forward*(*dist*) depends on the value that happens to be stored in the variable *dist* when this instruction is executed. This makes it extremely powerful in two ways. First of all, when you write the program, you don't even need to know what the value of *dist* will be; for example, it might be obtained by input from the user when the program is run. In that case, the same program can do something different each time it is run, depending on the value input by the user. Second, suppose that this instruction occurs in the middle

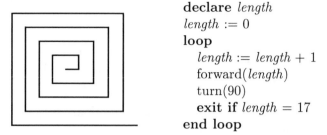

declare *length*
length := 0
loop
    length := *length* + 1
    forward(*length*)
    turn(90)
    exit if *length* = 17
end loop

Figure 6.2. *A program that uses a variable, assignment statements and a loop to draw the "square spiral" shown on the left. Although loops will not be introduced until the next section, you can probably follow how the loop in this program works. The instructions between* **loop** *and* **end loop** *are executed repeatedly. Each execution of the loop draws one line in the spiral. The assignment statement "length := length + 1" causes each line to be one unit longer than the previous line. The computer exits from the loop after drawing 17 lines.*

of a loop, so that it can be executed many different times while the program is running. It is possible for the value of *dist* to change from one execution to the next, so that the exact same statement in the same program might have a different effect each time it is executed. In fact, this is what makes a loop so powerful: It doesn't really "repeat the same thing over and over" in a simple sense. The situation in which the loop executes can change with each execution, so that each execution can have a different effect.

6.1.3. Input/Output Subroutines. Assignment statements are all you need to manipulate data inside the computer, but many programs require an exchange of data between the computer and the user while the program is running. For example, you might want your program to ask the user to enter a number, perform a calculation with that number, and then display the result of the calculation to the user. Two built-in subroutines called *AskUser* and *TellUser* are provided in xTurtle to make it possible to write such programs. The I/O facilities of xTurtle are rather limited—and a little bizarre—compared to those of most languages, but they are sufficient for all the examples we will look at.

If you just want your program to say "Hello" to the user, you can use the instruction

TellUser("Hello")

TellUser differs from all the other subroutines you have seen, since its parameter is a *string* (that is, a sequence of characters enclosed in quotes), rather than a number. When the computer executes this instruction, the string `Hello`, without the quotes, will appear on the screen.

TellUser allows you to output the value of a variable as follows: If the string contains the character #, the word after the # must be a variable name. When the string is displayed to the user, the value of the variable will be substituted for its name. Suppose for example that *Ans* is a variable. Then you could use the instruction

TellUser("The answer is #Ans")

in your program. If the value of *Ans* happens to be 17 at the time this instruction is executed, then the displayed string will be: `The answer is 17.`

Another subroutine, *AskUser*, is used to get a number from the user. It is a little more complicated than *TellUser* since you have to tell the computer where to put the number that the user types in. Of course, the only place where you can put a value is in a variable, and this means you must specify a variable where the subroutine is to dump the input. *AskUser* has two parameters: a string that will be displayed to the user and a variable in which the user's response is to be stored. For example, if *Amount* is a variable then the instruction

AskUser("How much money did you deposit?", *Amount*)

will display the question on the screen, wait for the user to type in a number, and store the number entered by the user in the variable *Amount*. That value can then be used by the remainder of the program.[5] Finally, then, here is a short but complete program that uses input and output:

> **declare** *Deposit, Amount*
> AskUser("Enter initial deposit.", *Deposit*)
> *Amount* := *Deposit* ∗ 1.06
> TellUser("After a year, you will have $#Amount.")

It should be clear what this short program does, but sometimes it can be a little difficult to think about and to write programs that use I/O. There are, after all, three different viewpoints that you have to keep in

---

[5] Note that the variable in *AskUser* is used in a very different way from the parameters in other subroutines we have seen. In the other subroutines, it was the value of the parameter that was being used. Here, it is the memory location of the parameter that is being referred to, since it is the *location* that the subroutine *AskUser* needs to know. The parameter in *AskUser* is used in the same way as a variable on the left-hand side of an assignment statement.

mind: yours (that is, the programmer's), the computer's, and the user's (that is, the person who interacts with the computer while the program is running). When you write a program like this one, you are often instructing the computer to give instructions to the user, and it is no wonder if it takes a while to get used to this.

6.2. Taking Control

In order to write programs that are more complex than just a sequence of simple instructions, we need to be able to group commands into loop and decision structures. In xTurtle, this is done with *loop statements* and *if statements*. These statements make it possible to control the order in which instructions are executed, by repeating a group of instructions several times or by choosing between alternative courses of action. The order in which instructions are executed in a program is known as the *flow of control* in the program, and **loop** statements and **if** statements are known collectively as *control structures*.

6.2.1. Loops. An example of a loop in an xTurtle program is shown in Figure 6.2. Loops in xTurtle are simple enough: To indicate that a group of instructions is to be repeated, you just type "**loop**" at the beginning of the group and "**end loop**" at the end. When the program is executed, the effect of the **end loop** instruction is to transfer the flow of control back to the beginning of the loop.

The computer will repeat a loop forever unless some way is provided for exiting the loop. This is done with an **exit** statement. An **exit** statement can occur only inside a loop. It tells the computer to check whether some condition is true or false. If the condition is true, the computer exits the loop by transferring the flow of control to whatever statement follows the **end loop**; if it is false, the computer just continues executing the loop. The syntax for an **exit** statement can be specified as

$$\textbf{exit if } \langle\text{condition}\rangle$$

Here, "$\langle\text{condition}\rangle$" does not appear literally in any program; in a real **exit** statement, $\langle\text{condition}\rangle$ must be replaced by a real condition that the computer can test. The most common conditions are simple comparisons between two quantities, such as "$length = 17$" or "$x > sqrt(y + 3)$". However, more complicated conditions can be constructed from simple conditions using the logical operators **and**, **or**, and **not**, as in

$$\textbf{exit if } x > 0 \textbf{ and } (y = 1 \textbf{ or } y = 2)$$

declare *count*
count := 0
loop
    count := *count* + 1
    ⟨statements⟩
    exit if *count* = ⟨max⟩
end loop

declare *count*
count := 0
loop
    count := *count* + 1
    forward(5)
    back(5)
    turn(10)
    exit if *count* = 36
end loop

Figure 6.3. *Above on the left is a template for a counting loop, and on the right is an actual program modeled on this template. The template has two "slots" called* ⟨statements⟩ *and* ⟨max⟩ *which can be filled in to give an actual loop. The purpose of a counting loop is to repeat a group of one or more instructions some specific number of times. In the template,* ⟨statements⟩ *stands for the list of instructions to be repeated, and* ⟨max⟩ *stands for the number of times that those instructions are to be repeated. In the program on the right, the statements in the loop are repeated 36 times. The picture produced by the program is shown as it would appear on a computer screen. It consists of 36 lines radiating from the center of the picture, one line for each pass through the loop.*

Among the many ways that loops can be used, the most common is when it is possible to determine in advance the number of times that the loop is to be repeated. In that case, it is only necessary to count off the repetitions of the loop and to exit from the loop when the required number has been reached. Figure 6.3 explains how a counting loop can be written and gives an example. Note that the counting variable *count* in this example starts out with value zero. The first time through the loop, its value is increased to one; the second time, to two; and so forth.

So, as the loop is executed, the value of *count* always represents the number of times the loop has been repeated so far.

6.2.2. BNF. Figure 6.3 includes what I call a "template" for a counting loop. A template provides an easy way of specifying syntax. Earlier, I used the template "**exit if** ⟨condition⟩" to specify the syntax of an exit statement.

You might already be getting tired of syntax rules; if so, you could hardly be blamed. The rules are so strict and the computer allows so little leeway in applying them that it is difficult to get everything straight when describing them in English. As the rules get more complicated, they only get harder to specify and harder to remember. Templates make things somewhat easier by replacing a long-winded and possibly vague English description with a kind of "picture" of what is being described.

Templates are used almost universally to describe programming language syntax. In general, the templates used are some variation of Backus-Naur Form (BNF). The original BNF was introduced by John Backus to describe the syntax of the early programming language ALGOL. Peter Naur later added some features to Backus' version.

Figure 6.4 contains a partial specification of the xTurtle programming language using BNF templates. Each BNF template defines a so-called *syntactic category*, such as a ⟨program⟩ or an ⟨if statement⟩. Syntactic categories are indicated by a word or phrase enclosed in angle brackets.[6] A template is written using the operator ::=, which can be read "is defined as." For example, the template

⟨exit statement⟩ ::= **exit if** ⟨condition⟩

says that an exit statement is defined to consist of the word "**exit**" followed by the word "**if**" followed by a ⟨condition⟩. What is meant by a ⟨condition⟩ must be defined in another BNF template or in an informal English description.

Several other features of BNF are used in Figure 6.4. It is possible to specify that part of a template is optional by enclosing it in brackets ("[" and "]"). For example, in the template for ⟨subroutine call⟩, which describes statements such as *forward*(5) and *PenUp*, the parameter list is optional. ("Optional" here means that it occurs in some subroutine call statements and not in others. As we know, *forward* requires a parameter

---

[6] BNF can be used to describe ordinary languages like English. In English, the syntactic categories would be things like ⟨sentence⟩, ⟨prepositional phrase⟩, and ⟨noun⟩.

⟨program⟩ ::= ⟨statement⟩ [⟨statement⟩]...

⟨statement⟩ ::= ⟨exit statement⟩ | ⟨declaration⟩ |
                ⟨assignment⟩ | ⟨subroutine call⟩ |
                ⟨loop statement⟩ | ⟨if statement⟩

⟨declaration⟩ ::= **declare** ⟨variable name⟩ [, ⟨variable name⟩]...

⟨exit statement⟩ ::= **exit if** ⟨condition⟩

⟨assignment⟩ ::= ⟨variable name⟩ := ⟨expression⟩

⟨expression⟩ ::= ⟨number⟩ | ⟨variable name⟩ | ⟨mathematical formula⟩

⟨subroutine call⟩ ::= ⟨subroutine name⟩ [(⟨parameter⟩ [, ⟨parameter⟩]...)]

⟨loop statement⟩ ::= **loop**
                    [⟨statement⟩]...
                end loop

⟨if statement⟩ ::= **if** ⟨condition⟩ **then**
                  [⟨statement⟩]...
                  [**or if** ⟨condition⟩ **then**
                    [⟨statement⟩]...]...
                  [**else**
                    [⟨statement⟩]...]
                end if

Figure 6.4. *A partial specification of the syntax of the xTurtle programming language using BNF. Certain categories, such as ⟨condition⟩ and ⟨variable name⟩ are left undefined here. Also, this specification does not include some syntax rules such as the fact that exit statements cannot occur outside of loops.*

list, and *PenUp* is not allowed to have one; these facts are not expressed by the BNF template.)

If the closing bracket is followed by three dots, then the optional stuff can be repeated any number of times. For example, the template

⟨declaration⟩ ::= **declare** ⟨variable name⟩ [, ⟨variable name⟩]...

says that a declaration consists of the word "**declare**" followed by a variable name, optionally followed by a comma and another variable name, optionally followed by a comma and another variable name, and so on.

The last BNF feature used in Figure 6.4 is the vertical bar ("|"), which is used to indicate a choice between alternatives. The rule for

⟨expression⟩, for example, says that an expression can be either a number or a variable name or a mathematical formula; whenever the category ⟨expression⟩ occurs in a template, it can be replaced by any of these things.

BNF is not quite powerful enough to describe all aspects of syntax. For example, it is impossible in BNF to express the fact that a variable must be declared before it is used. Still, it would be much more difficult to express complicated syntax rules without it.

6.2.3. Decisions. If you are wondering why I decided to introduce BNF at this point, take a look at the template in Figure 6.4 for an ⟨if statement⟩. This template includes several different pieces which are optional or which can be repeated. It is by far the most complicated syntax rule we have seen. Most actual **if** statements do not exhibit the full complexity.

The simplest type of **if** statement represents a choice between doing something and not doing it. Such a statement has the form:

if ⟨condition⟩ **then**
        [⟨statement⟩]...
end if

which is obtained by omitting the two optional parts of the template starting with "**or if**" and with "**else**." This is an instruction to the computer to test whether the condition is true or false. If it is true, then the computer will execute the statements between **then** and **end if**; if it is false, the computer will skip over these statements and proceed to whatever follows the **end if**. For example, when the computer executes the statement

if *YourGuess* = *MyNumber* **then**
        TellUser("Congratulations, you guessed it!")
end if

it will test whether the value of the variable *YourGuess* is equal to the value of the variable *MyNumber*. If so, the computer will display the message, "Congratulations, you guessed it!" on the screen.

Only slightly more complicated is an **if** statement that decides between two alternative courses of action. In this case, the part of the template starting with "**or if**" is omitted, but the "**else**" part is included. The statements after the word **else** represent the action to be taken if the condition turns out to be false. Figure 6.5 gives an example of this type of statement.

```
    if ⟨condition⟩ then              if TestTurn = 1 then
         [ ⟨statement⟩ ]...                turn(90)
    else                             else
         [ ⟨statement⟩ ]...                turn(−90)
    end if                           end if
```

Figure 6.5. *A simplified template for a two-way-decision* **if** *statement, and an example of such a statement. The computer tests the condition. If it is true, then the computer executes the first group of statements and skips the second. If the condition is false, the first group is skipped and the second is executed. In either case, the computer then proceeds to whatever follows the* **end if***. In the example, the turtle will be rotated left by 90 degrees if the value of the variable TestTurn is 1; otherwise, it will be rotated to the right by 90 degrees.*

Finally, when the entire template is used, the result is a complicated statement that makes a multi-way decision among several possible courses of action. Figure 6.6 gives an example. (Variations of this example might well be the second most common example in programming texts, following only a program for displaying the message "Hello World.") Multi-way choices are common enough in programming that it is useful to think of them as another type of tool available to the programmer, along with loops, two-way choices, assignment statements and subroutines.

6.3. Building Programs

It is fairly easy to understand what loops and **if** statements are meant to do. If only writing programs with them were so easy! Before leaving this chapter, we will work through the development of a few programs in some detail. Along the way, I will point out some techniques and strategies for developing programs.

In all but the most trivial cases, writing a program does not mean sitting down at a computer and starting to type. The quickest way to a working program is to begin with an analysis of the problem to be solved, followed by the design of a program based on that analysis. Of course, even careful analysis and design do not guarantee a totally error-free program, but they are likely to produce a program with fewer errors. More important, it is usually easier to track down and eliminate errors in a well-built program based on a clear design.

```
if Grade > 90 then
    TellUser("Excellent")
    Count_A := Count_A + 1
or if Grade > 80 then
    TellUser("Good")
    Count_B := Count_B + 1
or if Grade > 65 then
    TellUser("OK")
    Count_C := Count_C + 1
or if Grade > 50 then
    TellUser("Not satisfactory")
    Count_D := Count_D + 1
else
    TellUser("Failing")
    Count_E := Count_E + 1
end if
```

Figure 6.6. *An example of a multi-way-decision* **if** *statement. The computer evaluates the conditions one by one until it finds one that is true; it then executes the associated group of statements and jumps to whatever follows* **end if***. If all the conditions are false, then the group of statements following* **else** *is executed. Note that only one group of statements is executed, even if more than one condition is true, since the computer stops testing conditions as soon as it finds the first one that is true. In this example, if the value of Grade is 85, only the second group of statements is executed.*

6.3.1. Two Squares. We start with an easy problem: to write an xTurtle program that draws a picture of two squares, as shown on the left in Figure 6.7. Let's assume that the point where the squares meet is (0,0) and that each side is five units long. Although the problem of drawing these squares is simple, the solution will illustrate some important ideas.

Recall from the previous chapter that the sequence of steps in the execution of a program is called a process. A process is like a movie, with the program playing the role of a script. The individual "frames" of the process are called states. A state consists of all information relevant to the execution of the program at a given moment in time. This information would include, for example, the values of all variables and, in xTurtle, the position and heading of the turtle. The execution of each program instruction advances the computer from one state to another;

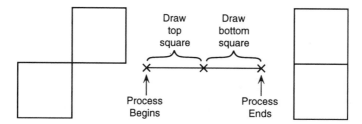

Figure 6.7. *The process of drawing the two squares shown on the left can be trivially broken into two steps: draw the first square, then draw the second square. On the right is the result of a failed attempt to draw the squares. A "picture" of a process that draws two squares is shown in the center. This picture is a timeline. The X's represent states of the computer, and the line segment between two X's represents the execution of the instructions that carry the computer from one state to the other.*

in fact, the only thing that defines the meaning of an instruction is its effect on the state of the computer.

This image provides an approach to program design. A problem can be stated in terms of the desired final state of the computer at the end of the program's execution. For example, the final state might be, "The screen is displaying a picture of two squares, arranged in such and such a way." In general, it is not possible to see immediately how a desired final state can be achieved, but it is usually easy to pick out a number of important intermediate states that occur along the way to that goal. These states break the process into a number of smaller pieces, and each piece can then be worked on separately. In the example, you might imagine drawing the top-right square, then drawing the bottom-left square. This leads to the image of the process shown in Figure 6.7.[7]

We could tackle the problem of drawing a single square in the same way, but here it is easy enough to construct an appropriate sequence of steps in terms of built-in xTurtle commands:

forward(5) turn(90) forward(5) turn(90)
forward(5) turn(90) forward(5)

---

[7] Even on a problem as simple as this, there are many, many ways of getting to the goal state, and you are free to script the process any way you like. For example, you might imagine drawing the line from $(-5,0)$ to $(5,0)$, then drawing the line from $(0,-5)$ to $(0,5)$, and then adding the two remaining sides of each square. This would lead to a completely different program.

This just draws a sequence of four sides, separated by 90-degree left turns. Now, can we construct a program for drawing the two squares by copying out these instructions twice? Unfortunately, it's not so simple. The picture produced by this strategy is shown on the right in Figure 6.7. The reason why this doesn't work is important: The effect of executing a sequence of instructions depends not only on the instructions but also on the state of the computer at the beginning of the sequence. Thus, the instructions will have the desired effect only if the required conditions are met before the instructions are executed.

Technically, the effect of the sequence of instructions is called its *postcondition*, and the conditions that are required to be true at the start are referred to as the *precondition*. The precondition describes the initial state of the computer before the instructions are executed; the postcondition describes the final state and shows how it depends on the initial state. We can rewrite the instructions for drawing a square, this time including a precondition and postcondition:[8]

> { precondition: turtle at (a,b), facing right, pen down }
>
> forward(5) turn(90) forward(5) turn(90)
> forward(5) turn(90) forward(5)
>
> { postcondition: turtle at (a,b), facing down, and a 5-by-5
> square is displayed with lower-left corner at (a,b) }

The postcondition describes the figure drawn by the instructions and says that the turtle ends up at the same point where it started, but facing in a different direction. (Having the name "(a,b)" for the initial position just makes stating the postcondition a little easier.) Note how the truth of the postcondition depends on the truth of the precondition. If the turtle is not facing to the right to begin with, then the square will not be drawn in the position stated in the postcondition. If the pen is not down, then nothing will be drawn at all.

Looking back at the problem of drawing two squares, we see that the postcondition that holds after drawing the first square does not match the precondition that would be required to draw the second square correctly. The turtle is not facing right and is not at the point $(-5,-5)$, the lower-left corner of the second square. To use the movie analogy again,

---

[8] In an xTurtle program, any text enclosed in set braces ("{" and "}") is ignored by the computer and is meant entirely for human readers of the program. The text is called a *comment* on the program. The ability to write helpful and informative comments is itself an important programming skill.

```
forward(5) turn(90) forward(5) turn(90)
forward(5) turn(90) forward(5)

face(0)
PenUp
moveTo(−5,−5)
PenDown

forward(5) turn(90) forward(5) turn(90)
forward(5) turn(90) forward(5)
```

Figure 6.8. *One of many possible programs for drawing the squares in Figure 6.7.*

it's as if Scene 1 ends with a shot fired on the docks at midnight, and Scene 2 opens with a knock on the door of the detective's office.

The script writer for the movie can rely on the moviegoer to understand the transition, but a programmer must spell out everything in complete detail for the computer. This means that we must insert extra code to set up the preconditions for drawing the second square. The command *face*(0) will achieve the precondition that the turtle is facing right. The condition that the turtle be at (−5,−5) can be achieved with *moveTo*(−5,−5), but we must be careful here: We need a *PenUp* before the *moveTo* command (because having the pen raised is a precondition for moving without drawing) and a *PenDown* after it (because having the pen down is a precondition for drawing the second square). The complete program is shown in Figure 6.8.

This is not the only program that solves the problem, nor is it necessarily the best. In this simple case, it might be easier just to write a new set of instructions for drawing the second square. (Changing the 90-degree turns to −90 degrees would work.) If the task were much more complicated than drawing a square, though, it would probably be more difficult to alter the existing code than to set things up so that the unmodified code will work.

Furthermore, in addition to being a tool for splicing together existing chunks of program code, preconditions and postconditions can be part of a strategy for designing programs. A precondition is a reminder that you need to do one of two things: Either examine the preceding instructions, to make sure that they have a matching postcondition; or insert an **if** statement into the program to test the condition, and write extra

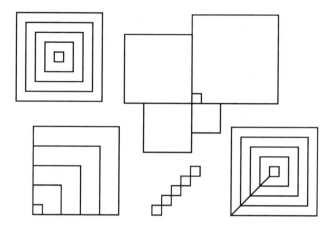

Figure 6.9. *Five nested squares, shown at the upper left, and the results of four incorrect attempts to draw them. All the incorrect attempts result from easy-to-make (but also easy-to-avoid) errors.*

instructions to handle the case where the condition fails. For example, consider the statement

$$Average := TotalOfItems \ / \ NumberOfItems$$

Since division by zero is not allowed, this statement has the obvious precondition that *NumberOfItems* should not be zero. Noting this precondition might lead you to realize that your program needs an **if** statement, "**if** *NumberOfItems* = 0 **then**... **else**...," so that it can take different actions in the cases where the value of the variable is, and is not, zero. Alternatively, if you don't expect the value zero to occur, you might be reminded to check the code that precedes the assignment statement, to make sure that the *NumberOfItems* cannot be zero.[9]

6.3.2. Nested Squares. Figure 6.9 shows another picture made up of squares, in this case a sequence of squares nested one inside the other. Let's assume that the smallest square is one unit on a side and that the distance between a square and the square that encloses it is one unit on all sides. We could draw the picture with five squares as shown in the figure by writing separate instructions for each square, but let's

---

[9] Even if you believe that the value of *NumberOfItems* is absolutely positively guaranteed to be nonzero, it might still be a good idea to include an **if** statement to verify the fact. This use of an **if** statement—to verify something that you think has to be true—is sometimes referred to as a ***sanity check***.

make things more interesting by supposing that the number of squares to be drawn will be input by the user. The program we write must be able to draw a different number of squares each time it is run.

It is still easy to imagine a process that will draw the squares. A timeline for such a process is shown in Figure 6.10. The timeline includes a segment for drawing each square, which can be done with the usual sequence of *forward* and *turn* commands. But, as we have learned, these instructions won't have the desired effect unless their precondition has been established, so the timeline includes a "setup" before each square is drawn.

As you have probably guessed, the sequence of repeated segments

setup, draw square, ... setup, draw square ...

can be folded into a loop, but doing so is not entirely trivial. First of all, as any programmer quickly learns, the setup for the first repetition of a loop is generally different from the setup for the remaining repetitions. This is almost inevitable, since the first setup splices the loop to whatever precedes it, while the others provide splicing from one repetition of the loop to the next. So, the program will have the general form:

{ get input from user }
{ setup for first square }
loop
    { draw square }
    { exit if all squares have been drawn }
    { setup for next square }
end loop

Now, the problem is to write code for the loop that will work no matter which square is being drawn. Since the squares are of different sizes, we need a variable to represent the length of the squares' sides. If this variable is named *length*, then the instructions for drawing a square are

forward(*length*) turn(90) forward(*length*) turn(90)
forward(*length*) turn(90) forward(*length*)

The precondition for these instructions is: (1) the turtle is at the lower-left corner of the square we want to draw, (2) the value of *length* is equal to the length of the sides of that square, (3) the turtle is facing to the right, and, of course, (4) the pen is down.

Let's assume that the lower left corner of the innermost square is at the point (0,0) and that the squares are to be drawn starting with the innermost square and working out. Then the the initial setup can be done by setting the value of *length* to 1. (The remaining conditions are

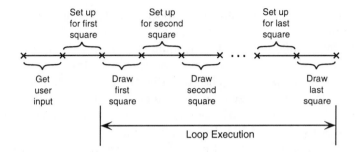

declare *count, HowMany, length*

AskUser("How many squares should I draw?", *HowMany*)

count := 0

length := 1

loop

       forward(*length*) turn(90)
       forward(*length*) turn(90)
       forward(*length*) turn(90)
       forward(*length*)

       count := *count* + 1
       exit if *count* = *HowMany*

       length := *length* + 2
       PenUp Move(−1,−1) PenDown
       face(0)

end loop

Figure 6.10. *A picture of the process that draws nested squares, and the program that implements this process.*

always satisfied when a program begins.) The setup between repetitions involves changing the value of length and moving and rotating the turtle.

Note that each square sticks out one unit on *each* side of the previous square, so that the length of its side is *two* units longer than a side of the previous square. After drawing one square, we can set up the value of *length* for the next square by increasing its value by two. This is done with the assignment statement *length* := *length* + 2.

To get the turtle into the correct position, we must move it from the lower-left corner of one square to the lower-left corner of the next. This can be done by moving the turtle one unit to the left and one unit down. That's exactly what is done by the command $move(-1,-1)$. Of course, we have to raise the pen before moving the turtle and lower it again afterwards.

Finally, of course, we can make the turtle face to the right with a $face(0)$ command. A complete program is shown in Figure 6.10. Note that the loop used in this program is an example of a counting loop of the type shown in Figure 6.3. The variable *count* is used in the program only to count how many squares have been drawn and to decide when to exit from the loop.

Getting all the details right in this program is by no means easy. Some of the errors that can occur, even when the basic loop structure is correct, are shown in Figure 6.9. The pictures in that figure were all produced by students trying to write the program (even the correct one!). In each case, the error can be traced to failure to set up one or more of the required preconditions correctly. Taking note of preconditions and dealing with them really can shorten the path to a correct program.

6.3.3. Nested Statements. The final example of the chapter deals with a simple little problem. The program that solves it illustrates an important, and perhaps surprising, feature of the xTurtle language. The BNF templates for xTurtle in Figure 6.4 show that **if** statements and **loop** statements are made up of, among other things, lists of ⟨statement⟩s. But when you check to see what a ⟨statement⟩ is, you find that among the possibilities are... **if** statements and **loop** statements!

What this means is that a **loop** statement can include an **if** statement nested inside it, an **if** statement can contain a loop, one loop can be nested inside another, and so forth. Furthermore, you can have even deeper nesting, such as a loop inside an **if** statement which is inside another loop. No limit is set on how deep such nesting can go. The templates for xTurtle are deceptively simple. In fact, they can produce programs of great complexity.

The program in Figure 6.11 provides a simple example of nesting: an **if** statement inside a loop. The odd looking test in the **if** statement

$$\textbf{if } N/2 = trunc(N/2) \textbf{ then}\ldots$$

is a way a testing whether the value of N is an even integer. The function *trunc* deletes the fractional part of a number. For example, $trunc(7.8)$ is 7, $trunc(3.5)$ is 3, and $trunc(8)$ is 8. The only way that $N/2$ can be

```
declare N, StepCount
AskUser("What is the initial value for N?", N)
StepCount := 0
loop
    exit if N = 1
    if N/2 = trunc(N/2) then
        N := N / 2
    else
        N := 3 * N + 1
    end if
    StepCount := StepCount + 1
end loop
TellUser("It took #StepCount steps to reach 1.")
```

Figure 6.11. *This program contains an* **if** *statement nested inside a* **loop** *statement. The syntax of the language allows nesting of statements to any depth, but programs quickly become difficult to write and difficult to understand when this feature is overused.*

equal to $trunc(N/2)$ is for $N/2$ to be an integer, with no fractional part, and in that case N is an even integer.[10]

Suppose that the user types in the number 3 in response to the question, "What is the initial value of N?" Since 3 is odd, the first time through the loop the condition in the **if** statement is false, so the statement $N := 3 * N + 1$ is executed. This changes the value of N to 10. Then, the next time through the loop, N is even, so the first alternative in the **if** statement, $N := N / 2$, is executed. This divides N by 2, so that its new value is 5. If we continue to trace the program, we see that N goes through the sequence of values

$$3 \quad 10 \quad 5 \quad 16 \quad 8 \quad 4 \quad 2 \quad 1.$$

Once N becomes equal to 1, then the next time the computer executes

---

[10] This discussion is strictly true in a mathematical sense, but it is not valid for large real numbers stored in a computer. The problem is that the computer does not store exact values of real numbers. It only stores a certain number of significant digits. For example, if the computer uses 10 significant digits, then it might be that when 1727356284831 and 1727356284832 are stored as real numbers, both are represented as 1727356285000. So the whole distinction between odd and even numbers breaks down for large numbers. This is not by any means the only problem that comes up when working with real numbers on a computer.

the exit statement, "**exit if** $N = 1$," the condition will be true, and the execution of the loop will end. The message in the *TellUser* statement will be displayed and the program will terminate. Since the variable *StepCount* counts the number of repetitions of the loop, the message in this case will be, "It took 7 steps to reach 1."

If the user enters a different initial value for N, then the sequence of values of N and the number of items in the sequence will be different. If the starting value is 7, then the sequence is

$$7 \ 22 \ 11 \ 34 \ 17 \ 52 \ 26 \ 13 \ 40 \ 20 \ 10 \ 5 \ 16 \ 8 \ 4 \ 2 \ 1$$

while if the initial value is 27, the sequence begins

$$27 \ 82 \ 41 \ 124 \ 62 \ 31 \ 94 \ 47 \ 142 \ 71 \ 214 \ 107 \ 322 \ 162\ldots$$

and goes on for 111 steps. Something interesting is happening here: Given the initial value, there seems to be no way to predict how long the sequence will go on. It's not just that when the initial number gets bigger, the number of steps also increases—the sequence starting with 28 has only 19 steps. Even such a short program can have unpredictable behavior.

The situation is even worse. It is not even obvious that the program will always terminate. It is conceivable that there is some positive integer such that the sequence starting with that number will go on forever, without ever reaching 1.

Perhaps it would be nice if I could tidy up the end of this chapter by saying, "But of course if we analyze the problem from the point of view of the mathematical theory of ...," and then tell you the answer. But I can't. No one knows. This little problem has been around for quite a while. So far, no one has found a starting number for which the sequence goes on forever (though programmers have tried all the possibilities up to very large values), and it has not been proved that no such numbers exist (though many mathematicians have worked on the problem). Once again we come to the conclusion we reached at the end of Chapter 4: Computation can surprise you. It's not naturally tidy. Personally, I prefer it that way.

Chapter Summary

A typical programming language makes available some basic commands, such as *assignment statements* and *built-in subroutines*, and a number of ways of combining them into complex *control structures*, such as loop statements and if statements. *Programming* consists of constructing solutions to problems using these basic building blocks.

To use a programming language, you must understand both its *syntax* and its *semantics*. Syntax, i.e., grammar, can be described conveniently and unambiguously using *Backus-Naur Form*. Semantics refers to the meaning of the language; it is generally more subtle and more difficult to describe than syntax.

Names play a fundamental role in programming since they, perhaps more than anything else, make it possible to hide low-level details. *Variables* are names used to refer to memory locations; their use frees the programmer from details of data storage. Similarly, a subroutine hides the details of a complex task behind a single name which can be used by the programmer to perform that task.

Although programming is not easy, the systematic approach known as *software engineering* can help to make problems manageable. For example, analysis of a problem in terms of *states*, *preconditions*, and *postconditions*, can help in piecing together a solution.

Questions

1. Discuss the similarities and differences between writing a complex program and designing a complex circuit.

2. Consider the built-in subroutine *forward*, which will draw a line on the computer's screen. Try to figure out what is happening inside the black box. What happens, on the level of machine-language instructions, when this subroutine is executed? Don't forget to think about how a line is represented on the screen.

3. This chapter mentions a number of style guidelines for programming, some of them in footnotes. Make a list of as many of them as you can find, and explain why each is justified. More generally, what is the use of worrying about "good style" in the first place?

4. What happens in the program from Figure 6.10 if the user enters a negative number for the number of squares to be drawn? (Remember that "the user" is assumed to be either very stupid or actively malicious.) A hidden precondition for the loop to work is that the number of sides is positive. Rewrite the program in two different ways to take this precondition into account. First, modify it so it does nothing when the number of sides is negative. Second, modify it by using a loop to get the user's input; the loop should continue until the user enters a positive number. (The program will also fail if the user enters a number that is not an integer, such as 2.5. Why? Can you fix this more subtle problem?)

5. Develop a program to draw the following picture of a "comb." Don't draw each line individually; use a loop. (Be careful: The number of vertical lines is not equal to the number of horizontal segments joining one vertical line to the next.)

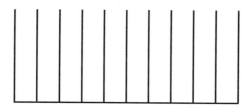

6. The English language has a complicated grammar, but it is still possible to describe at least part of that grammar using BNF templates. For example, all the ⟨sentence⟩s that can be formed using the following templates are legal English sentences, even though most of them don't make much sense.

⟨sentence⟩ ::= ⟨noun part⟩ ⟨verb part⟩

⟨noun part⟩ ::= ⟨proper noun⟩ | ⟨common noun phrase⟩

⟨proper noun⟩ ::= John | Mary | Richard Nixon |
                              The President of the United States

⟨common noun phrase⟩ ::= ⟨article⟩ ⟨common noun⟩ [who ⟨verb part⟩]

⟨article⟩ ::= a | the | some | every

⟨common noun⟩ ::= fish | dog | unicorn | man | woman

⟨verb part⟩ ::= ⟨intransitive verb⟩ |
                      ⟨transitive verb⟩ ⟨noun part⟩

⟨intransitive verb⟩ ::= runs | thinks | cries | is bald

⟨transitive verb⟩ ::= loves | hates | understands | knows | is

Give some examples of ⟨sentence⟩s produced by these rules. As you apply these rules, you have to make some choices. For example, when an example calls for a ⟨noun part⟩, you have to choose between a ⟨proper noun⟩ and a ⟨common noun phrase⟩. Try building sentences by making all such choices randomly, say by flipping coins or rolling dice. (These templates exhibit "nesting" similar to that discussed in the last subsection of the chapter. Can you see where?)

Chapter 7

Subroutines and Recursion

━━━━━━━━━━━

THE PROGRAMMER WHO doesn't understand how to write subroutines is like a mechanic who owns three general purpose tools—a wrench, a hammer, and a screwdriver—and tries to tackle every job with just those three tools. Perhaps in theory it is possible, but it is probably not pleasant. And as jobs become more complex, they will tend to become unreasonably difficult.

Subroutines are a tool for dealing with complexity. A subroutine is a chunk of code for performing some task, sealed in a black box and given a name. Once a subroutine exists, it can be used as a building block for constructing programs, or even other subroutines, that perform more complex tasks.

This chapter deals with writing and using subroutines in the xTurtle programming language. But more important, it discusses how subroutines can be used in any language to help in the construction of correct solutions to complex problems. The main purpose of going through all the gritty details of subroutine use is to give you an idea of exactly what type of building blocks they are.

The third section of the chapter deals with recursion, a particularly magical and wonderful example of subroutine use. Finally, the last section will give you some idea how subroutines can be implemented on real computers in terms of machine-language instructions.

7.1. Writing and Using Subroutines

The basic idea of subroutines is elegant and clear. As so often happens when dealing with computers, though, the many details of syntax and semantics easily can get in the way of understanding. I will cover many of the details, but it will be important for you not to get lost in them. The black box metaphor is a guide for keeping things straight. You should keep in mind the three aspects of subroutines considered as black boxes: their design, their use in complex programs, and their interface. Or to put it another way, the view from the inside of the box, the view from the outside, and the relationship between these two views.

A subroutine is designed to perform some task. The point of this is to allow the programmer, once the subroutine has been written, to think of that task as a single operation which can be performed with a single command. That command can then be used as a building block in a complete program, or even in another subroutine. A well-designed subroutine will perform a coherent task that is easy to think of as a single operation, and it will fit easily into place in a larger structure. This means that its interface—the way it communicates with the outside world—should be straightforward and easy to understand. The entire discussion of subroutines that follows is based on these principles.

We have already seen how built-in subroutines like *PenUp* and *forward* are used in an xTurtle program. Once a new subroutine has been defined, it is used in exactly the same way: by giving its name along with any required parameters. So, we just need to understand how to define new subroutines in the first place. For the record, the official syntax rules for defining xTurtle subroutines are given in Figure 7.1, but it will take most of this section to explain it all.

We start with a simple subroutine that draws a five-by-five square. The idea is to take the instructions for drawing the square, group them together, and give them a name. Using *Square5* as the name, we can do this in xTurtle as follows:

> **sub** *Square5*
> > forward(5) turn(90)
> > forward(5) turn(90)
> > forward(5) turn(90)
> > forward(5) turn(90)
>
> **end sub**

This is a *subroutine declaration*. The name of the subroutine and the list of instructions are bracketed between the words **sub** and **end sub**,

⟨program⟩ ::= ⟨program item⟩ [⟨program item⟩]...

⟨program item⟩ ::= ⟨statement⟩ | ⟨subroutine declaration⟩

⟨subroutine declaration⟩ ::= **sub** ⟨subroutine name⟩ [(⟨dummy parameters⟩)]

[⟨subroutine item⟩]...

end sub

⟨dummy parameters⟩ ::= [**ref**] ⟨name⟩ [, [**ref**]⟨name⟩]...

⟨subroutine item⟩ ::= ⟨statement⟩ | ⟨import list⟩

⟨import list⟩ ::= **import** ⟨variable name⟩ [, ⟨variable name⟩]...

Figure 7.1. *Further BNF templates for xTurtle, specifying the syntax
for subroutine declarations. The template for ⟨program⟩ given here replaces the template in Figure 6.4. The new version allows a program to
include subroutine declarations, as well as statements. The remaining
templates from Figure 6.4 remain valid. The upshot of all this is that
the inside of a subroutine looks just like a program, with two exceptions:
A subroutine cannot include another subroutine declaration (though it
can include subroutine call statements), and a subroutine can include
"import lists" while a program cannot.*

which mark the beginning and end of the subroutine.

When the computer encounters a subroutine declaration in a program, it remembers the list of instructions and associates them with the
specified name, which in this example is *Square5*. Later in the program,
if it come across the single word *Square5* used as an instruction, it will
recognize it as the name of a subroutine and will execute the associated
list of instructions. For example, a program consisting of the subroutine
declaration for *Square5*, as given above, followed by the instructions

Square5

PenUp MoveTo(−5,−5) PenDown

Square5

will draw the two squares shown in Figure 6.3 in the previous chapter.
It is important to remember that just *declaring* the subroutine does not
actually draw a square; it just defines the meaning of the subroutine
name for later use. Once declared, a subroutine can be reused in the
program any number of times, just by giving its name.[1]

---

[1] To clear up one possible confusion: The computer only remembers the
subroutine until the end of the program. If you want to reuse it in another
program, you must copy the entire subroutine declaration into that program.

7.1.1. Parameters. *Square5*, like *PenUp*, is a simple subroutine with no parameters. Recall that parameters, such as the variable *length* in the instruction *forward(length)*, add immensely to the power of a subroutine. A subroutine with no parameters performs one fixed task; when a subroutine has a parameter, it can perform a different task for each possible value of that parameter. *Square5* can only draw a square measuring five units on a side. If a square-drawing subroutine had a parameter for specifying the length of a side, it would be able to draw squares of all possible sizes.

You will be happy to know that you can write subroutines with parameters in xTurtle, as you can in almost all programming languages. As a first example, here is an improved square-drawing subroutine in xTurtle:

> **sub** *Square(side_length)*
>> forward(*side_length*) turn(90)
>> forward(*side_length*) turn(90)
>> forward(*side_length*) turn(90)
>> forward(*side_length*) turn(90)
>
> **end sub**

Once this subroutine has been declared in a program, the command *Square*(5) will draw a five-by-five square, whereas *Square*(1) will draw a square one unit on a side. And if *length* is a variable, then the command *Square*(*length*) will draw a square whose side is given by whatever value *length* happens to have at the time the command is executed.

Figure 7.2 shows this subroutine used in a complete program. No drawing occurs until the subroutine is called at the beginning of the loop. The first time through the loop, the value of *length* is 1, and a square of side 1 is drawn. After that, each time through the loop, the value of *length* increases and a bigger square is drawn.

The parameters of a subroutine are part of its interface. They provide a means of communication between the subroutine and the program in which the subroutine is used. In the command *Square*(5), the 5 is a message to the subroutine telling it how big a square it should draw. As we will see later, there is a way of doing back-door communication, without parameters. However, it is generally better to keep the communications

---

It might be nice if you could *permanently* teach the computer the meaning of a new word by defining a subroutine. This is not possible in xTurtle, but some more sophisticated languages do make it much easier to reuse subroutines in many different programs.

```
sub Square(side_length)
    forward(side_length) turn(90)
    forward(side_length) turn(90)
    forward(side_length) turn(90)
    forward(side_length) turn(90)
end sub
```

declare *count, HowMany, length*

AskUser("How many squares should I draw?", *HowMany*)

$count := 0$

$length := 1$

loop

  $Square(length)$

  $count := count + 1$

  exit if $count = HowMany$

  $length := length + 2$

  PenUp Move(−1,−1) PenDown

end loop

Figure 7.2. *Another xTurtle program for drawing nested squares. This program is equivalent to the one in Figure 6.10, but uses a subroutine to draw the individual squares.*

out in the open. First of all, it allows the computer to detect certain types of errors; for example, any attempt to use the command *Square* with the wrong number of parameters would produce an error message from the computer. Just as important, the presence of a parameter in a subroutine call will help any human reader to understand just what communication is taking place.

Parameters and variables are very different things. Consider, for example, *side_length* in the subroutine declaration for *Square*. Although it looks like a variable, it is not. It is what is called a **dummy parameter**, or sometimes a "dummy variable" or a "formal parameter." A dummy parameter is a place-holder for the **actual parameter**—such as "5" in the command *Square*(5)—that is provided when the subroutine is used. Inside the subroutine declaration, the dummy parameter acts a kind of stand-in for the unknown value of this actual parameter. When you tell the computer

sub *Square*(*side_length*)...

you are saying, "Here is what the command *Square*(*side_length*) would mean, if *side_length* were a variable: ...." The computer generalizes from this to the meaning of *Square*(5), *Square*(2 ∗ *Count* + 1), and so forth. You have to write the subroutine as if the dummy parameter already has some definite, though unknown, value. In fact, it doesn't really get a value until the subroutine is called during program execution, and then it is assigned the value of the actual parameter automatically.

One aspect of dummy parameters is especially confusing. A subroutine is supposed to be a black box. A dummy parameter is like a slot through which information—the value of an actual parameter—is passed into the box. When the box is viewed from the outside, the name of the slot is irrelevant. In fact, the name of the dummy parameter has no meaning at all outside of the subroutine declaration. In the program in Figure 7.2, *side_length* is never declared as a variable. If this name were used outside the subroutine declaration in that program, the result would be an "undeclared variable" error. Even stranger is the fact that it would be perfectly legal to declare an actual variable named *side_length* in the program, but that variable would have nothing to do with the dummy parameter of the same name. The dummy parameter and the variable would be on opposite sides of the box.[2]

Figure 7.3 gives another sample program that uses subroutines. Most of the program consists of the declarations of two subroutines, *petal* and *flower*. No drawing actually occurs until the last three lines, which use the subroutines to draw the three figures shown on the right in the figure. Let's try to understand how this program works.

A "petal" drawn by the subroutine *petal* is actually a rhombus, that is, a diamond shape with four sides of the same length. The two parameters for *petal* specify the length of a side and the angle between the sides that meet at one corner of the diamond. Since the first side of the rhombus is drawn in whatever direction the turtle happens to be facing,

---

[2] And here is the most confusing part (hidden safely in a footnote): It would be perfectly OK to use the command *Square*(*side_length*) in that program. While the subroutine is executing, the value of the program variable *side_length* would become the value of the dummy parameter *side_length* in the subroutine. But that would only be because the variable was used as the actual parameter in the command, not because they have the same name. The two identical names should be regarded as a harmless coincidence. Novice programmers tend to have a great deal of trouble using parameters correctly, partly because they fail to see a dummy parameter and an actual parameter as two separate things.

```
sub petal(angle, side)
    forward(side) turn(180−angle)
    forward(side) turn(angle)
    forward(side) turn(180−angle)
    forward(side) turn(angle)
end sub

sub flower(petalCt, size)
    declare count, angle
    angle := 360/petalCt
    count := 0
    loop
        petal(angle, size)
        turn(angle)
        count := count + 1
        exit if count = petalCt
    end loop
end sub

petal(5,30) Move(0,−8)
flower(8,3) Move(0,−16)
flower(24,5)
```

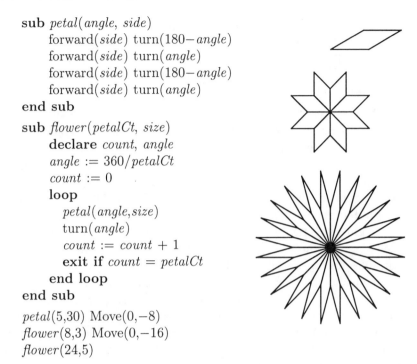

Figure 7.3. *A program containing two subroutines, and the picture drawn by the program. As this example shows, one subroutine can be used as an instruction inside another subroutine. Once a subroutine has been declared, it becomes part of the programming language and can be used throughout the remainder of the program in exactly the same way as a built-in subroutine. (This example also shows the syntax for defining subroutines with more than one parameter.)*

the orientation of the rhombus will depend on the heading of the turtle when the subroutine is called. When the subroutine ends, the position and heading of the turtle are left unchanged from their starting values.

A flower consists of a number of petals radiating out from the center. The definition of subroutine *flower* reflects this by calling subroutine *petal* repeatedly to draw each petal. The turtle rotates a bit after drawing each petal, so that each of the petals is drawn in a different orientation.

The parameters of *flower* specify the number of petals to be drawn and the size of the petals. The *size* parameter is simply passed on to *petal*, to be used as the length of the petal's sides. A counting loop is used to draw the specified number of petals; the *petalCt* parameter specifies the number of times this loop will execute. Note that the angle used for each petal is given by $360/petalCt$. This value is chosen so that the angles at the bases of the *petalCt* petals will add up to 360 degrees, that is, a full circle.

7.1.2. Gritty Details. You now know enough about subroutines to follow a discussion about how they are used in building complex programs. But before we go on to that, this subsection will cover some of the gritty details of internal construction and interface that a programmer needs to know to become an expert user of subroutines.

Look again at the subroutine *flower* in Figure 7.3. Note that it contains a **declare** statement that creates two variables, *count* and *angle*. As you might expect, these variables are part of the internal workings of the black box and are completely invisible from the outside.

Variables declared inside a subroutine are called *local variables* for that subroutine. Ordinary variables—that is, those declared outside any subroutine—are called *global variables*. It might be that a local variable has the same name as some global variable. There is nothing wrong with this. They are two different variables that just happen to have the same name. Their associated memory locations will be different, and changing the value of the local variable will have no effect on the value of the global variable.[3]

In fact, a local variable has an associated memory location only so long as the subroutine is being executed. That memory is released when the subroutine ends. It can even happen that when the subroutine is called again, its local variables will be assigned to completely different memory locations. Not only is a local variable inaccessible from outside the subroutine; it doesn't even exist except when the computer is actually executing the subroutine.

Of course, a subroutine is not completely cut off from the rest of the program. Parameters exist precisely to allow communication between the two sides of the black box. In the examples we have seen so far, the parameters are used for input. (That is, "input" from the point of view of the subroutine.) Sometimes, however, a subroutine produces new information which is meant to be used by the program after the subroutine ends. To get that information out of the subroutine and back

---

[3] Good thing, too. It would be as if when your refrigerator motor came on, it changed the channel on your television set. That would mean, of course, that your refrigerator was not a proper "black box."

to the program, we need a new kind of parameter, called a *reference* or **ref** *parameter*. A **ref** parameter can be used to output a value from the subroutine to the rest of the program.[4]

Here, for example, is a ridiculously short subroutine that computes the interest on a given amount of money, assuming an interest rate of six percent. ("Six percent" means "6 per 100," that is, 6/100 or 0.06.)

> **sub** *ComputeInterest*(*Amount*, **ref** *Interest*)
> $\quad$ *Interest* := *Amount* $*$ 0.06
> **end sub**

The word **ref** in front of the dummy parameter *Interest* tells the computer that this is a **ref** parameter. This allows the subroutine to change the value of the corresponding actual parameter, something which is impossible for non-**ref** parameters. For example, if *myInt* is a variable in the program, then the procedure call statement

> *ComputeInterest*(274.59, *myInt*)

will compute the interest on $274.59 and store the answer in the variable *myInt*. Since *Interest* is a **ref** parameter, the assignment statement in the subroutine will change the value of the actual parameter *myInt*.

Parameters represent slots or holes in the black box through which information can pass back and forth between a subroutine and the program that uses it. You might think that a black box should be completely sealed off from the outside, but if it were it would be of little use. It would go humming along, doing whatever it does, with no way of ever affecting or being affected by the rest of the world. Any black box needs an *interface* to connect it to the outside world. For subroutines, parameters are the obvious, straightforward part of the interface. There is nothing sneaky about them: A glance at the first line of a subroutine declaration will tell you exactly what parameters that subroutine uses.

Sometimes, though, it is useful to be sneaky—to smuggle information into or out of a subroutine through the back door, without passing it through a parameter. This is really only legitimate when it is done to avoid distracting the programmer who uses the subroutine with unnecessary details. Although you haven't thought of it in these terms, you have already been the beneficiary of such courtesy. Consider the command *forward*(5). This command draws a line. The parameter 5 gives

---

[4] We have already seen a **ref** parameter in the built-in subroutine, *AskUser*. Terminology gets a bit confusing here: *AskUser* requests the user to input a number; that number is in turn output by *AskUser* to the program. Remember that "input" and "output" are relative terms, depending on point of view.

```
declare InterestRate
sub GetInterestRate
    import InterestRate
    AskUser("What is the interest rate?", InterestRate)
end sub
sub ComputeInterest(Amount, ref Interest)
    import InterestRate
    Interest := Amount * InterestRate
end sub

declare Money, Int
AskUser("How much money do you have?", Money)
GetInterestRate
ComputeInterest(Money, Int)
TellUser("The interest on $#Money is $#Int.")
```

Figure 7.4. *A program to compute the interest on a given amount of money. Both of the subroutines in this program make direct use of the global variable, InterestRate. A subroutine gains access to a global variable with an* **import** *statement. In xTurtle, a global variable is invisible from inside a subroutine unless it is explicitly made visible with an* **import** *statement (or by being passed to the subroutine as a parameter).*

the length of the line, but the subroutine also needs other information to determine exactly what line to draw: It needs to know the position and orientation of the turtle. How does the subroutine know these values? They have to be stored somewhere "out there" in the computer's memory in something like global variables, and the subroutine must be able to access those variables. But as a programmer using turtle graphics, you deal only indirectly with these variables, through the turtle graphics commands. You don't need to think about them or mention them in your program.

Figure 7.4 shows how something similar can be done with user-defined subroutines in xTurtle. The extra information used by the two subroutines is stored in the global variable *InterestRate*.[5] From the point of view of the last five lines of this program, this variable is just "out there"

---

[5] In xTurtle, global variables are ordinarily invisible from inside subroutines. However, they can be made visible with **import** statements. (The **import** statement makes a "crack" in the black box through which the global variable is visible.) Note that a **declare** statement in a subroutine makes a new, local

somewhere and is used only indirectly, through the subroutines. Ideally, perhaps, the two subroutines and the variable *InterestRate* should be grouped together inside a black box that would give *InterestRate* some enforced protection from being tampered with by the rest of the program. Although this is not possible in xTurtle, the idea is an important part of some more advanced languages that will be discussed in the next chapter.

7.2. Real Programs

Our approach to understanding complex systems, including complex computer programs, can be summarized easily: Don't try to keep too many details in mind at one time. We have seen how complex systems can be built up, level by level, from extremely simple components. On each level, structures are built using black boxes from the levels below. These structures then become new black boxes for use on higher levels. If the step from each level to the next is kept small enough to be comprehensible, then very complex systems can be fully understood in this way.

The black boxes that make up complex systems are sometimes referred to as **modules**. A module is a more-or-less self-contained component of a larger system which interacts with other components in well-defined, easy to understand ways. In an xTurtle program, the modules are subroutines that interact by passing parameters and sometimes—at the risk of making the interaction less comprehensible—by using global variables. As mentioned at the end of the last section, other programming languages provide additional types of modules. But the idea is the same: Tackle a problem by dividing it into manageable pieces.

The sample programs in this book are quite short and, I hope, fairly easy to understand. In the real world, however, single programs that are as long as this book are common, and the most complex existing programs would fill it many times over. A program of that size is written by a team of many programmers, and no single individual understands the entire program in full detail. The software engineer in charge of the project will be familiar with the major program modules and their interactions but will trust the internal design of the modules to other team members. Individual programmers will be intimately familiar with

---

variable, but an **import** statement just makes an already existing variable visible. In many languages, global variables are automatically visible from inside subroutines.

the modules they work on but will be aware of other modules only as black boxes with certain carefully specified behaviors.

For an individual programmer writing a complete program of moderate complexity, there is no problem of coordinating the efforts of a number of different people. But the problem of coordinating the various components of the program remains, and it offers many of the same difficulties. In fact, it is sometimes useful for such a programmer to be a bit schizophrenic—to keep the details of different program components in different components of the mind, as it were. Much of my discussion here applies to programs written by individuals as well as by teams of programmers.

7.2.1. The Software Life Cycle. Some programs, especially those written as learning experiences, are meant to be used a few times by the programmer who writes them and then forgotten. Most "real" programs, on the other hand, are written for an audience and are meant to be used over a long period of time, possibly in changing circumstances. Such programs have a *life cycle* that begins with a specification of the problem to be solved and ends years later, after many revisions. The actual writing of the program is only a small part of this life cycle.

The software life cycle begins with an analysis of the problem to be solved. Often, an initial statement of a problem is far too vague to use as a basis for a program. The goal of problem analysis is to produce a *specification* of exactly what the program is expected to do. The specification should be complete and unambiguous, so that it will be possible to determine whether or not the program that is produced meets the specification.

Then, before any instructions are written, a design for the program is produced. A design is a kind of blueprint for the program, showing all the major components, their responsibilities, and how they will interact. In a large programming project, the design will exist as a separate, detailed document, stored on paper or in the computer. The design organizes the division of labor not just among program components but among programmers working on the project.[6]

---

[6] For an individual programmer (in my own case at least), the program design can be a skeletal version of the actual program, leaving details to be filled in as the program is gradually written. Think of an xTurtle program, for example, in which many subroutine declarations exist but do not yet contain any instructions. It is possible to write an outline of the entire program in this way and then to fill it in and test it bit by bit.

Once the design is complete, the program itself can be written. This part of programming—writing down instructions in some programming language—is sometimes called *coding*, with the implication that it is a merely mechanical translation of the program design into programming language. In fact, of course, coding is by no means a trivial skill.

Before a program can be called complete, it must be thoroughly tested to check that it is as error-free as possible and that it meets its specification. Since unplanned, haphazard testing is not likely to uncover all the errors in a program, a systemic testing strategy should be part of the program design from the beginning. It is rarely possible to eliminate all errors from a program, no matter how thoroughly it is tested, for the simple reason that it is impossible to test the program's responses in all possible circumstances. But it is certainly possible to increase the reliability of a program by careful testing.[7]

Analysis, design, coding, and testing do not necessarily take place independently or in strict sequence. Part of the advantage of a modular approach is that components can be worked on independently. One component might be coded and in the process of being tested while another is still being designed. Furthermore, problems that arise at any stage might force the process back to a previous stage. For example, questions of efficiency or even feasibility might be raised when programmers try to translate the design into program code, resulting in changes in the design. And testing might uncover errors in analysis, design, or coding that have to be fixed.

In most cases, a newly completed program has just begun its life cycle. Most programs are designed to be used over a period of years, and it is unlikely that they will remain unmodified. Instead, they will go through constant revision to add new features, to react to changing circumstances, and to correct newly discovered errors (and, too often, errors that are introduced into the program during revision). This part of the software life cycle is called *maintenance*, and it is usually responsible for a majority of the cost and effort that go into a program. A good program is designed to be as easy to maintain as possible.

---

[7] There is a great deal of interest in finding techniques for *proving* beyond any doubt that a program is correct, but existing proof techniques work only for fairly short programs. Furthermore, the most that can be proved is that a program meets its specification. Unfortunately, errors can occur in specifications as well, either because they don't exactly express what is really desired of the program, or because they fail to take into account some possible situations that the program will have to deal with.

The modular approach to programming is useful in all stages of the software life cycle. During coding, modularity permits different components of the program to be worked on independently. Independence of modules is also importing during testing. Testing does not have to be put off until the program is completely written. Well-designed modules can be tested individually, before the program is assembled, to make sure they meet their requirements. If each module is correct, and if the relationships among modules are straightforward and well-defined, then the entire program has a good chance of being correct.

Modularity is particularly important during maintenance. Recall the basic idea of the black box: As far as the outside world is concerned, only the behavior of the box is important. The inside of the box, the implementation, doesn't matter as long as it produces the correct behavior. The implication of this is that changes made to one module don't affect the rest of the program, as long as they don't change the module's behavior as seen from the outside. During maintenance, changes in implementation can be made without worrying about how they will affect the rest of the program. The other aspect of modularity—that the interactions among modules should be simple and well-understood—implies that when a change does affect other modules, it should be possible to determine exactly what the effect will be and to make changes in the other modules to account for it.[8]

7.2.2. Design Strategies. The advantages of the modular approach extend to the analysis and design stages of the software life cycle. It is, of course, easier to design a program as a collection of components, rather than all at once, as a massive jumble of detail. But, more than that, the modular view offers some definite guidelines about how to go about designing a complex program.

Remember that we view a program as a hierarchy with many levels of complexity. At the top of the hierarchy sits the program, considered as a whole. It is made up of components from lower levels of the hierarchy, which are themselves made up of components from even lower levels, and so on, down to the most primitive operations that the computer can perform. This view suggests two possible approaches to program design, which we can call *top-down design* and *bottom-up design*.

---

[8] I should note that the ideal of true modularity is rarely achieved. Many errors in programs, especially errors introduced during maintenance, occur because of unexpected or undocumented interactions among modules.

Top-down design is also called problem decomposition. The idea is to start with the overall problem to be solved and to break it into several subproblems. Each subproblem can in turn be broken into even smaller problems and so on, until the problems become trivial enough to be solved easily. The overall problem corresponds to the entire program, at the top of the complexity hierarchy. The subproblems correspond to the modules that make up the program.

In terms of xTurtle programming, the top-down strategy goes something like this: Start writing the program. When you come to something you don't know how to do easily, call it a subroutine and worry about writing it later. When you get to the end of the program, start working on the subroutines in the same way. As a trivial example, suppose you wanted to write a program to draw a house. You might start out by writing the instructions

> *DrawWalls*
> *DrawRoof*
> *DrawDoorsAndWindows*

and then go back and write the three subroutines *DrawWalls*, *DrawRoof*, and *DrawDoorsAndWindows*.

In bottom-up design, as I'm sure you've guessed, the complexity hierarchy is constructed starting at the bottom. At each stage, new components are assembled from components that have already been constructed. Obviously, there must be some overall direction to all this construction, and that direction must be derived from the problem at hand. But it doesn't come from dividing the problem into subproblems. Instead it comes from recognizing that a certain tool will be useful for solving the problem and then building that tool. After enough tools are built, the problem will be easy to solve. For example, if you want to draw a house, you know you will have to draw a roof, so why not work on a subroutine to do so. This looks less trivial when the distance between the top and the bottom of the hierarchy is larger: If you want to write a program to keep track of a mailing list, you know you will need tools for sorting a list of addresses, for inserting a new address, for changing an address, for printing out the list and so on. After a sufficient number of such tools are assembled, the task of finishing the program will be reduced to a manageable scale.

The term "tool" here is meant to imply something that can be applied in a wide range of circumstances, wherever the particular service that it performs is needed. Once a tool has been created, it can be reused in

```
sub Square(ref side_length)
    forward(side_length) turn(90)
    forward(side_length) turn(90)
    forward(side_length) turn(90)
    forward(side_length) turn(90)
    side_length := side_length + 2
    PenUp  Move(−1,−1)  PenDown
end sub

declare count, HowMany, length
AskUser("How many squares should I draw?", HowMany)
count := 0
length := 1
loop
    Square(length)
    count := count + 1
    exit if count = HowMany
end loop
```

Figure 7.5. *Yet another xTurtle program for drawing nested squares. Compare the subroutine in this program to the subroutine in Figure 7.1. The square-drawing subroutine in Figure 7.1 is much more likely to be useful in other programs.*

other programs. The writing and testing of the tool can be done once and for all. Each time the tool is reused, that much programming effort is saved. In fact, it might be worth the effort to write a more general-purpose tool than is needed in a particular program; such a tool is more likely to be reusable, and the effort saved when it is reused can more than make up for the extra effort it took to write it. For example, a tool for sorting a list of addresses will certainly have application beyond a single mailing list program. But a more general list-sorting tool, although harder to write, would be even more useful.

Of course, every subroutine is a tool in some sense, but it is always tempting to write subroutines that are so carefully sculpted to fit into a particular program that they will be of no use elsewhere. It is especially easy to do this when applying a strict top-down approach. Consider once again (last time, I promise!) the nested squares problem. Figure 7.5 shows another program for solving this problem. In addition to the instructions for drawing a square, the subroutine in this figure includes instructions that set things up for drawing the *next* square. In

the original version of the subroutine, these instructions were outside
the subroutine, in the loop. The new version is inferior because a subroutine to "draw a square of size *side_length*" is much more likely to be
reusable than a subroutine to "draw a square of size *side_length*, increase
side_length by 2, and move the turtle one unit left and one unit down."

The problem here is not only the lack of reusability. Even if it were
not reusable, the original version of subroutine *Square* would be prefer-
able because the description of what it does is simpler. This makes it
more likely that the original version will be used correctly in a program.
It also makes it easier for someone trying to read the program to understand what is going on.

In general, the interface of a subroutine should be straightforward
and easy to understand. One way to describe the interface is in terms of
preconditions and postconditions, which were introduced in the previous
chapter. The precondition of a subroutine represents the requirements
that must hold for it to work correctly. Its postcondition describes the
effect that the subroutine will have, provided that the precondition was
satisfied. A full statement of precondition and postcondition should always include a description of requirements and effects for all parameters
and global variables used by the subroutine. A subroutine is likely to
connect up well with the rest of the program, and to be reusable in other
programs, if the precondition is minimal and the postcondition can be
easily expressed.

7.3. Recursion

> *So, naturalists observe, the flea*
> *Hath smaller fleas that on him prey,*
> *And these have smaller still that bite 'em*
> *And so it goes, ad infinitum.*
> —Jonathan Swift

I have been describing a complex system as a hierarchy of components, in
which each component is constructed using components from the levels
below. In a program, the components are subroutines, and one subroutine uses another by referring to its name in a subroutine call statement.

In order to keep track of the structure of a program, it is sometimes
useful to diagram the relationships among its subroutines, as shown in
Figure 7.6. Note, however, that the lower diagram in that figure doesn't
represent a hierarchy at all, since it contains "loops" of subroutines that
call one another. A hierarchy has a definite top-to-bottom ordering; one

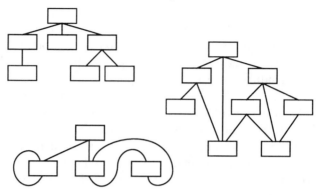

Figure 7.6. *The structure of a program can be visualized as a diagram in which each subroutine is represented by a box. The main program— the instructions that are not inside a subroutine—is represented by a box at the top of the diagram. A line is drawn between components to indicate that one component uses another. The diagram on the top left represents a program in which the subroutines are organized into a strict hierarchy. The diagram on the right includes some common complications: A subroutine can be used by several different subroutines, possibly on different levels of the hierarchy. The diagram on the lower left illustrates a surprising possibility: What happens if a program contains loops of subroutines that call each other, or even a single subroutine that calls itself?*

component can use another only if it lies above it in the hierarchy. Surprisingly, perhaps, nonhierarchical programs with loops of subroutines that call one another are allowed in most programming languages.[9]

A subroutine is called **recursive** if it is part of such a loop of subroutines. The simplest example of such a loop is a single subroutine that calls itself. Syntactically, this type of recursion is trivial: It just happens that one of the instructions in the definition of a subroutine refers to the very same subroutine that is being defined. But what could such a thing mean, and could it ever be useful?

In fact, recursion is a very useful and powerful programming technique that arises naturally from the idea of a subroutine as a black box. Recall that the task performed by a subroutine can depend on the parameters that it is passed and on the values of any global variables that it

---

[9] Douglas Hofstadter uses the term **tangled hierarchy** to refer to such hierarchies-with-loops. His wonderful book, *Gödel, Escher, Bach*, can be read as a 700-page investigation into the implications of tangled hierarchies.

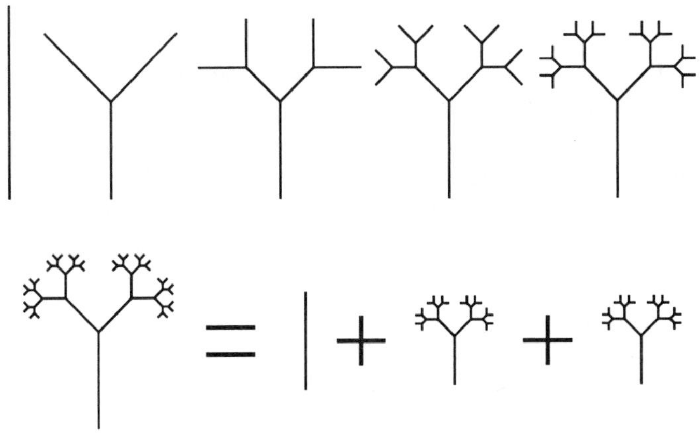

Figure 7.7. *A sequence of trees of increasing complexity. Each tree in the sequence has one more level of branching than the preceding tree. The "equation" in the bottom half of the figure shows how a tree can be constructed from three pieces: a trunk, represented by a straight line, and two identical branches. Each of the branches is really just a small tree, rotated 45 degrees from its usual orientation. Of course, this doesn't apply to the first tree in the sequence, which is just a vertical line with no branches at all.*

imports. For example, you would expect three subroutine calls *Tree*(4,3), *Tree*(2,1), and *Tree*(1,0) to have different effects, even though they all refer to the same subroutine. Now suppose it happens that part of the task performed by *Tree*(4,3) is exactly the same as the task performed by *Tree*(2,1). In that case it would make perfect sense for the execution of subroutine *Tree* (with parameters 4 and 3) to include a call to the same subroutine *Tree* (with parameters 2 and 1). *Tree*(4,3) and *Tree*(2,1) can be thought of as being different black boxes, and there is nothing wrong with one of the boxes using the other.

Figure 7.7 shows how this situation could arise in practice. Each tree, except for the first, is made up of a trunk and two branches. Each branch happens to be a scaled-down and rotated tree. It seems reasonable that a subroutine that draws such a tree should be able to call itself to draw the branches. The subroutine will have two parameters to tell it how large a tree to draw and how complex the tree should be. Note that the branches are smaller and less complex than the whole tree. When the subroutine is called, it receives certain values for the parameters; when it calls itself in turn to draw a branch, it must pass different values for the parameters.

sub *Tree*(*size, complexity*)

{ Draw a tree with base at the current turtle position, "growing" }
{ in the direction of the current turtle heading. *Size* is }
{ the (approximate) height of the tree. *Complexity* is the }
{ number of levels of branching in the tree; the value of *Complexity*}
{ must be greater than or equal to zero. At the end of the }
{ subroutine, the turtle is at its original position and heading. }

    if *complexity* = 0 **then**
        forward(*size*)
        back(*size*)
    else
        forward(*size* / 2)
        turn(45)
        Tree(*size* / 2, *complexity* − 1)
        turn(−90)
        Tree(*size* / 2, *complexity* − 1)
        turn(45)
        back(*size* / 2)
    end if
end sub

Figure 7.8. *A recursive subroutine for drawing binary trees. The comments inside curly braces give a slightly informal description of what the subroutine does. (The postcondition that the turtle is left in its original position and heading is essential if the branches are to end up in the correct position and orientation. The* back *commands and the final 45-degree turn are required to achieve this postcondition.)*

We can number the trees according to their complexity, starting with zero for the tree that has no branches. Note that for $n > 0$, the branches of a tree with complexity n are trees of half the size and of complexity $n − 1$. The first tree—with complexity zero—must be treated as a special case, since it consists of just a trunk with no branches. Figure 7.8 gives a subroutine, *Tree*, for drawing trees, written in the xTurtle programming language. If the parameter *complexity* is zero, this subroutine just draws a line; otherwise, it draws a tree consisting of a line and two branches. Each branch is drawn with a statement

$$Tree(size \ / \ 2, \ complexity \ - \ 1)$$

which calls the same subroutine to draw a smaller, less complex tree.

The trees in Figure 7.7 can be drawn with the commands *Tree*(10,0), *Tree*(10,1), *Tree*(10,2), and so forth.

Like most recursive subroutines, *Tree* uses an **if** statement to divide its task into two cases: a trivial case that does not require recursion, and the recursive case. The trivial case in a recursion is called the **base case**. If you think about it, you will see that everything is, in the end, built up from the base case. A tree of complexity 3 contains two trees of complexity 2, which in turn contain trees of complexity 1, which contain trees of complexity 0, which are just straight lines. Recursion is a wonderful example of building up complexity level by level starting with trivial components. Since the process of going from one level to the next is the same no matter which level is being considered, that process can be described once and for all—with a single subroutine, for example—and then repeated over and over to reach extraordinary levels of complexity.

7.3.1. Getting from A to B. Another example will be useful. This time, we consider a complex path from one point *A* to another point *B*. The easy way to get from *A* to *B* is to follow a straight line. In xTurtle, this would correspond to a single command *forward*(*dist*), assuming that *dist* is the distance from *A* to *B* and that the turtle is facing in the right direction.

If we want to add a little variety, we might take a detour to the left after traveling one-third of the distance. This path is shown in the upper right in Figure 7.9. It could be drawn with the xTurtle commands[10]

> forward(*dist* / 3) turn(60)
> forward(*dist* / 3) turn(−120)
> forward(*dist* / 3) turn(60)
> forward(*dist* / 3)

This path consists of four line segments. Suppose that in the middle of *each* of these line segments, we decide to take a little detour to the left. The resulting path is the middle example in Figure 7.9.

But why stop there? We can repeat the process of adding a detour in the middle of each line segment, and we can do this as often as we like, reaching truly ridiculous levels of complexity. Considering the number of line segments involved, it looks like the paths we get would be very difficult to draw in xTurtle. The idea of writing a *single* subroutine capable

---

[10] There is a bit of mathematics here that you don't necessarily need to worry about: The triangle with vertices at *C*, *D*, and *E* is equilateral, so that all its sides have length *dist* / 3. This also accounts for the 60-degree angles.

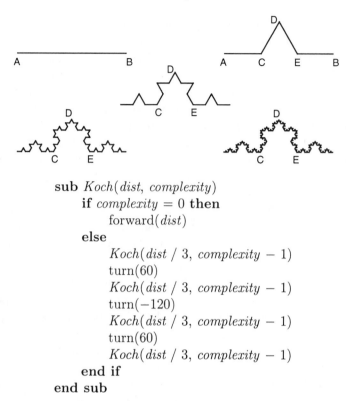

```
sub Koch(dist, complexity)
    if complexity = 0 then
        forward(dist)
    else
        Koch(dist / 3, complexity − 1)
        turn(60)
        Koch(dist / 3, complexity − 1)
        turn(−120)
        Koch(dist / 3, complexity − 1)
        turn(60)
        Koch(dist / 3, complexity − 1)
    end if
end sub
```

Figure 7.9. *Getting from A to B, along increasingly complex paths. The first path is a straight line. After that, each path is made up of four segments, and each segment is a one-third-size replica of the preceding path. If we number the paths by complexity, starting with zero for the straight line, then these paths can be drawn by the xTurtle subroutine Koch.*

of drawing *all* the different paths might seem out of the question—unless you know about recursion.

If you look at any of the paths in Figure 7.9, except for the straight line, it consists of four segments, separated by points C, D, and E. Each segment is in fact a one-third-size replica of the preceding path in the sequence. This is especially easy to see for the path with a single detour: Each segment is a straight line. In the next path, each segment is a path with a single detour, and so forth.

It follows immediately that we can draw the paths with a recursive subroutine. The base case, with a complexity of zero, is a straight line.

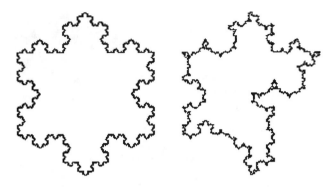

Figure 7.10. *The Koch snowflake and a Koch Island. These pictures and those in the next figure are taken directly from a computer screen, and so do not show detail at a level smaller than the size of a pixel. For these pictures this is almost an advantage, since it leaves you free to imagine a potentially infinite amount of detail within a single pixel.*

For complexity greater than zero, the path can be drawn by calling the subroutine recursively four times, once to draw each segment. The subroutine is shown in Figure 7.9.[11]

7.3.2. Random Recursion. There is something attractive about Koch curves, especially those with a high level of complexity. If three Koch curves are attached at their endpoints, the result is the beautiful "Koch snowflake" shown on the left in Figure 7.10.

The Koch curve is attractive because of its regularity and symmetry. Many things in the natural world are attractive in spite of, or perhaps because of, a lack of symmetry. The shapes of trees, clouds, mountains, and lightning are not symmetric, but neither are they entirely irregular. Their attractiveness seems to come from a combination of regularity and randomness.

The same combination can be achieved in a recursive subroutine by introducing an element of randomness. Often, the result has a surprisingly natural appearance, and computer artists have found this technique to be useful for producing realistic images. (Even if you have never visited an exhibit of computer art, you have seen their work in movies and television commercials.)

---

[11] It is called *Koch* after the mathematician Anders Koch, who studied these curves. Koch was actually interested in what happens if the process of adding detours is repeated an infinite number of times.

Figure 7.11. *A collection of images produced by recursive subroutines. The "coastline" on the upper left and the two trees incorporate an element of randomness that gives them a natural appearance. The drawing on the lower left is called a C-curve. (Look at it rotated −90 degrees.) On the lower right is a Sierpinsky triangle.*

The regular Koch curve is made by adding many levels of detours to a straight line. All the detours are to the left, starting with a 60-degree turn. We could just as easily have used detours to the right, starting with a turn of −60 degrees. Suppose that while drawing the curve, whenever it is time to make a detour, we make a random choice between detouring to the right and detouring to the left.[12] The result preserves much of the regular, "bumpy" appearance of the Koch curve, but now the bumps go in random directions. If we join three such random Koch curves at their endpoints, the result is the Koch island shown on the right in Figure 7.10. The random Koch curves do a fair job of simulating a rugged coastline.

Various types of randomness could be added to our tree-drawing subroutine to produce more natural-looking trees. For example, we could decide randomly on the number of branches, their lengths, and the angles they make with the trunk. Truly realistic images require more sophisti-

---

[12] A computer cannot generate truly random numbers, but there are techniques for generating sequences of numbers that look random. These numbers are called "pseudo-random," and are good enough for most purposes.

cated techniques than those discussed here, but the basic idea of using recursion to mix regularity with randomness is the same.

Recursion turns out to be a powerful programming technique, with applications far beyond turtle graphics. But few things are more effective at bringing home the power of recursion than looking at a beautiful, complex drawing and knowing it was produced by a short recursive subroutine. Figure 7.11 shows some of the variety of images that can be produced in this way.

7.4. Postscript: Implementation Issues

Since the central processing unit of a computer can directly execute only machine-language instructions, instructions in a high-level language must be translated into machine language before they can be carried out. It is not all that difficult to find machine-language instructions that are equivalent to assignments, loops, and if statements, at least in simple cases. A translation of a short xTurtle program into the machine language of xComputer is shown in Figure 7.12. (Of course, xComputer can only handle integers while xTurtle uses real numbers, but you get the idea.) Things are not so easy, however, when it comes to dealing with subroutines, especially recursive subroutines.

While a subroutine is being executed, storage space in memory is needed for its parameters and local variables. The block of memory locations used by a subroutine during its execution is called an *activation record*. This record is created when the subroutine is called. After the subroutine ends, it is no longer needed and can be reused for other purposes. Note that the activation record is simply the storage place for all information inside the black box that is the subroutine. Any global variables used by the subroutine are not in the black box and are not stored in the activation record.

In addition to parameters and local variables, there is one other item in the activation record. Recall that after executing the subroutine, the computer must pick up where it left off when the subroutine was called, by jumping back to the instruction that follows the subroutine call statement. It must keep track of where in memory that instruction is located, so that it will know where to jump. The location is called the *return address*. It is convenient to store the return address in the activation record.

declare x, y	0	LOD-C 0	
$x := 0$	1	STO 100	; $x := 0$
$y := 0$	2	STO 200	; $y := 0$
loop	3	LOD-C 80	; compute $80 - y$
exit if $80 < y$	4	SUB 200	
$y := y + 3$	5	JMN 13	; if < 0, jump to if
$x := x + 1$	6	LOD 200	; add 3 to y
end loop	7	ADD-C 3	
if $x < 10$ then	8	STO 200	
$x := 10$	9	LOD 100	; add 1 to x
end if	10	ADD-C 1	
	11	STO 100	
	12	JMP 3	; back to start of loop
	13	LOD 100	; compute $x - 10$
	14	SUB-C 10	
	15	JMN 18	; if < 0, skip to end
	16	LOD-C 10	; otherwise, $x := 10$
	17	STO 100	
	18	HLT	; end of program

Figure 7.12. *A translation of a rather useless xTurtle program into machine-language. Actually, the translated program is in assembly language; recall from Chapter 3 that each assembly-language instruction corresponds to a binary number, which is the actual machine-language instruction. The numbers on the left in the assembly language program give the location in the computer where each instruction is stored. In the translation, the variables x and y correspond to memory locations 100 and 200 respectively. The translation of the loop starts at location 3; the if statement starts at location 13.*

For example, suppose that a subroutine *ExampleSub* has two dummy parameters—a **ref** parameter named *p1* and a non-**ref** parameter named *p2*—and two local variables named *x* and *y*. Consider the subroutine call statement

$$ExampleSub(glob, 317)$$

where *glob* is some global variable. When the computer executes this instruction, the first thing it does is to create an activation record with space for five items—the two parameters, the two local variables, and the return address. It fills in values for the return address and for the two parameters. For the **ref** parameter *p1*, it fills in the address of the actual parameter *glob*. For *p2*, the value (317) of the actual parameter is copied into the activation record. And of course, the return address is filled in with the location of whatever instruction follows the subroutine call statement. Once the activation record has been set up, the computer jumps to the first instruction in the subroutine. When the subroutine ends, the computer jumps to the return address and destroys the activation record. ("Destroys" here only means "releases for other use." The memory is, of course, still there.)

7.4.1. The Stack. All this is complicated by the fact that while the computer is executing one subroutine, it might encounter a subroutine call statement that sends it off to execute another subroutine. And there is nothing to stop the second subroutine from calling a third, and the third a fourth. In fact, there is no limit on the length of such a chain of subroutine calls. The basic idea still works: When a subroutine is called, an activation record is created for it, and that record exists until the subroutine ends. It's just that when one subroutine calls another, a new activation record is created while the old one still exists. This means that the computer must be very careful about keeping track of what is stored where in memory.

The solution is the *stack*. All the activation records are "stacked up" in a region of memory set aside for the purpose. When a subroutine is called, its activation record is added to the end of the stack. While a subroutine is actually being executed, its activation record is the last one on the stack; any other record on the stack belongs to a subroutine that is suspended because it has called another subroutine. A memory location called the *stack pointer* is used to keep track of where the end of the stack is currently located. As activation records are created and destroyed, the stack grows and shrinks and the value of the stack pointer increases and decreases.

Figure 7.13 shows what a stack might look like. In this example, the end of the stack is at the bottom of the picture. Subroutine C is currently being executed. It was called by subroutine B, which was called by subroutine A. When subroutine C terminates, the value of the stack pointer will be changed to 1005, indicating the beginning of the activation record for subroutine B. This will effectively delete subroutine C's activation record from the stack.

The stack pointer always gives the address of the activation record for whatever subroutine is currently being executed. Whenever the computer needs to access that activation record—to read the value of a

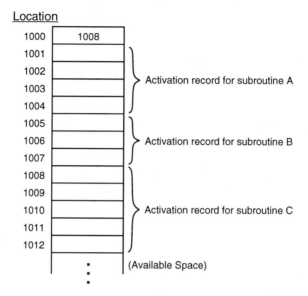

Figure 7.13. *A possible structure for the stack. The stack contains all the activation records for currently active procedures. In this example, subroutine A has called subroutine B, which has in turn called subroutine C. The stack starts at location 1001. Location 1000 contains the stack pointer, which holds the address of the activation record at the end of the stack. In this case, the stack pointer holds the address of the activation record for subroutine C.*

parameter or to change the value of a local variable, for example—it can simply check the stack pointer for the location of the activation record. The subroutine will work correctly no matter where on the stack its activation record happens to be stored.[13]

7.4.2. Implementing Recursion. The implementation of recursive subroutines requires no special treatment, but it can be difficult to follow exactly what is going on. Whenever a recursive subroutine is called, a new activation record is set up for it. This is true even when a subroutine calls *itself*.

---

[13] In most modern computers, the stack pointer is actually a register in the CPU, and there are specialized machine-language instructions for dealing with the stack. These instructions use a special addressing mode to make it easy to access items in the stack. This makes translating a subroutine into machine language much easier than it would be without such instructions.

If the subroutine is being executed, there is already an activation record for the subroutine. When it calls itself, both the existing record and the newly created one will be on the stack. The two records can contain different values for the return address, for local variables, and for parameters. In a sense, they represent two different black boxes, one inside the other. Of course, the nesting can proceed to deeper levels. For example, a call to *Tree*(8,4) will produce successive calls to *Tree*(4,3), *Tree*(2,2), *Tree*(1,1), and *Tree*(0.5,0). While the last of these calls is being executed, there will be five activation records for *Tree* on the stack. There is no limit on how deep such nesting can go.

It is probably better to stick to a black-box view of recursion. Executing the subroutine call *Tree*(8,100) involves drawing a line to represent the trunk and calling *Tree*(4,99) twice to draw the branches. That's all you need to know in order to write the routine. As soon as you try to open the box, you are faced with level after level of increasing complexity, with no limit in sight. But if you can control the vertigo for a moment, perhaps you can enjoy the view and savor once again the power we have acquired for dealing with complexity.

Chapter Summary

Complex systems are usually constructed from *modules*. A module is a black box with an *interface*, which defines the way it interacts with the rest of the system, and an *implementation*, which includes the details of its internal workings. *Subroutines* are one type of module used in constructing programs. A subroutine is a named chunk of code for performing some task; once a subroutine is defined, that task can be performed by *calling* the subroutine by name.

The main part of a subroutine's interface consists of its *parameters*, which allow communication between the subroutine and the program which calls the subroutine. A subroutine is written using *dummy parameters* which stand in for the *actual parameters* that will be passed to the subroutine when it is called. There can also be "hidden" communication using *global variables*.

Modularity, including the modularity provided by subroutines, is important throughout the *software life cycle*. The life cycle of a program includes *analysis* of a problem, *design* of a solution, *coding* of that solution into a program, and *testing* of that program. It also generally includes an extended period of use during which *maintenance* of the program is required to keep it up-to-date and to correct newly found errors. Modularity supports both *top-down* and *bottom-up* design strategies. Modules can be tested and coded separately and then assembled into a complete program. During maintenance of a well-designed program, individual modules can be modified without affecting the rest of the program.

The fact that one subroutine can call on another as a black box for performing some task leads to the idea of a subroutine that can call on itself. A subroutine that does this is said to be *recursive*. Recursion turns out to be a powerful and important programming technique (and not just because it can produce pretty pictures).

From the machine-language point of view, recursive subroutines are implemented in the same way as any other subroutine, that is, by using a *stack* of *activation records* to store the data required for each subroutine call.

Questions

1. Discuss the similarities and differences between programmer-defined subroutines and built-in subroutines such as *forward* and *penUp*.

2. The actual parameter corresponding to a **ref** parameter must be a variable. For a non-**ref** parameter, the actual parameter can be a constant, a variable, or a formula. Why the difference?

3. Write an xTurtle subroutine to draw a house. If you like, you can write and use other subroutines to draw the roof, windows, etc. Then, use your subroutine to draw a village consisting of several houses of different sizes in different positions. Your subroutine will need a parameter to specify the size of the house. There are two ways to handle the position: Either specify it with parameters, or write a subroutine that will draw a house at the current turtle position, whatever it is. Give a careful description of what your subroutine does, in terms of precondition and postcondition. Why is your subroutine superior to one that can only draw a single-sized house (even if the assignment had been to draw just *one* house)?

4. Write an xTurtle subroutine to draw a star (or substitute any other small object you like). Then write a subroutine to draw a row of stars, where the number of stars is given by a parameter to the subroutine. Your second subroutine should call the first. Finally, write a subroutine to draw a field of stars, that is, stars arranged into rows and columns in a rectangular grid. It should have two parameters, one to specify the number of rows and one to specify the number of columns. It should call your second subroutine to draw each row of stars. What subroutine call statement would you use to draw a six-by-eight field of stars?

5. Section 7.3 starts with a poem. Explain what it's doing there.

6. Draw the figures that would be produced by the subroutine calls $Bar(8,0)$, $Bar(8,1)$, $Bar(8,2)$, $Bar(8,3)$, and $Bar(8,4)$, if Bar is the following recursive subroutine:

```
sub Bar(length, complexity)
    if complexity = 0 then
        forward(length / 2)
        back(length)
        forward(length / 2)
    else
        forward(length / 2)
        turn(90)
        Bar(length / 2, complexity − 1)
        turn(−90)
        back(length)
        turn(90)
        Bar(length / 2, complexity − 1)
        turn(−90)
        forward(length / 2)
    end if
end sub
```

You can solve this problem by thinking "recursively," without trying to follow the execution of the subroutine in every detail. (However, if you want to understand the implementation of recursive subroutines, it would be a useful exercise to trace the execution of $Bar(8,2)$ step by step, keeping track of exactly what is stored on the stack.)

7. If recursion did not exist, the stack would not be necessary. Explain why. (Hint: Saying that a subroutine is recursive is equivalent to saying that it might have several activation records at the same time.)

Chapter 8

Real Programming Languages

ALREADY IN 1969, the proliferation of high-level programming languages was being compared to the Tower of Babel.[1] Since then, programming languages have continued to increase in number and complexity. A study of programming languages cannot hope to deal with all of these languages in detail, or even the most important of them. Instead, we will look at some of the themes and principles in their development and illustrate these with discussions of just a few languages.

The first section of the chapter is an overview of the development of high-level programming languages, including a brief survey of their history. The second and third sections cover two of the main trends in that development in more detail.

8.1. Virtual Machines

The native language of a computer is its machine language. In Chapter 3, we saw how machine-language instructions are executed directly, automatically, and mechanically by the hardware of the machine. Most programmers, however, write their programs in high-level languages. Such

---

[1] Jean Sammet, in her book, *Programming Languages: History and Fundamentals*, reported that, starting in 1960, "Over two hundred languages were developed in the next decade, but that only thirteen of them ever became significant in terms of either concept or usage."

programs must be translated into machine language before they can be executed, but the programmer doesn't have to think about machine language or even know anything about it. In fact, the programmer is free to imagine a computer that can directly execute high-level language programs. Such imaginary computers are called *virtual machines*.

Every programming language defines a virtual machine, for which it is the machine language. Designers of programming languages are creating computing machines as surely as the engineer who works in silicon and copper, but without the limitations imposed by materials and manufacturing technology.[2] In this sense, this chapter is just a continuation of Chapter 5, which dealt with the development of hardware machines.

8.1.1. Trends.   We should avoid the temptation to think in terms of an "evolution" of bigger and better programming languages, leading to some ultimate ideal language. First of all, different areas of application place different demands on languages. A good language for numeric computation would probably not be so good for writing artificial intelligence programs. A language designed to support the development of huge programs by large teams of programmers would seem cumbersome and restrictive to someone who just wants to knock off a quick program. Furthermore, there is no objective definition of what it means to be a good language. Programmers argue over the advantages of various languages, with opinions often based as much on fashion and individual style as on objective criteria.

Nevertheless, there are a few consistent trends that can be recognized in the history of programming languages. My own view of that history can be summarized in terms of three very general themes:

1. *Putting it in the language.* Actually, this might say it all. There is a sense in which all programming languages are equivalent, in the same way that all computers are equivalent: Ignoring restrictions of time and memory, they can all be used to solve the same class of problems. High-level languages are translated into machine language, and, in theory, any program could be written directly in machine language. But of course, no programmer could think exclusively in terms of individual machine-language instructions. A complex program, as we have seen over and over, has structure. In machine language, that structure exists almost

---

[2] Translating or interpreting a high-level language program to run on a real computer can then be seen as *simulating* the virtual machine on a real machine, in the sense of Section 4.1.

entirely in the mind of the programmer, and if the translation from mind to program is not perfect—well, that's the programmer's problem. In a high-level language, the structure of the program can exist as an aspect of the program itself. There is less distance between the "abstract" program in the programmer's mind and the real program. It is easier to make the translation without error, and when an error does occur, it is often possible for the compiler that translates the program into machine language to find it.

A structure that exists "in the mind of the programmer" is called an **abstraction**. The first trend in the development of programming languages has been the inclusion of increasing support for abstraction.

As an example, consider loops and decisions. I introduced these all the way back in Chapter 1 as structures that can be used to build complex programs. But, in fact, loops and decisions don't really exist in machine language. They are abstractions; machine language has only jump instructions. Jumps can be used to write loops and decisions, but they can also be used to write unstructured programs, sometimes called "spaghetti code," in which the jumps appear to go to random locations and in which it is impossible to identify blocks of code as loops or decisions. It is difficult to read such unstructured programs and almost impossible to modify them without introducing catastrophic errors. A high-level language, on the other hand, can provide **loop** and **if** statements, or their equivalent, which make it easy to program loops and decisions and difficult or impossible to write unstructured code. From this point of view we can say that loops and decisions are **control abstractions** and that they can be implemented in a language by **loop** statements and **if** statements.

Subroutines represent another form of support for abstraction, in this case **procedural abstraction**. The programmer starts with an abstract idea of a procedure for performing a certain task. A subroutine is a concrete expression of that procedure in some programming language. The term **algorithm** is often used to refer to the *idea* behind a program. A program is the expression of an algorithm in some computer language.[3]

---

[3] Technically, an algorithm is defined to be a definite step-by-step procedure that is guaranteed to terminiate after a finite number of steps. Unfortunately, in view of the unsolvability of the halting problem (see Chapter 4), there is no general way to tell whether a program will halt after a finite number of steps. So, it seems that it is not always possible to tell whether something is an algorithm or not!

Of course, when abstractions are implemented in a language, it should be done right. Correct use of the abstraction should be enforced by the language, rather than left to the programmer's respect for "good style." As an example, consider the treatment of global variables in the programming language Pascal. Recall that a global variable is a variable that is declared outside of a subroutine. For years, programming students learning the language Pascal have been told, "Don't use global variables in subroutines." The justification is that a subroutine is a black box that should have a simple, well-defined interface with the outside world. But in spite of this style rule, the language actually allows global variables to be used freely in subroutines. If there is really an absolute prohibition against using global variables in subroutines, then the language should enforce that prohibition; the compiler should label any attempt to do so as a programming error and should refuse to compile the program. If, as I would maintain, it is *usually* a bad idea to use global variables in subroutines, but sometimes necessary, then the language should make it possible to do so without allowing it automatically. The programmer should be forced to think consciously about violating the style guideline. This is the idea behind the **import** statement in xTurtle.

2. *Increasing respect for data.* The very first section of this book, Section 1.1, was about building complex structures of data, starting with individual bits as the fundamental building blocks. This is analogous to the way computers are built from transistors, and programs from machine-language instructions. And it is just as important. Since that first section, I have ignored data almost entirely. The same was true of early programming languages, which provided only a few basic data types, such as integers, real numbers, and characters, and one or two ways of combining them into structures.

Of course, programmers still had to work with very complex data structures, but once again these structures were only abstractions in the mind of the programmer. Newer languages, following the general principle that abstractions should be expressed explicitly in a program, have tended to provide much more support for data structures.

But more important has been a change in the way data is viewed. Traditionally, programs were thought of as made up of instructions that manipulate data. The data was seen as having a passive, secondary role. Writing a program was seen as finding the right sequence of instructions to solve a given problem. This is, I will admit, the view that I have presented of programs and programming.

More recently, though, data has come to be viewed as of equal importance with instructions. Often, in a reversal of the traditional view, a program, or a large chunk of it, can be most conveniently viewed as a data structure together with some subroutines that manipulate it. For example, in a program for maintaining a mailing list, it is the mailing list itself that is central. That list is manipulated by subroutines that can sort it, add a new address, and so forth. During program development, program designers are advised to begin by identifying the *data abstractions* required by the program. A data abstraction consists (in the mind of the programmer) of some data and the operations that can be performed on it. Many modern languages include support for representing a data abstraction as a type of module that can include both a data structure and the subroutines that manipulate it.

The development of the data-oriented view of programming is traced more fully in Section 2 of this chapter.

3. *Moving away from the machine.* A program written in machine language or in assembly language is closely tied to the design of a particular machine. The difficulty of writing such programs led to the creation of the first high-level languages. An important side effect of their creation was that it became possible to free the programmer from dependence on the details of a single type of machine. Since high-level languages must be translated into machine language in any case, it should be possible to translate the same high-level language program into a number of different machine language programs to be run on various machines. Obviously, this would save an immense amount of programming effort and make useful programs much more widely available.

A program that can be compiled to run on many different computers is said to be *portable*. One of the trends in the development of programming languages has been towards increased portability. Now, portability is not quite as easy or as automatic as it might sound. There is a wide range of possible computer designs, differing in the types of machine-language instructions supported, the representations used for data, and especially in the facilities provided for input and output. It is all too easy to design a language that depends on the features available on a particular type of machine; it is far harder to design a language that permits translation into efficient machine-language programs for many different machines.

Indeed, the problem is still not completely solved. The current situation is that it is possible to write programs that are close to universally portable, but such programs will not take advantage of advanced machine-specific features that are often most important to the user. Most languages have a "standard dialect" which conforms to a strict definition set by ANSI (the American National Standards Institute) or ISO (the International Organization for Standardization). Programs written in that dialect can be compiled to run on almost any machine. Unfortunately, the standard dialect can only include features that are available in a reasonably standardized form on most machines. As a result, there are many "local dialects" of a language, each specific to one type of computer. In practice, most programs are written in a local dialect, with some effort made to confine the deviations from the standard dialect to as small a part of the program as possible. Then, when the program is ported to a different type of computer, only that small part of the program will have to be changed.

There is another, more profound, way in which programming languages have moved away from the machine. In spite of their many differences, most computers are variations on the basic von Neumann machine; that is, they include a memory unit and a central processing unit that fetches instructions from memory and executes them one by one. Programs written in traditional languages reflect this design. They consist of instructions to be carried out in a step-by-step, sequential fashion.

There is no reason, however, why a high-level language could not in theory be based on a completely different model of computation. And it turns out that there are in fact other ways of describing a computation besides giving step-by-step instructions for carrying it out. The traditional style of programming, in which the programmer "commands" the computer to perform each individual step, is called *imperative programming*. Section 3 of this chapter introduces several *nonimperative programming languages*, which support very different styles of programs and program development.

8.1.2. A Very Brief History.   The history of programming languages starts at the same time as the history of general-purpose computing machines,[4] but the first high-level language in the modern sense was FORTRAN, the creation of John Backus and a team of programmers

---

[4] With a notation for writing programs developed by Charles Babbage and used by Ada Lovelace to write programs for the Analytical Engine. (Note: There are many textbooks on the design and implementation of programming languages. Most of them begin with a historical survey. In writing this section, I consulted [Horowitz] and [MacLennan] and, for information on C++, [Stroustrup].)

at IBM. The first version of FORTRAN was conceived in 1954, and the first compiler was released in 1957. Although it has been revised several times since then—the latest version is known as FORTRAN 90—FORTRAN is still in widespread use, especially for scientific programming.[5]

Before FORTRAN, it was not even clear that a compiler could produce high-quality, efficient machine-language code. Much of the effort in the original FORTRAN project went into making sure that the compiler could do just that, with such success that FORTRAN in particular and high-level languages in general were quickly accepted as the best way to write most programs.

FORTRAN was designed to create programs for the IBM 704 computer. Even before it was completed, though, it was clear that a more machine-independent language would be desirable, one that could be compiled to work on any computer. In 1958, an eight-member international committee met in Zurich, Switzerland to design such a language. A preliminary report describing a language known as ALGOL-58 was released, and comments and suggestions were collected. A final, revised report, incorporating many suggestions, was completed in 1960. That report, only fifteen pages long, is the single most influential document in the history of programming languages. The language described in the report is known as ALGOL-60. It was widely used in Europe but never became popular in the United States, where FORTRAN was already well established. Certainly, it never came close to becoming a single, universal programming language, as its creators had hoped. But it has influenced almost every language that was designed since 1960, and some of the ideas it introduced have become almost universal.

Among the important features in ALGOL were nested control structures such as loops and decisions, the requirement that all variables must be declared, a so-called "block structure" that amounts to a distinction between local and global variables, and recursive subroutines implemented using a stack of activation records. One curious omission was the lack of any standardized input/output facilities. Each implementation of the language on a particular machine would provide input/output facilities appropriate for that machine. The designers of ALGOL felt, probably correctly, that it was too early to define a standard version of input/output. The variation among machines was too large, and there was

---

[5] Generally, old programming languages never die, at least not if they have seen widespread use. The investment in programs written and programmers trained is too great to be lightly discarded.

not yet sufficient agreement on just what a standardized input/output facility should look like. Nevertheless, the lack of such a facility probably contributed to ALGOL's failure to win universal acceptance.

Another contribution of the ALGOL-60 report was the introduction of Backus-Naur form (BNF) for describing syntax. (See Subsection 6.2.2.) John Backus, the major force behind FORTRAN, was also on the ALGOL committee. The ALGOL-58 report used informal English descriptions of syntax. Backus had already developed a formal notation for describing syntax; when he presented a description of ALGOL-58 in this notation, Peter Naur, then editor of the *Algol Bulletin*, realized that his interpretation of the syntax of ALGOL-58 was different from Backus'. Obviously, this was a problem: If two people implementing ALGOL on different computers had different ideas about what the language description meant, they could easily end up creating, in effect, different languages. Programs would not be portable; one computer might be perfectly happy with a program that the other computer thinks is full of syntax errors. Naur recognized the problem and devised a variation of Backus' notation, which was adopted for the ALGOL-60 report.

Like FORTRAN, ALGOL was directed at the scientific community and was designed with numeric applications in mind. In 1959, the United States Department of Defense organized an effort to develop a language more suitable for the types of data processing required in business and government. The result of this effort was the language COBOL. The first COBOL compilers became available in 1960. For many years after that, COBOL was probably the most widely used computer language.

The most important innovation in COBOL was a method of describing complex data in a machine-independent way. COBOL introduced the *record*, a data structure that can contain several related items of data, such as an employee's name, address, age, social security number, and hourly wage. A *file* was introduced as a collection of records stored on some input/output device. This was the beginning of the database management systems that will be described in Chapter 9. More important, it was a step towards increased respect for the importance of data and towards the standardization of input/output.

The development of COBOL was led by Grace Murray Hopper, who first became involved in programming with the Harvard Mark I computer in the 1940s.[6] Hopper was a pioneer in the development of programming

---

[6] During her work on the Mark I, she helped to introduce the term *bug* to describe an error in a program. On one occasion, the Mark I stopped working

languages and was one of the major advocates of the computerization of the United States military.

All the languages described above were designed to be used for batch processing, in which there is no interaction between the user and the computer while a program is running. In the late 1960s, John Kemeny at Dartmouth College wanted to make it possible for students to program computers interactively. He created the BASIC programming language for this purpose.[7] BASIC, especially in its original version, is a very small programming language. When the first microcomputers were introduced, BASIC was small enough to fit into their limited memories, and it became perhaps the most popular language among nonprofessional programmers. Although programming language theorists do not consider it to be an interesting or well-designed language, many programmers still consider it a good choice for small programs written by individual programmers.

In the meantime, programming language theorists went on to design ALGOL-68 as a successor to ALGOL-60. Although ALGOL-68 introduced some important ideas, it was a very complicated language with almost unreadable documentation. It never achieved any popularity, and I am not even sure whether it was ever completely implemented. One member of the ALGOL-68 committee who didn't like the result was Niclaus Wirth, who had proposed much more modest changes to ALGOL-60. In 1968, Wirth began working on his own language, Pascal, embodying his ideas. The first Pascal compiler became available in 1970.

Pascal is a small but elegant language. It preserves many of the features of ALGOL-60, and it adds extensive support for data representation. Pascal was widely adopted for teaching purposes, and is still in widespread use in colleges and high schools. Pascal is covered extensively in Section 2 below.

Since the introduction of Pascal, there have been two more major rounds of innovation in programming languages, exemplified by the lan-

---

because a small insect had crawled into one of its mechanical relays. The computer had to be "debugged" before it would work again. After that, when a program didn't work correctly, the programmer could claim that the problem was probably a bug. From that time on, correcting the errors in a program has been known as debugging [Kurzweil, p. 178].

[7] BASIC stands for Beginner's All-purpose Symbolic Instruction Code. As for languages mentioned previously, FORTRAN stands for FORmula TRANslator, ALGOL for ALGOrithmic Language, and COBOL for COmmon Business Oriented Language. (Programming languages represent a fortunate corner of the world where the use of acronyms has actually declined; newer languages seem to be less likely to have an acronym as a name.)

guages Ada and C++. Like COBOL, Ada was developed under the auspices of the United States Department of Defense. It is named after Ada Lovelace. Ada is based on Pascal but incorporates many changes and many, many additions. The most important additions reflect new ideas about modularity that arose in the early 1970s. They make Ada more suitable than Pascal for writing large programs, and make it easier for programmers to reuse old work in new programs. Ada was first introduced in 1979. It was designed by a team at CII-Honeywell-Bull headed by Jean Ichbiah. In 1984, its use became mandatory for certain types of military software. Outside the military, its use is more limited but continues to grow.

C++ also addresses the issues of large programs and reusability, but it does so through *object-oriented programming.* (See subsections 7.2.3 and 7.3.1 below.) C++ was designed by Bjarne Stroustrup at Bell Laboratories in the early 1980s and was first used outside Bell Labs in 1983. It is based on an earlier language, C, designed by Dennis Ritchie, which is very much in the tradition of ALGOL and Pascal. C and C++ would probably be ranked as the most popular professional programming languages.[8]

There are many important languages that haven't even been mentioned in this brief survey. (Three of them, the nonimperative languages Smalltalk, LISP, and PROLOG, will be covered in Section 3.) In addition, one important trend, the increasing importance of concurrency and multiprocessing, will have to wait until Chapter 10. But I hope I have given you some sense of the wide variety of programming languages and how they have developed historically.

8.2. The Other Half of Programming

It was probably easy to ignore the whole issue of building data structures, at first. After all, it is so *obvious* that data has structure. A date is made

---

[8] One problem with both Ada and C++ is that they are extremely complex languages. Niclaus Wirth, who designed Pascal as an elegant alternative to the overly complex language ALGOL-68, designed another small language, Modula-2, incorporating many of the best ideas in Ada. His newest language, Oberon, is an object-oriented language and can be seen in some ways as an alternative to C++. By the way, I personally am not a fan of C, which I consider to be a rather ugly language and unnecessarily difficult to use. C++ has many nice features but still suffers from some of C's problems.

up of three parts, month, day, and year, no getting around it. A mailing list consists of a collection of addresses, and each address in the list has parts such as name, street address, and zip code. There is really no avoiding the structure, and just for that reason, it might not seem worth much fuss.

But it is one thing to say that data has structure, and quite another to say that that structure can be represented in a language. On the general principle that a program should reflect what exists in the programmer's mind as closely as possible, it makes sense to put explicit mechanisms for building data structures into a programming language. Inside the computer, of course, the data will still be just a jumble of bits, but in the program there might be dates, addresses, words, chess boards, tax records, airline flight schedules, or batting averages. It becomes easier to read programs and a little harder to make mistakes while writing them.

Data structures are built according to blueprints called *data types*. A data structure is really just a collection of bits; its data type is a roadmap telling how those bits are to be interpreted. When you declare a variable in a language that uses data types, you have to say what the data type of that variable is. The computer uses the data type to decide how much memory the variable needs and what each bit in that memory means. For example, a data type for representing dates might require three memory locations to hold the three parts (month, day, and year) of a date.

Every language provides some built-in data types, just as it provides built-in subroutines. Taking data seriously means providing the programmer with some way of creating *new* data types, just as new subroutines can be created. A programmer should be able to draw up a blueprint for a new type of data structure, even if no one has ever conceived of it before. This allows the data structures in a program to be crafted into whatever form is best suited to the problem at hand. Indeed, once data is taken seriously, it becomes clear that the crafting of data structures is every bit as important as the crafting of subroutines. If the data representation is well chosen, the program will tend to fall into place around it. As this has become clearer, the support in programming languages for data representation has grown.

8.2.1. Pascal and Data Structures. As a case study of data representation in programming languages, we will look at Pascal, which includes a large variety of mechanisms for building data structures and creating new data types.

```
program ThreeN;
var N, StepCount: integer;
procedure ComputeNext(var Num: integer);
  begin
    if odd(Num) then
      Num := 3 * Num + 1
    else
      Num := Num div 2
  end;
begin
  writeln('What is the initial value for N?');
  readln(N);
  StepCount := 0;
  while N > 1 do begin
    ComputeNext(N);
    writeln(N);
    StepCount := StepCount + 1
  end;
  writeln('It took ', StepCount, ' steps to reach 1.')
end.
```

Figure 8.1. *An example of a complete Pascal program. This program computes and prints out a sequence of numbers according to the "3*N+1" rule discussed at the end of Chapter 6. It is equivalent to the xTurtle program in Figure 6.11 (except that the xTurtle program did not print out the numbers in the sequence). The* **procedure** *defined in lines three through nine is Pascal's version of a subroutine.*

Control structures and subroutines in Pascal are similar in concept to those in xTurtle, although Pascal provides a greater variety of statements and uses a somewhat different syntax. Figure 8.1 gives an example of a complete program written in Pascal.

With just a little help, you can probably read this program. The first line simply gives a name to the program. The second declares two variables, *N* and *StepCount*, and tells the computer that the values of these variables will be integers. **Var** in this context is similar to **declare** in xTurtle, and *integer* is an example of a built-in data type.

The next seven lines define a **procedure**, the name used in Pascal for a subroutine. The instructions defining the subroutine are enclosed between **begin** and **end**. (**Div** here is the operator used in Pascal in place of "/" for dividing two integers.) *ComputeNext* is the name of the subroutine, and *Num* is the name of a dummy parameter to be used in the subroutine definition. (See Section 7.1.) Here, in front of a dummy parameter name, **var** is equivalent to **ref** in xTurtle; that is, it makes it possible for the procedure to change the value of the actual parameter provided when the procedure is called. (I would say that this use of the word **var** with two different meanings is a questionable design decision.)

Note that the data type of the dummy parameter is specified as *integer*. This implies that the actual parameter in a subroutine call statement must also be an integer. Pascal is what is called a **strongly typed** language: Every variable has a data type. The data type determines not just what the bits stored in the variable mean, but also what can legally be done with that variable in the program. For example, the data type of an actual parameter must be the same as the data type of the corresponding dummy parameter, and in an assignment statement, the data type of the value on the right must be the same as that of the variable on the left.[9] This is a safety feature: Usually, mixing data types just doesn't make sense. Doing so in any language would be a programming error; in Pascal it would be a *syntax* error that can be detected by the compiler.

The "main" part of the program consists of the instructions between the **begin** on the tenth line and the **end** on the last line. These are the instructions that the computer executes when the program is run. The main program uses Pascal's input/output routines, *writeln* and *readln*, to communicate with the user of the program. *Writeln*, pronounced "write line," displays output on the computer terminal; *readln* allows the user to type in a response, and it stores that response in a variable where it can be accessed by the program.

The five lines starting with "**while** $N > 1$" form a **while loop**. The computer repeatedly tests the condition "is $N > 1$?" and executes the instructions between the **begin** and **end** as long as the test is true. Pascal has two other types of loops. One is a counting loop, in which all the counting bookkeeping is done automatically. The other is similar to the while loop, except that the condition is tested at the end of the loop rather than at the beginning. Curiously, Pascal provides no way to exit from the middle of a loop.

---

[9] I am oversimplifying here. The actual requirement is that the types must be "compatible." For example, it is legal to assign an *integer* value to a *real* variable, even though *integer* and *real* are different data types. However, it is not legal to assign a *real* value to an *integer* variable.

The first thing you might have noticed about the program in Figure 8.1 is that it contains a lot of semicolons and a lot of **begins** and **ends**. Pascal uses semicolons to separate the individual instructions in a list, but the exact rules about where they are required, where they are allowed, and where they are forbidden are difficult to state. **Begin** and **end** are used to group instructions together. Whereas xTurtle has several ways of grouping instructions (**loop** and **end loop**; **if**, **else**, and **end if**; **sub** and **end sub**), Pascal relies almost entirely on **begin** and **end** for this purpose.

Pascal's overly complex rules for semicolons and its overuse of **begin** and **end** are responsible for many syntax errors in programs. (People have done studies on this; see [Horowitz, p. 69], for example.) This shows how even small design decisions in a language can be important. In Pascal's successor languages, Ada and Modula-2, the rules for semicolons have been cleaned up, and grouping of the type used in xTurtle has been introduced.

This brief look at one example program certainly does not give you enough information to write your own programs in Pascal. However, it should have given you a general idea of what Pascal is like. In particular, you should be able to follow a discussion of data types in Pascal, which is what really interests us here.

Standard Pascal has four simple built-in data types: *integer*, *real*, *char*, and *boolean*. Recall that data types are used to declare variables. The data type of a variable determines what type of value can be stored in that variable. *Integer* and *real* variables hold integers and real numbers, respectively. A *char* variable holds a single ASCII character. A *boolean* variable holds a single bit representing one of the logical values, `true` or `false`. (The *boolean* type is named after George Boole, who invented Boolean algebra.)

In addition, most dialects of Pascal have a more complex built-in data type called *string*, which for some reason is not included in standard Pascal. A value of type *string* is a sequence of characters. For example, 'Hello', 'Z', and 'Do it!' are examples of strings. A value of type *char* can only be a single character, such as 'Z'.

From these five built-in types, new data types of arbitrary complexity can be built up. When a new data type is created, it is given a name, which is used for declaring variables of that type. The newly created type can also be used as a building block in creating even more complex types. Of course, once a type has been created and named, it becomes a black box, or abstraction, which hides its complexity inside a single concept.

New data types can be defined in a Pascal program by specifying a name for the type and a description of the data structure it represents.[10] The formal syntax of data type declarations is shown in Figure 8.2, with some simplifications. Here is an example in which four new types named *Date*, *Game*, *League*, and *Schedule* are created:

> **type**
> *Date* = **record**
>   *month*: *integer*;
>   *day*: *integer*;
>   *year*: *integer*;
>   **end**;
> *Game* = **record**
>   *opponent*: *string*;
>   *when*: *Date*;
>   **end**;
> *League* = **array** [1..10] **of** *string*;
> *Schedule* = **array** [1..30] **of** *Game*;

The examples here use two different methods for building new data types from existing types: records and arrays.

As mentioned earlier in the chapter, a record is a data structure consisting of several related items of data (related, that is, in the programmer's mind). Each of the items is called a ***field*** of the record, and each field has its own name, which can be used to select it from among all the items in the record. In the example above, a *Date* is a record data type that can be used to create record variables. Each of those variables will be a data structure with three fields, named *month*, *day*, and *year*, and each field will hold an integer value. A variable of type *Date* would be declared as follows:

> **var** *Today*: *Date*;

This tells the computer to reserve memory to hold three integers. The variable *Today* is a collective name for the entire record. The indi-

---

[10] It is important to remember that a data type definition provides a blueprint for building a data structure, but no structure will actually be built until the type is used to declare a variable. The variable name (not the type name) is then used to refer to that structure. Furthermore, the blueprint can be reused to define several variables with the same structure; each of those structures will have its own variable name.

⟨type declarations⟩ ::= **type** ⟨type list⟩

  ⟨type list⟩ ::= ⟨type name⟩ = ⟨type definition⟩ ;
                   [⟨type name⟩ = ⟨type definition⟩ ; **]**...

  ⟨type definition⟩ ::= ⟨array type⟩ | ⟨record type⟩ |
                         ⟨pointer type⟩

  ⟨array type⟩ ::= **array** [⟨constant⟩ .. ⟨constant⟩] **of** ⟨type name⟩

  ⟨record type⟩ ::= **record**
                     [⟨field name⟩ : ⟨type name⟩ ; **]**...
                     end

  ⟨pointer type⟩ ::= ˆ ⟨type name⟩

Figure 8.2. *Simplified BNF syntax specification for data-type declarations in Pascal. Everything shown here is legal in Pascal, but many options and other complications are omitted. (Note: The square brackets used in the definition of* ⟨array type⟩ *are part of the syntax of Pascal. All other square brackets, shown in boldface, are part of BNF, used to indicate an optional item in a definition.)*

vidual integers—the fields of the record *Today*—would be referred to as *Today.month*, *Today.day*, and *Today.year*. For example, if *Birthday* is another variable of type *Date*, then the program could include the instruction

if (*Today.month* = *Birthday.month*)
                    and (*Today.day* = *Birthday.day*) **then**
        writeln('Happy Birthday!')

Furthermore, *Date* could be used as the data type of a dummy parameter in a subroutine, as in

      procedure *NextDate*(*Today*: *Date*; **var** *Tomorrow*: *Date*);

As this example shows, once a data type has been defined, it becomes part of the language and can be used in the same ways as a built-in type. In particular, it can of course be used in the definition of other types. The data type *Game*, the second example defined above, shows how data types can be combined to make complex, hierarchical structures. One of the fields in a record of type *Game* is itself a record. If a variable of type *Game* is declared with

            var *OurNextGame*: *Game*;

then *OurNextGame.when* is a record of type *Date*, which has fields such as *OurNextGame.when.day*. As you can see, names for the pieces of a data structure can get quite complicated, but the point is that you only need to use such names when you need to break into the black box. *OurNextGame* is a conceptual unit representing, presumably, someone's next game. If you need to look inside that conceptual unit to find out the date when that game will be played, you can refer to *OurNextGame.when*.

Arrays, which have been available in most programming languages from the very beginning, provide another method of chunking together pieces of data. They differ from records in two ways: In an array, the individual items must all be of the same type, whereas there is no restriction on what types of data can be combined to make a record. And the items in an array are referred to by number rather than by name. The declaration

type *League* = **array** [1..10] **of** *string*;

is a blueprint for a data structure consisting of ten items, numbered from 1 to 10. Each of those items will be a string of characters. If *TeamName* is declared to be a variable of type *League*, then the ten items that make up the variable *TeamName* are referred to as *TeamName*[1], *TeamName*[2], ..., *TeamName*[10]. Note that the item number is added to the variable name, enclosed in square brackets.

The really neat thing about arrays is that the item number doesn't have to be given as a constant number. It can also be specified by a variable or even by a mathematical formula. For example, if *i* is a variable of type integer, then *TeamName*[*i*] could be used to refer to any one of the items in the array *TeamName*. Which item will depend on what value happens to be stored in *i*. Inside a loop, *TeamName*[*i*] could refer to a different item each time through the loop. In fact, counting loops are often used to process arrays; each pass through the loop does the processing of one item in the array.

Since programmer-defined types are used in the same way as built-in types, there is nothing to stop a field in a record from being an array or the items in an array from being records, as the definition of type *Schedule* in the example above shows. A variable of type *Schedule* is an array of thirty items of type *Game*. If *G* is a variable of type *Schedule*, then *G*[7] is a data structure of type *Game*, which might be used to hold data about the seventh game of the season. *G*[7].*opponent* would be the name of the opposing team in that game, and *G*[7].*when* would be the date when it is scheduled to be played.

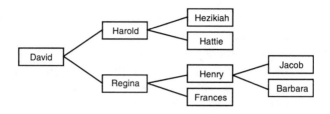

type *FamilyTree* = ^*FamilyMember*;
    FamilyMember = **record**
                name: *string*;
                MothersFamily: *FamilyTree*;
                FathersFamily: *FamilyTree*;
        end;
    var *ME*: *FamilyTree*;

Figure 8.3. *A "family tree" and its representation in Pascal. In the tree, each box holds a person's name and is connected to that person's mother and father (if the mother's and father's names are available.) This tree can be represented in Pascal using the data types shown. The fields MothersFamily and FathersFamily do not contain data. Instead, they contain "pointers," that is, addresses in memory where the data is to be found. (A special pointer value called **nil** is used when no data is available.)*

Array and record types can be used to build up very complex data representations in a structured, hierarchical way. However, not all data structures can be built naturally out of arrays and records. There are two problems. First of all, arrays and records both have definite, fixed sizes that are set in advance and cannot be increased without changing the program, recompiling it, and running it again. Consider a program designed to read a document and make a list of all the words in it. If the program stores the words in an array, it will run into trouble whenever it finds more words in a document than there are spaces in the array.

The second problem is more serious. Not all data structures look (in the mind of the programmer) like arrays or records. Consider a data structure containing your name and the names of your ancestors. The natural image of that data structure would be a kind of "family tree" like that shown in Figure 8.3. In Pascal, tree-like data structures, as well as structures of data with even more complicated interconnections, can be built using *pointer types*. Furthermore, those structures can grow to any size, limited only by the amount of memory available on the computer.

Figure 8.3 shows how a pointer type, *FamilyTree*, can be used to represent a tree structure. The value stored in a pointer variable is actually the memory address where some data can be found, rather than the data itself. The pointer variable "points to" that data. In this example, the value stored in the variable *ME* is the address of a record of type *FamilyMember*. That record can be referred to as *ME^*. (Think of this as telling the computer, "Get the value of *ME* and then follow the pointer.") The individual fields in that record are referred to in the usual way, for example, *ME^.name*.[11]

Pointers are an example of **low-level programming** in Pascal. They provide access to something that really exists at the "low" level of machine language, namely addresses of memory locations. Pascal does not provide support for tree structures as such; instead it provides access to the same mechanism that would be used to build such structures in assembly language. Of course, this tends to make pointers difficult to understand and use. On the other hand, it makes it possible to use many more different types of data structures than could possibly be built into a single language.

8.2.2. Abstract Data Types and Modularity.
The meaning of a data type is determined not just by the structure of the bits that make

---

[11] Of course, just declaring the variable *ME* doesn't automatically build an entire family tree. The program would have to include instructions for building the tree and entering names into it. I don't want to go into the details of how that would be done, but I will give an example of a procedure for processing a family tree once it has been built. Since a family tree can be described recursively as consisting of a name plus two family trees, it should not be too surprising that subroutines for processing trees are often recursive. Here is an example of a subroutine that will print out all the names in a family tree. (The symbol "<>" means "is not equal to.")

```
procedure OutputFamilyNames(Family: FamilyTree);
begin
  writeln(Family^.name);
  if Family^.MothersFamily <> nil then
    OutputFamilyNames(Family^.MothersFamily);
  if Family^.FathersFamily <> nil then
    OutputFamilyNames(Family^.FathersFamily);
end;
```

it up but also by the operations that can be performed on those bits. Being an *integer* means more than being represented by a certain number of bits in the computer's memory. Integers can be added, subtracted, multiplied, divided, and compared, and they can be input and output. All these operations are part of the abstract idea of "integer." In fact, of course, you don't even care that integers are represented by bits, as long as you can add them, subtract them, and so on—and get the right answers.

Suppose you come up with an idea for a new data type, something you want to use in a program you are writing. Of course, you have some idea about the kinds of things you want to do with that data. In fact, that's probably a lot clearer to you than the Pascal data structures you will need to represent the data. And although you know what operations you want to perform on the data, you don't yet know what Pascal instructions you will need to implement those operations. What you have "in mind" is called an *abstract data type*.

Your abstract data type is, conceptually, just an interface for a black box. Inside the box, once it is built, will be the implementation, the actual data representation and the subroutines that perform operations on the data. From outside the box, in the rest of the program, the implementation doesn't matter. All that matters is that you can do certain things with the data by calling the subroutines provided—and that those subroutines give the right answers.

Ideally, you should be able to represent your abstract data type as a module which chunks together both data structures and subroutines. Many newer languages, such as Ada and Modula-2, allow programmers to write modules of this type and to build programs from them. Standard Pascal does not, but many existing dialects of Pascal do, including THINK Pascal for Macintosh computers and Turbo Pascal for IBM PCs. In both THINK Pascal and Turbo Pascal, the modules are called *units*.

A unit consists of two parts, an interface section and an implementation section. Everything in the implementation section is hidden from a program that uses the unit. That program "sees" only what's in the interface. The interface can include types, variables, and procedures to be used by the program, but it does not include the instructions for carrying out the procedures. Those instructions will be in the implementation part, which can also include hidden variables that are used by the procedures but that are invisible from outside the unit.

Figure 8.4 shows a program that uses two units. The program reads a document specified by the user and prints an alphabetical list of all

```
unit WordList; { Makes an alphabetical list of words }
interface
   procedure BeginWordList;
   procedure AddWordToList(word: string);
      { word is inserted in correct alphabetical position }
   procedure PrintWordList;
implementation
   ... { Definitions of procedures go here! }
end.

unit WordReader; { Reads the words in a document }
interface
   procedure StartReading(DocumentName: string);
   procedure GetNextWord(var nextWord: string);
      { Note: returns an empty string ('') at end of document }
implementation
   ... { Definitions of procedures go here! }
end.

program ListWordsInDocument;
uses WordList, WordReader;
var word, document: string;
begin
   writeln('Enter name of document you want processed.');
   readln(document);
   StartReading(document);
   BeginWordList;
   GetNextWord(word);
   while word <> '' do
      AddWordToList(word);
      GetNextWord(word);
   end;
   PrintWordList;
end.
```

Figure 8.4. *Example of units in Turbo Pascal or THINK Pascal. The implementation parts of the units are omitted. The two units and the program would be stored in three different files, and each could be written and compiled separately. (Although you can probably follow what the program does, the main point here is just to show an example of how units are defined and used.)*

the words contained in the document. It does this by getting words one at a time from the document and adding them to a list; when the entire document has been read, the list is printed. All necessary operations on the list of words are performed by procedures from the unit *WordList*, and operations on the document are provided by the unit *WordReader*.

The implementation parts of these units, which contain the complete definitions of the operations, are not shown, but that should not affect your understanding of the program—even if you have absolutely no idea how those implementations could be written. That is, of course, the whole point. (The interface section of a unit should properly include a careful description of what each procedure does. In this example, I am counting on your being able to figure this out, more or less, from the procedures' names. But in real programming, understanding something "more or less" tends to lead to disaster.)

Units, and similar sorts of modules in other languages, are important software engineering tools. The main program, together with the interface section of each unit that it uses, represents the overall design of the program. Once that design exists, the implementation part of each unit can be written and tested separately. During program maintenance, units are replaceable parts: A unit can be removed and replaced with a new-and-improved or corrected version, as long as the new version has the same interface as the old.

Units are especially important in supporting reuse of existing code. A unit that has been carefully designed, written, and tested represents a resource that can be used in many different programs. A programmer can build up a library of units, representing work that has been done once and need never be done again. Ideally, no programming problem would be solved more than once.

That, at least, is the theory. In practice, the ideal is not at all easy to achieve.

8.2.3. Objects. In practice, it often happens that a unit can *almost* be reused but requires minor modification. The problem with this is that even a minor modification turns a carefully tested, perfectly working unit into an unknown quantity. Even a small change can introduce errors that have to be tracked down and eliminated. And even if no new errors were introduced, the unit must be thoroughly retested in order to verify that fact.

It would be nice if we could take an existing unit and add to or modify its behavior without changing the existing code. This might sound unlikely, and it is not possible with units. However, this is the basic idea behind *objects* and *classes*, the foundation of an increasingly important style of programming called *object-oriented programming*, or *OOP*.

An *object* is similar to a data structure, but in addition to data it also contains subroutines for performing operations on the data. Like a data structure, an object has a data type which can be thought of as a blueprint for building objects. The data type of an object is called its *class*. Since a class specifies both the data and the subroutines to be included in the object, a class is essentially an abstract data type.

When a new class is needed that is similar to an existing class, it can build on the existing class. Only the changes and additions will have to be programmed and tested, so that the work invested in the old class does not have to be redone. The definition of a new class can say in effect, "This class is just like such-and-such a class, except for the following additions and modifications...." The new class *inherits* the data representations and subroutines from the old class, but can add new data and subroutines. It can also specify a new definition for an inherited subroutine. The old definition is still there and is used for objects of the old class; the new definition applies only to objects of the new class.

Objects and classes have been around for a long time. They were first introduced in the language SIMULA in the 1960s. SIMULA was designed for writing programs to simulate complex systems such as an oil refinery or a battleship. The "objects" in a SIMULA program correspond to real objects in the system being simulated. In the 1980s, objects moved into the mainstream of programming, largely because they offered hope of a solution to the reuse problem. But their importance extends beyond that to a whole new way of looking at programs and programming, as we will see in the next section.

8.3. Escape from the von Neumann Machine

A single central processing unit, connected by a single data pathway to a memory unit and sequential, one-step-at-at-time execution of instructions—these are the characteristics of the von Neumann machine. When John von Neumann first put everything together in the proposal for the EDSAC computer, he laid the foundation of modern computer and programming technology. But now, half a century later, the limitations of the von Neumann machine have become more apparent.

There are, of course, the physical limitations. The single CPU of a von Neumann machine can never do more than one thing at a time. All instructions and data must be fed single file through the single pathway between the memory and the CPU.[12]

More important from the point of view of this chapter, however, are the conceptual limitations. Are detailed, step-by-step, beginning-to-end instructions really the only thing a computer can understand? When you are faced with a problem, is *looking* for such instructions always the best way for you to go about solving it?

8.3.1. Object-oriented Programming. In the previous section, I introduced the object-oriented approach to problem solving. In this approach, the first step in solving a problem is to identify the data objects that will be needed and the operations that will be performed on those objects. Let's twist this description just a bit. Instead of thinking of objects as passive things to be operated upon, think of them as active entities with behaviors. Instead of a list of addresses that you can sort or print by calling subroutines, think of a Mailing List that knows how to sort itself and how to print itself when requested to do so. Instead of issuing an instruction to the *computer* to sort the list, think about sending a **message** to MailingList, telling it to sort *itself*.

In true object-oriented programming, the model of computation is very different from the step-by-step instructions of the von Neumann model. A program consists of a collection of objects, which communicate with each other by sending and responding to messages. When you want to "run" the program, you send a message to one of the objects, asking it to perform some task. As it is doing so, it will probably send messages to other objects to get them to help out. Eventually, you will get a response to your original message.

Now, this new model of computation could conceivably correspond to a new reality, that is, to a non-von-Neumann computer. It is possible to imagine a computing machine with many processors, instead of a single CPU. On such a machine, each object could "live" at a different processing unit, sending messages over a large number of separate data pathways. Problems could be solved by many different objects working

---

[12] In fact, that pathway has become known as the "von Neumann bottleneck" because it has become difficult or impossible to shove enough bits through that pathway to keep up with the huge appetites of today's powerful CPUs.

and communicating at the same time. But even if a program is to be run on a standard von Neumann computer, the object-oriented model provides a very different way of thinking about the program, one which might lead to a quicker or better solution than the traditional model.

Many programming languages now include some support for object-oriented programming. C++ is the most popular of these languages, but both THINK Pascal and Turbo Pascal allow the programmer to create objects. In these languages, objects are an add-on, a tool that can be used in addition to traditional programming methods.

However, there are also completely object-oriented languages. The most prominent of these is Smalltalk, developed in the early 1970s as part of Alan Kay's Dynabook project at the Xerox Palo Alto Research Center. The Dynabook was an early and prophetic vision of a truly personal computer—a powerful, notebook-sized computer with a windows-oriented graphical user interface that inspired the Macintosh GUI and Microsoft Windows.[13] It is only now, two decades later, that we are coming close to realizing the Dynabook vision in full.

In Smalltalk, everything is an object, and nothing can be accomplished except by sending messages between objects. Even the expression $3 + 7$ is thought of as sending the message "add 7 to yourself and send back the answer" to the object 3. Programming in Smalltalk requires a thought process completely different from that used when programming in a language like Pascal.[14]

8.3.2. Functional Programming and LISP. There are other models of computation on which new programming languages and new problem-solving methods can be based. One of these "new" languages is actually almost as old as FORTRAN, the first high-level programming language. That language is LISP, and the model of computation on which it is based is called *functional programming*.

---

[13] Certainly, the rise of graphical user interfaces in the 1980s was partially responsible for the increasing acceptance of the object-oriented approach. In a GUI, the programmer is forced to deal with "objects" on the screen such as windows and menus. The computer screen itself becomes a visual image of an object-oriented world.

[14] I should probably admit that I have never become at all comfortable programming in Smalltalk, although I have found objects to be very useful in Pascal and in C++. I can only report other programmer's claims that it is possible and useful to develop a completely object-oriented mindset. The same remark applies to Prolog and logic programming, which are described below. (On the other hand, I am quite happy programming in LISP.)

LISP was designed by John McCarthy in the late 1950s for use in writing artificial intelligence programs, and ever since then, it has been the most important language in that field (although recently it has been challenged by Prolog). It is remarkable that a language has remained not just widely used but theoretically interesting for such a long time.

There are many different versions of LISP, and some aspects of syntax vary greatly among dialects. The most widely used version is probably Common LISP, but the dialect that best illustrates functional programming is called Scheme. My discussion here follows Scheme most closely, but much of it is true for any version of LISP.

A function is a rule that takes one or more values as input and produces an output value based on those inputs. The mathematical functions that you are already familiar with work with numbers, but more generally the input and output values can be anything at all. From the point of view of computer programming, a function is very similar to a subroutine, except that the purpose of a subroutine is to perform a task while the purpose of a function is to compute a value.

In pure functional programming, *everything* is accomplished by defining functions and by applying functions to input values to compute outputs. Furthermore, there should be no restriction on what types of things those inputs and outputs should be. In fact, to qualify as true functional programming, it must be possible to define functions whose inputs and outputs are other functions! A programmer can write one function whose purpose is to build other functions that can then be used to solve a problem. This is, in fact, possible in Scheme.

The advantage of functional programming is that its semantics is very simple. There is only one operation to understand: applying functions. This simplicity has a price: There are no variables or assignment statements in a pure functional language. LISP violates this rule, and in fact it is difficult to imagine a really practical programming language that does not.

Nevertheless, LISP is conceptually much simpler than other languages. Everything in LISP is still accomplished by calling functions, but some of those functions do more than just compute and return a value. They have "side effects," such as assigning a value to a variable, printing out a value, or reading a value typed by the user.

The simple semantics of LISP is matched by a simple syntax. Everything is either a number, a symbol, or a list. Numbers and symbols are called **atoms**; like chemical atoms, they cannot be split down any further. You can think of the symbols as being words, but there is no way to break down a symbol into individual characters. It is the symbol manipulation capability of LISP that makes it suitable for artificial intelligence applications. A list can contain numbers, symbols, and smaller lists. The items in the list are separated by spaces and enclosed in parentheses. For example,

> (*milk eggs apples cookies*)
> (*tom* (*class sophomore*) (*gpa* 3.2) (*friends* (*bill mary*)))
> (*sqrt* 9)
> (*plus x* 1)
> (*cons 'a '*(*b c*))
> (*if* (*equal x* 0) 1 2)
> (*lambda* (*x*) (*times x* 3))
> ()

are lists. The last one, a list containing zero items, is called the **empty list**.

The distinction between program and data breaks down in LISP. A symbol can be used as a word (an item of data) or as a variable (something in a program that holds data). A list can be a data structure or it can represent the application of a function to some input values. (Since lists can contain other lists, they can represent complex, hierarchical data structures.)

The first two sample lists above are pretty clearly being used as data structures. "*Milk*" is not a variable storing some value; it is itself a data value. However, if you ask LISP to evaluate *any* list, it will try to do so. It will succeed only if the first item in the list is a function and the remaining items are legal inputs for that function. The value of the list is just the output value computed by that function for those inputs. In the list (*sqrt* 9), for example, *sqrt* is the mathematical square root function. The value of this list is 3, the output value when *sqrt* is applied to the input value 9.

Real versions of LISP have many built-in functions, but only a few are really essential. There are functions such as *plus* and *times* for performing common operations on numbers, and other functions such as *cons* for operating on lists. *Cons* adds an item onto the beginning of an existing list. The value of the sample list (*cons 'a '*(*b c*)) is the list (*a b c*).[15]

---

[15] *Cons* is used to build lists; two other functions, *car* and *cdr*, are used to extract the component parts of a list. If *aList* is a list, then (*car aList*) is the first item in the list, and (*cdr aList*) is the list that remains after its first item is

```
(define (NextTerm N)
    (if (even N)
        (quotient N 2)
        (plus (times N 3) 1)
    ))
(define (Sequence N)
    (if (equal N 1)
        '(1)
        (cons N (Sequence (NextTerm N))) )
    ))
```

Figure 8.5. *Two functions, NextTerm and Sequence, defined in LISP. Together, these functions are essentially equivalent to the Pascal program in Figure 8.1. Sequence is used to build a "3N+1" sequence. For example, the value of (Sequence 3) is the list (3 10 5 16 8 4 2 1). There is enough information in the text for you to figure out everything that is going on here, but the main point is just to show what LISP functions look like.*

Each quote character in this example tells the computer not to evaluate the symbol or list that follows it; 'a is a way of writing "the symbol a itself," treated as a data value rather than as a variable. Similarly, '(b c) refers to the list (b c) itself rather than to the result of applying a function b to the value of a variable c.

LISP also has built-in functions that are similar to control structures such as **loop** and **if** statements. In fact, it could theoretically do without loops entirely, since anything that can be done with a loop can also be done by using recursion. It does need some way to choose between alternatives. The traditional **if** statement chooses between two alternative courses of actions; LISP's *if* function chooses between two alternative *values*. This can seem very strange to someone used to imperative programming. When the list (if (equal x 0) 1 2) is evaluated, its value will be either 1 or 2 depending on whether the condition (equal x 0) is true or false. This value could even be used in a larger expression such as

(plus num (if (equal x 0) 1 2))

which will have the value of num+1 if x is 0 and num+2 otherwise.

---

removed. The names of these two functions can be traced back to the machine language of the first computer on which LISP was implemented. Sometimes the more appropriate names *head* and *tail* are used.

Of course, things will only really get interesting when you know how to define new functions. This is done in LISP using *define*. For example,

$$(define\ (TimesThree\ x)\ (times\ x\ 3))$$

defines a new function *TimesThree* such that for any x, the value of (*TimesThree* x) will be computed as (*times* x 3). The symbol x is being used here as a dummy parameter. You can see that function definitions in LISP are similar to subroutine definitions in xTurtle.

In LISP, or at least in Scheme, a function is also a data object—a thing that can be copied, assigned to a variable, used as a parameter to another function, placed in a list and, so forth. The *define* statement above actually creates such an object and stores it as the value of the symbol *TimesThree*, but that object could also be created directly, independently of any *define* statement. This is done using the so-called **lambda notation.**[16] The value of the list

$$(lambda\ (x)\ (times\ x\ 3))$$

is "the function with input parameter x whose output value is given by x times 3." Consider the function definition

$$(define\ (MakeMultiplier\ N)$$
$$(lambda\ (x)\ (times\ x\ N)))$$

The value returned by *MakeMultiplier* is created using *lambda*. That is, the returned value is itself a function. Exactly which function depends on the value of the parameter N. The value of (*MakeMultiplier* 3) would be a function that multiplies a number by 3; that is, it would be exactly the same function as *TimesThree*. It could even be used in the same way, as in

$$((MakeMultiplier\ 3)\ 5)$$

which would be the same as (*TimesThree* 5) and would have the value 15.

With the ability to treat a function as an object and to perform operations on it, the distinction between data and program is almost destroyed. With this idea, we have reached a very advanced level of LISP programming. Of course, I have skipped all but a few high points along the way, but perhaps I have told you enough to give you some idea of the nature and power of LISP and of functional programming.

---

[16] This notation was invented by the mathematician Alonzo Church, who used it in his definition of computation. LISP is loosely based on Church's ideas about computation, in the same way that traditional languages are loosely based on Turing machines.

8.3.3. Logic Programming and Prolog. Object-oriented programming and functional programming are very different from traditional imperative programming, but at least they still carry a feeling of something happening, a *process*—whether it's objects responding to messages or functions computing output values. But there is another model of computation in which the whole idea of process disappears.

In *logic programming*, the computer is given a list of facts and can then answer questions based on those facts. The programmer does not specify any process for finding the answers; a program contains *only* facts and questions. The computer is supposed to deduce the answers logically, based on the facts it has been given.

The logic programming language Prolog was developed in France in the early 1970s by Alain Colmerauer, but it did not become popular until the 1980s. Like LISP, Prolog was developed for use in artificial intelligence programming. It is not a pure logic programming language, since in some cases the programmer must give the computer hints about how to go about answering a question, but it does come close.

There are two types of facts in Prolog, statements and rules. A statement is a simple statement of fact, such as that John is a parent of Jane. In Prolog, this might be expressed as "parent(john, jane)". The first word, "parent," is called the **predicate** in this fact. The predicate represents some relationship or condition that holds for the items in parentheses. Prolog makes a distinction between symbols and variables. Any word that starts with an uppercase letter is a variable. Thus, "John" would be a variable, but "john" is a symbol, that is, a data item.

A rule tells the computer conditions under which a statement will be true. For example, the rule

$$\text{father}(X,Y) :- \text{parent}(X,Y), \text{male}(X)$$

tells the computer that X is the father of Y if both X is a parent of Y and X is male. Since X and Y are variables, this rule holds for any values of X and Y whatsoever. The symbol ":–" can be read as "if" or, more properly, as "can be deduced if." A particularly powerful kind of rule can be made by introducing a new variable on the right hand side, as in

$$\text{grandparent}(X,Y) :- \text{parent}(X,Z), \text{parent}(Z,Y)$$

Here, the variable Z stands for any item that can be found that fulfills the condition. Thus, this rule says that X is a grandparent of Y if any value can be found for Z such that X is Z's parent and Z is Y's parent.

Figure 8.6 contains a short list of Prolog statements and rules. A complete program would follow this list by one or more questions. (In

parent(john, jane)
parent(mary, jane)
parent(john, bill)
parent(mary, bill)
parent(tom, mary)
parent(ann, mary)
parent(fred, ann)
male(john)
female(jane)
female(mary)
male(tom)
male(fred)
father(X,Y) :– parent(X,Y), male(X)
mother(X,Y) :– parent(X,Y), female(X)
grandparent(X,Y) :– parent(X,Z), parent(Z,Y)
sibling(X,Y) :– parent(Z,X), parent(Z,Y)
ancestor(X,Y) :– parent(X,Y)
ancestor(X,Y) :– ancestor(X,Z), parent(Z,Y)

Figure 8.6. *A list of Prolog facts that the computer can use as the basis for answering questions. Each of the last six lines gives a rule that can be used for making deductions. Note that the last rule is recursive.*

fact, Prolog is generally used interactively, so that the user could sit at a computer typing in facts and questions one after another.) The convention for asking a question is to precede it with the ":–" symbol. For example,

:– mother(mary, jane)

asks the computer whether mary is the mother of jane. The computer would answer yes, since the fact that mary is the mother of jane can be deduced from the information it has been given. But when asked

:– mother(ann, mary)

it would answer no, since this fact cannot be deduced using *only* the statements and rules in Figure 8.6.[17] It is important to remember that the computer knows nothing about the *meanings* of any of the symbols

---

[17] A person would see that mary's parents are fred and ann and that fred is male and would deduce that ann is mary's mother. However, this uses knowledge that is not in any of the rules that have been given to the computer. (It also uses the unstated assumption that ann and fred are not the same person.)

it is using. It just manipulates the symbols according to the rules you give it. If it has not been told a fact, and if it cannot deduce that fact logically from what it has been told, then it assumes that the fact is false. This is very different from the way people think.

If a question contains a variable, the computer will try to find values of that variable that will make the statement true. For example, to the question

$$:- \text{father}(X, \text{jane})$$

the computer will respond "X is john." And to

$$:- \text{father}(\text{john}, X)$$

it will respond, in succession, "X is jane" and "X is bill." The question ":- sibling(X,bill)" will produce the interesting pair of answers "X is jane" and "X is bill." Although bill would not usually be considered to be his own sibling, as far as the computer has been told, he would. In order to avoid this, the definition of sibling(X,Y) would have to include the fact that X is not equal to Y.

I will not explain how data structures can be dealt with in Prolog, or even how numeric computations can be performed. You should already be able to see that logic programming is very different from other styles of programming. It encourages the programmer to forget about how something can be accomplished and to concentrate on what knowledge is available. The details of the process by which new knowledge is deduced are left to the computer.

Chapter Summary

Many high-level programming languages have been developed since the first, FORTRAN, appeared in 1957. The history of high-level languages has been one of increasing support for *abstraction*, especially for *data abstraction*. An abstraction is essentially a specification of the behavior and interface of a black box. Programmers think naturally in terms of abstractions; a language that supports abstraction gives programmers a better chance of translating the ideas in their heads into working programs.

Support for data abstraction starts with the idea of *data types*. Data in a computer is represented as a sequence of bits; the structure of that data—which exists in the programmer's mind as an abstraction—is expressed in a program using data types. Every language provides some *built-in* data types, as well as ways of building *data structures* using the built-in types as a basis. The programming language Pascal, for example, provides *records* and *arrays*. It also provides *pointers*, which can be used to build data structures such as *binary trees* which are not supported directly by the language.

A full description of a data type includes not just the structure of the data but also the operations that can be performed on that data. All this information—leaving aside implementation details—forms an *abstract data type*. Some languages support abstract data types directly in the form of *modules* that chunk together both data types and subroutines that operate on those data types.

Traditional programming languages such as Pascal are based on the model of computation embodied in the von Neumann machine. Other models of computation are possible, and these lead to very different styles of programming such as *object-oriented programming, functional programming*, and *logic programming*.

Object-oriented programming in particular is becoming increasingly important. From one point of view, objects are a natural step in the process of adding support for data abstraction to programming languages. However, objects lead naturally to a model of computation in which problems are solved by self-contained, cooperating entities that communicate with each other by passing *messages* back and forth. This model supports new ways of thinking about problems and designing solutions. The real importance of nontraditional programming languages is their support for such new ways of thinking.

*   *   *

With this chapter, we have reached the end of the general survey of the fundamentals of computer science which was begun in Chapter 1. In the remaining four chapters of the book, we will look at some of the practical applications to which computers can be put.

Questions

1. State some principles that can be used as guidelines in designing a new programming language. What features would you include in a language if you were designing one yourself? Does your answer depend on the purposes for which the language is to be used? Should it?

2. Why is it important for the syntax of a language to be specified completely and rigorously, for example, by using BNF? There is no similar generally accepted formal method for describing the semantics of a language. What do you suppose the consequences of this would be? Do you have any suggestions for dealing with semantics?

3. Why might having several different instruction-grouping methods, as in xTurtle, be better than Pascal's use of a single method (**begin** and **end**)?

4. A computer science class has thirty students, and each student has three test grades. Design a data structure in Pascal that can be used to store information about all the students in the class. Start with a record type that can store a student's name and three test grades. What would you do if you don't know exactly how many students there are in the class, but you do know that there are not more than 100? What if you know no definite upper limit on the number of students?

5. If you were working in LISP instead of in Pascal, how would you represent the data in the previous question? How would you represent the data as a list of Prolog statements?

6. In Section 8.3.2, I say that anything that can be done with a loop can be done using recursion. Try to explain why this is true. Can you write a recursive subroutine in xTurtle that will draw nested squares without using a loop?

7. Is there any reason for a programmer to learn more than one programming language?

Chapter 9

Applications

THE FIRST EIGHT CHAPTERS of this book laid a foundation for an understanding of what computers are, what they can do, and how they do it. The rest of the book builds on that foundation by discussing some of the ways in which computers are commonly used.

It is possible to use computers as black boxes, without knowing much about what goes on inside. There is, of course, nothing wrong with this. It is a reasonable approach to dealing with complex technology—one that many people (including me) adopt when dealing with things like cars and microwave ovens. Still, opening the black box to at least some extent is much more intellectually satisfying, and it is essential if one wants to be more than a passive consumer of magic-like technology. This, I presume, has something to do with the reason you are reading this book in the first place.

So, my aim will be not just to describe computer applications but also to explain something of how the computer accomplishes the many complex tasks involved (although, in fact, I will do this mainly in Chapters 10 through 12). We begin in the first section of this chapter with a brief look at applications that are familiar to most users of desktop computers. The second section introduces some less familiar but important large-scale applications. The final, rather technical section returns briefly to theoretical computer science to address the questions of efficiency and practical limitations on computing.

The remaining chapters of the book tackle three major application areas of computer science in more detail: parallel and distributed computing, graphics, and artificial intelligence. Note that Chapters 9 through 12 can be read independently and in any order.

9.1. The Works

The desktop computers found in homes and offices tend to be used predominantly for running a rather small variety of application programs. The most common of these are sometimes bundled together by software companies into packages with appropriate names such as ClarisWorks or Microsoft Works. For many people, "the works" includes all the software their computer will ever need.[1] This section looks at applications commonly found in such packages.

9.1.1. Word Processing. Probably, the most familiar computer application is *word processing*, in which the computer is used for creating text documents. Word processing is to be distinguished from *text editing*, where the user enters simple lines of plain text. Text editing is often used to produce computer programs and data files—things meant mostly to be read or processed by a computer. A word processing program, on the other hand, lets a user format the text to make it more appropriate for humans, with frills like footnotes, underlined or italicized text, large-size text for headings, tables, and pictures.

A text editor is a comparatively simple program. It works with a sequence of characters, each represented by an ASCII code number, as explained in Chapter 1. The data for a word processing program is more complicated, since in addition to the text itself, the data structure has to include some encoding of the visual appearance and position of each item in a document. There are many different ways to encode such data, and every program uses its own encoding scheme. A word processing program can use a data file from another program only if it knows how to translate the data encoding used by that program into its own format. Most word processors can translate the data formats used

---

[1] I am ignoring here an important category of software for home (and maybe office) computers: games. In fact, the best games are sophisticated programs that stretch the limits of machine performance and programming talent. Many of the ideas I discuss in this book find application in computer games. Another major application area that I will avoid is educational software.

by a wide variety of other programs, but the only type of data that is automatically usable by any word processor is the same type of plain ASCII text used by text editors, without all the formatting information.

A step up from word processing is an application called **desktop publishing**, which tends to deal with documents with fancier layouts and more pictures, often meant to be published, or at least to look like professional publications. Desktop publishers use word processing to create their text, but they make use of a "page layout program" to arrange all the items on a potentially complex page. They might also use programs like those described in the next subsection to create and process pictures. Desktop publishing is one of the ways that computers have empowered people with only moderate resources to take on tasks that once required specialists with expensive equipment.

9.1.2. Painting and Drawing.   Some types of information can't be conveyed easily or at all in words. Scientific data is often best presented in the form of a graph. A picture of a person or scene, or an architectural drawing of a proposed building, can be understood more quickly and thoroughly than any verbal description. And visual artists create images that simply have to be *seen* in order to be appreciated. So it is not surprising that there is a wide range of programs for manipulating all kinds of images.

Most common on desktop computers are programs used for **painting** and **drawing**. With a painting program, the user applies color to the computer's screen the way a painter applies paint to a canvas. Generally, the computer's mouse plays the role of the brush. The data for a painting program is fairly simple: For each pixel in the image, there is a number representing the color of that pixel. Nevertheless, an image created by one painting program cannot automatically be used by another. The second program has to understand the type of data encoding that has been used to represent the image. First of all, there is the matter of deciding how the various pixel colors are to be encoded as numbers; usually, information about this encoding is included with the image data. More important is the fact that the image data is often **compressed**. Compression is used to reduce the amount of memory needed to store a data file.[2] Fortunately, there is only a small number of image-encoding

---

[2] For example, a simple form of compression called **run-length encoding** can be used on files that tend to contain long sequences of identical values. This is often true for image files. In a run-length encoded file, a string of fifty-seven threes would be replaced with the pair of numbers: 57, 3.

methods that are widely used for exchanging pictures between programs. These go by names like TIFF, GIF, PICT, and JPEG.

It is worth noting that, obviously, not all the images displayed on computers are created by hand. Any image—a photograph, a frame from a video, the Mona Lisa—can be converted into a list of pixel colors that can be used to display it (at least approximately) on a screen. Once the image is in numeric form, it can be manipulated by an *image processing* program, which is a kind of "digital darkroom" that, for example, lets the user enhance the image, adjust the contrast, edit the colors, or make a composite of several images.

Turning to drawing programs, we find that they relate to painting programs in much the same way that word processors relate to text editors. Instead of dealing with a simple sequence of pixel colors, a drawing program works with a complex data structure that represents objects in a scene. The basic objects are mostly simple geometric shapes like circles and rectangles, but they can be combined to make complex models such as a floor layout in an architectural drawing. The user edits the image by adding, rearranging, and deleting objects and by modifying their appearance (for example, by changing their size or color).

The ability to edit an image in this way gives drawing an advantage over painting for many applications. For example, sophisticated, high-precision drawing programs are used in *computer-aided design* (CAD), where they have largely replaced the traditional drafting table and pencil. And I created the illustrations for this book with a drawing program called Canvas. The principles and techniques behind such programs, including ones that can work with three-dimensional objects, will be covered in some depth in Chapter 11.

9.1.3. Spreadsheets. In 1979, a little program called VisiCalc transformed the way people thought about personal computers. What had been seen as impractical and slightly comical little boxes appropriate for hobbyists and visionaries suddenly became a vital tool for the forward-looking businessman. VisiCalc was the first spreadsheet.

A spreadsheet displays rows and columns of rectangular boxes, each box capable of holding a number. Not very exciting, it seems. But the little boxes—known more formally as *cells*—are not mere passive containers. A cell can actively compute a number based on the contents of other cells in the spreadsheet. For example, the cell in the top row, fifth over from the right, might compute and display the sum of the first four numbers in the top row. If you change one of those four numbers, the sum is recomputed automatically. That sum might in turn be used in computing the number in some other cell. If so, that number will also change, and the changes can cascade for many levels, as you watch. The numbers seem to have come to life.

Each cell in a spreadsheet has either an associated number or an associated mathematical formula,[3] which can be modified by the user of the spreadsheet program. A number is simply displayed in the cell; a formula tells how to compute the contents of the cell in terms of the contents of other cells. Behind the scenes, the computer keeps tracks of all the formulas, and whenever the user modifies the number or formula associated with a cell, it makes all the implied changes in the display.

Spreadsheets are used for *mathematical modeling*. A mathematical model consists of one or more quantities, together with mathematical formulas showing how those quantities are related. For example, there is a simple model that relates the amount of money you deposit in a bank account and the interest rate it will earn to the amount that will be in the account ten years from now. A more complex economic model might be used to relate a company's predicted profits or losses to such things as the cost of raw materials, the amount of merchandise it can sell, and the expected inflation rate. The formulas that define such a model can be entered into a spreadsheet, which can then be used to watch what happens when assumptions are changed. What if we cut the price of the widgets we manufacture by ten percent? What happens if inflation is a percentage point higher than we are assuming? It was the ability to do this type of modeling on a personal computer that made VisiCalc so popular. Modeling is important not just in spreadsheets and not just for economic models. In fact, we will see later in this chapter that huge amounts of computer time are devoted to various sophisticated mathematical models.

9.1.4. Databases. In Chapter 8, we encountered the idea of a data structure, which is a collection of data of specified types, organized so that it can be used in certain ways by a program. Data structures exist in a computer's memory while the program is running. If you imagine the same sort of thing stored in a file on the computer's disk, you have the idea of a *database*—with one major difference: A database tends to be larger and more complex, and to permit more complicated operations, than the data structures commonly used in programs.

---

[3] Or some text. Text is simply displayed for the information of human readers; it plays no active role in the spreadsheet.

On a desktop computer, the typical example of a database is a mailing list, consisting of a potentially large number of names and addresses. One particular name and address is called a *record*, and individual items such as the first name, last name, street address, city, state, and zip code are referred to as the *fields* of that record. For the mailing list to be useful, it should be possible to add new names and addresses to the list and to delete or modify existing items. More complex operations are also needed, such as sorting the list by zip code or printing out all the addresses in a particular state.

A database program should let the user manage not just mailing lists but data of many different kinds. A small business, for example, might want to keep track of inventory, suppliers, customers, sales, and customer accounts. Data for the inventory might consist of records containing the name of an item, the supplier from whom it is bought, the quantity on hand, and the price. Data for a sale would include things like the customer, the item purchased, the amount of the sale, the amount paid, and an invoice number. The operations that the user might want to perform on this data include things like finding all the sales made to a particular customer, or listing all the inventory items for which the quantity on hand is less than 100 and the supplier is from out-of-state.

The challenge in designing a database program is that there is no way for the designer to know what data all the various users of the program might want to store, or what they might want to do with that data. The solution is provide an abstract *data model* that will let the user describe the data to the program and a *query language* for specifying operations to be performed on the data. Together, the data model and the query language make a kind of specialized programming language, and using a database program (like using a spreadsheet) is something akin to programming.

A big advantage of using a specialized data model and query language is that it hides most of the complexity of what actually goes on in the database from the user. (This is another example of black boxes.) A database can contain a huge amount of information. Simply looking through that information one piece at a time would be impractical. So the data is not really stored as a simple list of records. It has a complex structure with extra information that is used to make searching through the data much more efficient.

A data model used in many database programs is the *relational database model*. A "relation" here is used to mean a list of records, where each record in the relation must have the same set of fields. The inventory data in the example above would be a relation. Customers' names and addresses would make up another relation, as would the data for sales. A database generally contains several different relations holding different types of data, as in this example. Each relation has its own name, and each field of the records in that relation also has a name. To create a new relation, a user simply has to provide these names, specify what type of data each field will contain, and then enter the data. An important point is that two different relations might have fields with the same name. Those fields are then taken to be the same. For example, the field name *ItemNumber* might appear in both an *Inventory* relation and a *Sales* relation. The same number in the *ItemNumber* field in both these relations would represent the same actual item. This sort of indirect relationship, through shared field names, is the only way that two relations are linked.

A **query** is a request to a database program to retrieve specified information from a database. A query language is used to form such requests. One widely used language is called **SQL** (Structured Query Language). In SQL, it is possible, for example, to make a request that amounts to, "Give me the names and address of all customers who have unpaid bills dating from before January 1, 1995, and sort them into alphabetical order." (The actual SQL query would would have to be much more formal, and it would refer to relations and fields by name.) Note that in satisfying this request, the program would have to collect data from at least two different relations.

9.1.5. Communications. As the final stop on this brief and incomplete tour of desktop computing, we look at communication facilities, which allow you—or more exactly, your computer—to communicate with other computers. Before any communication can take place, there has to be some sort of physical connection between your computer and another computer.[4] Computers in an office environment are often on a **network**, which can connect anywhere from a few computers to thousands or millions. A network connection gives a computer and its user access to resources made available by other computers on the network, such as data files, programs, and even computing time on their CPUs. A network also serves as a communications device that allows users of different computers to communicate with each other, for example by sending

---

[4] This is not quite true. There are "wireless" communication systems where the only physical link is provided by radio waves or infrared radiation. However, such communication still requires specialized hardware.

messages from one computer that can be read on another. Chapter 11 discusses the uses of networks and how they work.

Communication from a home computer generally uses a **modem**.[5] Two computers can communicate over regular telephone lines using a pair of modems. One way to use a modem is with a **terminal emulation** program. A terminal is an input/output device consisting of a keyboard and screen meant for providing access to a large, multi-user computer. Terminals are often called "dumb" terminals because all the actual processing is done on the computer; the terminal merely relays the user's keystrokes to the computer and displays the computer's responses on the screen. A terminal emulation program makes an expensive computer with a fancy graphical user interface act like a cheap, dumb terminal that displays only lines of ASCII characters.[6] This is more exciting than it sounds, because it gives you access to the resources of any computer that will accept your call. For many people, this means being able to use the main computer at their business or school from home.

For more people, though, in growing numbers, having a modem means begin able to connect to **bulletin board systems** and **online services**. A bulletin board system, or BBS, is just a computer running a program that accepts incoming calls via modem and lets the caller read and respond to messages left by other users. Users can post public messages that can be read by any user of the BBS. The public message area of a BBS is usually organized into a number of lively, ongoing discussions. Most systems provide other services as well, such as the ability to leave private messages for other users and to relay messages to users of other BBS's and computer networks. Often, users can obtain copies of software stored on the BBS (not, I'm afraid to say, always legally). Some BBS's are available free to the public. Others have a membership fee and restricted access. Although some of them are very large, most BBS's are set up by individuals as a hobby or business.

---

[5] Modem stands for modulator/demodulator. A modem takes a digital signal from the computer and "modulates" it into an analog signal that can be sent over a telephone line. In the other direction, it listens for signals coming over the phone line and "demodulates" them into the digital signals required by the computer.

[6] Until recently, the rate at which reasonably-priced modems could transmit data was too low to make them practical for much more than text. Within the last few years, inexpensive high-speed modems have made graphical user interfaces via modem feasible. The online services mentioned below have taken advantage of this with custom programs that provide a "user-friendly" interface to their services.

Most users, though, will probably get their computer connectivity through online services, such as CompuServe and America Online. These are the large-scale, commercial version of BBS's, catering to a huge range of interests and offering more different types of service—and somewhat less anarchy—than the typical BBS.

9.2. Off the Desktop

Not all computing is done on desktop computers, even today when a computer on your desktop can be more powerful than most large, "mainframe" computers were a decade ago. In this section, we will look at a few large-scale applications of computing that you should not expect to find on your typical home computer.

9.2.1. Weather and Other Dynamical Systems.

9.2.1. Weather and Other Dynamical Systems. Most people know that weather forecasts are produced by computers, without, perhaps, understanding how that could be. Computer weather forecasting is based on numeric *simulation* of the physical processes that produce actual weather. The idea is simple in theory: The Earth's atmosphere is governed by the laws of physics. Those laws take the form of mathematical equations. If you can solve those equations, you know exactly how the atmosphere will behave and you can predict the weather exactly. Obviously, things don't quite work out that way in practice.

Weather is an example of a *dynamical system*. In a dynamical system, future behavior is predicted based on knowledge of the current situation—technically referred to as the *initial condition* of the system—and an equation that governs how the situation changes with time. The so-called "dynamic equation" for weather is well known, but it is not an equation that can be solved exactly, the way you can solve $3x + 1 = 7$ to find that $x = 2$. The solution—that is, the prediction of what the weather will be at some point in the future—is obtained by simulating the atmosphere on a computer. The atmosphere is represented in the computer by a large set of numbers, each giving the value of a physical quantity such as temperature, air pressure, or humidity at some location. The dynamic equation is applied to these numbers to see how they will change with time. What happens to the numbers is an approximation of what will happen to the real physical quantities they represent. The abstract, simulated weather system inside the computer is called a *computer model* of the real thing. This is a large-scale version of the same type of modeling that can be done using spreadsheets.

There are several sources of error which make this model only an approximation rather than a perfect prediction of reality. First of all, an accurate prediction depends on knowing the initial condition (that is, the weather *now*). In practice, current weather is known only partially and inaccurately, from measurements made at a relatively small number of weather monitoring stations and other sources such as satellite data. The accuracy of the initial data puts a limit on the accuracy of the prediction that can be made.

More important, though, are the errors introduced because of the way dynamical systems are simulated numericly. A quantity like air pressure or temperature has a value at every location throughout the Earth's atmosphere, and at every moment of time. In mathematical terminology, they are "continuous" quantities. The numbers that the the computer manipulates are a so-called "discrete" approximation of these continuous quantities. Instead of dealing with every moment of time, the computer might jump from each hour directly to the next. Instead of working with each point in the atmosphere, it might represent with a single number the average conditions in a cube of air a mile on a side. Obviously, it will be missing something!

The more points in space and time that the computer uses, the more accurately its model will reflect reality. Unfortunately, the more points it uses, the more numbers it has to deal with, the more computation it has to do, and the longer it takes to run the model. As a result, weather forecasting consumes large amounts of computer time.

Weather is only one example of computer modeling and simulation. Computers can be used to simulate any system whose dynamic equation is known. In one particularly neat application, for example, two colliding galaxies are modeled as they interact over a period of millions of years. The equations in this case state the well-known law of gravity: Each star in the two galaxies is pulled and tugged by the gravitational attraction of each of the other stars according to a simple formula. The number of stars involved, though, makes this an application for massive computing power, and even then the model can include only a fraction of the billions of stars in real galaxies.

There are many other examples. The behavior of an airplane wing can be modeled on a computer so that many different designs can be tested without the expense of building a physical model of each. Simulating the flow of oil through the types of porous rocks where it is often found might help in the development of better techniques for extracting oil.

A model of wind and ocean currents might predict what will happen to oil that is spilled from a tanker. The acoustics of a new concert hall can be modeled and tested before it is built.

It is worth noting that a model is a reflection of some *theory* about the way the world behaves. In the examples I have given up to now, the theories are well-established physical laws. However, a computer model can be useful even if the theory involved is an unproved hypothesis. In fact, in this case the model can be seen as one way of testing the hypothesis. If predictions made using the computer model turn out to be true, that would count as evidence that the hypothesis is correct. In economics, for example, a model might relate quantities such as gross national product, interest rate, consumer price index, and money supply. The equations of the model would represent a theory about how all these quantities relate to and affect each other. Running the model on a computer would make a prediction about how the quantities will change over time. Correct predictions would tend to confirm the economist's theory, and even incorrect predictions might be useful, since the errors could suggest ways to improve the theory.

9.2.2. Optimization. Besides simulation, another general application area of computers is ***optimization***. This refers to finding, among a range of possibilities, the one that is "optimal," that is, finding the best possibility according to some specified criterion. For example, you might ask what is the best way to arrange your dishes in the dishwasher. The possibilities to be considered are all the different ways of arranging the dishes. The criterion, presumably, is cleanliness. That is, an arrangement is optimal if it gets the dishes as clean as possible. Unfortunately, this is not a problem that your computer is likely to help you with.

There are, however, many optimization problems that can be solved efficiently by computer.[7] The methods used are, for the most part, rather technical, and I will not attempt to describe them here. I will, however, discuss two types of problems that can be solved, to give you an idea of what can be done.

---

[7] "Efficiently" means in a reasonable amount of time. Often, it would be possible to find an optimum simply by testing all the possibilities and picking the best. In interesting problems, though, there are too many possibilities for this to be feasible. The question of efficiency is discussed below, in Section 3. The "corridor guard problem" discussed at the end of that section is an example of an optimization problem that cannot, as far as we know, be solved efficiently. Even for such problems, however, a computer can sometimes be used to find solutions that are reasonably good, even if not truly optimal.

My first example is scheduling of tasks. Suppose that a number of different tasks must be carried out to complete some overall project. Think, for example, of all the different tasks involved in building a house. Each task takes a specified amount of time. Several tasks can be worked on at the same time, but there are *constraints* that stipulate that certain tasks cannot be started until certain other tasks are finished. (The walls of the house can't be put up until the floors are laid; the floors can't be laid until the frame has been erected; the frame can't be erected until the foundation is in place.) The question then becomes, how can the tasks be scheduled so that the entire project can be completed in the shortest possible time?

Consider a sequence of tasks A, B, C, ..., such that B depends on A, C depends on B, and so on. Since A, B, C, ... must be performed in succession, the whole project obviously takes at least as long as the time required to perform this sequence of tasks. Among all such sequences of dependent tasks, choose one that takes the greatest amount of time. That sequence is called a "critical path" for the project, and the tasks in the sequence are called "critical tasks." It turns out that the time required for the entire project is the same as the time required for a critical path; all the other tasks can be scheduled around the critical tasks. A computer can be programmed to analyze the constraints, find a critical path, and create a minimum-time schedule for the project.

My second example concerns allocation of resources. As a typical problem, consider a steel company that can manufacture several different types of steel, each type requiring some particular combination of raw materials. The question is, from a given supply of raw materials, what amount of each type of steel should be produced in order to maximize the company's profit?

Let's say our steel company can produce just three types of steel, and that its profit is 3, 4, and 7 dollars a ton, respectively, on each type. If it produces x tons of the first type, y tons of the second, and z tons of the third, then its total profit would be

$$3x + 4y + 7z.$$

This is called the *objective function*. It is the function we want to maximize. Now, there are constraints on the amounts that can be produced, arising from the fact that only a limited quantity of each resource is available. Suppose that the company has 10,000 pounds of the metal vanadium. Let's say that the first type of steel contains 2 pounds of vanadium per ton, that the second contains 6, and the third contains 27.

Then the quantities, x, y, and z, of steel produced must satisfy

$$2x + 6y + 27z \le 10000.$$

This is a constraint equation, and there is a similar constraint for each of the other resources. We also have the obvious constraints $x \ge 0$, $y \ge 0$, and $z \ge 0$.

The formulas $3x + 4y + 7z$ and $2x + 6y + 27z$ are what mathematicians call linear functions. The linear objective function together with all the linear constraints form what is called a *linear program*. (The term "program" here is not related to computer programs.) Finding the maximum of the objective function, subject to the constraints, is called *linear programming*. The most common method of solution, known as the *simplex algorithm*, was invented in 1947 by George Dantzig.[8] Linear programming problems come up frequently in business and industry, and these real problems can easily involve hundreds or thousands of constraints. The computer programs that solve them save companies millions of dollars every year.

9.2.3. Beyond Numbers. So far in this section, I've only talked about numeric applications. Computers are good at number crunching. That is, they can perform massive calculations involving large collections of numbers. There is no shortage of numbers for processing. They are generated copiously from a variety of sources: information collected from people in surveys, digitally encoded pictures beamed back from satellites and space probes, measurements from scientific instrumentation, data produced by computer simulations such as those used in weather forecasting. All these numbers are churned and sifted by computer programs to produce something that *people* will find more directly meaningful: weather maps instead of columns of numbers, for example.

One way of extracting essential information from an unmanageable mass of numbers is *statistical analysis*. A "statistic" can be characterized as a number or small set of numbers that summarizes some aspect of a large set of data. A simple example would be the average of a list of numbers; the average gives some indication of the general character of the numbers, summarized in a single value. The average is more useful when combined with the standard deviation, a statistic that indicates how widely the numbers are scattered around their average value. This only scratches the surface of statistics. Computer programs are available that can perform many different types of statistical analysis.

---

[8] See [Karloff] for a full mathematical treatment of linear programming.

Still, a statistic is still a number. People are visual creatures, who can understand pictures much more readily than numbers. At this, we are much better than computers. In fact, sometimes the best way to find the pattern or meaning in long column of numbers is to represent them somehow as an image and show the image to some handy nearby human.

One example of this is **computed axial tomography** (CAT), a remarkable technique that is used to make a kind of three-dimensional X-ray, showing the full interior structure of a human body. Ordinary X-rays are taken from various directions. The data from these X-rays, converted into a set of numbers, are combined mathematically to produce a density measurement for each point in the interior of the body. Those measurements can then be used to construct a three-dimensional image, or any desired two-dimensional cross-section. CAT has proved to be a valuable tool in medicine—one that would be impossible without computers because of the large amount of computation involved.

Perhaps most exciting, though, are the images the computer shows us of things that we could never see otherwise. When a computer simulates a thunderstorm, it is manipulating numbers and mathematical equations. But it is capable of rendering those numbers into an animation showing, say, the air currents and temperatures in the evolving storm. Similarly, a program that computes the interaction between two molecules might display its results in a way that lets a scientist *see* how the molecules fit together. The computer might show an exploding star, continents drifting through eons of simulated geologic time, or strange forms defined only by abstract mathematical formulas. This making visible of the unseen is called **visualization**, and it is increasingly important as a scientific tool.

9.3. Postscript: Analysis of Algorithms

Chapter 4 dealt with one aspect of the theory of computation: the fundamental limits that apply to all computers, even given unlimited time and memory. It is important to know these limits, if only to keep you from trying to program computers to do something that they can never do. However, in real applications, time and memory often impose the real limitations on what programmers and computer users can do. The fact that a computer will eventually come up with the answer to a problem is not all that interesting if it will take it seven-and-a-half million years to do so.

So, there is another aspect of the theory of computation that studies the questions: How long will this program take to run? And how much memory will it need for storing intermediate results as it is running? The field that deals with these issues is called *analysis of algorithms*.[9] There is no general method that will answer these questions in all cases (except for the rather unsatisfactory one of running the program and finding out). But is often possible to analyze specific programs to obtain information about their running times or memory requirements.

The analysis of running time generally has received more attention than memory, and I will follow the same practice here. This is justified by the fact that many programs of interest have relatively modest memory requirements. Also, any program that uses extremely large amounts of memory automatically requires a lot of time—if only to store data in all the memory that it's using.

9.3.1. Big-Oh and Complexity Classes.   Most programs are designed to process some type of input data. In general, the more data a program has to process, the longer it takes to run. We can ask how the running time of the program depends on the amount of data it must process. As a simple example, consider a program that adds up a list of numbers. The numbers are the input to the program. The computer starts with zero and then reads each number in turn and adds it to the sum. We would expect the computer to spend the same amount of time processing each number, let's say a seconds.[10] If there are n numbers, that's a total of an seconds to process all the numbers. It also spends a certain amount of time, say b seconds, performing tasks that don't depend on the size on the input, such as initializing the sum to zero and printing out an answer. The total running time to add n numbers, then, is $an + b$ seconds. (We would expect the constants a and b to be very small, since computers can perform operations like addition very quickly. It might be more appropriate to use a different measure of running time than seconds, such as the number of machine-language instructions executed as the program runs.)

---

[9] Recall that an algorithm is just a step-by-step procedure for solving a problem, guaranteed to terminate after a finite number of steps. It is essentially a computer program, although it is more accurate to think of it as the *idea* behind a computer program.

[10] This is not necessarily true. For example, if the numbers are being read from a file, the time it takes to read a number might depend on how many digits are in the number. I will ignore such complications in this example. A more rigorous general discussion is coming up in a few paragraphs.

This analysis is fine, as far as it goes, but note that it doesn't really tell us the running time of the program unless we know the values of the constants a and b. These constants, which measure the time it takes for the computer to do certain operations, depend on the speed of the particular computer we are using. Different computers could have wildly different running times. All those computers, however, would still have in common the general character of the *relationship* between the size of the input and the running time, as expressed in the mathematical formula $an + b$. In analysis of algorithms, at least as a first approximation, we tend to study such relationships without worrying too much about the particular values of constants like a and b.

Once we stop worrying about particular constants, we can almost stop worrying about b entirely. As n—the size of input—increases, it is the term "an" in the formula "$an + b$" that drives the corresponding increase in running time. The "b" is less significant, and it becomes less and less significant as n gets bigger and bigger. We think of the running time as being of the form "some constant times n, plus some extra stuff," where the extra stuff becomes insignificant for large values of n. There is even a notation that gives this informal idea a rigorous basis: We say that the running time is $\mathcal{O}(n)$, pronounced "big-Oh of n."[11] Similarly, we would say that the running time was $\mathcal{O}(n^2)$ if it were of the form "some constant times n^2, plus some extra less significant stuff."

More generally, let's consider some particular program of interest. We assume that the program is an "algorithm," in the sense that it is guaranteed to halt eventually, no matter what input data it is given. We also assume that the program is to be run on some selected computer which will be fixed throughout the whole discussion of running time. If we change to a different computer, we could always find a program that performs the same task (since all computers are equivalent, as explained in Chapter 4), but the running times would be different. Provided that we stick to standard computers of the sort described in Chapter 5, though, the general form of the relationship between input size and running time would be the same. The same might not be true if

---

[11] More rigorously, if $f(n)$ is a formula involving n, we say that the running time is $\mathcal{O}(f(n))$ if there is some constant c such that, at least for large values of n, the running time is less than c times $f(n)$. The restriction to large values of n is a way of ignoring less significant terms, such as the b in $an + b$. Note that $\mathcal{O}(f(n))$ is an *adjective*, not a name for something. When we say that "the running time is $\mathcal{O}(f(n))$," we are saying that the running time has a certain property.

we were to change to some radically different type of computing machine, such as a Turing machine.

Another choice that we have to make is how to measure the size of the input. If the program reads input data from a file, we could count the number of characters in the file. This is a general definition of input size that would work for any program. However, all the programs that we will use as examples process lists of numbers, and so we adopt the *number of numbers in the list* as a more natural measure of the input size.

Now, in general, the running time of a program will depend not just on the size of the input but also on the specific input data. So that we can work with one definite value, we will consider the *maximum* running time (on our selected computer) of the program on any input of size n. This maximum value is called the **worst-case running time** of the program on inputs of size n, since the actual running time on any particular input of size n will be no worse than the maximum.[12]

With all these preliminary definitions out of the way, we come finally to the main definition: Let $f(n)$ be some formula involving n, such as n^2 or n or 3^n. We define the **time complexity class** TIME($f(n)$) to be the set of all programs which have worst-case running times that are $\mathcal{O}(f(n))$. For example, a program is in TIME(n^2) if its running time on an input of size n is less than or equal to some constant times n^2.[13] Note that any quantity that is less than or equal to cn is automatically less than the bigger number cn^2. Therefore, any program that is in the class TIME(n) is automatically in the class TIME(n^2). However, the converse is not true. There are many programs in TIME(n^2) that are not in TIME(n); such programs can be thought of as being strictly more complex than programs in TIME(n). We could write down an infinite chain of complexity classes, each class contained in the next and each containing programs of strictly greater complexity. For example,

$$\ldots, \text{TIME}(\sqrt{n}), \text{TIME}(n), \text{TIME}(n^2),$$
$$\text{TIME}(n^3), \ldots, \text{TIME}(2^n), \text{TIME}(3^n), \ldots.$$

It is desirable to have some idea in advance how long a program will take to run. Therefore, it is a useful exercise to analyze a program to

---

[12] It is also possible to study the **average-case running time**, which is defined as the average of the running times on all possible inputs of size n.

[13] If we wanted to deal with memory requirements instead of time, we would define the **space complexity class**, SPACE($f(n)$), in a similar way.

determine its complexity class. This is a large part of what analysis of algorithms is all about.

Now, suppose we have a program that performs some task. We could always speed up the program by running it on a faster computer model. However, this would only multiply the running time by a constant; it would not change the complexity class of the program. We would do better if we could find a different program, of strictly lower time complexity, that performs the same task. If we do this, the savings in time can be truly remarkable. To illustrate this, we look at two very standard examples: searching and sorting.

9.3.2. Searching and Sorting. Let's consider the problem of searching for some particular item in a list. For example, we might want to find a particular book in a list of all the books in a library. Here, we will consider the abstract problem of searching for some particular number in a list of numbers. The numbers in the list will be referred to as $A[1]$, $A[2]$, $A[3]$, ..., $A[n]$. (This is the notation for an "array" of numbers as used in the programming language Pascal, which was described in Chapter 8.) The number n here is the size of the input.

Suppose that the number that we want to find is S. There is an obvious method for searching for S in the list. First, check whether $S = A[1]$. If so, then we are done; if not, then check whether $S = A[2]$. If not, then check $A[3]$, and so on, until either S is found or the end of the list is reached without finding S. In the worst case, there are n steps. Since each step takes about the same amount of time, the running time is $\mathcal{O}(n)$, and the program is in the complexity class TIME(n). If we have no further information about the numbers in the list, this is about the best we can do.

But suppose that the numbers in the list are *sorted* into increasing order. That is, $A[1]$ is less than or equal to $A[2]$, which is less than or equal to $A[3]$, and so on. With this assumption, we can do much better than $\mathcal{O}(n)$, using a method known as *binary search*.

Start by comparing S to the number in the middle of the list. S could be less than that number, greater than it, or equal to it. If it is less, then, since the list is sorted, we can deduce that S cannot occur *after* the middle number in the list; we can eliminate the second half of the list from further consideration. Similarly, if S is greater than the middle number, we can eliminate the first half of the list from consideration. So, in either case, we have cut the number of numbers still to be considered in half. (Of course, if S is equal to the middle number, we've gotten lucky: We've already found S.)

This first step has reduced the size of the list we need to search from n to $n/2$. Applying exactly the same method to the reduced list (comparing S to its middle number) will eliminate half the remaining numbers and reduce the size of the list we still need to consider to $n/4$. The next step reduces the number further to $n/8$, then $n/16$, and so on. This will go on until either we find S or we reduce the size of the list to a single item.

The number of steps in this process is equal to the number of times you can divide n by two before getting an answer less than or equal to one. For large values of n, this number is *much* less than n—and the bigger n is, the more impressive the difference. For a list of a million items, for example, binary search requires only 20 steps. Searching through a million items one at a time would be infeasible even on a fast computer, if it had to be done very often. Using binary search, the search time becomes almost negligible in comparison.

The mathematical function that describes the running time of binary search is written as $\log_2(n)$, pronounced "logarithm, base 2, of n."[14] Thus, binary search is in the class $\text{TIME}(\log_2(n))$. Programs in this class have running times that grow very slowly with the size of their input.

Binary search requires a sorted list of numbers. In general, lists don't automatically come in sorted order. However, since sorted lists are often necessary, it's a common operation to start with a list of items in some unknown order and to rearrange them into an increasing sequence. For example, this process, which is called *sorting*, is used to put a list of names into alphabetical order. Sorting is another standard problem where the right choice of algorithm can lead to huge savings is run time.

The obvious sorting algorithms are in the complexity class $\text{TIME}(n^2)$. Since n^2 grows fairly rapidly as n increases, these algorithms become unacceptably slow even for reasonable values of n, such as $n = 1000$. However, a better choice of algorithm comes to the rescue. The best sorting algorithms are in the complexity class $\text{TIME}(n \cdot \log_2(n))$, a vast improvement over $\text{TIME}(n^2)$.

I will not discuss specific sorting algorithms here, but Figure 9.1 will give you some idea of the magnitude of the improvement that can be

---

[14] If $n = 2^k$, a power of two, then this function is defined by $\log_2(n) = \log_2(2^k) = k$. Notice that if you repeatedly divide 2^k by 2, you get the sequence $2^k, 2^{k-1}, 2^{k-2}, \ldots, 1$. This sequence has k steps.

$\log_2(n)$	n	$n \cdot \log_2(n)$	n^2
2	4	8	16
4	16	64	256
6	64	384	4096
8	256	2048	65536
10	1024	10240	1048576
13.3	10000	133000	100000000
16.6	100000	1660000	10000000000
19.9	1000000	19900000	1000000000000
29.9	1000000000	29900000000	1000000000000000000

Figure 9.1. *A table showing how* $\log_2(n)$, n^2, *and* $n \cdot \log_2(n)$ *grow as* n *increases. (In the last four rows, an approximate value of* $\log_2(n)$ *is used.)*

realized with the right choice of algorithm. When using this table to compare running times, keep in mind that the running time involves a constant factor that might affect the comparison. For example, the running times might be something like $0.003 \cdot n^2$ and $0.1 \cdot n \cdot \log_2(n)$, rather than n^2 and $n \cdot \log_2(n)$. In that case, the n^2 algorithm would actually be better for small values of n. But no matter what the constants are, the $n \cdot \log_2(n)$ algorithm would always be better for large enough values of n, and its advantage would continue to grow as n becomes larger and larger.

9.3.3. The P=NP Problem. Beyond TIME(n^2) are complexity classes TIME(n^3), TIME(n^4), TIME(n^5), and so forth, each class containing all the previous classes in the list. An algorithm that is in any one of these classes is called a ***polynomial-time algorithm***.[15] Thus, an algorithm is a polynomial-time algorithm if there is a constant exponent k and another constant c such that the running time of the algorithm on an input of size n is less than cn^k.

The class of problems that can be solved by polynomial-time algorithms is called $\mathcal{P}$. For example, the problem of sorting a list of numbers is in $\mathcal{P}$, since it can be solved by a program in the class TIME(n^2). In general, we can hope to solve problems in $\mathcal{P}$ in a reasonable length of time, at least for moderate input sizes.

---

[15] The variable n raised to a constant power, such as n^2 or n^{17} is an example of what is called in mathematics a "polynomial."

Now, there are certainly algorithms that are not polynomial-time. Here is an example: Imagine a labyrinth of intersecting corridors in a large building. The problem is to place guards at some of the intersections so that every corridor is under observation from at least one of its endpoints, and we would like to do this with the smallest possible number of guards. Let's take the number of intersections to be n, and use n to measure the size of the input. The obvious algorithm for solving this problem is to check *all* the possible ways of posting guards and to select the one that requires the fewest guards while satisfying the requirement of covering all the corridors. Unfortunately, there are 2^n different possibilities to consider,[16] so this algorithm requires 2^n steps. Now, 2^n grows faster than n^k for any constant exponent k, so our algorithm is not polynomial-time.

Of course, this does not settle the question of whether or not the corridor guard problem is in the class $\mathcal{P}$. Just because *one* algorithm for solving the problem is not polynomial-time, that doesn't mean that there isn't a *better* algorithm for solving the same problem. We have seen examples where choosing a different algorithm has yielded immense savings in run-time. Perhaps the same thing could happen here. At this time, however, no one knows whether this is possible; there is no known algorithm for solving the corridor guard problem that is appreciably better than checking each of the 2^n different ways of posting guards.

In fact, this question brings us to the most famous unsolved problem in computer science today: the "$\mathcal{P} = \mathcal{NP}$" problem. $\mathcal{NP}$ refers to the class of problems that are solvable by so-called ***nondeterministic polynomial-time algorithms***. What this means exactly is hard to state in a simple way,[17] but the corridor guard problem is a typical member of the class $\mathcal{NP}$. Every polynomial-time algorithm is also nondeterministic-polynomial-time, so that the class $\mathcal{P}$ is contained in the class $\mathcal{NP}$. The question is whether the reverse is true: Given any problem in the class $\mathcal{NP}$, is it possible to find a polynomial-time algorithm to

---

[16] Think back to Chapter 1: Code each intersection with a one if there is a guard there, and with a zero if not. Since there are n intersections, when you put the data for all the intersections together, you get an n-bit binary number. There are 2^n different n-bit binary numbers, and each one corresponds to a different way of posting guards.

[17] Roughly, the term "nondeterministic" means that the computer is allowed to make random guesses during the execution of a program. A problem is in the class $\mathcal{NP}$ if there is a *chance* that it will be solved in polynomial time, if the computer happens to make just the right random guesses at the right times.

solve it? No one has been able to answer this question yet, but the general expectation is that there are "intrinsically hard" problems in $\mathcal{NP}$, including the corridor guard problem, that are not solvable in polynomial time.

Is this a useful thing to know about? Well, in my case, there was a time when knowing it would have saved me some embarrassment. A mathematician friend of mine needed a program to solve a problem that was, essentially, the corridor guard problem. But some computer scientists told him it was "too hard." I said, "Gee, I could write that program easily," and proceeded to do so. My friend was impressed—until we both realized that the program would work only for small numbers of intersections. Even for as few as 20 intersections, the program took too long to be usable. It wasn't writing the program that was hard; it was the problem itself that was too hard for any known program! The point—the whole point, really, of analyzing the running time of algorithms—is that there are *practical* limits to what computers can do, as well as theoretical ones. Which is just what started us on this whole discussion.

Chapter Summary

Word processing programs are used to produce documents that consist mainly of text. Word processors are more than *text editors*; they deal with complex text styles and formats and allow the inclusion of non-text elements, such as tables and graphics. Therefore, the files used by word processors contain complex data structures, not just simple sequences of ASCII codes. Each word processor has its own *file format*, and knowledge of that format is necessary to decode the information it contains. The same is true for many types of application program.

Other applications that can be found on desktop computers include *spreadsheets*, in which tables of numbers represent models of real world problems; *painting and drawing programs*, which are used to produce graphics images; *database programs*, in which large, structured collections of data can be stored, manipulated, and queried; and *communication programs*, such as *terminal emulators* that can be used to connect one computer to another through a network or through a pair of *modems*.

Of course, there are still large-scale applications that consume processing power on a scale beyond that available on the desktop. *Weather forecasting* is an example of *simulation* where increased processing power can increase the accuracy of the simulation and therefore of the forecast.

Other computation-intensive applications include *computed tomography*, *scientific visualization*, and *optimization problems* such as those that arise in scheduling and resource allocation.

The question of practical applications of computing brings with it the question of practical, as opposed to theoretical, limits on what computers can do. The field of *analysis of algorithms* studies the running time and memory requirements of programs. Sometimes, using a different algorithm to solve a problem can dramatically reduce the time it takes to solve it. Such savings go beyond what can be achieved merely by speeding up the computer, since the percentage of time saved actually grows with the size of the problem.

Questions

1. Try to think of a way that you could use a database program (other than a mailing list). Describe the data that you would store in the database and what you would do with that data. What sort of operations would you want to perform on your data?

2. Why would it be easier to transmit text through a low-speed modem connection, rather than graphics? Can you make any suggestions for dealing with the problem? That is, would there be any way of providing a reasonable graphical user interface through a fairly low-speed connection?

3. The algorithm for searching through an unsorted list of numbers is in complexity class TIME(n). Can you think of any other algorithms in this complexity class? How would you characterize algorithms in TIME(n)?

Chapter 10

Cooperating Computers

NO AMOUNT OF COMPUTING power, it seems, is enough. Computers become more powerful each year, but that doesn't mean we need fewer of them. On the contrary, the more computing resources that are available, the more we seem to need. Each increase in power lets us do new things that were previously impractical, and there always seem to be really neat applications that are just waiting for the next ten-fold increase in computer speed or ten-fold decrease in computer cost.

Aside from waiting for newer and faster machines, there are two ways to increase the amount of processing power that can be brought to bear on a problem. The first is to use a computer that can execute more than one instruction at the same time. This is called *parallel processing*. The second is to connect a number of computers together so that they can communicate. A collection of communicating computers is called a *network*; when networked computers work together to solve a problem, they are doing *distributed processing*.

Instead of a single central processing unit, parallel processing computers have anywhere from two to thousands of processing units that can perform separate computations. Distributed processing is similar, except that the processing units happen to be in different machines. This tends to make communication between the processing units slower and less reliable, which in turn makes some of the techniques used in parallel processing inappropriate. But still, we will consider distributed processing to be one type of parallel processing.

295

At one time, parallel processing was associated mainly with *supercomputers*—large, expensive machines that use multiple processing units to achieve very high levels of raw computing power. But as the prices of computers fall, parallel processing is turning up in smaller computers and even in desktop models.

You can buy expansion cards that add parallel processing capability to personal computers, equipping them with computing power that a decade ago would have put them into the supercomputer class. And in fact, the latest generation of personal computers is based on microprocessors that actually incorporate a kind of parallelism on a single chip.

Furthermore, today's computers are more and more likely to be connected to networks, which range in size and complexity from two computers wired together and sharing data, to the *Internet*, a world-wide network that includes millions of computers. A networked computer can tap into computing power and information that can be spread around a room or throughout the world.

So, it seems, we must move beyond the image of an isolated CPU working its way through a task step by step, from beginning to end. Instead, we can imagine a "community" of processors working together. In this chapter, we consider how computing devices can be made to cooperate in this way.

10.1. Programming for Parallel Processing

When people work together on a project, it often seems that the actual productive work takes second place to the organizational problems: dividing up the project into tasks, assigning tasks to individuals to keep everyone busy, and making sure that things are done in the right order when one part of the project depends on other parts.

Getting computers to work together is, if anything, harder. The same organizational problems come up, and—as always when dealing with computers—the solutions must be spelled out in full detail. Some of the details are taken care of by operating systems and specialized compilers, but much of the work is left to the programmer, and programming for parallel processing can be very different from standard programming.

However, different doesn't necessarily mean bad. Recall the discussion of abstraction from Chapter 8. An abstraction is, more or less, an idea that a programmer has for solving a problem. That abstraction must be encoded into some specific programming language. This encoding will be easiest when the language offers support for the specific abstraction the programmer has in mind. Now, sometimes that abstraction might involve parallel processing in a natural way. In that case, it will be easiest to encode the abstraction in a programming language that offers explicit support for *parallel processing abstractions*.

The main abstraction needed for parallel processing is the *process*. In Chapter 5, a process was defined as the sequence of steps a computer goes through as it executes a program. A standard computer can execute only one process at a time. To deal with parallel processing, we generalize this to allow several processes to be going on at the same time.

As a simple example, consider a networked computer game program that supports several users playing against each other, with each player at a different computer on a network. A programmer designing such a program might well imagine a separate process for each user. Each process would handle the interaction with one user—detecting keystrokes, updating the screen and so forth—and it would communicate with the other processes when necessary. Players could easily be added to the game by creating new processes for them, or removed from the game by terminating their processes.

Once the program is conceived in this way, it can be most easily programmed in a language that supports some kind of "process abstraction." It should be possible to create and terminate processes that will all be executed simultaneously, and it should be possible for those processes to communicate in some way. Although interprocess communication might offer some difficulty, the programmer's design can be expressed most easily with such a process abstraction. Without it, the programmer would be forced to somehow weave the separate processes into the single thread of a standard process; this would probably be difficult, and the programmer's beautifully clear design would disappear into a clutter of implementation details.

Among major languages, the programming language Ada offers the most direct support for process abstractions of this type. Ada allows programmers to declare *tasks*. A task is similar to a subroutine with the following difference: When a program calls a subroutine, the execution of the program is suspended until the subroutine has finished executing; when a program starts a task, both the program and the task continue to execute simultaneously. A program can start many tasks, all of which can execute at the same time. These tasks can communicate by a mechanism called *message passing*, in which data is passed from one task to another.

Now here is a curious thing: Although Ada supports the creation of multiple processes to be executed simultaneously, Ada programs do not have to be executed on parallel-processing computers. As we saw in Chapter 5, a standard single-processor computer can use a technique called timesharing to simulate parallel processing. In timesharing, the single processor shifts its attention rapidly from one process to another, giving the illusion that all the processes are being executed simultaneously. In effect, the processes are being weaved into a single thread, but this is done automatically by the computer rather than laboriously by the programmer. In fact, the programmer doesn't have to know or care whether the program will be run using real or simulated parallel processing—this is just an implementation detail that is hidden by the abstraction.

The point here is that the ideas of parallel processing can be useful programming tools, even for writing programs that will be run on standard computers. Some problems can be solved more easily and more naturally using such tools than in any other way.

In the remainder of this section, we will look at some specific examples of problems that can be solved using parallel processing abstractions. In this discussion, I will use an extension of the xTurtle programming language that was used in Chapters 6 and 7. This extension allows the creation of processes and provides some basic support for communication among those processes. Keep in mind that it doesn't matter whether the processes are really executed by separate processors or by a single processor using timesharing. In this section, it is the parallel processing "mind-set" that is important.

10.1.1. Parallel Processing in xTurtle. A standard program in xTurtle consists of a sequence of commands that the computer executes one after another in a single stream. There can be loops and decisions that cause parts of the program to be skipped or to be executed more than once, but at any given time, only one thing is going on.

Most instructions in an xTurtle program tell the computer to do something with the turtle, such as rotate it in place or move it forward. Although the turtle is just a bunch of pixels drawn on the screen, it is easy to imagine that it is the turtle itself that is reading the instructions and carrying them out. That is, it is easy to think of the turtle as a kind of processor that can execute a program. In fact, this point of view will make it much easier to think about adding parallel processing capabilities to the xTurtle language: All we have to do is provide some way to create new turtles, and allow each turtle to execute a different sequence of instructions.

This new feature is provided by a built-in subroutine called *fork*, which tells a turtle to split into several copies of itself. For example, after the command *fork*(2) is executed, there will be two turtles where before there was only one. The parameter—2 in this example—determines how many copies there will be. *Fork*(3) will split the turtle into three copies, *fork*(4) into four copies, and so forth. After the command is executed, all the copies will continue to execute instructions, simultaneously and independently. They are, in effect, separate processors, running in parallel. For example, consider the short program

> fork(36)
> forward(5)

The first command splits the turtle into thirty-six copies. Then, each turtle goes on to execute the second command, which tells it to draw a line five units long.

Unfortunately, in this example the thirty-six turtles draw thirty-six identical lines, all on top of each other! This is parallel processing of a sort, but not very interesting. We need some way to make the turtles execute *different* instructions. This is made possible by a predefined variable called *ForkNumber*. After a *fork* command, each of the turtles will have a different *ForkNumber*. The value will be 1 for the first turtle, 2 for the second, 3 for the third, and so on. This is the only thing that distinguishes among the copies. Consider the program

> fork(36)
> turn(10 * *ForkNumber*)
> forward(5)

The first command produces thirty-six turtles which are identical except for their *ForkNumbers*. When these turtles execute the second command, each will perform a different action.

For the first turtle, *ForkNumber* is 1, and when it executes the command *turn*(10 * *ForkNumber*), it rotates 10 degrees. The second turtle, with a *ForkNumber* of 2, rotates 20 degrees. The third rotates 30 degrees. And so on, up to the thirty-sixth turtle, which rotates through a full 360 degrees. At this point, the turtles are facing in thirty-six different directions. Each turtle then goes on to execute the same instruction, *forward*(5), but since they are facing in different directions, each turtle draws a different line. The result is a picture with thirty-six lines radiating out from a central point.

In fact, the picture drawn by this three-line parallel processing program is the same as the picture shown in Figure 6.3. For Figure 6.3, the drawing was done with a loop, which draws the thirty-six lines in the picture one-by-one. That program was three times as long as the parallel processing version, and probably more difficult to write. Even this simple example shows the value of parallel processing as a programming tool.

The *fork* command makes it possible to do more than draw a large number of lines with one command. In fact, it is possible to use it to perform any tasks whatsoever in parallel. Suppose, for example, that you have two tasks that you want your program to perform simultaneously. Then your program can have the form:

> fork(2)
>
> **if** *ForkNumber* = 1 **then**
>
>   ⋮   { instructions for first task }
>
> **else**
>
>   ⋮   { instructions for second task }
>
> **end if**

The *fork* command creates two turtles. Each of these goes on to test the condition "**if** *ForkNumber* = 1." The first turtle, whose *ForkNumber* is 1, finds that this condition is true and so it goes on to execute the first task. At the same time, the second turtle, which has a *ForkNumber* of 2, finds that the condition is false, so it goes on to execute the second task instead. This example shows that *fork* is really a general-purpose command for creating processes.

A more interesting sample program is shown in Figure 10.1. This program uses thirty turtles to draw thirty eight-sided polygons, arranged into three rows of ten. The result is a pattern that looks something like bathroom tiles.[1] Note that the program contains two *fork* commands. The first divides the original turtle into ten copies. When these copies execute the command *forward*(*size* * *ForkNumber*), each copy moves

---

[1] Thanks to my colleague, Kevin Mitchell, for this example. Kevin is interested in the mathematics of this type of repetitive pattern, known in general as "tilings." He pointed out that the *fork* command in xTurtle makes them easy to draw.

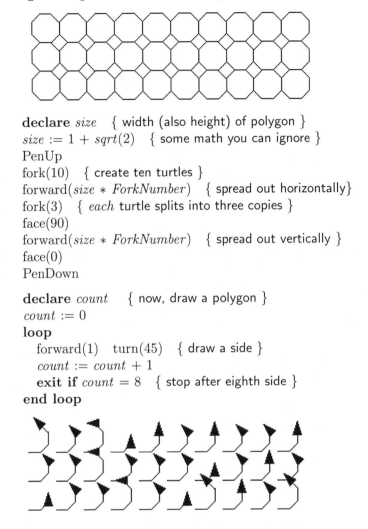

```
declare size   { width (also height) of polygon }
size := 1 + sqrt(2)   { some math you can ignore }
PenUp
fork(10)   { create ten turtles }
forward(size * ForkNumber)   { spread out horizontally}
fork(3)   { each turtle splits into three copies }
face(90)
forward(size * ForkNumber)   { spread out vertically }
face(0)
PenDown

declare count   { now, draw a polygon }
count := 0
loop
   forward(1)   turn(45)   { draw a side }
   count := count + 1
   exit if count = 8   { stop after eighth side }
end loop
```

Figure 10.1. *An xTurtle program that uses parallel processing to draw a picture containing thirty eight-sided polygons. The complete picture drawn by the program is shown above the program. Below the program is a snapshot taken while the program was being executed. Each of the thirty turtles (shown as small triangles) is drawing one of the polygons.*

forward by a different amount. This spreads the turtles out along a horizontal line. Then, each of the ten turtles executes the *fork*(3) command and splits into three copies. These copies then spread out vertically.

(Note that after the second *fork* command, *ForkNumber* refers to the most recent *fork*; the number from the first *fork* is lost.)

Once the thirty turtles are in position, each one draws an eight-sided polygon. These polygons are drawn simultaneously, but, as the snapshot in Figure 10.1 shows, they are not necessarily drawn at the same speed. Some of the turtles execute instructions faster than others, so that some might draw an entire polygon while others have drawn only a few sides. This difference in execution speed is not very important here, but as you can imagine, it becomes very important when processes have to communicate with each other. One process can make no assumptions about what another process is doing at any given time; the second process might be at any one of a number of points in the sequence of instructions it is executing.

10.1.2. Shared Variables. There is another subtle point in the example in Figure 10.1, having to do with the variables *size* and *count*. The variable *count* is declared after all the turtles have been created. This means that each turtle creates its own *count* variable. This is important because each turtle must count off the sides of its own polygon, so each must have a separate variable to do the counting. The variable *size*, on the other hand, is declared at the beginning of the program, while there is only one turtle. This means that there is only one copy of this variable, and that copy is shared by all the turtles.[2] The value of *size* is **shared data**, available to all the turtles. Shared data provides a somewhat primitive method for communication among the turtles: If one turtle changes the value of *size*, other turtles will be able to read the new value.

In the example, there is really no communication among the processes. Each turtle draws its polygon without reference to what the other turtles are doing. This is a very simple type of parallel processing. Things get more interesting and more difficult when processes are less independent. Consider an analogy to building houses: If three people want to build three houses, one way to do it would be to have one person build each house. The builders would be operating in parallel, but they would be completely independent, and there would be no need for them to communicate. They would be like the thirty turtles in the example, each drawing a separate polygon.

---

[2] This was a decision that was made when the xTurtle language was designed. The language could easily have been designed so that when a turtle is copied, all existing variables are copied as well. In that case, however, a different method would have to be provided for communication among the turtles.

However, this method is useless if the three builders want to work together to build a single house. In that case the tasks that the builders perform are not independent, and they have to communicate—with each other or with a supervisor—to see that all the tasks (walls, floors, wiring, plumbing, ...) get done in the right order.

Let's look at a simple example of interdependent tasks in xTurtle. Consider the somewhat silly program:

> **declare** *sum*
> *sum* := 0
> fork(3)
> *sum* := *sum* + *ForkNumber*

The variable *sum* is shared by three turtles. Each turtle, it seems, adds a number to this sum. The numbers added are 1, by the first turtle, 2, by the second, and 3, by the third. When the program ends, it seems that the value of *sum* should be 6. As it turns out, though, the value could be any number between 1 and 6!

The problem is that the command "*sum* := *sum* + *ForkNumber*" is actually executed as a sequence of three steps: (1) Get the value of *sum*; (2) Add *ForkNumber* to it; (3) Store the answer in the variable *sum*. Each of the three turtles executes these three steps, for a total of nine operations. The final value of *sum* depends on the order in which these nine operations are actually performed. Let's suppose that each turtle executes step (1) at about the same time. Then each turtle will read the same value: zero, which was originally stored in *sum*. Adding *ForkNumber* to this will give the answer 1, 2, or 3. Each of these answers will be stored into *sum*; the final value of *sum* will depend on which of the store operations happens to be performed last.

We need a way of letting a process take control of the shared variable *sum* for the whole time it takes to perform the entire instruction "*sum* := *sum* + *ForkNumber*." In xTurtle, this facility is provided by a **grab** command. For example:

> **declare** *sum*
> *sum* := 0
> fork(3)
> **grab** *sum* **then**
> *sum* := *sum* + *ForkNumber*
> **end grab**

The turtle that first executes the *grab* command has exclusive access to *sum* until it releases that variable by executing the **end grab**. If a second turtle tries to grab *sum* while the first turtle is using it, it will be forced to wait until the first turtle releases the variable. So in this example, each turtle grabs *sum* in turn and correctly adds its *ForkNumber* to it. The final value of *sum* will be 6.

A sequence of commands between **grab** and **end grab** form what is called a ***critical region***, that is, a section of a program where a process needs exclusive use of a shared variable. Critical regions provide ***mutual exclusion*** of processes: It is not possible for two processes to be in critical regions associated to the same variable at the same time.[3] Mutual exclusion is an important consideration whenever processes communicate by using shared variables.

The sample program that adds 1 plus 2 plus 3 is a silly example because the turtles don't really do anything significant in parallel: The **grab** command forces them to do the three additions in sequence. It would make more sense if, instead of just adding *ForkNumber* to *sum*, each turtle had to do some long computation to produce a number that would then be added to *sum*. The computations of the turtles could proceed in parallel, and the **grab** command would ensure that all the results were correctly added to the sum.

Controlling access to shared data is important in more realistic examples, too. Consider an airline reservation system used by several travel agents to book seats on a certain flight. Suppose that, at the same moment, two agents are performing the sequence of operations: (1) Check whether any seat is available; (2) If so, reserve the seat. If the shared data—that is, information about which seats have been booked—is not protected in some way against simultaneous use, it can happen that the same seat is reserved for two different customers. Or consider a program in which the shared data is the amount of money in your savings account. Suppose you and a friend, working at different automatic teller machines, each withdraw $100 from the account at the same moment, and that a process running on each machine records the withdrawal by executing the instruction "*amount* = *amount* − 100." Without mutual exclusion, it might happen that only $100 is effectively subtracted from your account, instead of the correct $200—something that you might

---

[3] Note that for this to work, *all* the processes that use the variables must restrict such use to critical regions. There is no way to stop a process from changing the value of the variable without first "grabbing" it, even though such badly behaved processes could cause serious and hard-to-fix errors in a program. Communication by message passing, as described later in the chapter, provides a safer method of communication between processes.

find perfectly OK, but that would probably cause the bank to fire its programmers.

10.2. Multiprocessing Computers

The previous section showed how some problems can be solved more easily or more naturally in a programming language that includes parallel processing abstractions. As far as programming goes, it doesn't matter whether multiple processes are really being executed at the same time, or if instead their parallelism is being simulated using timesharing.

But the major advantage of parallel processing—increased computation speed—can only be realized when two or more processors really do work on a problem at the same time. In this section, we consider how computers with multiple processing units make such actual parallelism possible.

10.2.1. SISD, SIMD, and MIMD. A standard von Neumann machine, with a single central processing unit and a single data path between memory and CPU, is said to be an *SISD*, or "single instruction, single data," machine. For parallel processing, we need a *multiprocessing computer*, one that has multiple processors that can perform separate computations simultaneously. There are many variations on how such a machine can work, but they can be classified into two broad types, *SIMD* ("single instruction, multiple data") and *MIMD* ("multiple instruction, multiple data"). Most of this chapter deals with MIMD, which is the most general type of parallelism, but SIMD is also very important.

SIMD is a relatively simple type of parallelism in which all the processing units in the computer execute the same instruction at the same time.[4] As an analogy, think of all the rowers in a boat pulling on their oars in lockstep. Such parallelism is useful because each of the processors can be working with different data (the oars in the analogy). For example, suppose that each number in a list of numbers is to be multiplied by two. This operation could be done in a single step on a SIMD computer: Each of the processors would operate on one of the numbers

---

[4] I should say, all the *active* processing units, because not all the processing units are necessarily used during every step of the computation. This is important for the programming of SIMD computers, but need not concern us here.

in the list. More generally, SIMD computers are good at manipulating lists and matrices of numbers. (A matrix is a just rectangular grid of numbers laid out in rows and columns.) Such data structures turn out to be very important in many applications that require large amounts of computation, such as weather forecasting and linear programming. (See Chapter 9.) And, in fact, the supercomputers with the greatest raw number-crunching power today are probably SIMD computers working on such applications.

We can consider SIMD a special case of parallelism in which all the processors execute the same sequence of instructions. If we relax this restriction so that different processors can execute different instructions, we get MIMD. It is in this context that the idea of multiple processes makes the most sense, since each processing unit can execute a different process. MIMD is required for problems that are more like building a house than like rowing a boat, problems where there is a variety of very different tasks to be executed in parallel.

Distributed computing—where the processing units are in separate computers on a network—is a kind of MIMD. Even when the processors are in a single MIMD computer, the individual processors must be sophisticated enough to independently execute a sequence of instructions. So each processor is really an almost complete computer, and MIMD computers have more in common with computer networks than with SIMD computers.

10.2.2. Control and Communication. For any type of parallelism, there are issues of control and communication. How is it decided what should be done and when? How does information, such as the result of a computation, get from one processor to another? These questions can be answered partly in terms of the computer hardware itself, partly in terms of the program that the computer is running, and partly in terms of the operating system (the basic software that is always present on the computer and that manages its basic functions). In some sense, of course, the program controls everything that goes on in the computer, but it can only do this by using facilities provided by the hardware and the operating system.

First, let's look a little more closely at how a parallel computer might be physically put together. A parallel computer has much in common with a standard computer. Programs are executed by a circuit that reads instructions from memory and carries them out. In a SIMD computer, this is done by a single circuit that drives all the processors; in a MIMD computer, each processor has its own circuit. Two types of memory are possible: shared memory that can be used by all the processors, and internal memory in the individual processors; both types might be found in the same computer. Shared memory, as we have seen, provides one method of communication between processors, but it requires careful management because of the possibility of simultaneous access by several processors. Internal memory is generally simpler and faster, but when it is used exclusively some other method of communication must be provided. On the hardware level, communication is provided by a connecting wire through which data can be transmitted.

There are many different ways that a bunch of processors can be wired together to provide communication. The two most obvious are: (1) Connect all the processors in a chain where each processor communicates with two neighbors, or (2) Connect every possible pair of processors directly. (See Figure 10.2.) In the first case, data must be relayed from one processor to another along the chain of connections until it reaches its destination. Except when the number of processors is very small, this slows down communication unacceptably.[5] The second method provides the fastest possible communication, since any processor can freely communicate with any other at any time. Unfortunately, this method is also impractical when the number of processors is large, because of the extremely large number of wires required.

A compromise is to provide direct connections only between certain pairs of processors. Processors that are not connected directly can still communicate, but the data must be relayed through a series of processors along a chain of direct connections. One neat way of organizing the network of connections is called a *hypercube*.[6] In a hypercube, the number

---

[5] A similar simple solution would be to connect all the processors to the same wire, so that any processor can communicate with any other along this wire. This connection method is called a "bus." (See Chapter 5.) This method is also unacceptably slow for large numbers of processors because the bus is a shared resource: A processor that wants to transmit data must gain exclusive use of the wire, and all the other processors must wait until it has finished its transmission before they can do any communication. Note that this is similar to the problem of shared data, which was discussed above. Because of its simplicity, this communication method is used on many computer networks, such as the Ethernet and LocalTalk networks that are mentioned below.

[6] The structure of a connected network of processors or computers is called its *topology*, a term borrowed from mathematics. Thus, you will see the hypercube referred to as a "network topology." The term "hypercube" itself is also borrowed from mathematics. In a hypercube with eight processors, the

of processors must be a power of two, that is, 2^n for some number n. A small hypercube might contain eight or sixteen processors, but there are hypercube computers with as many as 65,536—that is, 2^{16}—processors. In a hypercube, there is a simple rule that decides which pairs of processors are connected. The processors are numbered 0, 1, 2, 3 ..., and the numbers are written out in the binary number system. Two processors are connected if their binary numbers differ in exactly one bit. For example, there is a connection between the processors numbered 1010_2 and 1110_2, since the only difference between the two numbers is the second bit from the left. Even though not all processors are directly connected in a hypercube, there is always a reasonably short chain of connections leading from one processor to any other. In fact, as you can easily check, in a hypercube with 2^n processors, the longest chain that is ever needed will contain only n processors. A hypercube with eight processors is illustrated in Figure 10.2.

It might seem that in order to control all this hardware, the operating system for a parallel computer would have to be much more complicated than one for a standard computer. And highly specialized computers might indeed require highly specialized operating systems. The fact is, though, that much of the support for parallel computing, at least of the MIMD variety, was built into operating systems before parallel computers were ever used. Recall that timesharing was invented to allow several users to use a computer at the same time. Each user has an associated process, and the computer gives each user a share of its time by switching rapidly from one process to another. It is the operating system that has the job of creating a process for each user who "logs on" to the computer, for terminating a user's process when that user "logs off," and for scheduling all the processes so that each gets a fair share of execution time. The operating system also contains facilities for managing access to resources that are shared by all the users, such as the computer's main memory and output devices such as printers.

A simple extension of the idea of timesharing for multiple users is to allow a single user to have more than one process. A user might create— that is, give a command to the operating system to create—a process

---

connecting wires can be thought of as the edges of an ordinary cube, as shown in Figure 10.2. For larger networks, the connections correspond to edges in cube-like objects that exist in "higher-dimensional spaces." But let's leave the metaphysics of extra dimensions to a math class. What we are interested in here is just the pattern of connections.

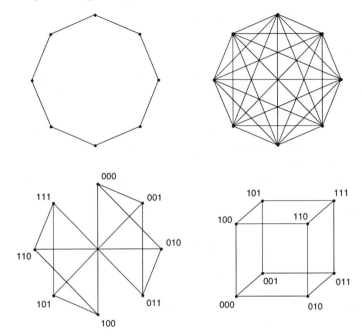

Figure 10.2. *Various ways of connecting eight processors so that they can all communicate. The processors are represented by small dots. On the top left, a single chain of connections includes all the processors. On the top right, there is a direct connection between every possible pair of processors. The bottom left shows a "hypercube." The processors in the hypercube are labeled with binary numbers from 000_2 to 111_2; two processors are connected if their binary numbers are the same except for exactly one bit. The picture on the bottom right is the same hypercube, with the nodes repositioned to show how the processors can be thought of as forming a cube.*

to handle a task such as printing a document while the user continues to work on something else. Or a user might run a program that creates several processes to handle different tasks. All this is so convenient that the capability to support multiple processes is now commonly found in operating systems meant for a single user.

The point, of course, is that it is not a great step from multiple processes sharing a single processing unit to multiple processes running on multiple processors. Some things do become more difficult; in particular, when several processes are *really* running at the same time, the management of shared resources such as memory requires greater care.

But the problems of creating, terminating, and scheduling processes for execution are not greatly changed. Even timesharing remains as an issue for the following simple reason: A multiprocessing computer has only a fixed number of processors. If more processes are created than there are processors available to execute them, then timesharing can be used to divide processing time fairly among them.

Many newer operating systems are designed to work with any number of processors, scheduling processes for execution on whatever processors are available. (See, for example, [Custer].) Adding more processors to a computer running such an operating system will speed it up by allowing more things to be done in parallel, but will not otherwise affect the way the computer is programmed or used. This is one strategy in the quest to produce ever-faster computers.

10.3. Computer Networks

The days of the isolated computer seem to be numbered. A computer today is likely to be just one of many *nodes* on a network. This is especially true for computers in business, educational, and governmental organizations. But it is increasingly true even for home computers, if only for the few hours a week that a home computer might be connected by telephone to a network.

It is true that networks do allow computers to cooperatively solve problems through distributed computing. But for most people, networks exist to allow them, not their computers, to communicate. A networked computer can provide some of the same functions as telephones, television, libraries, and the post office—and in the future it might well replace or merge with these services. This emergence of the computer as a *communication* tool is one of the surprises of the information age.

10.3.1. Protocols and Internets. Making a working computer network requires more than just laying down a wire and connecting some computers to it. First of all, there has to be an agreement about exactly *how* data will be transmitted. Such an agreement is called a *protocol.* A protocol is a specification of procedures to be followed for communication, such as the way that transmitted data will be represented or the method for specifying which machine on a network is to receive the data.

When computers communicate over a network, there are usually not just one but many protocols involved. Networks are complex things, and that complexity is handled—as usual—by multiple levels of structure.

Each level can have its own protocol, and protocols on higher levels build upon those on lower levels. From this point of view, a protocol is an interface to a black box. The protocol specifies the functions that must be implemented by the black box, but the details of that implementation are irrelevant from the point of view of the higher levels that use the protocol.

As an example, we consider some of the layers of protocols that are used in a typical network operation: transferring a data file from one computer to another. Let's assume that a person using one computer wants to copy a file from another computer, and that the method available for doing so is the high-level protocol called **FTP**, or File Transfer Protocol. FTP includes methods for opening a connection between two computers, for getting a list of files on the second machine, and for copying files from either machine to the other. Keep in mind that all these operations are implemented using lower-level protocols. But all that an FTP user sees is the set of commands needed to do file transfers.

FTP could be used on any network, provided that software is available that implements it on that network. But it is most closely associated with a network protocol called **TCP/IP**. TCP/IP is actually two protocols: the Transfer Control Protocol and the Internet Protocol. TCP works on a higher level than IP, and could in fact be used with a different low-level protocol. It is the job of TCP to get a collection of bits from one computer to another computer—more exactly, from a program running on one computer to a program running on the second. TCP knows nothing about the meaning of those bits; it is the job of the programs to interpret them. TCP also knows nothing about actually moving the data from machine to machine; that is the job of IP. The job of TCP is to supervise the transmission of a chunk of data and to make sure that it is received without error. (IP makes what is called a "best attempt" to deliver the data without error to its destination, but it is not guaranteed to succeed. TCP must detect any problems and fix them, for example, by retransmission.)

In our example, an FTP program takes a file (or a command or a list of file names) and delivers it as a sequence of bits to TCP. TCP then uses IP to transmit the bits. Since IP deals with "data packets" of a limited size, TCP will probably have to break the file into segments and have IP transmit the segments separately. The segments are received by IP software running on the second computer; they are passed on to TCP, which reassembles them into a single chunk of data and passes it on to FTP software which, finally, interprets it as a file being transmitted from the first computer.

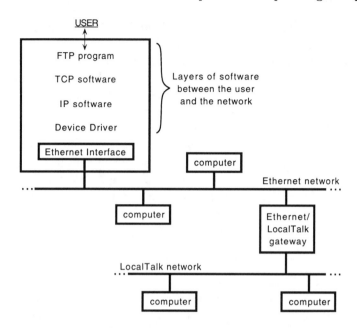

Figure 10.3. *Part of an internet—that is, a network formed by connecting two or more different kinds of networks together. Several computers are shown connected to an Ethernet network and a LocalTalk network, and the two networks are joined by a gateway. At the upper left is an expanded view of a computer, showing the interface that physically connects the computer to the net and several layers of software that might lie between the physical network and a person using the computer.*

This is already a complicated story, but it doesn't stop there. IP is not at the bottom level of complexity. IP has to use some kind of actual physical link, such as a wire, to transmit the data. There are at least two more levels here: On the bottommost level are the physical electric signals that represent the data and a ***physical transport protocol*** that specifies how such signals are to be sent; the physical transport protocol is implemented in a hardware interface device that connects a computer to a network. Finally, between IP and the physical hardware is at least one more level of software, a "device driver" that is used by IP to communicate with and control the network interface device.

On the physical level, there are a number of different types of network, each using a different protocol for data transmission. For example, Ethernet is one popular type of physical network. On an Ethernet network, several computers and other devices are connected to an Ethernet cable. Any computer on the cable can send data to any other, but only one computer can transmit at any given time. Because of this limitation, together with the fact that data can be reliably transmitted only over fairly short Ethernet cables, a single Ethernet network has to be fairly small—a few dozen machines at most. There are other types of networks, such as the LocalTalk networks that are often used by Macintosh computers, but all are limited to a fairly small number of machines.

Fortunately, it is possible to connect a number of small networks together to form a larger network. For example, two Ethernet networks can be connected by a *router*. The router has a connection to each network. When a computer on one network wants to send data to a computer on the other network, it sends the data to the router, which uses its connection to the second network to forward the data on to its specified destination.

It is often necessary to establish communication between two computers that are on completely different types of networks. It is possible to connect networks of different types with a *gateway*. A gateway between two networks has a separate connection to each network, and it runs software that allows it to understand the protocols used on both networks and to translate between them. This allows data to flow in both directions between the networks. The result of hooking up two or more networks with gateways is called an *internet*. The Internet Protocol, IP, is designed to get data from place to place across an internet, through as many routers and gateways as necessary. It is so effective at this that it can route data throughout the Internet (capital "I"), a world-wide TCP/IP internet that connects millions of computers on tens of thousands of individual networks.

A fragment of an internet (perhaps of the Internet?) is shown in Figure 10.3. This figure shows two networks, connected by a gateway. Any two computers on this internet can communicate, for example, to transfer files using FTP.

Each computer on an IP-based internet has an *IP address*, which is just a thirty-two bit number that must be different for every device on the internet. Every data packet handled by IP includes the address of the machine to which it is being sent. A computer that sends a data packet needs to know only the IP address of the destination. It does not need to know where the destination machine actually is physically—whether in the next room or in Paris—and it doesn't need to know the complicated path that the data packet must follow through the net to get to its destination. All that is handled by IP. All in all, IP is a great example of a "black box" that hides a lot of implementation detail behind a fairly simple interface. The same can be said about most of the hardware and software components that make the complexity of computer networks possible.

10.3.2. Distributed Computing. Networks provide the basis for distributed computing, in which processes running on several machines on a network cooperate in performing some task. The network is used as a black box for getting bits from one place to another, just as described above. But in this case, the bits sent from process to process represent the communication necessary for parallel processing.

In a sense, anything that involves two or more computers on a network is a type of distributed computing. For example, in an FTP file transfer, two processes—FTP software running on the two computers involved—cooperate to perform a task—copying a file from one computer to the other. The communication in this case consists of, first, a request for the file and, second, the file that is sent in response.

A similar model of communication can be used in more interesting examples of distributed processing: A process running on one machine sends some sort of request to a process on another machine and, possibly, gets back some sort of reply. This type of communication is called *message passing*. A message consists of a request to perform some task, along with whatever data is necessary for the task. When a process receives a message, it responds by executing the appropriate procedure. If that procedure generates some response, that response is sent back to the process that sent the original message.[7] Note that the process that sends the message does not necessarily have to wait, doing nothing, for a response; for real parallelism, it should go on working while the second process is handling the message.

The idea of message passing leads naturally to a form of distributed processing in which a "master" program on one machine sends messages to processes on other computers, asking them to perform various tasks.

---

[7] Distributed computing often uses a method called *remote procedure call* for communication. This is essentially the same as message passing. A process running on one machine calls a procedure (that is, a subroutine), but that procedure is actually executed on another computer. The parameters of the procedure can be used to transfer any data needed by the procedure and to return any result produced. This differs from message passing only in point of view: We might just as well say that one machine sends another the message, "Please execute such-and-such a procedure."

All these other processes just sit around waiting for incoming messages and responding to them as they come in. If a large computation can be broken down into independent tasks, the master program can hand off pieces of the computation to be done in parallel on other machines. For example, there is a method for computing realistic computer graphics images in which the color of each pixel in the image is computed separately. A program that wants to compute an image in this way can ask other machines on the network to work on different sets of pixels, and can then assemble the results returned by those machines into a complete picture. In fact, there are commercial computer graphics programs that work in just this way.

In a similar sort of application, we might imagine a small desktop computer connected to the same network as a supercomputer. The desktop computer might be able to handle most of its user's commands itself, but if the user tells it to perform some massive computation, it might send a message to the supercomputer asking it to perform the computation instead. The user might get back an answer in a matter of seconds instead of the days it would have taken the desktop computer to do the computation on its own. The resources of the supercomputer can be shared in this way by all the smaller computers on the network.

As a final example of distributed computing, I should mention *distributed databases*. A database is a collection of data, together with procedures for such operations as adding, deleting, and modifying data and searching through the data for specific information. In a distributed data base, data is spread over many computers on a network. For example, a bank might have several branch offices, and a network to connect the computers at the various branches. The bank could keep all its data on one large central computer, but if there are problems with that computer or with the network, all the branches will be cut off from the data they need to operate. If the bank uses a distributed database instead, each branch can keep its own data—such as information about the accounts of customers of that branch—on its own computer. The data, then, is closest to where it is needed most often and will be available unless that particular computer stops working. Yet, because of the network, the data can (if everything is working) be accessed from the other branches when it is needed.

To implement a distributed database, we might run a process on each computer to control the data on that computer. When a process needs to access data on another machine, it can do so by sending a message to the process on that machine. These processes might respond to messages such as, "Tell me Joe Smith's account balance," "Send me a list of customers with more than $10,000 in their accounts," and "Record a withdrawal of $100 from Mary Jones' account."

10.3.3. The Internet.   A bank's distributed database might be spread out over dozens of machines in several different cities or even in different states, and it would probably include many different kinds of financial information. This would probably be considered a fairly complex system. What, then, should we think of the Internet, with its millions of machines containing information on just about any topic you could name, and with very little overall control to keep things organized?

The Internet can, in theory, be used for distributed computing of any type, such as sending out pieces of a large computation to be done on a number of different machines. For example, in one research project, computers all over the Internet cooperated to help find the factors of a very large number.[8] But for most people, the Internet provides communication and information, both on a large scale. Here are some of the services you might find[9] on a computer connected to the Internet:

• *Electronic mail*, usually called e-mail, lets a user on one computer send a message to a specific user on another machine. The message will be waiting to be read the next time the recipient uses that machine.

• *USENET News* is a collection of several thousand "newsgroups," each dedicated to a different topic. The term "news" is misleading since a newsgroup is really a kind of bulletin board, where users can post messages to be read by anyone else on the Net who chooses to do so.

• *Telnet* allows a person using one computer to connect, through that computer, to another computer elsewhere on the Net. From my computer in New York State, for example, I can telnet to a computer at the Library of Congress in Washington DC, and then use that computer in exactly the same way as if I were accessing it directly. Ordinarily, before you can telnet to a computer, you need an account on that computer and a

---

[8] This might sound boring to nonmathematician, but factoring large numbers happens to be the way to break certain codes that are used to protect sensitive data. The people who use those codes are very interested in just how hard they are to break.

[9] "Might find," not "will find," because a service is available only if all the necessary software is available. This includes a program for you, as a user, to run. In addition, other software might be required to support communication protocols used by that program; without this support, the program will be useless.

password to identify yourself. But many places, such as the Library of Congress, have created public accounts that can be accessed by anyone.

• **FTP**, the file transfer protocol, was discussed above. *Anonymous FTP* is a common way of making information publicly available on the Internet. Like telnet, FTP ordinarily requires an account and a password. In anonymous FTP, files are made available in an account that anyone can access.

• *WWW*, the WorldWideWeb, is one of the newest and fastest growing information services on the Net. The Web consists of files on computers throughout the world. You can view these files with a "Web browser," a program that knows how to access files in the Web and display them on your screen. What makes the Web interesting is that a file can contain *links* to other files in the Web. With a Web browser, you can follow links from file to file until you find exactly the information that you want (or until you get thoroughly, but perhaps happily, lost).

The Internet has traditionally been difficult to use. New services such as WWW, and better interface software for old services like FTP, have begun to change that. And in the ocean of ASCII text that comprises most of the data on the Net, there are more and more islands of other types of information—such as pictures, sounds, and video—that require more storage space, more computational resources for processing, and faster network communication for transmission from place to place. So the Internet grows and changes. New computers and users come on line. Old, slower communication links are upgraded to fast links capable of carrying sound and video. New tools are introduced to make the Net easier for ordinary people to use.

We are seeing, perhaps, the beginnings of Cyberspace, the ultimate Net that would be a kind of alternate reality made of information— accessible through computers and built on layer upon layer of network protocols.

Chapter Summary

Several people working together on a large task can usually complete it more quickly than one person working alone. The same is true for computers. In *parallel processing*, several processing units work together on a problem. The processors might be part of a single *multiprocessing computer*, or they might be in separate computers on a *network*. The latter case is known as *distributed processing*.

Parallel processing is not appropriate for every problem. In some problems, each step depends on all the previous steps, and the only way to solve the problem is to perform all the steps in sequence. For many problems, however, there are subtasks that can be performed in parallel, and it is often easiest to program solutions to such problems in a language that supports *parallel programming abstractions*. Such language support the creations of multiple *processes*, and they provide some method of communication between processes, such as *shared variables* and *message passing*.

Processing units communicate by sending electric signals over wires. In a multiprocessing computer, you will probably find some elegant pattern of connections among the processors, such as the *hypercube topology*. Computer networks tend to be messier, often consisting of smaller networks connected by *routers* and *gateways*. Communication over these potentially messy networks involves multiple layers of *protocols*. High-level protocols, such as *FTP*, are used by people to perform meaningful communication such as copying a data file from one computer to another. High-level protocols use lower-level protocols such as *TCP* and *IP*, whose job it is to get bits from one place to another on a network.

The messiest network of them all—gloriously messy, you might say— is the *Internet*, a world-wide TCP/IP network. The Internet is a democratic sort of place, where anyone who wants to post information on the Net can have a voice. It is very different from broadcast services such as newspapers and television, where a central source sends out information to a large number of mostly passive recipients. There is a great debate going on right now over the nature of the universal information network that will probably arise in the near future. The question is: Will it be democratic and participatory in the spirit of the Internet, or will it just mean five hundred television channels in place of the forty or so we have now?

Questions

1. In Chapter 4, it was claimed that—except for considerations of memory and speed—all computers are equivalent in the problems they can solve. Does this apply to parallel processing? That is, are there problems that can be solved by multiprocessing computers that cannot be solved by traditional computers? Justify your answer.

2. Subsection 10.1.1 contained an example of three turtles adding 1, 2, and 3 to a variable *sum*, in parallel. In the absence of a **grab**

statement, it was claimed, the final value of *sum* could be any number between 1 and 6. It was explained how the final values 1, 2, and 3 could be obtained. Explain in detail how 4, 5, and 6 could be obtained as answers. While you are at it, explain in more detail the banking example from the end of Subsection 10.1.2, where it was claimed that, "Without mutual exclusion, it might happen that only $100 is effectively subtracted from your account, instead of the correct $200."

3. Distributed databases, implemented using message passing, were discussed at the end of Subsection 10.3.2. How is the mutual exclusion problem in Question 2 solved in such a distributed database? That is, what prevents two simultaneous $100 withdrawals from being incorrectly recorded?

4. The program in Figure 6.10 uses a **loop** to draw a sequence of nested squares. Write a program that uses parallel processing to draw the same picture. Each square should be drawn by a separate turtle.

5. The program in Figure 6.11 counts the number of steps it takes for a certain sequence, starting from an integer N, to reach 1. Consider the question, "What is the largest number of steps in the sequence for any starting number N between 1 and 100?" This question can be answered as follows: Declare a variable *max*, and set it equal to zero. Then, for each number N between 1 and 100, compute the sequence starting from N, and let *StepCount* be the number of steps in that sequence. If *StepCount* is greater than the current value of *max*, then change the value of *max* to *StepCount*. After all the numbers N have been processed, the value of *max* will be the number of steps in the longest sequence. Write an xTurtle program that uses parallel processing to implement this procedure. Part of your program can be copied from Figure 6.11. In order to work correctly, the program will need a **grab** statement.

6. In this chapter, message passing was discussed as a method of communication in distributed computing. The idea of messages also arose in Chapter 8, where it came up in connection with object-oriented programming. Review Subsection 8.3.1 and then discuss the possible relationship between object-oriented programming and distributed processing.

Chapter 11

Graphics

===========

COMPUTERS HAVE ALWAYS been good at numbers and words, numbers because they are built into the very structure of the machine, and words because letters can be so easily coded into numbers.

Images are another story. Although a picture can be easily represented as a long sequence of numbers giving the color of each pixel, those numbers don't represent the *things* in the picture. A computer can use the numbers to show the picture on its screen. But it can't perform operations such as "Delete the tree in the middle of the picture" in the same way that it could, for example, easily "Delete the third word in the sentence."

A human painter would be able to paint the tree out of the picture. There are *painting programs* that allow a computer user to interact with an image on the screen in much the same way that a painter interacts with a canvas. The computer plays a passive role, and the user does most of the work. Such programs are useful, but they are only one small aspect of *computer graphics*, which deals with all aspects of the composition and manipulation of images on a computer.

In a more sophisticated computer graphics program, the computer maintains a symbolic representation, or data structure, of the objects in a scene. The image that the computer displays is still just a bunch of colored pixels, but the image is only a way of *viewing* the symbolic representation. If the scene changes, and the representation is modified, then a new image can be computed and displayed.

With this sort of program, it is easy to remove a tree: Just remove the tree from the data structure and compute a new image. It is also easy to modify the image in other ways: by adding or moving an object, by viewing the image from a different point of view, or by changing *attributes* of objects, such as color and size. From here, it is a simple step to *computer animation*. Animated films are created by human artists by drawing each frame of the film by hand. In computer animation, the sequence of images is produced by a computer, with small changes in the scene from one image to the next.

In general, then, there are two stages in the production of computer graphics images. In the first stage, a representation is constructed of the scene which is to be displayed. The representation is sometimes called a *model*, and the process of creating it is known as *modeling*. The model is really a data structure, which contains information about the objects in the scene rather than the pixels on the computer's screen. In the second stage, the actual visual image of the scene is produced by the computer, based on the model that has been constructed. This process of computing an image from a symbolic representation is called *rendering*.

The quality of graphics and animations produced on computers has increased from simple line drawings in the 1960s to highly complex and realistic-looking images today. This can be attributed partly to increased computing power but mainly to intensive research into methods for producing such images. Later in this chapter, we will look at some of the newer techniques that this research has produced. But we will start with the basics.[1]

11.1. Mathematical Foundations

Most of the fundamental techniques of computer graphics are based in mathematics, especially in geometry. This foundation is often hidden from the users of computer graphics programs, but a real understanding of what those programs do requires some familiarity with the mathematical ideas on which they are based.

We will concentrate on the type of computer graphics where the goal is to produce an image of a scene containing a number of objects. The

---

[1] The material of this chapter is covered in greater detail in almost any textbook on computer graphics, such as the classic [Foley, *et al.*].

objects might be abstract geometric shapes such as spheres and cubes, or they might be real things like trees or chairs. But in fact, trees and chairs are too complicated for typical graphics programs to deal with directly. They must be broken down into simpler components, such as the trunk of a tree or the leg of a chair. Where does this decomposition end? With abstract geometric shapes! In many programs, for example, scenes must be composed (at least in the computer's internal representation) entirely of polygons.[2] Other programs might allow curved surfaces such as spheres. But in any case, look deeply enough and you will find geometry. In fact, the process of modeling a scene in a computer graphics program is sometimes referred to as "building a geometry."

In this section, we look at some of the geometric techniques for modeling scenes. We want to be able to deal with fairly complex scenes, and "deal with" here means not just rendering the scene but also building it in the first place and modifying it when necessary. The approach we use follows our general method for dealing with complexity, that is, building complex systems from simpler components that are used as black boxes, without regard to the details of their internal construction.

Suppose, for example, that a scene contains a chair. There are two things here that we should keep separate: the chair itself and the role that the chair plays in the scene. We start by building a description of the chair. The description is a model of a scene consisting of a single chair in some standard position and location. Once this chair-scene is in hand, we can use it as a component in a more complex scene by specifying things like the location, orientation, and size of the chair in the scene.

There are several advantages to this approach. Moving the chair is just a matter of specifying a new location for the chair-scene, rather than building a new chair from scratch in a different position. If the scene contains more than one chair, we can simply reuse the same basic chair-scene several times. And we get the conceptual advantages of having multiple levels of complexity: The chair itself is not a simple object. It consists of simpler components, such as a seat, a back, and four legs. These components might in turn be composed of polygons and simple curved surfaces. So, from simple components, we can build complex scenes without being overwhelmed by the details.

The basic operation here is to take a component—either a simple geometric shape or a model that has already been constructed—and specify

---

[2] A polygon is a flat geometric shape whose boundary is made up of straight line segments. Triangles and rectangles are examples.

its size, position, and orientation in a scene. There is a surprise here: Much of the emphasis in computer graphics is not on drawing things but on operations such as moving them, rotating them, and changing their size. These are mathematical operations which are usually called *transformations* or *geometric transformations*.

11.1.1. Transformations in Two Dimensions.

We start with two dimensions, that is, with flat figures that all lie in the same plane. The ideas we encounter in two dimensions generalize easily to the more realistic three-dimensional case. If we think of the plane as being the computer's screen, then each point in the plane can be assigned an x-coordinate, giving its horizontal position, and a y-coordinate, giving its vertical position. These numbers form a *coordinate system* on the plane. The point with coordinates $(0,0)$ is called the *origin* of the coordinate system. Usually, we will assume that the origin is at the center of the screen, although it wouldn't have to be. We used the same sort of coordinates in Chapter 6 for the xTurtle programming language.

When we want to model an object, we should think of it as being drawn in some conveniently chosen standard position. For example, the origin might be right at the center of the object. Or, if the object is a square, the origin might be at the lower-left corner. The object then can be modified to fit into a scene by applying transformations to it. Transformations that can be applied in two dimensions include *scaling*, *translation*, and *rotation*. Some examples are shown in Figure 11.1.

Scaling refers to a change in size. For example, scaling a one-by-three rectangle by a factor of two will result in a two-by-six rectangle. Mathematically, a figure in the plane can be scaled by a factor of s by multiplying each x-coordinate and each y-coordinate in the figure by the number s. So scaling can be identified with the equations:

$$x_{new} = s * x_{old}$$

$$y_{new} = s * y_{old}$$

where (x_{old}, y_{old}) indicates the coordinates of a point in the figure before the transformation is applied, and (x_{new}, y_{new}) indicates the coordinates of the corresponding point in the transformed figure. There is also a more general version of scaling in which a figure is scaled horizontally and vertically by different amounts. Scaling by a factor of two in the horizontal direction and by a factor of one-half in the vertical direction would transform a two-by-two square into a four-by-one rectangle. The equations for this transformation would be $x_{new} = 2 * x_{old}$ and $y_{new} = (1/2) * y_{old}$.

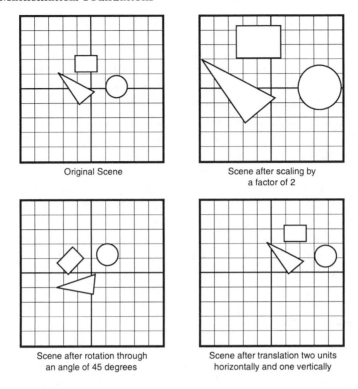

Original Scene

Scene after scaling by
a factor of 2

Scene after rotation through
an angle of 45 degrees

Scene after translation two units
horizontally and one vertically

Figure 11.1. *A simple two-dimensional scene, and the effect that three different transformations have on that scene. The scene consists of a triangle, a square, and a circle. The coordinate system is shown as a grid of lines.*

Translation refers to change in position. A translation by a units horizontally and b units vertically is accomplished by adding a to the x-coordinate and b to the y-coordinate of each point. This translation can be identified with the equations:

$$x_{new} = x_{old} + a$$
$$y_{new} = y_{old} + b$$

For example, a translation by 3 units horizontally and 2 units vertically simply displaces a figure three units to the right and 2 units up.

Rotation refers to changing the orientation of a figure by pivoting it about the origin. The amount of rotation is specified as the angle through which the figure pivots. It turns out that a rotation through θ degrees can also be identified with a pair of equations:

$$x_{new} = \cos(\theta) * x_{old} + \sin(\theta) * y_{old}$$
$$y_{new} = \cos(\theta) * y_{old} - \sin(\theta) * x_{old}$$

You don't need to know anything about the mathematical functions sin and cos, except that $\sin(\theta)$ and $\cos(\theta)$ are certain numbers that work. That is, applying these equations to all the points in a figure will rotate that figure by θ degrees around the origin. For example, if θ is 90 degrees, then $\cos(\theta)$ is 0 and $\sin(\theta)$ is 1. In this case, the equations for the transformation are $x_{new} = y_{old}$ and $y_{new} = -x_{old}$.

These are the basic transformations used in computer graphics. It is possible to apply a sequence of operations to an object, one after the other, to achieve the effect we want. We might start with a square centered at the origin, change its size with a scaling operation, then change its orientation with a rotation, and finally move it to a new position with a translation. The result of applying a sequence of transformations is also considered to be a transformation, and it has its own equations that can be computed easily from the equations of the transformations that go to make it up. Any transformation created in this way will have equations of the form:

$$x_{new} = a * x_{old} + b * y_{old} + c$$
$$y_{new} = d * x_{old} + e * y_{old} + f$$

for some set of numbers a, b, c, d, e, and f. Transformations of this form are called **affine transformations**. They play a central role in computer graphics. Figure 11.2 gives an example.

The point here is that an entire sequence of transformations can be accomplished in a single step, by applying the equations for the combined transformation. The operation of placing an object into a scene can always be computed using a single transformation, no matter how many transformations were originally used to specify its placement.

This is especially important when complex scenes are built up in several stages from simple components. Consider one of the legs on a chair that is itself just one of the objects in a complicated picture. (In this example, I am returning for the moment to three-dimensional space.) When the chair is constructed in its standard position, a transformation is used to specify the placement of the leg in the model of the chair. When the chair is used as part of a scene, another translation is applied to the chair as a whole. What about the leg, considered as a part of this final scene? Its placement is specified by a sequence of two transformations: one which places a leg into position on the chair, and a second that moves the chair (carrying the leg along with it, of course) into place. When the

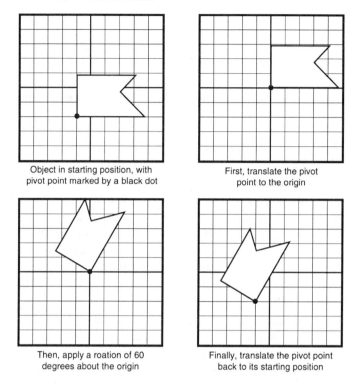

Object in starting position, with
pivot point marked by a black dot

First, translate the pivot
point to the origin

Then, apply a roation of 60
degrees about the origin

Finally, translate the pivot point
back to its starting position

Figure 11.2. *A sequence of three transformations can be used to rotate an object about the point $(-2, -1)$ instead of about $(0, 0)$. The combined transformation is given by a single pair of equations that can be computed from the equations of the component transformations.*

computer actually draws the leg, it can combine these transformations and compute the placement of the leg in a single step. Even if the chair is part of a dinette set which is part of a kitchen which is part of a house, the leg *still* only requires one transformation!

11.1.2. Animation. Transformations also turn out to be central in computer animation. A transformation changes the position, orientation, or size of an object *all at once*. To get an animation, all we have to do is change the object *a little at a time* and make an image of each step. Instead of moving an object three units to the right, we move it one-tenth unit, then another one-tenth, then another... for thirty steps. When the images are played back in rapid succession, the eye will perceive an object in continuous motion.

This step-by-step motion is easily accomplished mathematically. To make things simple, we assume that the changes take place at a constant rate (even though it might be more realistic for things to start slowly, speed up, and then slow down to a stop at the end). The placement of the object at each step is given as a transformation from its standard position. Let's suppose that we are given a transformation specifying its initial placement and another transformation specifying its final placement. Then, at every step in between, the placement of the object is given by an "interpolation," or weighted average, of the initial and final transformations.

Suppose that an object starts out rotated 30 degrees from its standard position and ends up rotated 100 degrees. Halfway through the process, its rotation is given by the average, $\frac{1}{2} \cdot 30 + \frac{1}{2} \cdot 100$ degrees. One-tenth of the way along, we would use the *weighted* average, $\frac{9}{10} \cdot 30 + \frac{1}{10} \cdot 100$ degrees, consisting of "nine parts out of ten initial position plus one part out of ten final position." A similar formula, $(1 - t) \cdot 30 + t \cdot 100$, applies to any fraction t between zero and one.

The same technique can be used to show an object in motion or changing in size. Combined motions, such as an object that rotates as it moves to the right, are no problem: We simply apply weighted averages of each of the component transformations. We can even deal neatly with animations of complex, structured scenes. Consider a bicycle moving along a road. The wheels of the bicycle are rotating and are also taking part in the overall motion of the bicycle. We can construct this scene by first creating a model of a rotating wheel; in this model, the wheel just sits in standard position, rotating about its center. Next, we build a model of the bicycle, incorporating a few rotating wheels. Finally, we apply a translation animation to the bicycle to set it in motion—the wheels will be carried along with it automatically!

11.1.3. Three-Dimensional Viewing.

In two dimensions, the position of a point is described by two numbers. To specify a point in three-dimensional space, we need one additional number. So, we just add a z-coordinate to the x- and y-coordinates used on a plane. Again thinking of the computer's screen as the plane, you can think of z as representing distance in front of the screen (or behind the screen if z is negative).

Translation and scaling work as you would expect in three dimensions. Three equations are required to specify a transformation instead of one, but the form of the equations is familiar. The equations for scaling

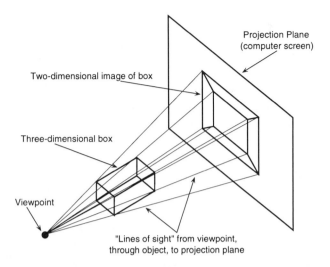

Figure 11.3. *Projecting a three-dimensional object onto a plane. Note that the cube is distorted by the projection. The side of the cube closest to the viewpoint is projected onto a larger square than the far side of the cube. This distortion is called "perspective," and it is one of the ways by which images of three-dimensional scenes are made to look realistic.*

by a factor of s, for example, become: $x_{new} = s * x_{old}$, $y_{new} = s * y_{old}$, and $z_{new} = s * z_{old}$. Rotation in three dimensions comes with a slight twist: When a solid object, such as the earth or a spinning top, rotates, it has an **axis of rotation**, a line that stays fixed while the object rotates around it. When a figure rotates in two dimensions, it rotates around a single fixed *point*. The repertoire of three-dimensional transformations includes rotations about the x-axis (the horizontal line running across the screen through the origin), or about the y-axis (the vertical line through the origin), or about the z-axis (a line pointing from the origin directly out of the screen). Rotations about other lines are possible, but they can be built up out of these three basic rotations plus some translations.

Complex scenes and animations can be handled in exactly the same way in three dimensions as in two—there are just a few more numbers to play with. There is one big area of difference, though: the matter of getting an image of the scene onto the computer's screen. It's easy to draw a two-dimensional scene on a two-dimensional screen. A three-dimensional scene, on the other hand, has to be *projected* onto the screen.[3] See Figure 11.3.

The projected image is essentially what would be seen by a camera located at some point in space. That point is called the *viewpoint* or the *center of projection*. In order to determine what image would actually be recorded by the camera, we must also specify what direction the camera is pointing and how the camera is oriented (since the camera will record a different image if it is tilted or turned upside-down).

It is useful to think of the camera that is viewing the scene as part of our model of the scene. Moving the camera, tilting it, or pointing it in a different direction will give a different image. We can even have animations in which the camera moves, imitating a movie where the camera pans in for a close-up or a film shot from the window of a moving airplane.

In this section, you have learned enough about computer graphics and animations to appreciate the geometry involved. The next time you see an advertisement with three-dimensional letters flying across the screen, you can imagine how those letters were assembled from polygons, how they were translated and rotated into position, and how they were set into motion by applying a sequence of transformations or by floating an imaginary camera through a mathematical model of the scene.

This is, however, only part of the story. Once the geometry of a model has been set up, there is still the matter of making the image produced from it look realistic. This is the topic of the next section.

11.2. Realistic Images

The abstract geometric framework of a scene can be visualized as a *wireframe model*, a simple representation which shows only the edges of the polygons in the model. Wireframe models show the shapes and positions of objects in a scene. They can be computed and drawn very quickly on a computer screen, and most computer graphics programs allow the user to preview graphics images and animations in this form.

---

[3] Projection in computer graphics is an imitation of what happens when you look at an object: The object is projected onto the two-dimensional retinas in your eyes. In effect, each of your eyes registers a two-dimensional image, and your brain reconstructs an impression of a three-dimensional world from those images.

For a realistic image, though, a wireframe model must be fleshed out with things like color, surface textures, and lighting effects.

For such images, we need to add more information to the model. When the images are rendered, a lot of computation is required to take all this information into account. It is not unusual for a computer to take several hours to render a single high-quality image, or several days for a few seconds of animation.

11.2.1. Object Attributes. Suppose we have a scene consisting of a single cube. The geometric information in the model tells us how large the cube is, how it is oriented in space, and from what point it is being viewed. This is enough to make a simple line drawing of the edges of the cube, but for a realistic image we need need information about the properties of the cube that determine its visual appearance. Such *attributes* of objects are stored, along with the geometric information, as part of the model of a scene.

In the simplest case, an object has a single, uniform color. Even this is not as simple as it sounds, because color turns out to be subtle thing. When light strikes an object, it can be either reflected or absorbed—it is the reflected light that we see when we look at the object. Light comes in various colors, ordinary white light being a combination of all colors. An object will be seen as red, for example, if it tends to reflect red light and absorb light of other colors. As it turns out, we can get an adequate representation of the color of an object by specifying just three numbers: the percentage of red light that it reflects, the percentage of green light, and the percentage of blue light. (This explains why, if you magnify the screen of a color television, you will see that it is made of red, blue, and green dots.)

This is still not enough to distinguish between the shiny red of a new car and the dull red of an old brick. This difference can be modeled by distinguishing between two different types of reflection: *specular reflection* and *diffuse reflection*. In specular reflection, a ray of light bounces off an object just as a thrown ball bounces off a wall. Diffuse reflection is more like a water balloon, which bursts on the wall and splatters in all directions. The diffuse reflection from an object is visible from all directions, but a specularly reflected light ray is visible only from a certain angle.

When you are driving and are blinded by the sun glinting off a red sportscar in front of you, it is because you are seeing the specular reflection of the sun's rays. You can still see the rest of the sportscar—the parts that are not in the right position to reflect the sun's rays directly to your eyes—because the car also reflects some light diffusely. A mirror reflects essentially all of the light that hits it specularly. (The word "specular" comes from the Latin word for mirror.) A red brick reflects very little light specularly; it reflects some incoming red light diffusely, and it absorbs the rest of the light that hits it. A red car reflects some red light diffusely, but it also reflects a lot of the incoming light specularly.

We see, then, that we need six numbers to describe the color of an object: the percentages of red, green, and blue light that it reflects specularly and diffusely. It might be, of course, that different parts of an object are different colors, so that we should allow models in which each polygon in the model has its own associated color data.

Such models are adequate for many purposes, but they tend to produce images with a plastic or metallic look—in fact the classic look of computer graphics and animation. Real objects often have distinctive surface textures which arise from variation in color, such as the patterns seen in woodgrain or granite (or for that matter in a photograph of the Statue of Liberty). In computer graphics, texture can be achieved by applying a *texture map* to a surface. A texture map is simply an image of any kind, represented as a grid of pixel colors. A woodgrain texture map, for example, could be obtained by "scanning" a photograph of an actual piece of wood into the computer. This could be considered cheating, since we are making realistic computer graphics images by using images of real objects, but the process of applying the map—stretching it, rotating it, transforming it to fit onto the surface—still requires a lot of computer processing.

Textures can also arise from small variations from perfect smoothness, such as the bumps on the skin of an orange or the weave of threads in a piece of cloth. This type of texture can be simulated by a *bump function*, which specifies small changes in the orientation of a surface from point to point.

One further object attribute that we might add to our repertoire is *transparency*. Instead of being reflected or absorbed, it is possible for light hitting an object to be transmitted through it. A sheet of glass transmits most of the light that hits it, although some of the light is reflected specularly. Dirty glass would have some diffuse reflection as well, and colored glass would transmit different colors of light to different degrees. Besides all this, there is the fact that a ray of light changes direction when it passes from one medium, such as air, into another, such as glass. This bending of light rays should be taken into account when an image is rendered.

11.2.2. Lighting. Adding attributes such as color, texture, and transparency to the geometric model of an object produces a realistic description of the object itself, but does not determine how the object will actually appear in an image. For that, we need to know about the environment in which the object appears, starting with the lighting conditions. An object looks different when direct sunlight is falling on it than it does on a dim, cloudy day. It would look different again if it were illuminated with a red spotlight.

The model of a scene will have to include information about any light sources. The easiest types of light sources to deal with are *point sources* and *directional sources*. In a point source, all the light radiates out from a single point; this is a reasonable model of a small light bulb. A directional source is one that, like the sun, is so far away that all the light rays from it are effectively parallel. *Extended light sources*, such as a long fluorescent light, are generally dealt with only by advanced rendering techniques such as those discussed at the end of this section.

Besides position or direction, we need to know the intensity, or brightness, of each light source. We allow for the possibility of colored lights by specifying a separate intensity for red, for green, and for blue.

Finally, a model should include *ambient light*—once again given as separate intensities for red, green, and blue—which represents some general level of light that comes from no particular source and that illuminates everything in the scene uniformly. Ambient lighting can be used to approximate the light of a cloudy day. It can also be thought of as including light that has reflected and re-reflected from so many surfaces that it has become impossible to keep track of its original source. Note that without ambient light, shadows would be absolutely black.

11.2.3. Rendering. So far, we have been talking only about constructing a model of a scene. In practice, this construction is generally done by a person with the aid of a computer program. That program provides the user with a method for defining and positioning objects, setting their color, specifying what texture maps are to be applied, and so forth. The method can be as simple as a specialized language for describing scenes, or as fancy as a graphical user interface in which the user can build and manipulate the objects on screen. In any case, once the scene is set up, it is up to the computer to render an image of it, as it would be seen by a viewer at some specified viewpoint.

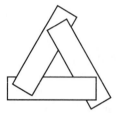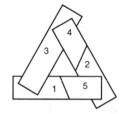

Figure 11.4. *The figure at left is supposed to show three rectangles arranged in space (not flat on the page) so that the first covers part of the second, the second part of the third, and the third part of the first. On the right, two of the rectangles have been subdivided, producing a total of five polygons. These five polygon can be drawn from "back to front" in the order indicated.*

Let's assume that the model is one in which everything is built up, ultimately, from polygons.[4] Rendering the image is not a simple matter of drawing all the polygons. First of all, only some of the polygons are visible from the viewpoint. Some are wholly or partly obscured from view by other objects, while others are not visible simply because they are on the back sides of objects as seen from the viewpoint. These unseen parts of objects are called **hidden surfaces**. The problem is to make sure that the hidden surfaces are not, in fact, shown in the rendered image.

Polygons on the back sides of objects are not a real problem, since it is possible to keep track of which way each polygon is facing and to avoid drawing those that face away from the viewpoint. The **painter's algorithm** is one way of handling the surfaces that are hidden from view by other objects. A painter might paint a mountain in the background and a house in front of it; when the house is painted, it simply covers up the part of the mountain that is hidden behind it. It doesn't matter that the hidden part of the mountain was drawn—except for the waste of paint and effort—because it doesn't appear in the final image.

When applied to computer graphics, the painter's algorithm says to draw the polygons from back to front, starting with those farthest away from the viewpoint and working gradually forward from there. Unfortunately, some strange things can happen because the polygons

---

[4] A curved surface can be approximated by a large number of small polygons. Some computer graphics models can include curved surfaces of certain types, but the basic ideas are still the same as those I cover here.

can be tilted into any orientation in space. For example, it is possible for a scene to contain three polygons where the first covers part of the second, the second covers part of the third, and the third in turn covers part of the first. (See Figure 11.4.) There is no place to start the painter's algorithm in this case, since no one of the polygons can be said to be in back of the other two. Fortunately, there is a simple fix. It is always possible to divide some of the polygons in a scene into smaller polygons to make the painter's algorithm apply.[5]

It is sort of wasteful to do all the rendering computations for a polygon that is just going to be painted over by another polygon that lies in front of it in the scene. It is possible to determine which polygons are actually visible from the viewpoint, and to render only those. (This determination can be done by applying the painter's algorithm mathematically, without actually rendering the polygons.) Polygons that are partly visible and partly hidden can be further subdivided so that only the visible parts will be rendered.

This method of dealing with hidden surfaces can also be used to deal with shadows in an image. A light source does not illuminate everything in a scene, because some objects lie in the shadows cast by other objects. But the objects that are illuminated are precisely those that would be visible to a viewer at the position of the light source. Everything else is in shadow. So, solving the "shadow problem" for a light source turns out to be the same as solving the hidden surface problem from the point of view of the light source.

So finally the time comes to actually render the polygons that will make up the image. Let's concentrate on some one particular polygon. Our problem is to compute a color for each of the pixels that make up the

---

[5] There is a procedure for deciding how to subdivide polygons. Pick any polygon. That polygon lies in some plane—an infinite sheet dividing space in two. The painter's algorithm says that we should draw everything that is behind the sheet, then draw the polygon that lies on the sheet, then draw everything that is in front of the sheet. A problem arises when some polygon is cut by the sheet, and lies partly in front of it and partly behind it. The solution is obvious: whenever this happens, divide the polygon into two pieces, the part lying in front of the sheet and the part lying behind. Now, doing this for one particular sheet does not completely solve the original problem of drawing the scene, but it does divide the problem into two smaller problems: drawing the part of the scene that lies behind the sheet, and drawing the part in front of the sheet. If necessary, we can attack each of these smaller problems in the same way, by choosing a polygon and using it to further divide the scene. (This is, in fact, a recursive procedure. See Section 7.3.)

image of the polygon. We know which light sources, if any, illuminate it, and we know the general level of ambient lighting in the scene. We have information about the color of the polygon—more exactly about its diffuse and specular reflection of light of various colors. (Or, alternatively, we have a texture to be mapped onto the polygon, effectively a different color at each point.) To this we can add one further item of information: the orientation of the polygon in space. This is needed to compute the amount of light that is reflected specularly in the direction of the viewer.

From all this information about light sources and the reflective properties of the polygon, we can compute a color for each pixel. The colors of different pixels can be different for two reasons. First of all, the intensity of illumination from a light source depends on distance from that light source, and different parts of a polygon will generally be at different distances from a given light source. Second, specular reflection of a light source is seen only near those points where the angles between viewpoint, surface, and light source are just right.

The exact color at a given point on the polygon can be computed as the sum of the light reflected diffusely from that point, plus the light reflected specularly from that point in the direction of the viewpoint. And the amount of reflected light depends on the incoming light (ambient lighting plus light from any light source that illuminates the polygon), together with the intrinsic attributes of the polygon that determine how much of the incoming light is reflected. Whew!

Because it takes a lot of computation to do these calculations for each pixel, a compromise is often made between rendering time and quality of image. A low-quality image can be rendered fairly quickly if the same color is used for every pixel in the polygon. The color to be used can be computed, for example, by computing the true color of just one sample point in the middle of the polygon. This method is referred to as *constant shading*.

A step up in quality is obtained by computing the true color at each of the vertices of the polygon, and then computing colors at other points in the polygon as weighted averages of the vertex colors. Using this method, known as *Gouraud shading*, the computer has to calculate a different average for each pixel in the polygon, but this computation still takes a lot less time than the complicated calculation needed to determine the true color. Often, the flat polygons in a model are only approximations for curved surfaces. Gouraud shading does not deal very well with this curvature. Another polygon shading method, *Phong shading*, uses a more sophisticated averaging of vertex information to take surface curvature into account—but, of course, this is done at the cost of still more computation time.

And so, after all the polygons have been rendered, we have an image. You should have noticed that at each step along the way there was approximation and compromise. Few objects are really made of geometrically flat polygons. Light is not really made up of just three colors. Light sources are not really points. Diffuse and specular reflection are not so neatly separated in reality as they are in our model. In spite of all this, the methods discussed here can produce fairly realistic images of certain types of scenes.

Furthermore, we should consider that realism is not always a goal of computer graphics. When an image is created of a building that does not yet exist, a crude plastic-looking rendering is good enough to convey the structure of the building and to help spot any problems. When a chemist makes an animation of two molecules undergoing a chemical reaction, visual realism is not an issue—realistically, molecules are too small to see! And for the artist, of course, computer graphics is a medium that, like any medium, has its own look with whatever advantages and disadvantages that implies.

11.2.4. Ray Tracing and Radiosity. Rendering of the type discussed in the previous section can be thought of as the "classic" approach to computer graphics. After some preprocessing to deal with hidden surfaces and shadows, polygons are rendered into the image one by one. Two other rendering methods, *ray tracing* and *radiosity*, take a more global approach and can often produce higher quality images (at the cost of greatly increased computation time).

Standard rendering uses a fairly simple model of the way light behaves. It assumes a background of uniform ambient illumination, plus light from point and directional sources. Light from these sources is essentially tracked until it hits an object; whatever fraction of it is reflected from the object is assumed to become part of the ambient illumination. Both radiosity and ray-tracing are, at least partly, attempts to track that light through multiple reflections—with radiosity concentrating on diffuse reflection and ray-tracing on specular reflection. In addition, each method can deal with aspects of reality that are handled poorly or not at all by classic rendering. Ray-tracing has no problem with transparent objects or with the reflection of one object in another. Radiosity can deal with extended light sources, such as long fluorescent lights and brightly illuminated windows. It is even possible to use a combination of the two techniques to get the advantages of both; some of the highest quality computer graphics images have been produced in this way.

To understand ray-tracing, you should imagine a set of objects lying behind a transparent computer screen. Consider one of the pixels on the screen. The problem is to determine what you will see at that pixel. In ray-tracing, this is computed by following a ray of light backwards from your eye, through the pixel, until it hits some object in the scene. This tells you what object is visible at that pixel. Now the question is, what color will be seen at that point?

To determine this, we continue tracing the light that hit your eye backwards to the time *before* it left the object. Part of this light is reflection of ambient light, and since that comes from all directions, we just take it into account without worrying about where it came from. Another part of the light is specular reflection, which comes only from a specific direction. We trace a ray back in that direction to see where it came from. The color of that incoming ray depends on what we find at its source. If the object is transparent, another contribution is made by a light ray transmitted through the object from its far side. Again, we follow this transmitted ray back to its source to discover its color. Finally, part of the light can come from light sources that illuminate the object. To check on this part, we follow a ray from the object in the direction of each light source. If that ray hits something before it gets to the light source, then the object is in shadow; otherwise, we add in the contribution from that source. The final color that is seen at a point depends on all these incoming rays, together with the intrinsic attributes of the objects.

Something interesting happens when we trace a specularly reflected ray, or a ray transmitted through a transparent object. When we find the source of that ray, we need to know its color. But this is the same problem we started with: find the color of a light ray emitted from an object in a particular direction. To find the color, we could apply the same technique again, following the ray back even further in time. Of course, we have to put some limit on how far back we are willing to look, but it is this ability to track multiple reflections that gives ray-tracing its power.

The main point of radiosity is to replace the mysterious ambient light that we have used in our models with something more realistic. Whereas ray-tracing starts with the pixels in an image, radiosity starts from the objects in the scene. The objects in this case can include light sources, which are treated in exactly the same way as other objects. The term "radiosity" refers to the rate at which light leaves a surface. It can be thought of as the color that you would see when you look at the surface. This can include light emitted by the surface, as well as light from other sources that it reflects.

Think of a scene made up of a large number of small polygons, and consider one of those polygons. Light radiation is constantly arriving at and departing from the surface of the polygon. The amount departing must be equal to the amount that arrives, minus the part of the incoming radiation that is absorbed by the polygon, plus—if the polygon is part of a light source—any radiation that is emitted by the polygon.[6] This gives a mathematical equation: "Outgoing radiation = Incoming radiation." We get one such equation for each polygon. The incoming radiation can be written as a formula involving the outgoing radiation from all the other polygons in the scene (as well as some factors that depend on the geometry of the scene). Then the only unknown quantities in the equations are the levels of outgoing radiation for all the polygons in the scene. All we have to do is set up this huge set of equations and solve them for these values! The answers that we get are the colors we need when we render the objects.[7] However, since radiosity does not take into account the *direction* in which light is reflected from objects, it does not deal well with specular reflection. For a scene in which specular reflection is important, it can be added in by a second round of computation using ray-tracing techniques.

*   *   *

This chapter has not covered all of computer graphics, by any means, but it does contain an overview of many of the fundamental ideas in the field. Beyond these fundamentals lies a world of applications in which computer graphics and animation play important roles.

Images and animations—computer generated or otherwise—can be combined with sound and text to make **multimedia** presentations that can be viewed on a computer. The idea is that some types of information

---

[6] This is not always true. It is not true, for example, for the fraction of a second after you turn on a light bulb in a room. However, unless the lighting of the scene is changing very rapidly, it is at least approximately true.

[7] In practice, only approximate solutions are found, and even for that the amount of computation that has to be done is very large. Better approximations essentially take into account more levels of reflection and re-reflection of light.

can be most effectively conveyed using a combination of media, instead
of through words alone.

Our impression of a three-dimensional world arises to a large extent
from the fact that we have two eyes, and each eye sees the world from a
slightly different viewpoint. A realistic three-dimensional effect can be
achieved with computer graphics by rendering two *stereoscopic views*
of a scene—one showing the scene from the viewpoint of the left eye
and one from the viewpoint of the right eye. The two images must be
viewed with some sort of apparatus that will present one image to each
eye of the viewer, such as a headset that holds a separate small computer
screen in front of each eye.

When we build a model for computer graphics, we create a mathematical representation of some real or made up scene. We then choose a
viewpoint and render the scene as it would appear from that viewpoint.
Now, there is nothing to stop the viewpoint from being *inside* the scene.
Imagine a person wandering through the scene, looking around in different directions. We could easily render a series of stereoscopic views that
show just what that person would see, and play those views back as an
animation on a headset. In fact, if we can compute fast enough, we can
render each view and show it on the headset at the same moment that
the person is seeing it. We could use some sort of sensor to determine
where the person is looking, so that we can get the view just right. And
then. . . why not let this person we are imagining wear the headset!

This is the basic idea behind *virtual reality*. In fact, of course, it is
the person who is real and the scene that is a mathematical simulation.
But we can track the movements of a real person, construct a continuously changing image of the scene as it would be seen if it were real, and
display that image on a headset. The person experiences the scene as it
would appear if it were real (within the limitations of computer graphics,
of course). Virtual reality can include other senses besides vision, and
the long-term goal is to immerse the user in a complete virtual world,
indistinguishable from "real reality." This would surely be the ultimate
user interface!

Chapter Summary

Computer graphics images are produced in two stages, *modeling* and
rendering. A model of a scene is a data structure containing geometric
information about the sizes, shapes, and positions of objects in the scene,

and about *attributes* of the objects such as color and surface *texture*. In the rendering phase, an image is computed that shows the scene as it would appear from some chosen *viewpoint*.

The geometry of a model can be constructed from simple components, such as polygons, using *geometric transformations* to specify the placement of each component in the scene. The basic geometric transformations include *scaling*, *translation*, and *rotation*. Complex scenes can be constructed using *hierarchical models*, in which objects built from simple components can themselves be used as components in more complex scenes. Computer *animation* can be created by applying a series of small transformations and rendering an image of each step.

When an image of a three-dimensional scene is rendered, the computer must take into account illumination from any *light sources* in the model and from *ambient light*. It must ensure that *hidden surfaces* in the model do not appear in the image. The *painter's algorithm* is one approach to the problem of hidden surfaces. A similar technique allows the computer to take into account *shadows* cast by objects in the scene.

When the time comes to render a polygon, its appearance should be determined pixel by pixel using all the information available. Since this requires so much computation, approximate methods such as *constant shading*, *Gouraud shading*, and *Phong shading* often are used instead.

The alternative rendering methods *ray-tracing* and *radiosity* are used to produce very-high-quality computer graphics images. These methods achieve greater realism by taking into account multiple levels of reflection and re-reflection of light in a scene.

Questions

1. This question is about building a model of a two-dimensional scene from basic components and geometric transformations. Suppose that you have three types of basic components to work with: a line segment extending from the point $(-\frac{1}{2}, 0)$ to $(\frac{1}{2}, 0)$, a circle of diameter 1 with its center at the origin, and a one-by-one square centered at the origin. For geometric transformations, you have rotation, scaling, and translation. Given all this, how would you build a "wheel" like that shown in Figure 11.5? (What are the basic components you would use? What transformations would you use to arrange them into a model of the wheel?) Once you have invented the wheel, how could you make the simple wagon shown in Figure 11.5?

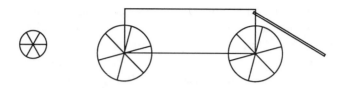

Figure 11.5. *A "wheel" and a "wagon" for use in Question 1. You can assume that the wheel on the left has diameter 1 and that the two identical wheels on the wagon have diameter 2. (From this, you can approximate the sizes of the body and the handle of the wagon.)*

2. Discuss the similarities between writing a computer program and building a model of a complex scene for computer graphics. In particular, compare the role of subroutines in programming to sub-scenes in model-building. (A **scene description language** is a language used to give formal specifications of scenes for use by computer graphics programs. If you are feeling ambitious, try to devise a simple scene description language that would allow you to specify scenes like those in Question 1. Your language will probably be very much like a programming language in some ways.)

3. When you apply a scaling transformation to an object centered at the origin, it just gets bigger (or smaller). When the object is not at the origin, it also moves farther from (or closer to) the origin. This effect can be seen in Figure 11.1. Why does this happen? Suppose that some object is centered at the point (3,5) and that you would like to increase its size by a factor of 2, *without moving its center*. What sequence of transformations could you use to do this? (Hint: See Figure 11.2, which shows how rotation about a point other than the origin can be performed by a sequence of basic transformations.)

4. I have said that objects in computer graphics images often look plastic or metallic. What are the properties of plastic and metallic surfaces that allow them to be represented so well in computer graphics images? And what is it—in terms of the object attributes discussed in this chapter—that makes plastic and metal appear different in such images?

5. Ray-tracing is a *recursive* procedure. Where does the recursion come into it? (If necessary, review the definition of recursion in Section 7.3.)

Chapter 12

Artificial Intelligence

SOMETIMES, SITTING IN FRONT of a computer, it is hard to avoid the feeling that we—we humans—are no longer alone in the world. The computer is responsive. It often seems to have goals and motivations. It can use logic and solve problems. And at times, it seems deliberately obstinate.

We know that this appearance is a kind of illusion. Deep down inside, at the bottom of multiple layers of complexity, all that is going on inside the computer is the purely mechanical, purely automatic manipulation of bits. But we really know very little about what goes on deep down inside *ourselves*. How can we be sure that we are really fundamentally different from our machines?

I do not believe that today's computers running today's programs can be called "intelligent" in the usual sense of the term. Although they are complex, their complexity is well within our comprehension. We can see the tricks on which the illusion is built, and we can pretty much locate whatever cleverness our machines display in the humans who build and program them.

But how much confidence should we have that this situation will continue? As we learn more about the "tricks" used by the human mind, and as we teach new tricks to newer, more complex machines, will there come a time when the illusion of machine intelligence and the reality of human intelligence become indistinguishable? If our creations awaken to true intelligence, how will we even know?

In 1950, Alan Turing, the inventor of Turing machines, published an article called "Computing Machinery and Intelligence." In it, he proposed a way of testing machines for intelligence. This test has come to be known as the Turing Test. Although it is not accepted by everyone, no one has come up with any obviously better, general method for testing a computer for intelligence.

Turing proposed a game to be played by a computer and a human, with a second human as a judge. The judge and the two players are all in separate rooms. Without knowing which player is which, the judge communicates with the players by typing questions into a computer terminal and getting back typewritten answers. After some time, the judge is required to make a determination as to which of the players is a computer and which is human. The task of the computer is to try to fool the judge. If a computer, playing with a variety of opponents and judges, manages to fool the judge as often as not, then the computer passes the Turing Test.[1]

No limits are put on the questions the judge can ask, or on the strategies that the players can employ. To fool the judge, the computer would need wide-ranging knowledge about the world and about human interaction. It would have to understand the incredible intricacies of human language, with its ambiguities, metaphors, puns, sarcasm, and poetry. It would have to dissemble about its own ability to calculate faster than any human could.

Words like "knowledge," "understand," and "dissemble" would not ordinarily be used to describe a machine (except as metaphor!), but they would be hard to avoid in the case of a machine that could pass itself off as human. You might argue that the computer, whatever the appearance, is still a machine executing a program, with no more choice or feeling than a rock rolling down a hill—and no more alive or intelligent. But could you really stay convinced of that if the computer displayed all the resourcefulness, wit, and empathy of a good friend or respected teacher?

---

[1] This is the test as it is most often stated, but it is not exactly what Turing proposed. Turing first described a game played by a man and a woman. The man would pretend to be a woman, and the judge would try to determine which was which. The game between a machine and a human is then a variation of the man/woman game. Turing would say that the machine is intelligent if it could win playing against a human as often as a man could win playing against a woman. However, interestingly, Turing did not prejudge how often that would be.

For the moment, the idea of such a machine is fantasy, and there is no real evidence that standard bit-pushing, instruction-following computers will ever achieve such intelligence. The research that goes under the name "artificial intelligence" has, for the most part, more immediate and limited goals. But always present in the background, most often unspoken and sometimes even denied, is the quest to create thinking machines that will equal or exceed our own intellectual abilities.

12.1. Good Old-fashioned Artificial Intelligence

One common definition of *artificial intelligence*, or *AI*, says that it is the attempt to program computers to perform tasks that, when performed by humans, would generally be acknowledged to require intelligence. This definition captures only one aspect of a term whose full meaning draws on all the many connotations of the words "artificial" and "intelligence," as well as a long history of artificial creatures in mythology and literature,[2] but it does have several advantages. First of all, it does not prejudge whether the computer will be a true, man-made (one meaning of "artificial") intelligence or merely a simulation (another meaning). Second, it allows us to talk about degrees of intelligence; a computer that is only somewhat intelligent or that captures only some small aspect of human intelligence would nevertheless qualify as AI.

Finally, this definition focuses attention on standard computers and computer programs, which have played the dominant role in the history of AI. As we will see later, some other approaches to machine intelligence are becoming important, but in this section I will restrict attention to traditional, mainstream AI research—what the philosopher John Haugland has called *Good Old-Fashioned Artificial Intelligence*, or GOFAI.

Artificial intelligence was given its name by John McCarthy—the inventor of the programming language LISP—at a conference held at Dartmouth College in the summer of 1956. A number of researchers had already recognized the ability of computers to do more than crunch numbers and had begun to work on ways to program them to display

---

[2] Such as the Pygmalion myth, the story of the Golem, and the novel *Frankenstein*. See the first chapter of [McCorduck]. By the way, the subtlety of meaning and the multiplicity of connotation of almost any term in a language like English indicates the difficulty of programming a computer to pass the Turing Test, and explains why Turing chose language use as a test for general intelligence.

intelligence. The Dartmouth conference brought together many of these early researchers, and it marked the beginning of AI as a recognized scientific field.

Since its inception at the Dartmouth conference, AI has gone through several periods of great optimism as new techniques were discovered and programs displaying new types of intelligent behavior were created. In each case, though, the limitations of the new techniques soon became apparent and the optimism faded. Some critics of the AI enterprise claim that the fundamental assumptions of the field are flawed and that there will never be any breakthrough to true artificial intelligence. AI supporters, on the other hand, point out that in spite of the setbacks, significant progress has been made. I will describe some of that progress in this section and leave a discussion of the criticisms of AI to the following section.[3]

12.1.1. The Physical Symbol System Hypothesis. The basic claim of GOFAI can be simply stated: Intelligence is based on the very sort of activity that goes on inside a computer. That activity, which is usually called computation, is to be seen in this context as *symbol manipulation*. (See the beginning of Chapter 1.)

In this view, intelligence has two aspects: a data structure built out of symbols that are in themselves meaningless, and rules for manipulating that structure in a definite, mechanical way. The symbol structure and the rules for manipulating it form a ***symbol system***. If we add to this a physical object such as a computer (or a brain) that can store the symbols and perform the manipulations, we get a ***physical symbol system***. The claim that intelligence is just a physical symbol system is called the ***physical symbol system hypothesis***. According to this hypothesis, knowledge is represented as a symbol structure, thinking is just the mechanical manipulation of those symbols, and AI is the quest to build a symbol system as complex and subtle as that represented in the human brain.

Whether or not the full range of human intelligence, including such paramount features as creativity and consciousness, can really be explained in terms of symbol manipulation, it is at least clear that it plays an important role. The words of our language are, after all, symbols— meaningless in themselves but carrying a heavy freight of meaning be-

---

[3] The history of AI, including minimally technical accounts of major achievements, is covered in [Crevier], [McCorduck], and [Kurtzweil]. A much fuller, but quite technical, survey of traditional AI is given in [Barr and Feigenbaum].

cause of the way they are conventionally used. The sentences we speak or write are symbol structures constructed according to the rules of grammar in order to communicate knowledge and ideas. Perhaps the knowledge and ideas that we express in language are already present as symbol structures stored in some physical form in the brain. As I write this sentence, perhaps I am duplicating a fragment of my own internal symbol structure in the form of language; as you read it, perhaps that fragment is being recreated in your brain; as you think about what you have read, perhaps symbol structures are being compared and new structures created.

We should, then, investigate just how much *can* be accomplished by symbol manipulation, and how. It is precisely that investigation that constitutes the history of GOFAI.

12.1.2. Search and Problem Solving. A major aspect of intelligence is *problem solving*. Problems can be abstract, such as selecting a good move in a chess game or finding a proof for a mathematical theorem. Or, they can be more practical, such as deciding what to cook for dinner or getting the most benefit from a three-hour study session for a computer science test. Often, problem solving can be seen as *searching* through all available courses of action, looking for one that solves the problem.

Consider first an example that seems to have little to do with computers: deciding what to cook for dinner. This can be rephrased as searching for a selection of dishes that meets some criteria. For example, you might require that each dish can be made from foods already available in your kitchen, that they contain certain levels of calories and nutrients, and that you haven't eaten the same thing recently. Now, a computer could be provided with a list of all the foods in your kitchen, recipes for a large number of dishes, and so forth. It could then be programmed to select a dinner menu that meets all the specified criteria.

One straightforward way of programming the computer to do this would be to have it generate every possible dinner menu, one after the other, and test each one to see whether it meets the criteria. As soon as it finds one that does, the problem is solved. This method of searching through every possibility is called *brute force search*. For many problems, there is a relatively simple brute force search procedure that will find a solution. The problem is that for almost any *interesting* problem, the number of possibilities that must be checked is so vast that searching through them all would take an unreasonable amount of time (such as longer than the age of the universe), even for an incredibly powerful computer. In practice, then, it must be possible to limit the search to a smaller number of possibilities, if there is to be a reasonable chance of actually finding a solution.

In our dinner example, there are certainly ways to proceed that do not involve looking at every possibility. For example: Choose some food that is available in the kitchen, and look up recipes that use that food as an ingredient. Or select a successful meal from some time in the past and check whether ingredients are available to recreate it; if not, try making substitutions using similar ingredients that are available. A human solving the problem undoubtably uses "rules of thumb" like these. Technically, such rules of thumb are called *heuristics*. In a *heuristic search*, heuristics are used to limit the number of possibilities that must be considered or to guide the search towards those possibilities that are more likely to represent a solution to the problem at hand.

An average person trying to imagine an intelligent computer is more likely to imagine it playing chess than selecting a dinner menu. Playing chess well seems to require a good deal of intelligence, and AI researchers have been programming computers to play games such as chess from the very beginning. Such programs are based on a type of heuristic search.

The problem for a chess-playing program can be stated as follows: given the position of all the pieces on the board, select the best possible move. Now, there can be only a small number of legal moves, so the computer just has to evaluate each move and select the best. "Evaluating moves," though, is not so easy. It is certainly possible to make up a set of heuristic rules that computes a numeric value for each possible move. Simple rules might, for example, count each side's pieces and check which pieces are under attack. The computer would then simply choose the move with the highest numeric value.

However, it should be clear that the computer could improve its play by looking ahead to see how its opponent might reply to each of its possible moves. That is, for each of its own moves, the computer should determine the best possible countermove that its opponent can make and evaluate the state of the game after that countermove; to find the best countermove, it must search through all the possibilities. But surely, to evaluate any given countermove, it should look at each of its own legal *counter*-countermoves to determine what its best move will be in each case—and so on until the computer has looked ahead all the way to the end of the game!

So, to find the perfect strategy, the computer must, in effect, search through the set of *all possible chess games* that start from the current board position, to find one in which each player makes the best possible move on each turn. For a trivial game like tic-tac-toe, the number of possible games is so small that it is possible to examine them all by brute force search. In chess, the number of games is huge, and brute force search is literally impossible. Instead, the computer looks ahead only a certain number of moves and countermoves; at the limit of this look-ahead, it bases its evaluation of each possible move on simple heuristic rules rather than further look-ahead. To make better use of the time available for calculation, it might use other heuristic rules to decide that certain moves are more promising than others; it would then look further ahead while evaluating those rules than it does for less promising moves. Chess-playing computers that work in this way can defeat most human players, but the ultimate goal of a computer as world chess champion is still out of reach.

It is fair to ask where all these heuristic rules are supposed to come from. In general, they are hand-crafted by a programmer based on knowledge and intuition about the problem to be solved. Ideally, though, an intelligent computer would be able to learn new rules, based on experience. Not surprisingly, **machine learning** has proved to be one of the most difficult problems in AI. But some progress has been made. In fact, one of the first game-playing programs, a checkers program written by Arthur Samuel in the late 1950s, was able to learn in a limited way. Samuel's program was provided with a number of heuristic rules for evaluating moves. The weight given to each rule in the evaluation was adjustable. After each game it played, the program would adjust the weights based on its analysis of its performance in that game. As it played game after game, the program's performance gradually improved until soon it could regularly beat its creator.

Samuel's checkers program was one of several early successes in AI that led some researchers to predict that computers would soon achieve human-level intelligence. One of the most influential of these programs was the immodestly named GPS (General Problem Solver), written by Alan Newell and Herbert Simon. GPS was based on an analysis of human problem-solving methods, and it marked the beginning of Newell and Simon's efforts to model human cognition.[4]

---

[4] Cognition means, roughly, the process of thinking, whether conscious or subconscious. A branch of psychology known as **cognitive science** tries to

Given descriptions of an initial situation, a desired "goal" situation, and a set of operations for making changes, GPS would search for a sequence of operations that could be applied to transform the initial situation into the goal situation. Such a sequence of operations would constitute a *plan* for achieving the goal. In searching for a plan, GPS used a very general heuristic called *means-ends analysis*, which involved finding the differences between a given situation and the goal and looking for an operation that reduces those differences. Applying such an operation would produce a new situation, closer to the goal; GPS could then apply the same heuristic to the new situation to find the next operation in the plan. Often, of course, it would find a situation in which no available operations would be useful; in that case, it would *backtrack* to some previous situation and try to find a different operation to apply in that situation.

12.1.3. Microworlds and Robots. Now, it is important to keep in mind what programs like GPS are really doing: purely mechanical manipulation of data structures. True, those data structures might be thought of as representing knowledge about some real or made-up world, and the manipulation of those data structures might correspond to thinking about that world. But it is not clear how much the terms "knowledge" and "thinking" here have in common with human knowing and thinking. Furthermore, the amount of knowing and thinking going on is rather small.[5]

Consider the following list of facts, written in a format appropriate for use with the programming language LISP; think of this as representing part of the knowledge of some program:

(box (size 7) (on table) (color red))
(box (size 3) (on floor) (color blue))
(table (size 50) (on floor))
(ball (size 4) (on floor) (color red))

Here, the first line can be interpreted as saying that there is a red box whose size is seven (inches, perhaps) on the table. The remaining lines

---

explain cognition as a form of computation. Cognitive science is closely related to the branch of artificial intelligence that tries to imitate human cognition. There is, of course, another branch of AI that merely seeks to produce intelligent behavior by any available means; for example, the methods used by the chess-playing programs described above bear little relation to methods used by human chess players.

[5] Certainly true for GPS and arguably for any existing program, but see Subsection 12.1.4 below.

can be interpreted similarly. The computer might use such facts to answer such questions as, "Where is the red box?" or to respond to commands such as, "Put the ball into the box on the table."

Now, symbols like "box" or "red" do not in themselves have any meaning for the computer. Look at it this way: It would make no difference to the computer if the above list of facts were written as

(G17 (G42 7) (G2017 G18) (G69 G101))
(G17 (G42 3) (G2017 G105) (G69 G107))
(G18 (G42 50) (G2017 G105))
(G19 (G42 4) (G2017 G105) (G69 G101))

In this form, this list looks a lot less like knowledge and a lot more like a symbol structure! What meaning there is comes from the *structure*— the fact that "size" or "G42" is used as the second item in each list, for example—and from relationships built into the program, such as the one associating the symbol "box" or "G17" and the English word spelled with the letters B-O-X. Unfortunately, all the meaning tied up into the English word is unavailable to the program, unless that meaning can somehow be explicitly coded into additional symbol structures.

Obviously, full understanding of the world would require very complex structures. For practical purposes, AI researchers have generally limited their programs to dealing with stripped-down, simplified artificial worlds known as **microworlds**.[6] The most famous example of a microworld was **Blocks World**, the focus of several projects undertaken at the Massachusetts Institute of Technology under the direction of Marvin Minsky (one of the organizers of the Dartmouth conference) and Seymour Papert.

Blocks World consisted of toy blocks of different shapes, sizes, and colors. Blocks could be moved around and stacked up, with certain restrictions such as the fact that nothing can be stacked on top of a pyramid-shaped block. Some projects used real blocks; for others, the blocks were just represented by drawings on the computer's screen or symbol structures in the computer's memory. If all the projects had ever been combined into one large system, the result would have been a

---

[6] The word "microworld" was used in the 60s and early 70s. A microworld was seen as a starting point, capturing knowledge about some small aspect of the world but capable of being gradually scaled-up to represent more and more of the real world. Scaling turned out to be much harder than many people expected and the word largely fell out of use. It is still true, however, that existing AI programs deal with microworlds of one sort or another.

"robot" adapted for life in Blocks World: That robot would be able to observe a table full of blocks (by analyzing a television image), move the blocks around and stack them up (with a mechanical arm), and carry out commands and discuss what it was doing in (typewritten) English. None of this is easy for a computer.

When a computer analyzes a television image, all it has to work with is a long sequence of numbers representing the color of each pixel in the image. From those numbers, the computer must extract knowledge about objects and their positions in three-dimensional space. Blocks were used in early computer vision experiments because of their simple shapes and straight edges. Provided that the scene was carefully lit and not too complex, the computer could extract information about edges and their intersections from the pixel data and then use that edge and intersection data to determine what it was looking at. It took several research projects to produce computational methods for accomplishing this much. Developing a computer-controlled mechanical arm that could then manipulate the blocks was another, and much larger, project, but eventually a system called Copy-Demo was produced that could look at a structure built of blocks and duplicate it [Crevier, p. 94].

Natural-language communication between user and computer was the subject of another Blocks World program known as SHRDLU, written by Terry Winograd. ("Natural language" here refers to a human language such as English, as opposed to the much simpler "artificial" languages ordinarily used in computer programming.) SHRDLU could have only limited conversations about blocks, and so was very far from passing the Turing Test, but it was hoped at the time that it would be a step in the right direction. What it could do was impressive.

If given an instruction such as, "Put the small red pyramid on the blue block," SHRDLU could use GPS-style problem solving to plan a sequence of actions to carry out the command. This might include, for example, removing an object from the top of the block to make room for the pyramid. (These actions would be carried out not with real blocks but with a simulation drawn on the computer's screen.) SHRDLU could answer questions about its actions. For example, it might respond to "Why did you pick up the pyramid" with "so that I could put it on the blue block." It could even learn in a limited way. For example, if instructed to "Build a steeple," it would respond, "Sorry, I don't know the meaning of the word 'steeple'." But if it were told, "A 'steeple' is a stack which contains two cubes and a pyramid," SHRDLU would then be able to build such a steeple. ([Hofstadter, p. 586–593] is a long sample conversation with SHRDLU.)

Computer vision, robotics, and natural language processing continue to be major areas of AI research. Industrial assembly-line robots have been developed which are essentially computer-controlled mechanical arms, and some of them use vision systems similar to the one developed for Blocks World. Mobile robots have also been built, and research continues with the goal of producing a robot that can independently explore environments such as the surface of Mars or the interior of a volcanic cone.

Natural language processing programs have been written to allow users to interact with computers in English, provided the subject area is sufficiently limited and simple (such as an airline reservation system). Some progress has been made on computer translation of text from one natural language to another, with programs that can produce readable—though far from polished—translations of sufficiently straightforward prose. An important research goal in the area of natural language processing is a program that can analyze and extract information from English text. A program that completely solves this problem would probably also be able to pass the Turing Test, but there is some hope for useful partial solutions in the near term.

12.1.4. Expert Systems. Although SHRDLU could deal with Blocks World with reasonable competence, it suffered from at least two problems. One was the practical problem that it was difficult to extend its abilities. This was because it was very complex, with both knowledge and rules for manipulating that knowledge hand-crafted into the program. The second problem was one of public relations: SHRDLU was, after all, only playing with blocks; surely for AI to achieve real respect it would have to come up with more obviously interesting applications.

Both these problems were addressed with the development of *expert systems*. An expert system is a program that encodes many of the rules that a human expert uses in some particular area of expertise.[7] For example, the first expert systems DENDRAL and MYCIN were developed in the late 1960s and early 70s. They dealt, respectively, with analysis of mass spectrograms of complex organic molecules and with diagnosis of infectious blood diseases. (You don't need to know what these are, but

---

[7] The question of the degree to which human expertise is actually based on applying rules is very controversial. I will discuss this controversy below.

this gives you an idea of the specialization of expert systems.) By 1980, research into expert systems had produced a major commercial success with XCON, an expert system for configuring the computer systems manufactured by Digital Equipment Corporation. Although the enthusiasm of the early 80s—which was fueled by overly optimistic predictions that expert systems could replace human experts in many fields—has faded somewhat, expert systems continue to be a useful technology for many practical applications.

The expert knowledge in an expert system is expressed in the form of *production rules*. Each production rule contains a condition to be tested and an action clause that will be executed when the condition is true. The action clause represents a conclusion that can be drawn or an action that should be taken when the condition holds. For example, an expert system for playing poker might include rules like these, encoded, of course, in a manner more suitable for a computer:

> IF:
>> hand contains a card with card-value X
>> AND hand contains another card with card-value X
> THEN:
>> record that hand contains a pair with card-value X.

> IF:
>> hand contains a three-of-a-kind
>> AND hand contains a pair
>> AND the card-value of the pair is different from
>>> the card-value of the three-of-a-kind
> THEN:
>> record that hand is a full-house.

> IF:
>> hand is a full-house
>> AND game-state is first-betting-round
> THEN:
>> place big-bet.

Such rules are similar to **if** statements in an ordinary computer language, but the flow of control in an expert system is very different from that in a traditional program. In an expert system, the conditions in the various production rules are not tested sequentially in some predetermined order; instead, any rule can be activated at any time, as its condition becomes true. This can be understood by analogy with a blackboard.

Imagine a blackboard on which is written all the information available to the expert system, and think of each production rule as an active agent that constantly monitors this blackboard to see whether the condition in the **if** part of the rule is true. When some rule sees that its condition is true, the action clause of the rule is executed; this results in changing the information written on the blackboard. As soon as the information changes, other rules might be activated because their conditions have just become true. This causes further changes to the information on the board, which activates further rules, and so forth until some rule writes the solution to the problem on the board. (In practice, of course, there must be some overall control of the system, to decide, for example, what happens when several rules are activated simultaneously.)

In many applications, the independence of the individual production rules makes it easier to encode knowledge in an expert system, rather than to construct a traditional program where everything depends on a careful sequencing of instructions. Furthermore, it is easier to add knowledge to the expert system, simply by adding new rules. Indeed, the XCON expert system succeeded where several previous attempts to apply traditional programming methods had failed due to the complexity of the problem. And XCON was successfully expanded from an original system containing 300 rules in 1980 to a 10,000-rule system in 1987 [Kurtzweil, p. 292].

12.1.5. The More Knowledge the Better.   One problem with expert systems and other AI programs is their *brittleness*. This refers to that fact that programs that operate reasonably well in a limited domain are easily "broken" as soon as they are applied to situations outside that domain. This is not surprising for a chess-playing program; we would probably not expect such a program to know how to play tic-tac-toe, let alone discuss the joy of victory or the agony of defeat. However, when a program like SHRDLU seems so happy playing with blocks, it can be a disappointment to find that it knows nothing about sandboxes, balls, or playmates.[8] When a program like MYCIN can analyze the symptoms of a patient with an infectious blood disease and recommend treatments

---

[8] Earlier, I noted that SHRDLU would understand the definition "A 'steeple' is a stack which contains two cubes and a pyramid." However, if told that "A 'steeple' is a pointed roof on a church," it would merely respond with "Sorry, I don't know the meaning of the word 'pointed'." In fact, as someone pointed out in a reference I can no longer find, SHRDLU is quite capable of responding to "Sorry, I thought you were smarter than you are" with "Sorry, I don't know the meaning of the word 'Sorry'."

as effectively as a human doctor, it might be surprising when it tries to interpret the symptoms of a patient who has a cold, or is pregnant or even dead, as if that patient were suffering from some infectious blood disease.

This is a problem we have seen before: In order to display *general* intelligence—not merely limited competence in a microworld—a program must have access to something approaching the full range of human knowledge. And it is not enough just to give the computer a list of facts. Those facts must be linked together into a symbol structure that encodes all the associations and relationships among the facts, and the program must somehow be able to make effective use of what would surely be a huge mass of data.

Early AI researchers, with their emphasis on problem-solving, did not seem to realize the importance and difficulty of this issue of **knowledge representation**. However, it has come to be the central issue in traditional AI. One person who has faced the full extent of the problem is Douglas Lenat, who is leading a multi-year project with the aim of building a symbol structure containing enough knowledge, in a usable form, to support something like general intelligence. The project is called **CYC**, short for "encyclopedia," but the goal is not simply to store all the facts from an encyclopedia into a computer. The real problem, as Lenat puts it, is to represent all the facts that are *not* in any encyclopedia because they are just common sense—things that are too obvious to mention to any person, such as the fact that when people walk they move their legs, or that Napoleon had a mother. CYC also includes programs that manipulate its huge, linked data structure and make it easier for humans to add new facts. Ultimately, Lenat hopes, the human role will be reduced or eliminated as CYC becomes capable of learning—that is, extracting new facts—from the ordinary English found in books and newspaper.

CYC is an ambitious project, and it might well represent the last hope for good old-fashioned artificial intelligence, the ultimate test of the idea that true human-level intelligence can be embodied in a physical symbol system. This, as we will see in the next section, is an idea that has been hotly debated from the start.

12.2. The Philosophical Debate

In the 1950 paper in which he proposes that machines might be made to exhibit artificial intelligence, Alan Turing also takes note of nine possible objections to the idea and attempts to refute them. Some of them he does not take very seriously, such as what he calls the "Heads in the Sand" Objection, that "The consequences of machines thinking would be too dreadful. Let us hope and believe they cannot do so." To this, his reply is, "I do not think that this argument is sufficiently substantial to require refutation. Consolation would be more appropriate." But among the other objections he lists are some that have been central in a long-running and still ongoing debate about whether thinking machines are even possible.

There are many positions in this debate, ranging from those who think that superhuman intelligent machines are inevitable in the near future, to those who believe that no machine could ever be truly said to think. There are those who accept the possibility of a man-made intelligence but deny that that intelligence could be based on programmed symbol manipulation. Some accept the Turing Test as the best way to assess intelligence, while others argue that the test is invalid. Those who think it invalid break further into two camps, one claiming that the test is too strong—because an intelligent machine would be so alien that it would not be able to think enough like a human to pass the test—and the other camp claiming that it is too weak—because a machine that passed the Turing Test would be merely simulating intelligence rather than displaying the real thing.

With such a variety of "expert" opinion, it can be difficult for an outsider to make any judgment about what to believe. My own best guess, for what it's worth, is that the pure symbol-manipulation approach of traditional AI is unlikely to lead to true intelligence (although a final judgment will have to wait for the completion of Lenat's CYC project). My impression is that a majority of workers in the field have come to accept this. Even if this is true, of course, it does not mean that traditional AI has no future. It has already proved its worth in practical applications, such as expert systems, that fall far short of general intelligence.

Nor would it mean that the dream of creating intelligence is dead. There are other approaches to AI besides symbol manipulation, and several of these are currently generating a great deal of excitement. Some of these alternative approaches are introduced in the next section. The remainder of this section surveys in more detail some of the arguments that have been used against traditional AI.

12.2.1. The Limits of Logic. Turing's own work on computationally unsolvable problems (see Chapter 4) is one of several mathematical results that have been used to argue against AI. Turing showed that there are problems that cannot be solved by running a program. Since running programs is all that computers do, there are problems that are forever beyond the ability of computers to solve. On the other hand, so the argument goes, when people are faced with problems, they are not limited to blindly following programs. People are creative; they can come up with novel approaches to problems and therefore can do things that no programmed computer can. The problem with this argument, as Turing was quick to point out, is that it is based on an unproven assumption that people are not subject to the same sorts of limits as computers.

The built-in limitations of symbol manipulation were first demonstrated in a theorem proved by the mathematician Kurt Gödel in 1931.[9] Mathematicians like to make lists of assumptions, which they call **axioms**, and then use those axioms and the rules of logic to prove other statements, which they call **theorems**. The axioms and theorems are made up of symbols, and these are to be mechanically manipulated according to definite logical rules. This is a kind of computation, and indeed once a set of axioms has been selected, it is possible to program a computer to generate all the theorems that can be proved from those axioms.

Before Gödel came along, it was hoped that a single, finite set of axioms could be found that could be used to prove *all* mathematical truths. Gödel showed that this hope can never be realized by proving that any sufficiently complex, consistent mathematical theory is incomplete, that is, it includes true statements that cannot be proved within the system. The level of complexity required to prove incompleteness is rather modest: Gödel's Theorem applies to any system that includes ordinary integer arithmetic.

Now, this result seems to apply only to mathematical systems, but as noted above, any such system can be programmed as a physical symbol system in a computer. Conversely, the working of a computer can be described in terms of logical rules applied to binary numbers, and with a little effort can be expressed in terms of a "mathematical system" to which Gödel's Theorem applies. So, the theorem can be applied to

---

[9] Two useful overviews of the debate about Gödel's Theorem and AI, from opposite sides, can be found in [Hofstadter] and [Penrose].

computers and therefore to any artificial intelligence based on mechanical symbol manipulation. It proves a certain type of limitation on any such intelligence.

For people who want to use Gödel's Theorem to argue against AI, the main point is that a human mathematician, Gödel for example, standing *outside* a mathematical system can analyze it and find specific, true statements that cannot be proved *within* the system. It looks as though human intelligence is innately superior to any physical symbol system; the human mind can find limitations in any such system and go beyond those limitations.

The problem with this argument is that it is still subject to Turing's counterargument, as given above: There is no proof that human intelligence is not subject to the same sort of limitations imposed by Gödel's Theorem. If in fact the human mind *is* a physical symbol system, then there is no way for that mind ever to step outside *itself*. Any analysis that the mind does of itself is inside the system, and subject to its limitations; those limitations would simply be invisible to the mind. That such a mind could analyze other systems would be no more surprising than the fact that one computer program can analyze another.[10]

In the end, neither side in this argument is likely to be convinced by the other, since the evidence is not strong enough to change opinions based on deeply held beliefs about human nature and the nature of intelligence. This accounts, no doubt, for the passion with which the debate has often been waged.

12.2.2. Always Already in a Situation. Perhaps the most acrimonious segment of this debate has been that between philosopher Hubert Dreyfus and the AI community. Dreyfus was one of the first to attack the whole AI enterprise, in a paper called "Alchemy and AI," later expanded and published in 1972 as the book *What Computers Can't Do*. In it, he claims that the whole symbolic approach to AI is flawed, that AI researchers are naive for ever believing it could work, and that if they would just pay attention to the wisdom of Dreyfus' brand of philosophy they would see the error of their ways. Although his actual language wasn't quite so blunt, Dreyfus' attitude was clear and won him no friends in the AI community, which generally considered his brand

---

[10] Think back to the proof of the unsolvability of the Halting Problem in Chapter 4, which at its heart is based on the inability of a program to analyze *itself*. By the way, this hints at the deep connections between Gödel's results and Turing's.

of philosophy to be a "ball of fluff." (This is reported in [McCorduck], which devotes an interesting chapter to the Dreyfus controversy.)

In fact, Dreyfus was attacking not just AI but what he identified as the Western philosophical tradition, which provided a background of beliefs that made it possible to think that intelligence could be reduced to calculation. Already in the sixteenth century, the philosopher Thomas Hobbes believed that "Reason is nothing but reckoning," and in the next century, Gottfried Leibnitz, who built an early calculating machine, sought to develop a system of calculation that could be used to settle all questions of truth. Once such a system were found, Leibnitz said, "If someone would doubt my results, I would say to him: 'Let us calculate, Sir,' and thus by taking pen and ink we would settle the issue" [Dreyfus, p. 69]. When George Boole invented Boolean algebra in the nineteenth century, he was continuing this quest to reduce reason to calculation. It is no wonder that when general-purpose computing machines based on Boolean algebra were invented, it was expected that they would soon be able to equal and surpass human reasoning ability.

Dreyfus is from a very different philosophic tradition called *phenomenology*, which views a person as an integral part of a natural world, shaped by evolution and experience to interact with that world with an unselfconscious competence that has nothing to do with calculation.

In the Western tradition—that is, the scientific tradition—the world itself is seen as kind of physical symbol system, consisting of simple, basic components that interact according to definite rules. An intelligence makes its way in the world by forming an internal representation of that system and using that representation—that is, calculating with it—to understand, predict, and control external reality. When that intelligence finds itself in a new situation, it can attempt to deal with it by extracting the relevant facts, adding them to its internal symbol system, and then using that system to calculate its response. This is the standard AI approach to problem-solving.

For Dreyfus, this is nonsense. There are simply too many possibly relevant facts to consider, and which ones are actually relevant depends on contexts and meanings that are inaccessible to a symbol system. People, Dreyfus believes, do not deal with new situations by extracting facts and calculating a response. People are always *already in a situation*. That is, they experience any situation as part of a continuing interaction with a world full of meaning and context. They react to the relevant features of their environment without having to sift out those features from the huge background of irrelevant information. This, computers can never do.

Computers can only follow rules, and while Dreyfus acknowledges that people are capable of mechanically following rules, he believes that their competence in a real, complex world is not and cannot be based on rule-following, either conscious or subconscious. Dreyfus acknowledges that computer programs such as SHRDLU and expert systems can display useful but limited competence in stripped-down microworlds where all the facts are given and all the rules are made explicit. But he does not believe that such programs could ever be scaled up to true general intelligence.[11] Whatever one thinks of his philosophy, his pessimism about traditional AI has proved to be justified, at least in the short term.

12.2.3. The Chinese Room. Dreyfus believes that it is impossible to produce human-level competance using facts and rules. Other philosophers have argued that even if a computer could be programmed so that its performance was indistinguishable from a person's, the computer would still not be truly intelligent. The argument is that a *simulation* of intelligence is not the same as the real thing, and would not, for example, confer on a seemingly intelligent computer the moral status of a human being.

One of the most famous arguments along these lines was given by John Searle, who describes the following thought experiment: Let's assume that you don't know a single word of Chinese. You are locked in a room with a large number of books, a lot of scratch paper, and a slot in the wall. People outside the room pass in pieces of paper with meaningless-looking squiggles written on them. Your job is to process the squiggles according to definite rules, which are contained in the books that have been locked up with you. After a certain amount of processing, the rules tell you to draw certain squiggles on a piece of paper and pass it to the people waiting outside. As far as you are concerned, you are mechanically following meaningless rules.

Now, let us imagine that the squiggles are actually Chinese words and that to the Chinese-speaking people outside, the papers being passed into and out of the room make up a pleasant and natural conversation in Chinese. By blindly following rules and processing meaningless squiggles, you have managed to seem like a native Chinese speaker, but you have done this without knowing Chinese!

---

[11] It is interesting that Terry Winograd, SHRDLU's programmer, is something of a convert to Dreyfus' point of view. See [Winograd and Flores].

According to Searle, your position in this experiment is the same as that of a computer trying to pass the Turing Test. Even if the computer were to pass that test, it would not be evidence that the computer "knows English" any more than your performance in the experiment is evidence that you know Chinese. The question here is not whether passing the Turing Test is possible. Searle's argument is that the test itself is invalid since the test cannot distinguish between intelligence and mere simulation of intelligence.

I should point out that Searle's position looks incomprehensible or even silly to most AI researchers. These researchers might start by pointing out how complicated the books of rules would have to be and how long it would take you to form each reply. But even taking the experiment on its own terms, their response would be that while of course *you* don't know Chinese, the whole *system*, including the books of rules and the scratch paper, does in fact know Chinese. Searle in turn finds this response silly.

12.2.4. The Problem of Consciousness.   It looks very much as though for both Dreyfus and Searle there is something about human intelligence that cannot be duplicated in a computer, something that depends on our biological nature and our evolutionary history. They are far from alone in feeling that there is a fundamental difference between people and rule-following machines. The perceived disabilities of such machines include things like emotion, creativity, free will and—most fundamentally—*consciousness.*

Consciousness is the awareness that we all have of ourselves and of the world. It is an odd sort of thing, since while we are each unavoidably and undeniably aware of our own consciousness, we have no direct evidence that anyone else is self-aware in the same way. Consciousness distinguishes emotion from mere physiological response; it distinguishes creativity from mechanical generation of novel symbol structures; and it distinguishes free will from blind rule-following. Can rule-following machines ever be conscious? If not, it might be difficult to accept them as truly intelligent, no matter how closely they can simulate human behavior.

Some proponents of AI regard consciousness as a fundamentally simple thing, merely the result of one part of the brain monitoring the activity of some other part. (See, for example, [Minsky].) Machines would be as good at this as people, or better. This would perhaps have been Alan Turing's position. He was well aware of the problem of consciousness. In his view, if a machine can pass the Turing Test, then it is useless to deny that it is conscious. It would be like one person denying that any other person is self-aware, an absurd but perfectly consistent philosophical theory known as *solipsism*. In practice, we believe that other people are self-aware on the basis of purely external evidence that they think and feel emotion just like we do.

But other people are *like us* in a way machines are not. Other people are biological creatures, built in the same way we are. It is natural to believe that they think and feel in the same way. Things are not so clear in the case of machines. It is not surprising, then, that some people think that biology—and not just intellect—is required for true intelligence. This idea has been vindicated to some extent by some of the recent developments in the field of AI that are discussed in the next section.

12.3. AI in the World

While traditional AI has seen many successes and has spun off important applications, it has always failed to live up to the most optimistic predictions, and it has not yet come close to producing true general intelligence. One of the surprises along the way has been the difficulty of getting computers to do things that people do easily, without even thinking about them—things like picking a familiar face out of a crowd or walking across a cluttered room. Computers can excel at logic and can cope with stripped-down microworlds, but when it comes to existing in a real, complex world, they are outclassed by, say, a cockroach.

In the traditional AI view, a mind—artificial or natural—understands the world by building an internal symbolic representation. Its connection with the outside world is really rather tenuous. Its input from that world is a stream of data that must be filtered, interpreted, and integrated into its internal representation before that input is of any use. When the mind needs to act, it manipulates the internal representation to compute a "plan," which is actually a detailed program for the sequence of actions it will take; actually performing the actions is something of an anticlimax.

The quest to create artificial intelligences that can cope with the real world has led some researchers to move away from this physical symbol system approach. These researchers note that the way people and cockroaches deal with the world is not so much by thinking about it as by reacting and adapting to to it. Why make a representation of the world when the world itself is right there in plain view? Why make a detailed plan (which is likely to be frustrated by complex reality in any case) when you can just go ahead and *act* to achieve your goals? This view has something in common with Hubert Dreyfus' idea of the way a person exists in the natural world, but now it is being proposed by people who want to build artificial entities that will be at home in the world in a similar way. The rest of this section looks at some of the approaches these people are taking. It is too early to tell whether these new approaches will ever lead to true artificial intelligence, but they do offer some hope of overcoming problems that traditional AI seems unable to handle.[12]

12.3.1. Neural Nets. The brain is composed of large numbers of neurons; each neuron gets inputs from other neurons, performs some computation on those inputs, and sends an output on to yet other neurons. There is a superficial similarity here to a computer, with neurons corresponding to transistors or logic gates. But the similarity is only superficial, even leaving aside the fact that the brain operates in a complex chemical broth whose effects we only partly understand.

First of all, neurons do not perform simple logical operations such as AND and OR. The computations they do are much more complex than that, so much so that a single neuron is more like a complete central processing unit than a simple logic gate. The brain as a whole, then, is more like a huge network of computers doing massively parallel processing than it is like a single computer. (Parallel processing is discussed in Chapter 10.)

Neurons are also like computers in that their behavior can change over time. The output of a neuron depends not just on the current values of its inputs but also on the history of previous inputs. That is, neurons have a kind of memory or internal state.

Since the brain is the only natural object we know that exhibits intelligence, it makes sense to use it as a model for artificially intelligent systems. Most people assume that if we could make an *exact* physical model of the brain, it would share all of the brain's properties, including intelligence. Unfortunately, the brain is exceedingly complex, far beyond our ability to model in detail. However, the structure of the brain pro-

---

[12] These "new" approaches are not actually new. Some of them have deep historical roots. However, until recently the AI field has been so dominated by symbol manipulation that alternatives have received little attention. Today, that is no longer true. For further reading on the subjects covered here, see [Levy, *Artificial Life*], [Waldrop], [Caudill and Butler], [Brooks], and [Holland].

vides inspiration for a kind of stripped-down, simplified model called a *neural net*.

A neural net is made up of a number of processing units that I will call *neurodes*. (This name is not standard; I have adopted it from [Caudill and Butler].) A neurode is meant to be a simplified model neuron. Each neurode has several inputs and computes an output based on the values of its inputs and on its internal state. The inputs can come from other neurodes or from outside the neural net; similarly, the output of a neurode can be connected to other neurodes or to the outside world. The neural net as a whole, then, is a kind of computational device that takes some input values and computes one or more outputs. The structure of a neural net is shown in Figure 12.1.

Each input to a neurode can be an arbitrary real number in some range of values, let us say between -1 and 1.[13] The output of the neurode is computed as follows: First, each input value is multiplied by a number called a *weight*, and the results of these multiplications are added together. A different weight can be used for each input. This gives what is called a *weighted sum* of the inputs. The value of the sum is then adjusted according to some fixed formula to give the value of the output. (This adjustment ensures that the output value is in the correct range; the exact form of the adjustment is chosen to imitate the way that real neurons work.)

The important point here is that the weights used in the weighted sum are part of the internal state of the neurode. If the weights are changed, then the neurode will perform a different computation. A given neural net can perform many different computations, depending on the weights used by each of its neurodes. A net could be programmed to do some desired computation by setting the values of these weights. What is remarkable—and what makes neural nets so different from other approaches to AI—is that nets are not programmed at all. Instead, they are "trained." They learn from experience!

---

[13] Because neural nets operate on real numbers rather than on zeros and ones, they are what are called "analog computers" rather than the standard "digital computers" that we have considered in the rest of the book. Real neurons are also analog rather than digital devices. A digital computer can approximate an analog computer to any desired degree of accuracy, and indeed neural nets are generally simulated on standard digital computers. But there is an intrinsic *inexactness* in the computations of analog computers, and a simulation can therefore never be perfect. Although it is unlikely, it is at least theoretically possible that this *im*perfection of analog computation plays some essential role in intelligence.

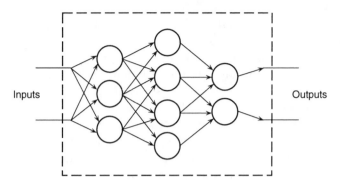

Figure 12.1. *A diagram showing the structure of a small but typical neural net. Each circle represents a neurode. Arrows pointing into the neurode represent its inputs; each arrow pointing out represents the output that the neurode computes from its inputs. The neural net as a whole has two inputs entering from the left, and it computes two outputs which exit on the right. Not represented here is the important fact that neurodes can be modified by changing their internal states. A neural net can be "trained" to do some desired computation by adjusting the internal states of its neurodes.*

The idea is to start with a neural net in which the weights are assigned randomly and then to test it on sample data, for which the desired output is known. Of course, the random net will almost surely give the wrong answer. When it does this, the weights in the net are adjusted so that it comes closer to giving the correct answer. The adjustments depend in a straightforward way on the difference between the correct answer and the output that the net actually gives, so that there is no need to analyze *why* the net gave the wrong answer. (There is a mathematical technique called **backpropagation** for adjusting the weights, but the details are not important here.)

This process is repeated on a number of different sample inputs. The samples are presented to the net over and over. Each time it gives the wrong output, the weights are adjusted. Eventually, assuming the net is large and complex enough, it will give the correct answer for each of the sample inputs. More important, it will also tend to give correct answers for similar inputs that were not among the samples.

As an example, consider a problem to which neural nets have been successfully applied: recognizing hand-printed letters. The image of a letter can be given as a grid of pixel colors; each pixel provides one input for the neural net. The output might be eight bits representing the ASCII code of the letter. This problem is one that is easy for people but difficult for computers.

A traditional AI program working on this problem might start by analyzing the pixel data looking for certain features, such as vertical lines, closed curves, and free-floating dots. The features that it finds make up a symbol structure that contains the relevant information about the input data. This symbol structure could then be analyzed by a set of rules like those in an expert system. Or it might be compared with stored symbol structures representing typical letters. Because of the wide variation in the appearance of hand-printed letters, each step in this procedure would be difficult and error-prone. It would certainly require a large amount of careful programming to come up with a program that will work for a large fraction of possible inputs.

With the neural net approach, there is no programming at all. A few hundred sample images are used to train the net, as described above. When the training is complete, the net would be able to identify the letter represented by each sample image. It would also be able to identify other images of letters, with a high degree of accuracy.

Neural nets can solve problems that are hard for traditional AI, and they do so without being programmed with rules or symbol structures. Of course, it is possible that a careful analysis of a neural net might show that it is implicitly using rules and symbols. For example, in the net described above, we might find that one particular neurode has output 1 when the input image contains a closed curve and output -1 when it does not. This output, then, is a symbol whose meaning is the presence or absence of a certain feature in the input.

Even if this is true, though, something interesting would be going on. The rules and symbols, after all, were not carefully programmed in by a human programmer. Instead, they emerged naturally from a simple training process.

12.3.2. Complex Systems, Emergence, and Artificial Life.
Throughout this book, complexity has been portrayed as something that arises by deliberate, planned, step-by-step construction. That is how computers are built and how programs are written. But that is not the only way complexity can arise. Sometimes, as in the case of neural nets, complexity can *emerge* in systems consisting of simple components interacting in simple ways. Somehow, the complex behavior of an ant colony emerges from the relatively simple behavior of individual ants.

Life emerges from the interactions of simple chemicals, and then continues to increase in complexity through the natural process of evolution. The complex economy of a large city emerges from the decisions of a large number of independent individuals acting on the basis of limited, local knowledge. In each case, something *qualitatively* new arises on a high level from simple interactions on a lower level.

This process of emergence in complex systems is something that we are only beginning to understand. This new understanding is generating an immense amount of excitement in a surprising variety of fields, including economics, psychology, physics, biology, and, of course, artificial intelligence.

This approach to AI can be seen in a new field called ***artificial life***. The object of artificial life research is to create artificial systems that display some of the characteristics of living things. In a way, this is what traditional AI does—intelligence, after all, is one of the characteristics of at least some living things. But traditional AI, as we have seen, imitates the computer-like symbolic processing aspect of intelligence and has a great deal of trouble with the seemingly simple skills that make it possible for a living organism to exist in the natural world.

One species of artificial life consists of robots created by Rodney Brooks and his coworkers at the Massachusetts Institute of Technology. Traditional AI has produced its own robots, with computer brains that operate on a symbolic representation of the world. But these intellectual robots have trouble dealing with the real world.

Brooks wants to create intelligent robots that don't use symbolic representation. So far, the robots that have been built in his lab are not particularly intelligent. Their abilities might be compared with those of insects, and in fact one of them looks very much like a foot-long cockroach. But Brooks argues that getting robots to do the kinds of things that insects can do is a long first step towards intelligence. He points out that in the three-billion-year history of life, intelligence appeared only in the last few million years. "This suggests," he writes, "that problem solving behavior, language, expert knowledge and application, and reason are all pretty simple once the essence of being and reacting are available. That essence is the ability to move around in a dynamic environment, sensing the surroundings to a degree sufficient to achieve the necessary maintenance of life and reproduction. This part of intelligence is where evolution has concentrated its time—it is much harder" [Brooks, p. 141].

Brook's robots are constructed from fairly simple components that can each have their own inputs, internal states, and behaviors. For example, the leg of a robot insect might be capable of behaviors like "raise," "lower," "move forward," "move back," and "keep still." Its internal state would determine which behavior it is pursuing. That state might change when a sensor in the leg indicates that the leg has hit an obstacle, or because of a signal from another component that has detected a large threatening object moving nearby. The components in the robot make up a hierarchy in which high-level components can influence or control those on a lower level, just as the leg in our example can be influenced by a danger-detecting sensor. But nowhere is there a central intelligence that thinks and plans. The behavior of the robot emerges from the interactions of its components with each other and with the world.

12.3.3. The Genetic Algorithm.

The behavior of Brook's robots can be surprisingly lifelike, but they lack an essential aspect of life: They cannot reproduce. And because they cannot reproduce, they cannot evolve. But there are other artificial life projects that deal with both reproduction and evolution. The "organisms" in these projects are simulated on a computer and "live" in a computer-simulated world. These simulations can be thought of as a way of studying some of the general characteristics of life and evolution. But from the point of view of AI, evolution can be thought of as a way of automatically generating and testing new ideas. It can be used to find solutions to problems without explicitly programming those solutions. Although evolution is a fundamentally simple process, it allows structures of great complexity to emerge in a world—simulated or natural—where it operates.

Many people have experimented with simulated evolution, starting in the 1950s. But the subject is most closely associated with John Holland, who put it on a firm mathematical foundation in a 1975 book called *Adaptation in Natural and Artificial Systems*. Holland investigated a process called the *genetic algorithm*. He starts with a population of individuals operating in some environment. Each individual has a *fitness value*, which is just a number indicating how well it performs in the environment. The individuals can reproduce, and the new individuals generated in this way replace existing members of the population.

Evolution can occur because of two factors that affect reproduction. First, individuals with higher fitness values have a greater chance of reproducing. To put it another way, fitter individuals produce more offspring. This means that the average fitness of the population tends to increase. Second, when an individual reproduces, its offspring is not necessarily an exact copy of itself. Reproduction really means "reproduction with variation." The variation is produced by what Holland calls *genetic operators*. Examples include *mutation*, in which a small random copying error occurs during reproduction, and *cross-over*, in which traits from two different individuals are combined in novel ways. Genetic operators allow the genetic algorithm to generate new traits and new combinations of traits to be tested against the environment.

In an actual application, an individual might be represented by a sequence of zeros and ones that somehow encode its behavior, appearance, or other information relevant to its fitness. This sequence of zeros and ones is referred to as a *chromosome*, by analogy to the structures in living cells that carry genetic information. With this type of representation, the mutation and cross-over operations are very simple. Mutation corresponds to changing a zero to a one or a one to a zero as a chromosome is copied during reproduction. In cross-over, a chromosome for a new individual is constructed from pieces of the chromosomes of two existing individuals.

In a static environment, the genetic algorithm can be thought of as a way of searching for an optimal individual. The fitness of the population will tend to move towards a maximum value, at which point the population will consist entirely of near-optimal individuals, and evolution will slow down and stop.

Things become more interesting when the environment itself changes over time, since then the population must continually adapt to the changing environment. The most interesting case is when the population is considered part of the environment, since then the environment changes automatically as the average fitness of the population increases. For example, suppose that the members of the population compete among themselves. Perhaps they engage in simulated combat, or they might compete for resources that they need to reproduce. This competition has the potential to drive the evolving population to ever-increasing levels of sophistication and complexity.

The genetic algorithm can be used to solve difficult, practical problems. For example, suppose the problem is to find the optimal shape for the wings of a certain type of airplane. Once some way is found to encode the shape as a sequence of zeros and ones, the genetic algorithm can be applied. Fitness just measures the actual performance of a wing. (This can be simulated on a computer; you don't have to build legions of airplanes!) People are even using the genetic algorithm to try to evolve programs that can predict the behavior of the stock market.

More interesting from my point of view, however, are simulated computer worlds in which the evolving entities are lifelike simulated organisms. For it is in such systems that we see hints of the real power of evolution to generate complexity.

*   *   *

The view of the mind as a logic machine, detached from the world and engaged in a precise exercise in abstract reasoning, has a kind of cold elegance. But the reality, I think, is messier and more interesting. If an artificial mind ever looks out with understanding on the world, it will probably be filled with echoes of SHRDLU and CYC alongside shadows of neural nets and genetic algorithms and other things not yet imagined. I suspect that it will be a complex, almost jury-rigged, affair, and that no one will really understand exactly how it works—not even itself. In this, it will be very much like us.

Chapter Summary

Can computers be programmed to be intelligent? If the requirement is just that computers perform tasks that are ordinarily considered to demand some intelligence, then the answer is surely yes. Artificial intelligence in this sense has had significant successes, with more to come. But true general intelligence has not yet been achieved in computers, and it is not clear whether it ever will be. Certainly, no computer has yet come close to passing the *Turing Test*, proposed by Alan Turing in 1950 as a way of testing machines for intelligence.

The traditional approach to AI is based on the *physical symbol system hypothesis*. Knowledge is represented as a data structure containing symbols that are manipulated according to programmed rules. Existing programs deal only with *microworlds*, but the *CYC project* is attempting to build a data structure containing enough facts to support general intelligence. (It is not yet clear how close it will come to success.) Successful applications of traditional AI include *expert systems* and some *natural language processing* programs.

From the beginning, there has been controversy about whether true artificial intelligence is even possible. Mathematical results proved by Kurt Gödel and Alan Turing put certain absolute limits on what computers can do. Hubert Dreyfus says that computers, which can deal only with facts and rules, can never interact with the natural world in the way that people do. John Searle claims that even if a computer seemed to be intelligent, it would be mere simulation, different in kind from the intelligence of a conscious, feeling human being.

Inspired by the failures of traditional AI, and perhaps by these philosophical criticisms, some researchers are using new techniques that are informed by the ways in which people and other organisms exist in the natural world. Many of these approaches make use of the fact that complex behavior can *emerge*—without complex programming—from simple components interacting according to simple rules. Examples include *neural nets* and the *genetic algorithm.*

This chapter brings *The Most Complex Machine* to an end on a philosophical note. Computation, which seemed at first a simple and even simple-minded thing, turns out to have hidden depth—to the extent that some people have seriously proposed that the universe itself is a kind of ongoing computation. It might be, we are told, that we ourselves are fundamentally similar to the computers we have created, our intelligence a kind of program being executed by the brain.

Some people are frightened by this idea that we might be machines—*mere machines*, they would say. But even if, in the end, we do turn out to be machines, we are very complex machines indeed, and it would only show that machines are capable of exceedingly strange and marvelous things.

Questions

1. There are several possible opinions on the Turing Test. You might think that computers will eventually pass it, and that when they do they will have to be considered intelligent. You might think that it is impossible for a computer ever to pass it. You might think that a computer could pass it without necessarily being intelligent. You might imagine a super-intelligent computer that nevertheless could not pass the test. What justifications can be given for each of these opinions? What is your own opinion?

2. In traditional AI, a concept such as "dog" must be represented as part of a symbol structure. The "dog" concept might be linked to other concepts such as "mammal," "pet," or "fur." Give a more detailed description of a symbol structure that represents the concept "dog." (You might try drawing a structure in which linked symbols are connected by lines.) To what extent do you think the structure captures the meaning of the word "dog"?

3. Imagine a computer program that is supposed to understand children's stories. (Programs that attempt to do this have been written.) The program will need rules about how typical things found in such stories might behave. One such rule might be, "All birds can fly." If the story is about Polly, a bird who escapes when its cage is left open, the program can deduce that Polly probably flew away even though that fact is not explicitly stated in the story. Such deductions are part of what it means to understand. The problem is that the rule isn't true. Not all birds can fly. For example, penguins are birds but cannot fly. List as many other exceptions to the rule as you can find, even silly ones such as, "A bird that is too afraid to fly cannot fly." Might the exceptions you list be relevant to understanding a children's story? What does this example show about the difficulty of encoding human knowledge as rules and symbol structures?

Answers

EACH CHAPTER in this text ends with a list of questions for your consideration. These questions are meant to be thought about and/or discussed, and many of them don't really have single, definite, right answers. However, here are some thoughts of my own on possible answers—along with, in a few cases, extra discussion of interesting points not covered elsewhere in the text. These answers are meant to be read after you have already thought about the questions, but of course, you can use them as you like.

Chapter 1 Answers

1.1. How can we convert a base-ten number to the base two? For a power of two, the answer is easy. You just get a one followed by the appropriate number of zeros. For example, $2^5 = 100000_2$. The next observation is that in base two, it is trivial to add up powers of two provided that all the powers are different; each power of two just contributes a one to the final answer. For example, $10000_2 + 1000_2 + 10_2 = 11010_2$. So, the method of breaking a number down into a sum of distinct powers of two, converting each power of two into binary, and then adding the resulting numbers does always work.

Of course, you must have distinct powers of two for this to work easily. It is true that $10 = 4 + 4 + 2 = 100_2 + 100_2 + 10_2$, but this leaves us with the problem of adding $100_2 + 100_2$, which is easy enough in this case, but not so easy as adding numbers with ones in different positions. The problem, then, is to systematically pull powers of two out of a base ten number without any duplications. Starting with the largest power of two contained in the number is one way of doing this. (Once you have pulled out the largest power of two, what's left over will be a smaller number that cannot contain a second power of two of the same size.)

1.2. Note that the question here is simply to find the number of different sequences made up of k letters, where each letter is A, T, C, or G. Although the question talks about DNA, that's really just an application of the answer and has nothing to do with finding the answer.

For binary numbers, we found that increasing the number of digits by one would double the number of possible sequences of digits. This was because we could take each sequence of k digits and produce two sequences of length $k + 1$ from it, by tacking on either a zero or a one.

We can do something similar here. From each possible sequence of k letters, we can produce four different sequences of length $k + 1$ by tacking on either an A, a T, a C, or a G. For example, from the sequence ATAAC, we can make ATAACA, ATAACT, ATAACC, and ATAACG. It follows that the number of sequences of $k + 1$ letters is four times the number of sequences of k letters. Since there are 4 sequences consisting of just one letter, there will be 4×4 sequences of length two, $4 \times 4 \times 4$ of length three, and so on. In general, there will be 4^k sequences of length k.

1.3. For a circuit with k input wires, there are 2^k different ways of setting these wires to be on or off. The easiest way to see this is to note that when we think of on as being the same as 1 and off as being the same as 0, then the setting of the k wires represents a k-bit binary number. Since there are 2^k different k-bit binary numbers, there are 2^k different possible settings of the wires.

The second question, dealing with the number of possible circuits with k inputs, is even more abstract and therefore more difficult. Think of it like this: You are given a table listing all the possible combinations of k inputs, where each input can be either off or on. The problem is to figure out how many different ways there are to fill in the outputs. For two inputs, the table would look like:

Input 1	Input 2	Output
off	off	
off	on	
on	off	
on	on	

The question is, in how many different ways can the last column be filled in with on's and off's? But this isn't so hard after all. There are four spaces, each of which can be filled in in two ways. The number of ways of doing this is the same as the number of 4-bit binary numbers, that is, 2^4. In general, if there are n rows in the table, then the number of ways of filling in the column of output values will be 2^n.

To finish this, we have to know what n is. Suppose that there are k input wires. The number of rows in the table is just the number of different ways that the values on these wires can be set. From the first part of the problem, we know that this number is 2^k. That is, n, the number of rows in the table, is 2^k. So, 2^n, the number of ways of filling in the output values, is 2^{2^k}, which is our final answer.

Even for small values of k, this can be very large number. For circuits with five inputs and one output, 2^k would be 32, and the number of different input/output tables would be 2^{32}, which is more than four billion. For $k = 10$, the number is 2^{1024}, which is almost unimaginably huge.

1.4. If you build a three-input AND gate from two regular two-input AND gates, the circuit you build contains eight transistors—four in each two-input AND gate. By building the three-input AND gate directly from six transistors, you save two transistors. Obviously, if you are going to be using a lot of three-input AND gates, the savings will be substantial. On the other hand, we gain a great deal in conceptual simplicity by building everything up from the three basic kinds of gates, and we can do so without knowing anything about transistors at all. The trade-off, then, is between conceptual simplicity and the cost of the physical components of the circuit.

There is often such a trade-off, and it is not always obvious how the conflict between them should be resolved. But conceptual simplicity is important and can often help save development and maintenance costs. Often, this will more than make up for the costs of the components used.

Diagrams of the two possible ways of constructing a three-input AND gate are shown in Figure A.1.

1.5. After a subroutine ends, the computer must jump back to the point in the program from which the subroutine was called. This point is called the *return address* and is just a binary number. (The computer can get this number from the program counter before it jumps to the start of the subroutine.) While the computer is executing the subroutine, it must remember the return address. It might store this data in some particular memory location, say, memory location number 38,543. Then, every subroutine could end with the instruction, "Go back to the return address stored in memory location 38,543."

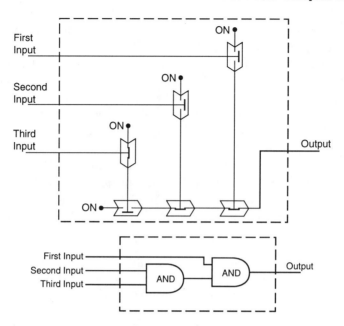

Figure A.1. *Two ways of constructing a three-input* AND *gate. The top circuit is constructed from four transistors; the one below, from two two-input* AND *gates. The symbol used for an* AND *gate in the lower diagram is introduced in Chapter 2.*

Using a single memory location will not work, however, if one subroutine calls another. The problem is that when the return address for the second subroutine is placed in location 38,543, it will erase the return address for the first subroutine. The computer will then have no way to get back to the point in the program from which the first subroutine was called. One solution would be to use a different memory location for each subroutine. The subroutine is itself stored in memory. The computer could use the location just after the end of each subroutine to store the return address for that subroutine. The instruction at the end of the subroutine would say, "Go back to the return address stored in the *next* memory location."

This works fine except for one subtle but surprisingly important possibility. What happens if a subroutine calls *itself*? This is called **recursion**, a subject that you will encounter again in Chapter 7. The problem here is that if the return address is simply stored in memory after the end of the subroutine, then the second call to the subroutine will erase the return address for the first. The solution is for the computer to keep a list of all the return addresses of currently active subroutines, stored in a portion of memory set aside for this purpose. When a subroutine is called, a new return address is added to the end of the list; when the subroutine ends, the last return address in the list is used. This list might contain several different return addresses for the same subroutine, if that subroutine calls itself. This is discussed in more detail in Section 7.4.

The last part of the question—to explain why it is essential for a subroutine to be able to make use of other subroutines—is related to the idea of a complex system as having many different *levels* of complexity. On each level, new components are made by chunking together simpler components from the levels below. The step from one level to the next has to be small enough to be comprehensible, so that real complexity cannot be achieved in just one step. If subroutines could not use other subroutines, we would be limited to just one level of chunking, and our ability to program solutions to complex problems would be greatly limited. In fact, we can write subroutines to solve fairly easy problems, and then use them in subroutines to solve slightly complex problems, which can be used in turn to solve moderately complex problems and so on to as many levels as we need.

1.6. Structured complexity is everywhere. In biology, an organism is made up of organs, which are made up of cells, which are made up of smaller components. In the other direction, individual organisms can be grouped into species, which are grouped into genera, then into families, and so forth.

Books are made up of chapters, sections, subsections, paragraphs, sentences, words, and letters—on different levels of complexity. Political organizations are often divided into national, state, county, and municipal levels. Armies have divisions, brigades, and platoons. Time can be measured in eons, millennia, centuries, years, days, hours, minutes, or seconds.

A planet or star is just a lot of atoms, organized in the right way. Stars and planets can get together and make solar systems. A bunch of solar systems make a galaxy, while galaxies themselves can be organized into clusters.

There are lots of examples. Just look around. And think about how dealing with an organized world, instead of with a chaos of details, makes your life easier.

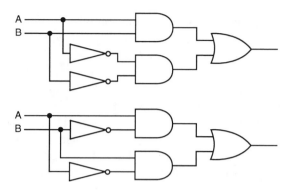

Figure A.2. *The top circuit corresponds to the expression (A* AND *B)* OR *((*NOT *A) AND (*NOT *B)). Its output is on whenever its inputs are the same. For the bottom circuit, the outputs are on whenever the inputs are different, that is, when A is true and B is false or when A is false and B is true.*

Chapter 2 Answers

2.1. The circuit whose output is on whenever its two inputs are the *same* is shown in Figure A.2. A circuit with two inputs whose output is on whenever the two inputs are *different* corresponds to the expression *(A* AND (NOT *B))* OR *((*NOT *A)* AND *B)*. This circuit is also shown in the figure.

Now, saying that the two inputs of a circuit are *different* is exactly equivalent to saying that they are NOT *the same*. Given a circuit that computes whether its inputs are the same, we could feed the output from that circuit through a NOT gate. The output from the NOT gate would then be on precisely when the inputs to the circuit are different. That is, if we feed the output from the top circuit in Figure A.2 through a NOT gate, we obtain a circuit equivalent to the bottom circuit in that figure.

Suppose we have a large input/output table in which most of the outputs are specified to be **true**. The best way to proceed is to build a circuit that does exactly the *opposite* of what that table specifies! That is, we build a circuit whose output is **on** precisely when the table says that the output should be **off**. The circuit that we really want can then be obtained by feeding the output from the circuit we have built through a NOT gate. This will produce a circuit that is smaller than the one that we would have obtained by following the specifications in the table directly.

A	B	NOT $(A$ AND $B)$	$($NOT $A)$ OR $($NOT $B)$
false	false	true	true
false	true	true	true
true	false	true	true
true	true	false	false

Figure A.3. *A truth table that verifies DeMorgan's law, namely that* NOT *(A* AND *B)* ≡ *(*NOT *A)* OR *(*NOT *B). The last two columns of the table show that these two expressions have the same value for any possible combination of input values.*

2.2. I will leave it as an easy exercise to draw the circuits representing the two sides of DeMorgan's Law. Figure A.3 shows a ***truth table*** which demonstrates that the two sides of DeMorgan's laws have the same value for any possible combination of inputs. (A truth table is simply a systematic way of listing all possible inputs to an expression of Boolean algebra and finding the value of the expression in each case. Truth tables are effective ways of verifying that the laws of Boolean algebra are in fact true.)

An English example of DeMorgan's law is the statement, "This card is not the ace of spades." This can be rephrased as, "It is NOT true that both (this card is an ace AND this card is a spade)." Now, ask yourself how a card can fail to be *both* an ace and a space. It can do so *either* by failing to be an ace OR by failing to be a spade. Thus, a card is "not the ace of spades" if and only if either "it is not an ace" or "it is not a spade" (or if it is neither, which is included in the meaning of the logical operator OR).

As another example, we would say that it is NOT a warm and sunny day if it is NOT warm OR if it is NOT sunny.

There are actually two parts to DeMorgan's law. The second part says that NOT $(A$ OR $B)$ ≡ $($NOT $A)$ AND $($NOT $B)$. You can easily verify this with a truth table. For an example in English, saying "It is neither warm nor sunny" is equivalent to asserting that *both* "It is not warm" and "It is not sunny."

2.3. An input/output table for a full adder is shown in Figure A.4. The circuit built from this is quite complicated, and I leave it as a straightforward but annoying exercise.

A circuit built directly from the table in Figure A.4 is much more complicated, in the sense of having more gates, than the circuit we built

A	B	Carry-in	Sum	Carry-out
0	0	0	0	0
0	0	1	1	0
0	1	0	1	0
0	1	1	0	1
1	0	0	1	0
1	0	1	0	1
1	1	0	0	1
1	1	1	1	1

Figure A.4. *A table showing the two outputs of a full adder circuit for each possible combination of values of its three inputs. The outputs are the two digits of the sum obtained when the three input bits are added. For example, the sum $1_2 + 1_2 + 0_2 = 10_2$ is represented by the seventh row of the table.*

from two half-adders. Therefore, it would be more expensive and consume more power. In this practical sense, it certainly makes a difference which version we use. On the other hand, the two circuits have exactly the same input/output behavior. In that sense, they are completely interchangeable, and in this theoretical sense it makes no difference which one we use.

In general, we should prefer the "simpler" solution to a problem, but it is not always clear what that means. When cost is paramount, the simpler circuit is the one with fewer gates. But if we are primarily interested in understanding what is going on, then conceptual simplicity is more important, even if the result is a circuit with more gates.

2.4. Given any logic circuit that does not contain a feedback loop, it is possible to write down an expression of Boolean algebra that gives the output of the circuit as a function of its inputs. (I am assuming here that the circuit has only one output; if it has several, then one Boolean expression is needed for each of its outputs.) The key observation is that we can actually write down expressions for the outputs from all of the individual gates in the circuit; the final output from the circuit is just a special case.

The first step is to label the inputs with letters, such as A and B. Then, we go on to label each output wire from each gate in the circuit with the logical expression computed by that gate. Pick any gate in the circuit such that the input wires to that gate are already labeled (either with individual letters or with expressions computed by other gates). Suppose that the gate is a NOT gate and that the label on the input wire is P. Then label the output of that NOT gate with "(NOT P)". If the gate is an AND gate and if the two inputs to the gate are labeled P and Q, then label the output with "(P AND Q)". An OR gate is treated similarly. Repeat this process until the output from every gate is labeled, including the final output from the entire circuit. A circuit labeled in this way is shown in Figure 2.3.

How do we know that all the output wires will eventually be labeled? Well, if there's a feedback loop in the circuit, they won't be. It is not possible to label the output from a gate until after its inputs have been labeled. If the gate is part of a feedback loop, however, one of the inputs to the gate is connected, directly or indirectly, to the output from the gate. This means that that input cannot be labeled until sometime *after* the output is labeled. This gives a contradiction: We can't label the output unless the input is already labeled, but the input depends on the output.

If there is no feedback loop (and assuming that all the input wires to all the gates in the circuit are in fact connected to something), then our method for labeling outputs works. Essentially, a loop is the only thing that can go wrong. Actually proving this requires a bit of mathematical thinking. (Read this if you want.)

We have to show that as long as there are *any* gates in the circuit whose outputs are unlabeled, there must be at least one gate whose inputs are all labeled but whose output is unlabeled. Pick any gate, G_1, whose output is unlabeled. If it has an unlabeled input, let G_2 be the gate that produces that input. If G_2 also has an unlabeled input, then let G_3 be the gate that produces that input, and so forth. There can't be any repetitions in this list because a repetition would be a loop (some G_n gets input from G_{n+1}, which gets input from G_{n+2}, ..., which gets input from G_n). If there are no repetitions, the sequence G_1, G_2, ... can't continue forever since there are only a finite number of gates in the circuit. So, the list must end eventually with some gate that has no unlabeled inputs. This is what we wanted to show. Finding a gate whose inputs are labeled allows us to label its output and to continue the labeling process.

2.5. If a NOT gate is sitting by itself, unconnected to anything, then there is no power being supplied to its input; its input is off. Since the NOT gate reverses its input, the output is on. (Remember that the NOT gate has an internal power supply that produces the voltage on its output wire.) Now, suppose that you connect the output wire of the NOT gate to its input wire.

At the very moment you do this, the input to the gate is still off, but a tiny fraction of a second later the electric impulse from the output wire reaches the input. When the input to a NOT gate is turned on, its output goes off. (Again, only after the small period of time it takes for the signal to pass through the gate.) So, now the output is off. But the output is connected to the input, so this turns the input off. But when the input goes off, the output turns on again. But when the output turns on, it turns the input on.…

This cycle repeats regularly. The output from the gate alternates between on and off. The time it takes to complete an on/off cycle is just the time it takes for an electrical signal to pass through the gate and over the wire connecting the output to the input. The NOT gate is really a kind of clock that turns its output wire on and off as it "ticks."

2.6. A multiplexer circuit is shown in Figure A.5. The second circuit in that figure uses four multiplexers and a four-bit adder to produce a circuit that can either add or subtract, depending on whether the control wire, Select-subtract, is off or on. Note that Select-subtract is connected to the Select wire of each of the four multiplexers and is also connected to the Carry-in input wire on the right end of the addition circuit. (Refer to Figures 2.9 and 2.10 if you have forgotten the details of how addition and subtraction circuits work.)

When Select-subtract is off, the input data for the calculation is fed unchanged into the addition circuit, and the Carry-in at the left of the addition circuit is turned off. So, the addition circuit simply computes the sum of the two four-bit inputs as usual.

If Select-subtract is on, then the ones complement of the second four-bit input is fed into the addition circuit. Furthermore, the Carry-in wire is turned on. This is the setup for doing subtraction, as shown in Figure 2.10.

We have thus arranged for the same circuit to be used for both addition and subtraction. To complete the redesign of the ALU, we need only make a minor modification in the circuit shown in Figure 2.13, to account for the fact that the addition and subtraction circuits have been consolidated. A simple way of doing this is to replace the wires labeled "from Subtraction Circuit" and "from Addition Circuit" with a single wire that comes from the combined circuit.

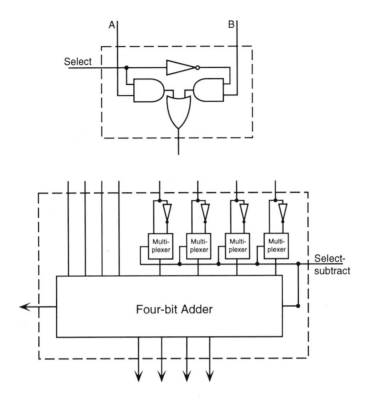

Figure A.5. *The top circuit in this figure is a multiplexer. Its output will be equal to the value of input A if the* Select *wire is on, and will be equal to input B if the* Select *wire is off. The bottom circuit can perform both additions and subtractions, as explained in the answer to problem 2.6. (Refer to Figures 2.9 and 2.10 for the original addition and subtraction circuits.)*

Because of the complexity of an addition circuit, these modifications will significantly reduce the size of the ALU without changing its function. (But, in fact, the main reason for working through this problem is to further your understanding and intuition about the way control wires and gates can be used to control the flow of data through a circuit.)

Chapter 3 Answers

3.1. We cannot connect the ALU's input wires directly to the output from the accumulator. The problem is that when the ALU performs a computation, the Load-AC-from-ALU control wire is turned on to load the answer into the accumulator. All this takes time, and the value in the accumulator will change *before* Load-AC-from-ALU is turned off. The output from the accumulator will change at the same time. If the output from the accumulator were used directly as input to the ALU, then the input to the ALU would change as well. But this might then cause the output from the ALU to change (from the right answer to something else), which can cause a further change in the contents of the accumulator, and so on.

In effect, as long as Load-AC-from-ALU is on, we have created an uncontrolled feedback loop that will have unpredictable (and useless) results. The X register attached to the ALU's input stops this loop from forming. With the X register in place, a loop could be formed only if both the Load-AC-from-ALU and the Load-X-from-AC wires were turned on at the same time, opening up both "information gates" that control the flow of information in the loop. That will never happen.

3.2. This one I'm not going to do for you. A complete drawing of xComputer is pretty complicated. All the interconnections between the various components are indicated in Figures 3.1, 3.4, and 3.6. It would be useful to put it all together, maybe with pretty colors.

3.3. If all programs were written correctly the first time, it would never happen that a meaningless instruction code would be loaded into the instruction register. In the real world, though, it could easily happen. For example, a JMP instruction might incorrectly jump to a memory location that contains data instead of part of the program. Ideally, the computer would be able to indicate in some way that an error has been detected. In our simple model computer, perhaps the best that can be done is to have the computer halt. This is certainly better than having the computer ignore the instruction and go on as if nothing has happened! It is usually better to get no result at all than to get an incorrect result.

In the design of xComputer as given in this chapter, no account is taken of the possibility of illegal instructions. For example, the leftmost two bits of a legal instruction code, which indicate the addressing mode for that instruction, must be 00, 01, or 10. A value of 11 is not allowed. It is completely predictable what would happen when an illegal instruction code beginning with 11 is loaded into the instruction register, but only with a detailed analysis of the construction of the computer. In Figure 3.14, for example, both of the wires Indirect and Constant—which indicate the addressing mode—will be turned on for an instruction beginning with 11. This will cause all those control wires to come on that would ordinarily be turned on for *either* constant or indirect addressing. Although something definite and predictable would happen, it would probably look pretty random.

To avoid this, the Control circuit should be redesigned so that every illegal instruction is treated exactly like a Halt instruction. This is no different in principle from the way we designed the Control circuit in the first place, but the logic circuit that controls the **Stop-clock** wire will be more complicated. (If you would prefer to have xComputer ignore illegal instructions, you could have it turn on **Set-COUNT-to-zero** instead of **Stop-clock** when such an instruction is detected. You would still have to redesign the Control circuit to do this.)

3.4. The Control circuit in xComputer consists of 26 subcircuits, each responsible for turning one control wire on and off as necessary to execute machine-language instructions. This problem asks us to "design" the subcircuits for the **Load-PC-from-IR** and **Load-PC-from-memory** control wires. As explained in Section 3.3, we can begin by looking at the lists of steps for executing each instruction, and we can use these lists to write down a Boolean expression that specifies when each control wire is to be turned on. The Boolean expressions are given in terms of the outputs from the decoder circuits shown in Figure 3.14. These Boolean expressions *are* in fact the designs for the circuits that we want.

Load-PC-from-IR is used during step 4 of the executions of the JMP, JMZ, JMN, and JMF instructions, as shown in Figure 3.11. This control wire is used for the direct-addressing versions of the commands; it moves the location number specified in the data bits of the instruction from the instruction register to the program counter. For the conditional jump instructions, this is done only if some condition holds. The wires AC=0, AC<0, and FLAG=1 in Figure 3.14 are used to test the conditions for the JMZ, JMN, and JMF instructions. So, the expression that determines when **Load-PC-from-IR** is to be turned on is:

$$\text{Load-PC-from-IR} = \text{Step}_4 \text{ AND Direct AND}$$
$$(\text{ JMP OR (JMZ AND AC=0)}$$
$$\text{OR (JMN AND AC<0)}$$
$$\text{OR (JMF AND FLAG=1))}.$$

(You have to remember that Step_4, Direct, JMP, AC=0, and so on are just the names of *wires*, from Figure 3.14, that are available as inputs to the circuit that we are designing.)

Load-PC-from-memory didn't show up in any of the lists of steps given in Chapter 3. This is because it is needed only for the jump instructions that use indirect addressing, JMP-I, JMZ-I, JMN-I, and JMF-I. The lists of steps for these instructions were left as an exercise. In direct addressing, the data bits in the instruction specify the location in memory to which the computer should jump when the instruction is executed. In indirect addressing, the data bits again specify a location in memory, but the *contents* of *that* location specify *another* location to which the computer should jump. That is, the new value for the PC comes from memory, not from the instructions register. The data from the instruction register is loaded into the address register to specify where the data for the PC is to be found. (Got that?) The steps for executing JMP-I are

Step 4 (JMP-I): Turn on Load-ADDR-from-IR.
Step 5 (JMP-I): Turn on Load-PC-from-memory.
Step 6 (JMP-I): Turn on Set-COUNT-to-zero.

The steps for JMZ-I, JMN-I, and JMF-I are similar but include a test in step 5 to see whether the appropriate condition is true. The Boolean expression for Load-PC-from-memory is thus

$$\text{Load-PC-from-IR} = \text{Step}_5 \text{ AND Indirect AND}$$
$$(\text{ JMP OR } (\text{JMZ AND AC=0})$$
$$\text{OR } (\text{JMN AND AC<0})$$
$$\text{OR } (\text{JMF AND FLAG=1})).$$

3.5. The xComputer was designed to manipulate sixteen-bit binary numbers (as data), six-bit numbers (as instruction codes), and ten-bit numbers (as addresses for specifying locations in memory). For example, each memory location holds a sixteen-bit number, and the main memory has sixteen data input wires and sixteen data output wires for reading and storing numbers. But it has only ten address wires for specifying locations.

The ALU is designed with sixteen-bit inputs and outputs. On the other hand, the program counter and the address register, which both hold addresses of locations in memory, are ten-bit registers.

The limitation to ten address wires was more or less forced on us by two other decisions: the decision to represent a machine-language instruction with a single sixteen-bit number (rather than using two consecutive memory locations to store a single instruction, for example) and the decision to use six-bit instruction codes, leaving room for only ten data bits in our sixteen-bit instructions.

Label	Instruction		Label	Instruction	
	LOD	Packed		LOD	Char1
	SHR			SHL	
	SHR			SHL	
	SHR			SHL	
	SHR			SHL	
	SHR			SHL	
	SHR			SHL	
	SHR			SHL	
	SHR			SHL	
	STO	Char1		OR	Char2
	LOD	Packed		STO	Packed
	AND-C	255	Packed:	data	
	STO	Char2	Char1:	data	
Packed:	data		Char2:	data	
Char1:	data				
Char2:	data				

Figure A.6. *Two assembly-language programs for manipulating ASCII character codes. Although we think of it as representing a character, an ASCII code is really just an eight-bit number. The program on the left takes a sixteen-bit number, initially stored in the memory location labeled* Packed, *breaks it into two eight-bit numbers, and stores them in the memory locations labeled* Char1 *and* Char2. *The second program reverses the process. It combines two eight-bit numbers from* Char1 *and* Char2 *and stores the result in* Packed.

We could easily redesign xComputer to use data with more than sixteen bits. Making, say, a thirty-two-bit adder is no more conceptually difficult than a sixteen-bit adder. Essentially, we would double the size of most of the components used in building the computer. Once we do this, we could have more address bits in our instructions. Assuming that we still use six-bit instruction codes, that would leave twenty-six bits that we could use to specify an address. We could then use a main memory with up to 2^{26}, or about 67 million, locations.

3.6. Figure A.6 shows programs for converting characters between "packed" and "unpacked" format. The first program extracts two eight-bit numbers from a single sixteen-bit number. It assumes that the sixteen-bit number is stored in the memory location labeled *Packed* before the program is run. If the original sixteen-bit number is

$$a_1 a_2 a_3 a_4 a_5 a_6 a_7 a_8 b_1 b_2 b_3 b_4 b_5 b_6 b_7 b_8$$

where the a's and b's stand for zeros or ones, then shifting it right eight times converts it to $00000000a_1 a_2 a_3 a_4 a_5 a_6 a_7 a_8$. This gives us the first eight-bit number we want. The second eight-bit number is computed as

$$0000000011111111_2 \text{ AND } a_1 a_2 a_3 a_4 a_5 a_6 a_7 a_8 b_1 b_2 b_3 b_4 b_5 b_6 b_7 b_8$$
$$= 00000000 b_1 b_2 b_3 b_4 b_5 b_6 b_7 b_8$$

where "AND" here means a sixteen-bit AND operation. Note that in the program, 0000000011111111_2 is given in base-ten form as 255.

For the second program, we are given two eight-bit numbers in memory locations *Char1* and *Char2*, and the object is to combine them into a single sixteen-bit number and store them in the location named *Packed*. Let's suppose that the given numbers are $00000000a_1 a_2 a_3 a_4 a_5 a_6 a_7 a_8$ and $00000000 b_1 b_2 b_3 b_4 b_5 b_6 b_7 b_8$. Shifting the first left eight times converts it to $a_1 a_2 a_3 a_4 a_5 a_6 a_7 a_8 00000000$. We can then combine this with the second number using a sixteen-bit OR operation:

$$a_1 a_2 a_3 a_4 a_5 a_6 a_7 a_8 00000000 \text{ OR } 00000000 b_1 b_2 b_3 b_4 b_5 b_6 b_7 b_8$$
$$= a_1 a_2 a_3 a_4 a_5 a_6 a_7 a_8 b_1 b_2 b_3 b_4 b_5 b_6 b_7 b_8$$

This gives the result we want to store in *Packed*.

Working through this example can help you gain some understanding of why the shift operations and the sixteen-bit AND, OR, and NOT operations should be included in a computer's instruction set.

3.7. Implementing subroutines on xComputer is not all that hard, and it provides a natural use for the otherwise odd-looking instruction JMP-I. (Recall that JMP-I N tells the computer to fetch the contents of memory location N and to jump to the address indicated by the number it finds there.) We decree that the memory location immediately following a subroutine will be used to store the return address. The program that calls the subroutine is responsible for storing the return address there before jumping to the start of the subroutine. In outline, the subroutine would look like this:

Label	Instruction	Comment
Sub:	...	;start of subroutine
	...	;instructions for subroutine
	JMP-I RtnAdr	;jump to location stored in RtnAdr
RtnAdr:	data	;holds the return address

The dots represent whatever instructions constitute the subroutine. The subroutine actually ends with the JMP-I instruction. The next location, labeled *RtnAdr*, is where the program must put the return address.

The instruction "JMP-I RtnAdr" means "jump to the memory location whose address is stored in location number $RtnAdr$."

The program would call this subroutine with the three instructions:

$$\begin{array}{ll} \text{LOD-C} & \text{Next} \\ \text{STO} & \text{RtnAdr} \\ \text{JMP} & \text{Sub} \\ \text{Next:} \quad \dots \end{array}$$

The line labeled $Next$ can contain any instruction. This is where the program will pick up after the subroutine has been executed. Remember that the label $Next$ is really a number. The instruction "LOD-C Next" will load that number into the accumulator. From there, it is stored into location $RtnAdr$, where the JMP-I at the end of the subroutine expects it. Once the return address has been set up, the JMP instruction will begin execution of the subroutine.

By the way, sometimes a program and a subroutine must pass data back and forth. Such data can be handled in the same way that we have handled the return address. If the program must provide some data for the subroutine, it can load it into a location that follows the subroutine in memory, and the subroutine can access it from there. Data to be passed back from the subroutine to the program can be handled similarly.

3.8. A complete assembly-language program for multiplying two numbers is shown in Figure A.7. As explained in Subsection 2.2.4, multiplication can be performed as a sequence of shift operations and additions. You should look at the example in that section again and work some additional examples.

If $N1$ consisted entirely of ones, then we would multiply another number $N2$ by $N1$ by repeatedly shifting $N2$ to the left and adding up all the numbers we generate in this way. The number of digits in $N1$ would tell us how many times to do this. For example, if $N1 = 1111_2$,

$$1111_2 \times 1101_2 = 1101_2 + 11010_2 + 110100_2 + 1101000_2.$$

(Shifting $N2$ to the left is the same as multiplying it by 10_2, so that $1101000_2 = 1101_2 \times 1000_2$, for example. Combine this with the fact that $1111_2 = 1_2 + 10_2 + 100_2 + 1000_2$ to see why this method of multiplication works.)

If $N1$ contains a zero, it just means that we should omit the corresponding term on the right of the sum. To keep things straight, though, we still should shift $N2$ left for each step:

$$1010_2 \times 1101_2 = (0 \times 1101_2) + 11010_2 + (0 \times 110100_2) + 1101000_2.$$

Label	Instruction	
start:	LOD-C	0
	STO	ANS
loop:	LOD	N1
	JMZ	done
	SHR	
	STO	N1
	JMF	doAdd
shift:	LOD	N2
	SHL	
	STO	N2
	JMP	loop
doAdd:	LOD	N2
	ADD	ANS
	STO	ANS
	JMP	shift
done:	HLT	
N1:	data	
N2:	data	
ANS:	data	

Figure A.7. *A program for multiplying two numbers. The numbers must be stored in the locations labeled N1 and N2 before the program is run. The product of these two numbers will be placed in the location labeled ANS. This will only give the correct answer if that answer can be expressed with sixteen or fewer bits.*

So there is really nothing mysterious here. We need a loop that will repeatedly shift $N2$ to the left and either add or not add the result into a sum, depending on whether the next bit in $N1$ is one or zero. Testing the bits of $N1$ requires some ingenuity, and it gives a chance to actually use the FLAG register and the JMF instruction. Recall that when the ALU is used to shift $N1$ to the right, the rightmost bit will "fall off" into the FLAG register. The JMF instruction can then be used to test whether that bit was a zero or a one. In our multiplication program, we repeatedly shift $N1$ to the right at the same time that we are shifting $N2$ to the left. Each time we do this, we test whether the bit that falls into the FLAG register is one. If it is, we add the (current) value of $N2$ into the answer and then shift $N2$ to the left. If the bit in the flag register is 0, we skip the addition but still do the left shift. We know we are done when the value of $N1$ becomes zero (because we have then accounted for all the ones that the original number contained).

All this is hard enough to say in English. Getting it into assembly language is something of a chore, but at least the result is unambiguous. I encourage you to trace the step-by-step execution of the program in Figure A.7 for a few examples.

Here is a brief summary of how this program works: The first two instructions in the program put a zero in memory location ANS; this is the starting point for the sum that will be the answer at the end of the program. The five instructions beginning with *loop* test whether $N1$ is zero (which tells us our answer is complete), shifts it to the right, and tests whether the bit that falls off the end is a one. If it is, then the instructions beginning with *doAdd* will add the current value of $N2$ to the sum. Whether or not the addition is performed, the instructions beginning with *shift* will shift $N2$ to the left and then jump back to the beginning of the loop.

Chapter 4 Answers

4.1. This problem asks you to "play computer." That is, you are supposed to follow a definite, step-by-step procedure in which the actions you perform and the the decisions you make are based *only* on the explicit instructions you are given and the very small amount of data you can inspect at a given time. When deciding what to do next, you are not allowed to remember what has happened in the past, and you cannot let yourself be influenced by the meaning of what you are doing. The fact that computers operate in this way is one of the things that makes writing programs for them so difficult. Playing computer can help you get a feel for just how simple-minded and literal-minded computers are, and that can help to make programming easier.

You should sit down with Figure 4.1 and a pencil. Work through the six-step procedure, writing in changes to the values listed in the various memory locations. Start with step 1: Cross out the 0 in location 1 and put a 1 there. For step 2, put a 0 in location 0. (There is already a 0 there, so this doesn't change anything this time around.)

For step 3, look at each input value in turn, in locations 4, 8, 10, 14, and 16. For each of these values, check the output value that is its source. For example, the value in location 4 is the input to a NOT gate, which is attached—as specified in location 5—to the output wire whose value is in location 1. Since the value in location 1 is 1, you have to change the value in location 4 to match this. So, cross out the 0 in location 4 and write in a 1. As you go on to check each of the other input values, you will find that the value listed in location 16 for the second input of the OR gate also changes.

In step 4, check that the output values stored in locations 3, 7, and 13 are correct for the given inputs to each gate. Location 3 represents the output from a NOT gate. The input for this gate (in location 4) is listed as 1, so the output should be 0. Since the output is listed as 1, you have to cross out the 0 in location 3 and write in a 1. Also, according to the directions in step 4, you should cross out the 0 in location 0 and write in a 1. The output value for the OR gate also changes; the output of the AND gate does not.

Then, in step 5, the fact that there is a 1 in location 0 means that you have to return to step 2 and repeat steps 2 through 5 again.

Soon enough, after doing this for a while, you should say, "Oh yeah, now I see how it works." At that point, of course, you have accomplished the purpose of the exercise. You have extracted the meaning from the details of the individual steps in the program.

4.2. The reason we don't do this is that a Turing machine can't do anything *interesting* by staying in the same cell. The action of a Turing machine at a given time is completely determined by the state it is in and by the symbol that it reads. If it did sit on the same cell for a while, its ultimate action—writing some symbol and then moving left or right or halting—would be completely determined by the *initial* symbol that it saw in that cell and the *initial* state it was in when it first entered that cell. Whenever it encountered the same symbol in the same state, it would go through the same sequence of operations before performing the same ultimate action. So, we might as well make it skip the intermediate steps and go directly on the ultimate action it would take eventually in any case.

By the way, even if the Turing machine sat on the same cell calculating forever, it would still not be doing a particularly interesting calculation. There are only a finite number of different symbols, and the machine has only a finite number of states. If it stays in the same cell forever, rather than straying over its infinite tape, only the single symbol in that one cell will ever have any effect. Eventually in the course of its infinite calculation, the Turing machine must find itself in the same state and reading the same symbol as at some previous time. Once that happens, it will just go through the same series of steps again and again, returning to the same situation over and over in an infinite cycle.

4.3. The first table in Figure A.8 is a specification for a Turing machine that subtracts one from its input. The assumption is that the input is a binary number and that the machine is started on the rightmost digit of that number. This is a fairly simple machine that will leave leading zeros in the answer on the tape. (For example, on input 1000, it will output 0111 rather than just 111.)

If the rightmost digit is a 1, all that is necessary to subtract 1 from the input is to change that rightmost digit to a 0. In this case, when the machine is started in state 0, it will see the 1, write a 0, move right and change to state 1. In state 1, it will encounter a blank, move left, and halt.

If a number ends in a sequence of one or more 0's, each of those 0's should be changed to a 1, and the 1 immediately to their left should be changed to a 0. The second line of the specification table takes care of changing the 0's to 1's, and then the first line takes care of changing the 1 to a 0. After that, lines three and four will move the machine back to its original starting point, where it will halt.

If this machine is started on a number consisting of just a sequence of 0's, it will move left, converting those 0's to 1's until it sees a blank. At that time it will take the default action of moving to right and halting. (It is not clear what it *should* do in this case anyway!)

The much more complicated second table in Figure A.8 adds two binary numbers. It does this by repeatedly subtracting 1 from the second number and adding 1 to the first number until the second number becomes 0. It then erases the second number so that only the answer remains on the tape. Embedded in this machine are modified versions of the subtraction machine and the addition machine from Figure 4.2. Essentially, the subtraction is done in state 0 and the addition in state 4. States 2 and 3 erase the second number after it becomes zero. (When this happens, state 0 will convert all the 0's to 1's and then encounter a blank; at that point, the machine enters state 2.) State 1 moves the machine left from the second number to the rightmost digit of the first, while states 5 and 6 move it right from the first number back to the rightmost digit of the second, where the calculation returns to state 0. I encourage you to trace the action of this machine for a few sample inputs.

4.4. I will not try to do this for you. Here is a recipe for the copying machine described in the problem; I leave the details to you.

Current State	Current Cell Contents	New Cell Contents	Direction of Motion	New State
0	1	0	R	1
0	0	1	L	0
1	1	1	R	1
1	#	#	L	h

Current State	Current Cell Contents	New Cell Contents	Direction of Motion	New State
0	1	0	L	1
0	0	1	L	0
0	#	#	R	2
1	1	1	L	1
1	0	0	L	1
1	#	#	L	4
2	1	1	R	2
2	#	#	L	3
3	1	#	L	3
3	#	#	L	h
4	0	1	R	5
4	1	0	L	4
4	#	1	R	5
5	0	0	R	5
5	1	1	R	5
5	#	#	R	6
6	0	0	R	6
6	1	1	R	6
6	#	#	L	0

Figure A.8. *Tables of rules for two Turing machines. These machines are discussed in the answer to Question 2.3.*

Assume that the machine is started on the y. It should erase the y and move left one cell. If it sees a 0 or a 1 in that cell, then it has to copy that digit to the left end of the tape. For example, suppose it sees a 0. It should write a y to mark its spot, move left, and change to state 2. In state 2, it should move left until it sees the z, and then continue to move left (in state 3) until it finds a blank space. It should write a 0 in that space, then it should move right to the y (in state 4). It should replace the y with a 0, move left, and return to state 0.

In state 0, if the machine sees a 1 instead of a 0, it should copy the 1 is a similar way using states number 5, 6, and 7. Finally, if it sees a blank when in state 0, it should write a y and halt, since the number has been completely copied.

4.5. If we can make "definite rules" for answering some question, then we should be able to program a computer to follow those rules. The rules would have to be spelled out in great enough detail to be complete and unambiguous. Otherwise, how would it be possible to sure that they are correct? But if they are complete and unambiguous, then following those rules is a *calculation* rather than a thoughtful, creative process, and a computer should be able to follow them as well as a human could.

At least, this is true if the Church-Turing Thesis is correct. The Church-Turing Thesis is the assertion that anything that can reasonably be called computation can be done by a computer, and hence by a Turing machine. We cannot prove this thesis; we can only give evidence for it. But the evidence—that all definitions of computation that have been proposed are equivalent to computation by a Turing machine—is rather strong.

4.6. Dr. McCoy is an interested party here, and he has set the rules. Whatever answer Mr. Spock gives, Dr. McCoy can do the opposite of what he predicts. Spock has no chance of being right. He can't logically predict the future if the future depends on his prediction.

This is the same problem that is at the heart of the proof of the unsolvability of the Halting Problem. The machine H cannot make a correct prediction about the result of a calculation if that calculation is rigged to do the opposite of whatever it predicts.

Perhaps Spock's best response would be to throw both the rock and Dr. McCoy into the lake. But I guess that wouldn't be logical.

Chapter 5 Answers

5.1. It could easily be argued that the ENIAC computer was computationally universal. Certainly, it could solve any problem that a modern computer could solve (subject as always to limitations such as the size of its memory). However, the modifications necessary to change the

ENIAC's program seem to me to be very close to actually building a new machine. We wouldn't say that a box of transistors was computationally universal just because we could build a variety of computing machines from them. Well, all right, that's not being fair to the ENIAC either. But when we program a modern computer to solve a new problem, we don't have to make any physical change to the machine itself. All we do is load a new program into its memory. Even the Analytical Engine would have been programmed just by dropping a new set of cards into its card reader. The ENIAC was not programmable in this more interesting sense.

5.2.   It actually does make sense to use general-purpose microprocessors running permanent, special-purpose programs. It is much easier to write a special-purpose program than it is to design a special-purpose computer chip. It is relatively cheap to mass-manufacture identical microprocessors. These can then be loaded with various programs to adapt them to particular tasks.

The program for such a microprocessor can be stored on a chip called a PROM, or programmable read-only memory. Such chips are actually not quite "read-only." A program can be stored in such a memory—but only once. After that, the contents of the PROM can be read but not modified.

By the way, it is becoming more economical to produce small batches of special-purpose computer chips, largely because of the application of computers to the design and manufacturing process.

5.3.   It seems reasonable for the mouse's buttons to work something like a keyboard. That is, when the user presses a mouse button, an interrupt signal is sent to the computer so that the operating system can respond immediately to the mouse click.

It is not so obvious how the mouse can control a cursor on the screen. Your first guess might be that the mouse periodically sends a report of its position to the computer, but that can't be right because it's not the position of the mouse that matters. The cursor moves only when the mouse is rolled across a flat surface. If you pick it up and move it, the cursor will stay fixed on the screen even though the mouse has changed position.

In fact, as the mouse rolls across a table, it sends out an interrupt to the computer every time it moves a certain distance back or forth or up or down. The computer responds to these interrupts by moving the cursor. In general, this response is handled automatically by a device driver or some other part of the operating system, without the intervention of any application program that might be running. Such a program can, if necessary, ask the operating system where the cursor is. (It would do this by calling some subroutine in the operating system that exists for just this purpose.)

As to the actual drawing of the cursor, this can be handled in various ways. The video controller that draws the image on the screen might be programmed to automatically substitute an image of the cursor for part of that image. It would simply ignore the data in video memory that are currently "covered" by the cursor. Alternatively, the CPU might be directly responsible for storing the image of the cursor into the appropriate position in video memory. The CPU would have to save a copy of the data that were originally stored there, so that it can restore the data when the cursor moves.

5.4. Two identical machines can, in fact, execute exactly the same machine-language instructions, even if those machines are running two different operating systems. The problem is that any practical program for a real computer is, by itself, incomplete. Such a program will do part of its work, perhaps even most of it, by calling subroutines from the operating system. If that program is run on a machine with a different operating system, then the subroutines that it needs won't be available. The only programs that could be run on both machines would be those without any "jump-to-subroutine" instructions that call subroutines that are not part of the programs themselves.

In practice, there are also other difficulties. For example, different operating systems use different techniques for storing programs in files, and they generally store extra, system-specific information in the file along with a program. One operating system might not even recognize a file from another system as *being* a program in the first place!

5.5. *Frankenstein* is the archetypical story of technology gone out of control. The scientist who seeks knowledge and power without considering the consequences is destroyed by the "monster" he creates. It is a story still worth reading and considering.

The story in the original novel is rather different from the version popularized in the movies. The monster in the book is no unthinking brute; it is articulate and explains its motivations even as it drives its creator to his destruction. The monster claims that it could have been a force for good as easily as for evil, and that Dr. Frankenstein, by creating it and then abandoning it, is responsible for what it has become.

It has always seemed to me that *Frankenstein* is about the obligation of scientists and other seekers-after-knowledge to try to understand all the consequences of what they create and to take responsibility for it. In Section 5.3, I have argued that this is certainly true for computer technology, which is in itself neither good nor evil, but which has the capacity for both.

5.6. If you start making a serious list of computerized databases that might contain information about you, it will probably soon grow longer than you initially expect. Furthermore, it will almost certainly be incomplete. This is because data can propagate so easily from one computer to another. Most people understand how easy it is for a name and address to find its way onto the mailing list of a mail order company, magazine, or political organization. They might be less aware of (and more disturbed by) the extent to which data such as credit information and court records are publicly available to those interested in obtaining them.

Chapter 6 Answers

6.1. A major theme of this book is that complexity can be handled by building up complex systems level by level from simpler components. Complex programs and complex circuits are just two examples of complex systems, and the analogies between them are strong. In the case of programs, instructions are chunked together into structures such as loops, decisions, and subroutines; these are then available to be used as black boxes for building more complex programs. In circuits, the basic building blocks are transistors or logic gates, but once some of these are assembled into a circuit, that circuit can become a building block in even larger circuits.

There are some differences, of course, largely owing to the fact that a circuit is a physical object, while a program is just a just a collection of information. For example, it is not possible for one circuit to "call" another in the way that one subroutine can call another subroutine— the first circuit must physically contain a copy of the second. Still, the similarities outweigh the differences.

6.2. A line on the screen consists of a set of pixels whose color has been changed to make it different from the background color. As we have seen, the color of a pixel is simply a reflection of a number stored in the computer's video memory. In order to draw a line on the screen, the CPU must change the number in memory corresponding to each pixel on the line. So, we might guess that somewhere inside the implementation of the *forward* statement is a loop that changes individual pixels on the line, one by one. Each time through the loop, a *store* instruction is executed that changes the color of one pixel.

For this to work, the CPU must be able to determine where the line starts and ends. So, at all times, it has to keep track of where the turtle is and what its current heading is; this information must be stored in memory. Using this information together with the distance specified in the *forward* command, the CPU can compute the endpoints of the line.

If the turtle is displayed on the screen, then the CPU must start by erasing the turtle from its current position on the screen, which itself involves changing the color of many pixels. It can then draw the line and redraw the turtle in its new position. Finally, it must change the stored turtle position in its memory (so that it doesn't lose track of where the turtle is located).

Of course, to you as a programmer, all this looks like a single simple operation: The turtle moves forward a specified distance in response to a single command. All the complexity is hidden in the "black box."

6.3. Here are three style guidelines that I mentioned: (1) Programs should be laid out on the page so that they are easy to read. This is called **formatting** the program. Using indentation, spaces, and line breaks can help to make the structure of the program obvious. (2) Variables should be given meaningful names, related to their purpose in the program. (3) Informative, helpful comments should be used to help a reader understand the program. I might also have mentioned: (4) Statements such as loops and if statements should not be too deeply nested inside each other, since that would require a reader to keep too many levels of complexity in mind at once.

Good style exists purely for human readers. The computer would accept a randomly formatted program with no comments and with variables named $x1$, $x2$, ..., $x237$, but no person would ever be willing to read it. (Keep in mind that the principal human reader of a program that you write is likely to be you yourself, a few days, months, or years later!)

6.4. In the program in Figure 6.10, the value of the variable *count* is initialized to zero before the loop begins. Each time through the loop, 1 is added to the value of *count*, so that it takes on the successive values 1,

2, 3, 4, ... The loop ends when the value of *count* becomes equal to the value of the variable *HowMany*—if that ever happens. If the user inputs a negative value for *HowMany*, then *count* will never become equal to *HowMany*, and the loop will never end. The computer will continue drawing larger and larger squares forever. The same thing will happen if the value of *HowMany* is not an integer, since the only possible values for *count* are integers.

So, the loop in this program has a precondition: *HowMany* must be a positive integer. As mentioned in Subsection 6.3.1, there are two ways to deal with a precondition: Either use an **if** statement to check that it is true, or change the preceding instructions so that the precondition you need is a postcondition of those instructions (that is, something that is guaranteed to be true after those instructions are executed).

Using an **if** statement to test the precondition leads to a program that simply ignores an illegal value and does nothing when the user inputs a bad value:

> **declare** *count, HowMany, length*
> AskUser("How many squares should I draw?", *HowMany*)
> **if** *HowMany* > 0 **and** *trunc(HowMany)* = *HowMany* **then**
> { Insert rest of program from Figure 6.10 }
> **end if**

The function *trunc* used in the **if** statement was introduced in Subsection 6.3.3. *Trunc* converts its parameter into an integer; if that parameter is already an integer, *trunc* doesn't change it. Thus, the test "*trunc(HowMany)* = *HowMany*" checks whether the value of *HowMany* is an integer.

A more satisfactory solution is to guarantee that the precondition holds. One way to make sure that a condition holds is to use a loop whose **exit** statement tests that condition. Then the only way that the loop can ever end is for the condition to test true. Applying this strategy leads to a program like

> **declare** *count, HowMany, length*
> AskUser("How many squares should I draw?", *HowMany*)
> **loop**
> **exit if** *HowMany* > 0 **and** *trunc(HowMany)* = *HowMany*
> AskUser("Please enter a positive number.", *HowMany*)
> **end loop**
> { Insert rest of program from Figure 6.10 }

After the loop ends, the value of *HowMany* is definitely known to be a positive integer. (By the way, we have no way of guaranteeing that the loop will actually end—the user might just sit there forever typing in 3.14159 over and over! A computer scientist would say that this program is "partially correct," meaning that if it halts it gives a correct result, but there is no guarantee that it will halt. You might want to modify the program so that it gives the user only, say, ten chances to enter an acceptable input.)

6.5. When I say "develop" a program I mean more than just "write" one! You should always approach a problem thoughtfully and systematically. The most basic approach is to try to break the problem down into simpler subproblems. One way to do this is to think of a series of *states* that the program might go through on the way to a complete solution. When you do this, you are designing a *process* that the computer might go through to solve the problem. You can then try to write the "script" for that process by finding the program instructions that will move the computer from one state to the next.

If the problem is to produce a picture, then you can try to imagine the steps you would go through to produce the picture by hand. The "comb" you are supposed to draw in this case consists of eleven vertical lines connected by ten horizontal line segments along the bottom of the picture. Let's suppose that the vertical lines are five units long and that the connecting segments are each one unit long. One way to decompose the problem is like this:

> Draw a vertical line;
> Draw a horizontal segment;
> Draw a vertical line;
> Draw a horizontal segment;
>
> $\vdots$
>
> Draw a horizontal segment;
> Draw a vertical line.

Since the process repeats itself, we can collapse it into a loop. Each repetition of the loop will draw one vertical line and one horizontal segment. We have to draw one extra vertical line outside the loop—this can be done either at the beginning or the end. Now the process looks like this:

> Draw a vertical line;
> **loop**
> > Draw a horizontal segment;

Draw a vertical line;
exit if ten lines have been drawn
end loop

We have to use a *count* variable to keep track of how many times the loop
has been executed. We also have to be careful to set up preconditions
involving the position and heading of the turtle before we draw each
line. Before drawing a vertical line, the turtle must be facing up, with a
heading of 90. Before drawing a horizontal segment, the turtle must be
facing to the right and must be at the bottom of the picture. Taking all
this into account, we get the program:

```
declare count
face(90)
forward(5) { Draw a vertical line }
loop
   back(5)   { Return turtle to bottom }
   face(0)
   forward(1) { Draw a horizontal segment }
   face(90)
   forward(5) { Draw a vertical line }
   count := count + 1
   exit if count = 10
end loop
```

6.6. For example, we can produce the sentence "Mary runs" because a ⟨sentence⟩ is a ⟨noun part⟩ followed by a ⟨verb part⟩, a ⟨noun part⟩
can be a ⟨proper noun⟩ which can be "Mary", and a ⟨verb part⟩ can be an
⟨intransitive verb⟩ which can be "runs". (Remember that a vertical bar
in a rule indicates that you have to make a choice among alternatives.)

Other ⟨sentence⟩s include "The President of the United States understands John," "The unicorn loves a woman," and "John is a fish who
thinks."

When applying BNF rules such as those given in this problem, it is
customary to write out each step. For example, using the symbol → to
mean "becomes":

⟨sentenct⟩ → ⟨noun part⟩⟨verb part⟩
        → ⟨proper noun⟩⟨verb part⟩
        → John ⟨verb part⟩
        → John ⟨transitive verb⟩⟨noun part⟩
        → John is ⟨noun part⟩

$\rightarrow$ John is ⟨common noun phrase⟩

$\rightarrow$ John is ⟨article⟩⟨common noun⟩ who ⟨verb part⟩

$\rightarrow$ John is a ⟨common noun⟩ who ⟨verb part⟩

$\rightarrow$ John is a fish who ⟨verb part⟩

$\rightarrow$ John is a fish who ⟨intransitive verb⟩

$\rightarrow$ John is a fish who thinks

In each step here, just one rule is applied. In the second line, for example, ⟨noun part⟩ is replaced by ⟨proper noun⟩ using one of the options in the rule

⟨noun part⟩ :== ⟨proper noun⟩ | ⟨common noun phrase⟩

Every ⟨sentence⟩ can be generated in this way.

One interesting note about these rules is that they can produce an infinite number of different sentences. This is because they include a circular definition (the "nesting" referred to in the question). A sentence consists partly of a ⟨noun part⟩. Now, among the things a ⟨noun part⟩ can be is a ⟨common noun phrase⟩, which can optionally end with "who ⟨verb part⟩." Finally, a ⟨verb part⟩ can include a ⟨noun part⟩, completing the cycle. This means you can make sentences like

- John knows the dog who loves Mary.
- Mary loves the cat who knows the dog who hates John.
- John understands the unicorn who loves the woman who knows the cat who loves the fish.

You can make sentences as long as you want, all of them different and all of them perfectly grammatical. Having a finite number of rules that generate an infinite number of different sentences (or programs) is what makes BNF so powerful and useful.

Chapter 7 Answers

7.1. Once a subroutine has been written by a programmer, it can be used in exactly the same way as a subroutine that is built into the language. In each case, the subroutine is simply called by name and passed any necessary parameters. A subroutine of either type is a black box for performing some specific task and can be used as a building block in complex programs. The main difference, then, is just that one type of subroutine is, in fact, written by the programmer and can be changed by the programmer if necessary; built-in subroutines are given and cannot be changed.

7.2. The point of a **ref** parameter is that the value of the actual parameter can be changed by the subroutine. It just doesn't make sense for the actual parameter to be anything other than a variable, since that is the only kind of parameter that has a value that can be changed. A subroutine with a **ref** parameter is something like an assignment statement. In fact, we could define the really trivial subroutine

> **sub** *assign*(**ref** *variable, value*)
> *variable* := *value*
> **end sub**

Then, the subroutine call "*assign*(x,17)" is equivalent to the assignment statement "$x := 17$," which changes the value of x to 17. It would make no more sense to say "*assign*(3,17)" than it would to try to change the value of the constant 3 to 17.

7.3. If you want to write a subroutine to draw a house, you should first make sure you know how to draw one by hand. A drawing of a very simple house is shown in Figure A.9. It is made up of a large square, one unit on each side, containing three rectangles representing a door and two windows. The large square is topped by a triangular roof. The lower-left corner of the house is at the point (0,0). This house can easily be scaled to any other size by multiplying all the coordinates by any given number.

A subroutine to draw such a house can simply draw four rectangles and then two more lines to represent the roof. Since we have to draw so many rectangles, we might as well start with a rectangle-drawing subroutine. Let's assume we've already written a subroutine $rect(w,h)$ that draws a rectangle w units wide and h units high. Assume that after the rectangle is drawn, the turtle is left at its original position and heading. (This postcondition is important! You have to pay attention to such things.)

A house-drawing subroutine using *rect* is shown in Figure A.9. Since this subroutine draws the house using only *move, forward,* and *back* commands, it will correctly draw a house no matter what the initial position of the turtle. The house will be drawn with its lower-left corner at the current turtle position. (This assumes that the turtle starts out facing to the right; if the turtle is facing some other direction, the subroutine will draw a "tilted" house.) After the house is drawn, the turtle will be restored to its original position and heading.

Once the subroutine *House* has been written, it can be used to draw more complicated pictures. For example, it could be used to draw a

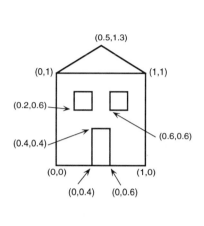

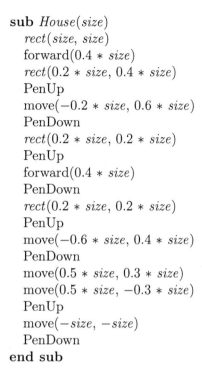

```
sub House(size)
    rect(size, size)
    forward(0.4 * size)
    rect(0.2 * size, 0.4 * size)
    PenUp
    move(−0.2 * size, 0.6 * size)
    PenDown
    rect(0.2 * size, 0.2 * size)
    PenUp
    forward(0.4 * size)
    PenDown
    rect(0.2 * size, 0.2 * size)
    PenUp
    move(−0.6 * size, 0.4 * size)
    PenDown
    move(0.5 * size, 0.3 * size)
    move(0.5 * size, −0.3 * size)
    PenUp
    move(−size, −size)
    PenDown
end sub
```

Figure A.9. *A drawing of a house, with some points labeled with their coordinates. We can scale the house to any size by multiplying all of the coordinates by some number. The subroutine can draw houses of different sizes. It uses another subroutine, rect(w,h), which draws a rectangle of width w and height h.*

small "village" consisting of three houses of various sizes:

```
PenUp  MoveTo(−8,−4)  PenDown
House(6)
PenUp  MoveTo(−1,2)  PenDown
House(4)
PenUp  MoveTo(2,−6)  PenDown
House(8)
```

7.4. The point of this problem is to build up a series of increasingly complex subroutines, one fairly easy step at a time. One possible solution is shown in Figure A.10. The hardest part is to draw a star, since it is probably not obvious what angle the turtle must turn through after drawing each of the five lines in the star. However, if you think about

sub *Star*
  turn(72)
  forward(1) turn(144) forward(1) turn(144)
  forward(1) turn(144) forward(1) turn(144)
  forward(1) turn(144)
  turn(−72)
end sub

sub *RowOfStars(NumberOfStars)*
  declare *count*   *count* := 0
  loop
    Star
    PenUp forward(2) PenDown
    count := *count* + 1
    exit if *count* = *NumberOfStars*
  end loop
  PenUp back(2 ∗ *NumberOfStars*) PenDown
end sub

sub *FieldOfStars(NumberOfRows, StarsPerRow)*
  declare *count*   *count* := 0
  loop
    RowOfStars(StarsPerRow)
    PenUp move(0,2) PenDown
    count := *count* + 1
    exit if *count* = *NumberOfRows*
  end loop
  PenUp move(0,−2 ∗ *NumberOfRows*) PenDown
end sub

Figure A.10. *Subroutines for drawing a star, a row of stars and a field of stars. All of these subroutines are designed to return the turtle to its original position and heading after execution.*

the process, you will see that the turtle turns through a total of *two* full circles as it draws a star, for a total of 720 degrees. Since it makes five individual turns while doing so, each turn is 720/5, or 144, degrees. (In my subroutine, I have added a turn of 72 degrees at the beginning to make the star come out in its usual orientation; this is balanced by a turn of −72 degrees at the end of the subroutine to return the turtle to its original heading.)

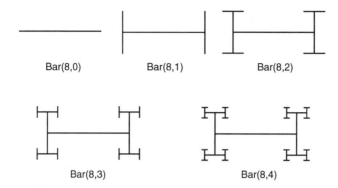

Figure A.11. *Some of the drawings that can be produced using the subroutine Bar defined in Question 6 from Chapter 7.*

Note that the subroutines *RowOfStars* and *FieldOfStars* are very similar. *FieldOfStars* uses the subroutine *RowOfStars* as a black box in almost exactly the same way that *RowOfStars* uses the subroutine *Star*. The basic idea of lining up a given number of identical pictures is the same. The only difference is that in one case they are lined up horizontally and in the other, vertically.

7.5. Jonathan Swift's image of big fleas that are plagued by little fleas that are plagued in their turn by littler fleas, and so on forever, is a pretty illustration of recursion, since he describes an infinitely complex situation in just a few words. The image you get from his poem might be similar to an image of the Koch curve or a binary tree, even though a little less abstract. "Big detours have small detours, which themselves have smaller detours, and so on *ad infinitum.*" (Of course, there is also Swift's wry commentary on the human condition, which you can take as a kind of bonus.) (And if you suspect there might be some analogy between the fleas and the bugs in a program, you might just be onto something.)

7.6. Figure A.11 shows the drawings produced by the subroutine calls *Bar*(8,0), *Bar*(8,1), and so forth.

When the value of the parameter *complexity* is zero, the turtle simply goes forward *length*/2 units, then back *length*, and then forward *length*/2. The result is that the turtle returns to its original position and heading after drawing a line *length* units long. The midpoint of that line is the original position of the turtle, and the line is oriented in whatever direction the turtle happens to be facing. (This postcondition, *the turtle at the center of the figure in its original position and heading*, turns out to be true for this subroutine no matter what parameters it is given, and it is what makes the pieces of the drawing fit together properly when the value of *complexity* is greater than zero.)

When *complexity* is greater than zero, the instructions executed by the turtle include two recursive calls to *Bar* with actual parameters *length*/2 and *complexity*−1. This means that *Bar*(8,1) will contain two copies of the figure produced by *Bar*(4,0), that *Bar*(8,2) will contain two copies of the figure produced by *Bar*(4,1), and so forth. This makes it easy to build up the sequence of drawings in Figure A.11 one step at a time: Each figure is made of two scaled-down copies of the previous figure in the sequence, together with some extra line segments. (This uses the fact that *Bar*(x/2,n) is just a half-size copy of *Bar*(x,n). This is not automatic, but it is easy to see that it is true in this case since all the forward and backward motions of the turtle are scaled with the *length* parameter.)

If we look in more detail at the instructions executed when *complexity* is greater than zero, we see that the turtle first moves forward *length*/2 units. It then makes a right-angle turn and draws a half-size copy of a *Bar* of smaller complexity; when it finishes this it is back at its starting position and heading. It then reverses its right-angle turn and backs up *length* units, putting it at the other end of a line *length* units long. It draws another small *Bar* at right angles to that line and finally returns to the center of that line by executing a *forward*(*length*/2) command. It ends up in the same position and heading as when it started the whole procedure.

7.7. For this answer to this question, you should look all the way back to the answer for Question 5 in Chapter 1. If a subroutine is not recursive, we can simply use one *fixed* set of memory locations as an activation record for that subroutine (that is, for its local variables, parameters, and a return address). Once a nonrecursive subroutine has been called, it cannot be called *again* until the first call has been completed. Once the first call completes, the data in the activation record for that call are no longer necessary, and there is no reason why the second call should not use the same locations in memory for its activation record.

The problem with a recursive subroutine is that it can be called a second time (and a third, or a fourth...) *before* the first call has completed.

Each call needs its own activation record, in its own segment of memory. The stack provides a neat way of organizing all this memory—so neat that it is even used for nonrecursive subroutines.

Chapter 8 Answers

8.1. A major principle of programming-language design is that the language should make it possible to express concretely the abstract ideas in the programmer's mind. To some extent, this will depend on the applications for which the language is designed. A language designed for scientific calculation does not need the same features as a language such as LISP that supports symbolic processing. This is simply because programmers working in two such different areas will have different sorts of ideas that need to be expressed.

A second principle might be that the language should be designed so that as many errors as possible can be caught by the compiler before a program is even run. As I noted earlier, this is why, in most languages, variables must be declared before they are used.

Third, the language should support good programming style. For example, it should allow long, meaningful variable names, and it should allow a programmer to lay out a program on a page to show its structure.

8.2. A rigorous specification of syntax makes it possible for everyone who uses the language or writes compilers to be absolutely sure about what is and is not acceptable. A program that runs on one machine when translated by one compiler should also run on another machine when translated by a different compiler.

Since semantics is generally specified more informally than syntax, it is harder to be sure that everyone agrees about just what a program actually means. That is, even though the program runs on many different computers, it might not give exactly the same results in each case. Obviously, this is something we would like to avoid, but semantics is a difficult subject, and the problem of specifying the semantics of a language completely and rigorously is not yet solved.

8.3. This is an application of the general principle that the compiler should be able to detect and point out as many errors as possible. The more exact the compiler can be when describing an error, the easier it will be for the programmer to find and fix it. A message such as "missing **end sub**," which you might get in xTurtle, is more informative than the message "missing **end**," which is what you would get in Pascal. The Pascal statement makes you search through all the while loops, if statements, record declarations, and subroutine definitions in your program to find the one that is missing the **end**. In xTurtle, the message "missing **end sub**" would send you on a search through the subroutines only.

8.4.   Here is a type declaration for a Pascal data structure that can store information about thirty students:

> **type** *StudentRecord* = **record**
>   *name*: *string*;
>   *grades*: **array**[1..3] **of** *real*;
>   **end**;
> *StudentData* = **array**[1..30] **of** *StudentRecord*;

This does not actually create the data structure. To do that, you have to declare a variable of type *StudentData*. For example, you could say:

> **var** *sd*: *StudentData*;

The variable *sd* will consist of thirty pieces named $sd[1]$, $sd[2]$, ..., $sd[30]$. Each of these pieces is a record containing the name of a student and that student's three test grades.

This works fine if there are exactly thirty students. If all we know is that the number of students is less than or equal to 100, then we have to allow space for 100 students. We can do this by changing the definition of *StudentData* so that it has 100 pieces instead of thirty:

> *StudentData* = **array**[1..100] **of** *StudentRecord*;

However, that is not enough, because we have not provided any way for the program to keep track of exactly how many students there are. For example, if you wanted to find the average on the first test, you would have to add up all the grades on that test and divide by the number of students. The program needs a variable to represent the number of students. So, in addition to the variable *sd*, you should declare a variable

> **var** *NumberOfStudents*: *integer*;

In fact, since *NumberOfStudents* and *sd* are actually part of the same abstract concept, a neater solution would be to chunk these two variables together into a record.

Finally, if you don't know any upper limit on the number of students, the only solution in Pascal is to use pointers. That is, you can put the data for each student into a record and link all the records together using a pointer from each record to the next. The pointer is necessary because it will provide the only way of ever finding the data again in memory. A data structure of this type is called a *linked list*.

8.5. In LISP, there is only one answer about how to represent something: as a list! You can represent the data about a single student as a list containing that student's name and three grades. For example: "(Fred 87 75 93)." Or, you might prefer to represent the name as a list containing a first name, middle initial, and last name: "((John Q Doe) 73 67 94)." The lists of data for individual students can then be strung together into one long list:

$$(\text{(Fred 87 75 93)} \\ \text{(Jane 83 85 91)} \\ \dots)$$

Note that there is no set limit on the number of students in the list. Similarly, this structure could accommodate differing numbers of grades for each student. What is harder here than in Pascal is accessing the individual entries in the data structure.

In Prolog, the data must be represented as a list of facts that associate each student with that student's grades. For example:

```
gradeOnFirstTest(fred,87)
gradeOnSecondTest(fred,75)
gradeOnThirdTest(fred,93)
gradeOnFirstTest(jane,83)
gradeOnSecondTest(jane,85)
gradeOnThirdTest(jane,91)
      ⋮
```

8.6. Recursion is a kind of repetition. When a subroutine calls itself recursively, the computer starts executing the subroutine again from the beginning. This is similar to returning to the beginning of a loop, similar enough that any loop can be replaced with a recursive subroutine. Consider a loop that has the form:

> **loop**
> ⟨some statements⟩
> **exit if** ⟨condition⟩
> ⟨more statements⟩
> **end loop**

We can write a subroutine that does the same thing as this loop:

> sub *ImitateLoop*
> ⟨some statements⟩
> **if not** ⟨condition⟩ **then**
> ⟨more statements⟩
> *ImitateLoop*
> **end if**
> **end sub**

The actual loop given above can be replaced in a program by a call to this subroutine. In the subroutine, if the ⟨condition⟩ is false, then the recursive call to *ImitateLoop* at the end of the **if** statement sends the computer back to the beginning of the subroutine. If the ⟨condition⟩ is true, however, the body of the **if** statement is skipped and the subroutine ends.

There is one complication. In practice, the statements inside the loop would refer to some variables. These variables must be passed to the subroutine as parameters. Figure A.12 shows the nested square program from Figure 6.10 rewritten to use a recursive subroutine instead of a loop. Note that *count* and *length* are passed as **ref** parameters since their values are changed by the subroutine. *HowMany*, whose value does not change, is passed as a regular parameter.

8.7. This is one of those yes-and-no questions. In a sense, all programming languages are equivalent just as all computers are equivalent. Anything that can be done in one language can be done in any other. So, in theory, learning one language is enough. However, languages are certainly not equivalent when it comes to actually writing programs. Some languages are easy to use, and some, like machine language, are almost impossible. You might think that it should still be possible to find one really good language and stick to that. Some programmers do just that, but the fact remains that there is no language that is ideally suited to every task. (See the answer to Question 8.1.) A good programmer understands this and learns a variety of languages.

Chapter 9 Answers

9.1. What you, personally, would do with a database depends, of course, on what your interests are and whether you have any collection of data that would be worth storing on the computer. For example, you might want to store information about your audio compact disk

```
sub NestOfSquares(ref count, ref length, HowMany)
   forward(length)  turn(90)
   forward(length)  turn(90)
   forward(length)  turn(90)
   forward(length)
   count := count + 1
   if count < HowMany then
      length := length + 2
      PenUp  Move(−1,−1)  PenDown
      face(0)
      NestOfSquares(count, length, HowMany)
   end if
end sub

declare count, HowMany, length
AskUser("How many squares should I draw?", HowMany)
count := 0
length := 1
NestOfSquares(count, length, HowMany)
```

Figure A.12. *The nested squares program from Figure 6.10 rewritten to use a recursive subroutine instead of a loop. Anything that can be done with a loop can be done with recursion instead, as explained in the answer to Question 6 from Chapter 8.*

collection. For each CD, you could store the title, artists, and list of selections. You might add the date of publication and the purchase date. As for the operations you might want to perform, you could easily query your database to get a list of all the CD's in your collection by a specific artist. A more complicated query could tell you whether you have any song in your collection performed by three different artists.

All this might be interesting, but it is questionable whether it would be useful for anyone with a nonprofessional interest in compact disks. Even more questionable is whether you would, or should, have the discipline to keep the database up to date. I suspect that most potential personal uses for database programs would be similarly inappropriate. One reason for studying computer applications, of course, is to get some idea of where they can be used effectively.

9.2. It simply takes less information to fill an area on your screen with text than to fill it with graphics. Think of a single character. It takes only eight bits of information to specify a character's ASCII code, but it occupies perhaps forty or fifty pixels on the screen. Even simple black and white graphics use one bit for each pixel (to say whether that pixel is black or white). Color graphics typically use between four and twenty-four bits per pixel, so filling the screen area occupied by a character with color graphics instead could take twenty or a hundred times as much information. And transmitting that information from the other end of a modem connection would take twenty to a hundred times as long as transmiting the character's ASCII code.

Some speedup could be obtained by compressing the the graphics data so that fewer bits are used to represent the same image. But then, compression could be used for text as well. If the objective is to get some unique image from one computer onto the screen of another, then there is not much else that can be done.

However, in the case of providing a graphical user interface, much of the graphics that appears on the screen will *not* be unique. Many interface elements, such as "icons" that represent choices available to the user, will appear over and over. These can be transmitted just once, or they can be provided by the graphical user interface program that the user is running so that they don't have to be transmitted at all. If this is done, it will take very little information to display such standard interface elements: just a short code number to specify which item is to be displayed, and an indication of where on the screen it should appear. Transmitting this information will take very little time. (By the way, this is sort of what's done with text. What you see on your screen is a picture of a character that your computer knows how to draw. The ASCII code of the character tells the computer which of these character-pictures to draw.)

9.3. An algorithm is in TIME(n) if there is a constant c such that the running time for input of size n is less than or equal to cn. Searching an unsorted list is in TIME(n) because every item has to be checked (in the worst case), and because checking each item takes the same amount of time. If the processing time for one item is c, where c is a constant independent of the number of items in the list, then the time for processing n items is cn.

More generally, if an algorithm processes each item of input in some way, and if the time it spends on each item is (less than or equal to) some constant that is independent of the number of input items, then the algorithm is in TIME(n). This is just another way of stating the definition, but concentrating on the processing time *per item* gives a nice characterization.

Other problems that can be solved with constant per-item processing time include: finding the maximum or minimum in an unsorted list of numbers, checking whether a list of numbers is sorted (you just have to check whether each number is less than or equal to the one after it in the list), inserting a number into its proper place in a sorted list, and computing the average of a list of numbers.

By the way, you might be wondering why the processing time per item would change as the number of input items increases. This could easily happen if the input numbers are not processed in isolation. In sorting a list, for example, the basic operation is comparing *two* numbers, to see which one should come first in the list. Unless you are careful, you might end up comparing each of the n input numbers to each of the other $n-1$ inputs. That's $n-1$ comparisons for each of the n inputs, for a total of just under n^2. This explains why the most obvious sorting algorithms are in complexity class TIME(n^2), although with some ingenuity, a sorting algorithm can have per-item processing time that grows like $\log_2(n)$ rather than like n.

Chapter 10 Answers

10.1. Parallel processing increases the effective speed of computers, but it does not increase the range of problems that they can solve in theory. The reason for this was actually mentioned several times in the text: Parallel processing can be *simulated* on an ordinary, single-processor computer. Instead of running each process on a different processor, multitasking can be used to divide computing time on a single processor among all the processes that need it. Multitasking allows a single-processor computer to do anything that can be done through parallel processing.

However, it is certainly possible that some problems that cannot be solved by a single-processor computer *in a reasonable amount of time* might be quickly solved by applying massive parallel processing. But this is a practical, not theoretical, difference.

10.2. Each of the three turtles performs three operations: (1) Get the value of *sum*; (2) Add *ForkNumber* to it; (3) Store the answer in *sum*. The variable *sum* starts out with a value of zero. Altogether, the three turtles perform a a total of nine operations, which can be interwoven in various ways. For example:

Turtle #1: Get *sum*   (reads 0)
Turtle #2: Get *sum*   (reads 0)
Turtle #2: Add *ForkNumber*   (adds 2 to 0, giving 2)
Turtle #2: Store answer in *sum*   (stores 2)
Turtle #3: Get *sum*   (reads value 2, stored by Turtle #2!)
Turtle #1: Add *ForkNumber*   (adds 1 to 0, giving 1)
Turtle #3: Add *ForkNumber*   (adds 3 to 2, giving 5)
Turtle #1: Store answer in *sum*   (stores 1)
Turtle #3: Store answer in *sum*   (stores 5)

Each turtle performs its own three operations in the same order, but—for whatever reason—Turtle #2 manages to perform its calculation before Turtle #3 ever reads the value of *sum*. Since Turtle #3 is the last to set the value of *sum*, the value that it computes, 5, is the final value of *sum*.

Other orderings of these operations will give different final values. If the roles of Turtles #1 and #2 are interchanged in the above list of operations, for example, then the final value of *sum* would be 4 (computed by Turtle #3 by adding 3 to 1). If Turtle #1 completes all three operations before Turtle #2 does anything, and Turtle #2 then completes its operations before Turtle #3 does anything, then the final value of *sum* will be 6.

The example at the end of Section 10.1.2, dealing with two simultaneous withdrawals from a bank account, shows how a similar problem might arise with shared variables in a real situation. Suppose that a process in an automatic teller machine performs the operation "deduct $100 from the account" in the following sequence of operations: (1) Get the account balance (from the central bank); (2) Subtract 100; (3) Store the answer (back to the database in the central bank). The problem is that the account balance, which is stored in one location on the central computer, is shared by many processes running in many different automatic teller machines. If two processes perform this operation at the same time, they might perform these operations in the order:

Process #1: Get the account balance
Process #2: Get the account balance (reads same value)
Process #1: Subtract 100
Process #2: Subtract 100 (gets the same answer)
Process #1: Store the answer (original balance, minus 100)
Process #2: Store the answer (just stores the same number)

declare *HowMany*

AskUser("How many squares should I draw?", *HowMany*)

fork(*HowMany*)
PenUp
MoveTo(−*ForkNumber*, −*ForkNumber*)
PenDown
forward(2 ∗ *ForkNumber*)   turn(90)
forward(2 ∗ *ForkNumber*)   turn(90)
forward(2 ∗ *ForkNumber*)   turn(90)
forward(2 ∗ *ForkNumber*)   turn(90)

Figure A.13. *Solution to Question 10.4. This program draws nested squares by creating one process for each square that is to be drawn.*

The final answer is just $100 less than the original balance, rather than the correct $200. Needless to say, this is not the way things are done by real banks. Something like the **grab** command in xTurtle might be used: One process can gain control of the account balance and force the other to wait until it has completely finished its transaction. This makes an interleaving of operations, as shown above, impossible.

10.3.   The message-passing mechanism has an automatic, built-in solution to the mutual exclusion problem. Suppose that two processes both want to subtract 100 from an account balance and that each process sends the message "Subtract 100 from the account balance" to the central computer, where the account balance is stored. Even if these messages are sent at exactly the same time, the central computer will only process one message at a time. This means that one message will be completely processed before the processing of the next one starts. Each message correctly subtracts $100 from the account balance.

Note that in this case, the account balance is not really a shared variable. It is accessible to one just one process—the one running on the central computer. Other processes can't access the balance directly; they can only "ask" the central computer to do it for them.

10.4.   An xTurtle program to draw nested squares using multiple processes is shown in Figure A.13. After determining how many squares to draw, the program creates a separate turtle to draw each square. Each turtle moves to the lower-left corner of the square it is supposed to draw, and then draws the square as usual, with a sequence of *forward* and *turn*

```
declare max   { shared variable }
max := 0
fork(100)   { create 100 processes }
declare N, StepCount
StepCount := 0
N := ForkNumber   { starting point for sequence }
{ Now, count steps in sequence starting from N }
loop
    exit if N = 1
    if N/2 = trunc(N/2) then
        N := N / 2
    else
        N := 3 * N + 1
    end if
    StepCount := StepCount + 1
end loop
grab max   { take control of shared variable, max }
    if StepCount > max then
        max := StepCount
    end if
end grab
```

Figure A.14. *Solution to Question 10.5. This program will find the largest number of steps in the "3N+1" sequence starting from any integer between 1 and 100.*

commands. Note that to write this program, I had to figure out how big the squares would be ($2 * ForkNumber$) and where the lower-left corners would be. This is a bit of thinking that I didn't have to do for the program in Figure 6.10. On the other hand, for this new version I didn't have to write a loop or deal with the variables *length* and *count*. I find the parallel processing version easier to understand and more elegant, but this is to some extent a matter of taste.

10.5. The "3N+1" sequence starting from an integer N is defined by the operation: If N is even, then divide N by two; otherwise, multiply N by three and add 1; and repeat this until N becomes equal to 1. The program in Figure A.14 computes the 3N+1 sequence for every number between 1 and 100, and it does these computations simultaneously by creating a separate process to handle each different starting number.

Each process creates its own variables, *StepCount* and *N*, which are used in this program in exactly the same way that they were used in Figure 6.11. However, all the variables share a single copy of a variable called *max*. Each process runs a **loop** to count the number of steps in its assigned sequence; at the end of this loop, the value of *StepCount* is equal to the number of steps in the sequence.

After the loop, the process "**grabs**" the shared variable *max*, checks its value, and possibly changes that value. The **grab** command is necessary because several processes could be performing this operation at the same time, and there is the possibility for "interleaving" of operations, just as described in the answer to Question 10.2. Suppose, for example, that one process checks the value of *max* and decides to change it. Without the **grab** command, it is possible that some *other* process will change the value of *max* while the first process is thinking—so the value that the first process replaces might not be the value that it checked! It might even replace the true maximum value with a lower value, and the program as a whole will end up with the wrong value stored in *max*.

(Note, by the way, that we have no easy way to *check* the value of *max* at the end of the program. A *TellUser* statement won't work, since each process will execute the statement, and we'll end up getting 100 messages, with different values of *max*, instead of just one. Obviously, the xTurtle language should have some feature to deal with this problem— some way to "reunite" the processes after they have all done their work.)

10.6. This question is almost answered in Subsection 8.3.1. The only problem is relating what is said there to the idea of distributed processing. In an object-oriented system, we can imagine (or arrange in fact) that each object is really a *process* that receives messages from other objects (that is, other processes) and carries them out. Each object has control over the data that it contains, and other objects can manipulate that data only by sending messages. It makes little difference, from the programming point of view, whether the objects are all in the same computer or are distributed over many computers on a network. (Compare the answer to Question 10.3, where the bank account balance might well be a Bank Account Object in a distributed, object-oriented system.)

Chapter 11 Answers

11.1. The object here is to construct a wheel from circles, lines, and squares using certain geometric transformations. Squares don't make

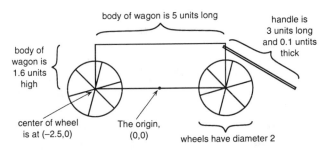

Figure A.15. *A wagon constructed from transformed squares and wheels. Note that the wagon is assumed to be positioned with the origin at the location shown.*

very good wheels, but we can use a circle to represent the rim of the wheel and line segments to represent its spokes. We start with the standard circle of diameter 1, centered at the origin. The wheel has six spokes, and we could use six separate line segments to draw them. But it's easier to see the six spokes as paired into three diameters and to just use three line segments. One of the diameters—the horizontal one—is the line that extends from the point $(-\frac{1}{2}, 0)$ to $(0, \frac{1}{2})$. This is one of our basic components, and we can simply include it in the image. The other two diameters can each be obtained by rotating our standard line segment through the proper angle. Thus, an image of a wheel can be built from four parts: a standard circle, a standard line segment, another standard line segment rotated 60 degrees, and one more standard line segment rotated 120 degrees.

Now, we turn to the construction of a "wagon," as shown in Figure A.15. We have already built a wheel, so we can freely include wheels, with any required transformations, as components in the wagon. To make the wheels used in this particular wagon, we have to magnify them by a factor of 2 and rotate them a bit—say, by 15 degrees. These transformations leave the wheels centered at the origin, so we finish by applying a translation to each wheel to move its center to the desired point at one corner of the wagon.

There are still two pieces to account for in the image: the large rectangle that makes up the body of the wagon and the very thin, rotated rectangle that forms its handle. We can make a rectangle from a square by scaling it by different amounts in the horizontal and vertical directions. Using the measurements shown in the figure, we can make the body of the rectangle by starting with the standard one-by-one square centered at the origin; we translate it vertically by one-half unit so that the origin lies at the center of its lower edge; then we scale it by a factor of 5 in the horizontal direction and a factor of 1.6 in the vertical direction. And finally, we can make the handle as follows: Start with the standard square; translate it by one-half unit horizontally so that the origin lies on its left edge; scale by a factor of 3 in the horizontal direction and 0.1 in the vertical direction; rotate by −30 degrees; and translate 2.4 units horizontally and 1.5 units vertically.

11.2. A subroutine is a set of instructions packaged into a black box and given a name so that it can be used as a component in building more complex subroutines and programs. The same subroutine can be designed once and then used over and over in many different situations.

Building complex images is similar. A "sub-scene" can be designed once and for all and then used as a black box in constructing larger images. As always, this sort of thing is essential for dealing with complexity: the task is divided into manageable sub-tasks which can be worked on separately. In the example, the task of building a wheel is done once and for all. Then, wheels can be included as components in a wagon or in any other image without redesigning them each time.

A scene description language should provide support for the creation and use of sub-scenes. It should also provide some basic components. And there should be some way of applying geometric transformations to components. Let's agree that in our language, each component will have a name. The basic components are named *circle*, *square*, and *line*. New components can be defined as sub-scenes and given names. A scene or sub-scene is specified by listing the names of the components it contains; these names can be modified by a list of geometric transformations to be applied to them. For example,

circle

line

line rotate 60

line rotate 120

describes a scene made up of four components: a circle, a line, a line rotated by 60 degrees from its standard position, and another line rotated by 120 degrees. This is, in fact, the same description of a "wheel" as that given in the answer to Exercise 11.1. Note that "*line rotate* 60" means a line rotated by 60 degrees. In addition to *rotate*, we allow the transformations *translate* and *scale*. Several transformations can be

define *wheel*

[

    circle

    line

    line rotate 60

    line rotate 120

]

wheel scale 2,2 *rotate* 15 *translate* −2.5,0

wheel scale 2,2 *rotate* 15 *translate* 2.5,0

square translate 0,0.5 *scale* 5,1.6

square translate 0.5,0 *scale* 3,0.1

                  rotate −30 *translate* 2.4,1.5

Figure A.16. *A wagon specified using the scene description language that was invented in the answer to Exercise 11.2. The first seven lines define what is meant by a "wheel." Then come five lines that specify the wagon itself.*

strung together. For example,

        square translate 0,0.5 *scale* 5,1.6

specifies a square that is first translated 0.5 units vertically and then scaled by a factor of 5 horizontally and by a factor of 1.6 vertically. (Note that *translate* and *scale* each require two "parameters.")

Finally, our language needs some syntax for defining a sub-scene. This should be similar to defining a procedure in a programming language. Figure A.16 shows one possibility. Here, a sub-scene is defined and given the name *"wheel."* This makes *wheel* into a component that can then be used later in the definition of the main scene.

11.3. When a scaling transformation is applied, all distances are increased or decreased. When a figure is scaled by a factor of two, for example, the distance from the origin to any given point in the figure is doubled. The origin itself is fixed; every other point moves away from it. The size of the figure is doubled. If the center of the figure— whatever that might mean—is at the origin, then the figure increases in size *symmetrically* around the origin, so it is still centered at the origin. But if the figure is at some distance from the origin, then it will end up at twice that distance after the scaling operation.

Suppose that the object is centered at the point (3,5) and that we want to double its size without moving its center. If we just scaled by a factor of two, the center would move to the point (6,10). However, if we first apply translation by -3 units horizontally and -5 units vertically, then the center will be at the origin. Scaling by a factor of two will leave the center at the origin. Finally, we can return the center to the point (3,5) with a translation by 3 units horizontally and 5 units vertically. This sequence of transformations—translate, then scale, then translate back—scales the figure by a factor of two and leaves its center at the point (3,5).

11.4. Computer graphics can deal most easily with surfaces that are flat and that have the same properties at each point. For such surfaces, there is no need for "bump mapping" or "texture mapping." Plastic and metal surfaces are perfect examples, and so these surfaces often look realistic in computer graphics images. The same cannot be said of more visually interesting surfaces such as—to use a standard example—a beat-up old couch.

The main difference between plastic and metal surfaces is that metal has a high degree of specular reflection and little diffuse reflection. Plastic, on the other hand, generally has a high degree of diffuse reflection; its specular reflection can range from moderate (for shiny plastic) to almost zero (for a very dull, "matte" surface). Note that a metal surface can look very interesting, at least in a ray-traced image where specular reflection is handled correctly, but its interest is "borrowed" from the things that it reflects.

11.5. A recursive procedure is one that calls itself. That is, in the course of solving some problem, a subproblem is encountered that has the same general form as the big problem. A subroutine written to solve the problem can call itself to solve the sub-problem.

In ray-tracing, the basic problem is to determine the color of the light ray emitted by a surface in a given direction. At the "top level," the ray that we are interested in is one that leaves the surface and strikes the eye of a viewer. But the color of this ray is determined, at least partly, by the colors of certain other light rays—such as the one that strikes the surface at just the right angle and is specularly reflected to the viewer's eye, or the ones from light sources that hit the surface and are reflected diffusely by it in all directions (including towards the viewer's eye).

So, to determine the color of the ray that really interests us, we must first determine the color of several other light rays. The recursive procedure "Find the color of a given light ray" calls itself to find the color of each of the other rays that contribute to that color.

As with any recursive procedure, this could go on forever if we let it, tracing rays further and further back in time. In practice, of course, there has to be a limit. We look back so many levels and no further. In the subroutines in Chapter 7, a parameter named "complexity" was used to control the number of levels of recursion. A recursive ray-tracing subroutine could work in much the same way.

Chapter 12 Answers

12.1. The debate on the Turing Test has been going on for almost fifty years, and the opinions put forth by knowledgeable people cover the whole range of possibilities. So, you needn't be shy about forming your own opinion.

The argument that a super-intelligent computer might not be able to pass the test is certainly valid, since such a computer might have no ability whatsoever to use English language. This is, however, sort of beside the point, as Turing points out early in his paper. Turing does not claim that *every* intelligent entity can pass his test, merely that any computer that *does* pass it can definitely be said to be intelligent. This leaves open the possibility of an intelligent computer (or extraterrestrial) that cannot pass the test.

It is possible, however, that no computer will ever pass the test. The Turing Test is enormously difficult to pass. The difficulty seems to have surprised many people, and in fact, one of the lessons of a half-century of artificial intelligence research has been an appreciation for the difficulty of tasks that people perform easily. Attempts to reduce these tasks to rules and symbols have resulted in programs that can do some interesting things, but not in programs that can operate with anything like the flexibility and naturalness that people display in doing everyday tasks.

Still, the continued rapid advance in computer hardware and software raises the possibility that computers with the information storage and processing capabilities of the brain will exist some time in the not-so-distant future. With the right program, why wouldn't such computers be as intelligent as we are? Perhaps they will be, but it is not clear that the "right program" can ever be written. It is not even clear that people are running a program in their heads when they think.

And even if some future computer running some extraordinarily complex program can pass the Turing Test, would that entitle it to be called

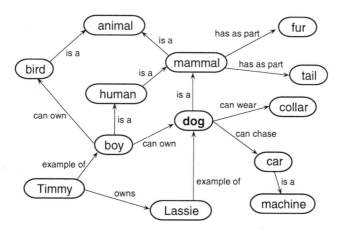

Figure A.17. *A semantic net including the symbol "dog" along with symbols to which it is linked in various ways. Each link is labeled to show the type of relationship it represents. Links might be used by a computer to deduce information that is not stored explicitly in the semantic net. For example, we can deduce that a dog has fur from the facts that a dog is a mammal and a mammal has fur. A much larger net might contain everything there is to know about dogs—or at least enough for a computer to work "intelligently" with the concept.*

intelligent? Some people, like John Searle, would say no. Their argument is that a computer following a program and pushing symbols around can never be intelligent, no matter how impressive the result, because it has no understanding of what it is doing, nor does it have a choice to do anything else.

Personally I think I would have to accept any computer that were to pass the Turing Test as intelligent. Human use of language is so intricate and so laden with meaning that I don't believe this test could ever be passed *without* real understanding of what is being said. I tend to doubt, however, that any traditional rule-following, symbol-pushing computer will ever pass the test. As I indicate at the end of Chapter 12, that still leaves open the possibility of other approaches that might yet create real artificial minds.

12.2. Figure A.17 shows a small part of a symbol structure in which the symbol "dog" is linked to many other symbols. Some of these symbols represent other general concepts, such as "mammal" and "car"; others represent specific individuals such as "Lassie" and "Timmy." Links are labeled to show different types of relationships between symbols.

This symbol structure is an example of a ***semantic net***. The word "semantic" refers to meaning, and its use here is a claim that somehow the meaning of a word is represented by the way it is linked to other words in the net. In evaluating this claim, you should remember that most of your *own* understanding of the example in the Figure A.17 comes from your previous experience with the word "dog," with all its connotations and connections to your own life. Try to imagine the net labeled with words from a language you have never heard of. Obviously, you would have no idea that it was about dogs! If there is a semantic net inside your head, then the word "dog" must be linked to a lot more than other words. It must also be linked to images of dogs you have known, memories of cuddling a puppy, sounds of barking, some stupid pet tricks from David Letterman's TV show, the fear you have felt of a growling dog on a deserted street, the sight of a wagging tail, ...

12.3. If we try to list all the exceptions to the rule that all birds can fly, it is hard to find an end to the list. All birds can fly, except. . .

- If the bird is a penguin, then it can't fly.
- If the bird is an ostrich, then it can't fly.
- If the bird is dead, then it can't fly.
- If it's a baby bird, then it can't fly.
- If its wings have been clipped, then it can't fly.
- If it's sick, then possibly it can't fly.
- If it is chained to its perch, then it can't fly.
- If its feet are nailed to the table, then it can't fly.
- If it's a hawk wearing a hood, then it can't fly until the hood is removed.
- If it has eaten too much, then possibly it has become too fat to fly.
- If it's a toy bird, then it can't fly.
- If it's really an airplane (called a "bird" by metaphor) and it has no fuel, then it can't fly.

I have done this exercise with classes I have taught. I like to end with the example of a bird who can't fly because it is afraid, and ask the class if they agree that this is a silly exception to the rule that "all birds can fly." Then I imagine a children's story about a bird who is afraid to fly but learns to overcome that fear. Here, the "silly" exception is vitally important to understanding the story! And then, I ask whether that story is *really* about birds at all, or is it about the process of dealing with fear and growing up?

Obviously, encoding the full range of human knowledge into a set of rules would be extremely difficult, if not impossible. Almost any definite rule you state will have exceptions and qualifications. These exceptions are, of course, just more rules, and they can have their own exceptions. (A penguin can fly in an airplane.) It is easy to believe that the accumulation of rules will never stop, and easy to doubt that it will ever add up to real understanding in any case.

When I use this example in class, it is a starting point for an understanding of the difficulty of passing Turing's Test, and of an appreciation for the depth and complexity of human intelligence.

Annotated Bibliography

Aspray, William. *John von Neumann and the Origins of Modern Computing.* MIT Press, Cambridge, Massachusetts, 1990. [Von Neumann was a mathematical genius who made many contributions to computer science, physics, and economics. This biography concentrates on his work in computer science from 1943 to 1952.]

Augarten, Stan. *Bit by Bit: An Illustrated History of Computers.* Ticknor and Fields, New York, 1984. [A useful history, with lots of pictures. It ends with the introduction of the IBM PC in 1981.]

Barr, Avron and Edward A. Feigenbaum, editors. *The Handbook of Artificial Intelligence*, volumes I, II, and III. William Kaufmann, Inc., Los Altos, California, 1982. [An exhaustive survey of artificial intelligence, covering basic techniques and significant programs. It is rather technical but not unreadable.]

Boole, George. *An Investigation of the Laws of Thought, on Which are Founded the Mathematical Theories of Logic and Probabilities.* Dover Publications. Reprint of the 1854 edition. [Boole begins his work with a statement of his intent to "investigate the laws of those fundamental operations of the mind by which reasoning is performed; to give expression to them in the symbolical language of a Calculus, and upon this foundation to establish the science of Logic and construct its method." This book introduced the mathematical system now called Boolean algebra, which is fundamental to the design of logic circuits.]

Brooks, Rodney A. "Intelligence without Representation." In *Foundations of Artificial Intelligence*, edited by David Kirsh. MIT Press, Cambridge Massachusetts, 1992. Pages 139–160. [Brooks, who has built "artificial insects" and other robots at MIT, explains how complex behavior can be achieved without the explicit representation of knowledge in symbol systems. Brook's work is one example of "artificial life." (See Levy's book on the subject.)]

Caudill, Maureen and Charles Butler. *Naturally Intelligent Systems.* MIT Press, Cambridge, Massachusetts, 1990. [An introduction to the theory of neural nets and their applications.]

Cooper, Doug and Michael Clancy. *Oh! Pascal!*, second edition. W. W. Norton, New York, 1985. [One of the standard introductory textbooks in Pascal programming.]

Custer, Helen. *Inside Windows NT.* Microsoft Press, Redmond, Washington, 1993. [A survey of the design of the new operating system, Windows NT. This is a technical book, but it might be worth looking at, if only to get an idea of what goes into the construction of a complex operating system.]

Crevier, Daniel. *AI: The Tumultuous History of the Search for Artificial Intelligence.* Basic Books, New York, 1993. [A generally balanced and readable history of AI, concentrating on the traditional, symbol-system approach. (In the last few chapters, though, Crevier yields to the temptation to make the same kind of optimistic predictions about the future of AI that have proved in the past to be wrong, or at best premature.)]

Dreyfus, Hubert L. *What Computers Still Can't Do.* MIT Press, Cambridge, Massachusetts, 1992. [Dreyfus is a long-time critic of artificial intelligence. This is the latest edition of a book first published in 1992, with a new introduction in which Dreyfus essentially claims that he has won the debate. Much of the book is difficult philosophical argument, but the introductions to the various editions and the summary sections are useful.]

Foley, James D., et al. *Computer Graphics: Principles and Practice*, Second Edition. Addison-Wesley Publishing Company, Reading, Massachusetts, 1990. [A large, technical, standard textbook on computer graphics.]

Forester, Tom, editor. *Computers in the Human Context.* MIT Press, Cambridge, Massachusetts, 1989. [I found this collection of articles and the two that follow to be particularly useful. Forester has selected articles from a range of perspectives on a large number of topics relating to the social impact of computer and information technology. His short introduction to each article gives a fair summary of the author's argument and puts it into the context of a larger debate. It is worth reading Forester's longer introduction to each collection to see how the prevailing views changed over the course of the 1980s.]

Forester, Tom, editor. *The Information Technology Revolution.* MIT Press, Cambridge, Massachusetts, 1985.

Forester, Tom, editor. *The Microelectronics Revolution.* MIT Press, Cambridge, Massachusetts, 1981.

Gibson, William. *Neuromancer.* Ace Books, New York, 1984. [A science-fiction novel that introduced the term "cyberspace" and set it in a near-future technological dystopia. This book helped set the tone for discussion of networking, cyberspace and virtual reality.]

Gibson, William and Bruce Sterling. *The Difference Engine.* [A historical science-fiction novel set in a nineteenth century in which Charles Babbage completed his Analytical Engine and launched the Information Revolution in the midst of the Industrial Revolution. This fictional world is just the background for a (not tremendously innovative) mystery story, but some interesting ideas are developed.]

Goldstine, Herman H. *The Computer from Pascal to von Neumann.* Princeton University Press, 1972. [I have seen this book called the "standard academic history of computers." Goldstine worked as a mathematician on the ENIAC and EDVAC during World War II, and later at Princeton. He gives an insider's view of that work. There is more mathematics in this history than in most. Most of the British wartime work was still classified when this book was written and is not covered.]

Haugland, John. *Artificial Intelligence: The Very Idea.* MIT Press, Cambridge, Massachusetts, 1985. [Artificial intelligence from a philosophical perspective, concentrating on the "physical symbol system hypothesis" that is the basis of what Haugland calls Good Old-Fashioned Artificial Intelligence.]

Hodges, Andrew. *Alan Turing: The Enigma.* Simon and Schuster, New York, 1983. [This biography of Turing covers his work, as well as his life, and so contains some interesting information on the history of computers. (Hodges, a mathematician, is clearer about the theoretical capabilities of the machines he describes than are most authors I have looked at.) Turing made fundamental contributions to computer science and to the British war effort during World War II. He also happened to be gay, and he was convicted under British antihomosexual laws and sentenced to be treated with feminizing hormones. He completed the sentence but died a short time later, an apparent suicide, at the age of 42.]

Hofstadter, Douglas R. *Gödel, Escher, Bach: An Eternal Golden Braid.* Vintage Books, New York, 1979. [A hard book to describe. Perhaps it is mainly an investigation into the nature of intelligence and how it might be programmed into a machine, but the book is so wide-ranging that that only begins to explain what it is about. Not a particularly easy book, but very much worth reading.]

Holland, John H. *Adaptation in Natural and Artificial Systems.* MIT Press, Cambridge, Massachusetts, 1992. [This is a reprinting, with one new chapter, of a 1975 book in which Holland set forth the mathematical theory of the genetic algorithm. It is only recently, as interest in complex systems has grown, that the importance of Holland's work has been recognized. The book is very technical and highly mathematical. More accessible introductions the the genetic algorithm can be found in [Waldrop] and [Levy, *Artificial Life*].]

Horowitz, Ellis. *Fundamentals of Programming Languages.* Computer Science Press, Rockville, Maryland, 1984. [Undergraduate textbook on programming language design and implementation.]

Hyman, Anthony. *Charles Babbage, Pioneer of the Computer.* Princeton University Press, 1982. [It is an injustice to Babbage that he is usually thought of as a man who *failed* in the chief undertaking of his life. In fact, as Hyman's biography makes clear, he made many contributions to science and mathematics, and he was, and was known to be, one of the great men of his time.]

Karloff, Howard. *Linear Programming.* Birkhäuser, Boston, 1991. [A mathematically oriented textbook at the advanced undergraduate level that discusses the algorithms for linear programming, a type of optimization problem mentioned in Chapter 9.]

Kurtzweil, Raymond. *The Age of Intelligent Machines.* MIT Press, Cambridge, Massachusetts, 1992. [A flashy sort of book, concentrating on artificial intelligence but ranging over the whole field of computing, its history, and its applications. It includes some interesting essays by various people, but on the whole I found it unfocused and, in a few cases at least, inaccurate.]

Levy, Steven. Artificial Life. Pantheon Books, New York, 1992. [Describes attempts to build artificial systems that have lifelike properties. Covers some of the same topics as [Waldrop]. A very good book that only occasionally descends into hype.]

Levy, Steven. *Hackers.* Anchor/Doubleday, New York, 1984. [A lively and interesting history of hackers, with insight into the culture of these people who devote large parts of their lives to computers for the pure satisfaction of knowing the machine. Hackers have contributed a lot to the development of computers, including the lasting influence of their open-access, hands-on ideology. (The term "hacker" has been stolen to refer to people who break into computer systems illegally; that is not what this book is about.)]

Lewis, Harry R. and Cristos H. Papadimitriou. *Elements of the Theory of Computation.* Prentice Hall, Englewood Cliffs, New Jersey, 1981. [An advanced college-level textbook covering Turing Machines and related topics in a rigorously mathematical way.]

MacLennan, Bruce J. *Principles of Programming Languages*, second edition. Holt, Rinehart and Winston, New York, 1987. [Undergraduate textbook on programming language design and implementation. (A bit more readable than [Horowitz].)]

McCorduck, Pamela. *Machines Who Think.* W.H. Freeman and Company, San Francisco, 1979. [A very readable, nontechnical account of artificial intelligence, covering its historical roots and its development through the 1970s. Like many of the people who were working in the field at the time, this book has proved to be overly optimistic about the potential of artificial intelligence (in the near term, at least).]

Minsky, Marvin. *The Society of Mind.* Simon & Schuster, New York, 1985. [Minsky is known as one of the "gurus" of artificial intelligence. That means that it is his job to have fascinating and inspirational ideas and then leave all the details to other people. In this book he presents his speculations on how intelligence and even consciousness could arise from a large number of evolving, communicating structures in the brain. (Read the postscript first, which is the only place in the book where Minsky acknowledges just how highly speculative the whole thing is.)]

Moseley, Maboth. *Irascible Genius: A Life of Charles Babbage, Inventor.* Hutchinson of London, 1964. [It seems surprising, given the place that Babbage has assumed in the standard history of computers, that this was the only biography available until recently. Hyman's biography is more recent and, I think, superior.]

Penrose, Roger. *The Emperor's New Mind: Concerning Computers, Minds, and the Laws of Physics.* Oxford University Press, New York, 1989. [Penrose, a well-known physicist, questions the assumptions of the field of artificial intelligence. He suggests that the laws of quantum physics might make possible a *mind* that could never be duplicated in a *machine*. His review of the AI controversy is good, but his own theories don't seem to be very well-supported. (I am told there is now a sequel.)]

Rosenberg, Richard S. *The Social Impact of Computers*. Academic Press, 1992. [Provides a complete (if somewhat dry) survey of most of the issues one could think of related to computers and society. Because its coverage is so broad, it is not always as deep as might be desired, but it does provide extensive lists of additional readings organized by topic.]

Schaffer, Cullen. *Principles of Computer Science*. Prentice Hall, Englewood Cliffs, New Jersey, 1988. [An introductory textbook which covers some of the same material as does mine. However, it continues the low level approach, which I cover in my first few chapters, throughout the book.]

Siegel, Lenny and John Markoff. *The High Cost of High Tech*. Harper and Row, New York, 1985. [Subtitled "The Dark Side of the Chip," which pretty much says it. Although it has a large number of disturbing facts, this book is not anti-technology as such. It argues that all people must learn and practice "computer citizenship" if the dark side of technology is to be defeated.]

Stein, Dorothy. *Ada: A Life and Legacy*. MIT Press, Cambridge, Massachusetts, 1985. [This biography of Ada Lovelace challenged the usual view, found in Moseley's book, for example, that she was a great mathematician who saw the potential of Babbage's machines more clearly even than he. Stein says that Moseley's biography of Babbage is "almost perversely inaccurate, distorted, and fabricated." Stein's book is itself controversial.]

Stroustrup, Bjarne. *The C++ Programming Language*, second edition. Addison Wesley, Reading, Massachusetts, 1991. [This introduction to C++ and object-oriented programming by the designer of the language is directed towards people who already know a lot about programming. It is rather dry and technical, with no pictures and only one joke that I could find. Given that, however, it is very well-written and informative.]

Swade, Doron D. "Redeeming Charles Babbage's Mechanical Computer." *Scientific American*, February 1993, p. 86–91. [Describes the construction of a Difference Engine No. 2, from Babbage's original designs, at the London Science Museum in 1989–91.]

Tanenbaum, Andrew S., *Computer Networks*. Prentice-Hall, Englewood Cliffs, New Jersey, 1988. [A well-written textbook on the theory of computer networks, concentrating on "layered protocols."]

Toole, Betty A. *Ada, the Enchantress of Numbers: A Selection from the Letters of Lord Byron's Daughter and Her Description of the First Computer*. Strawberry Press, Mill Valley, California, 1992. [Although this consists mostly of letters, Toole has added enough narration to qualify this as a biography. Toole sees Ada Lovelace as someone who reconciled the poetical heritage of her father, the poet Lord Byron, with a scientific view of the world. She argues against the views in Stein's book.]

Turing, Alan M. "Computing Machinery and Intelligence." In *Mind*, Number 59, 1950, pages 434–460. Reprinted in *Computers and Thought*, edited by E. Feigenbaum and J. Feldman, McGraw-Hill, New York, 1963, pages 11–35. [The paper in which Turing asks whether machines can think and proposes a way of testing a machine for intelligence. Turing lists nine possible objections to the idea of thinking machines, and gives counterarguments to each. His discussion foreshadows much of the debate about artificial intelligence that has gone on over the past half century, and it holds up remarkably well.]

Turkle, Sherry. *The Second Self: Computers and the Human Spirit.* Simon and Schuster, New York, 1984. [This is an interesting and well-written book by a psychologist/sociologist who focuses her expertise on cultures that have grown up around computers. It has some interesting things to say about the relationship of people to their machines, and how that relationship affects their ideas of themselves. (The book might be a bit overly influenced by the particular computer culture at MIT, where Turkle is a professor, but that is at most a minor flaw.)]

Waldrop, M. Mitchell. *Complexity: The Emerging Science at the Edge of Order and Chaos.* Simon & Schuster, New York, 1992. [A very readable and exciting account of recent work on complexity, which refers here to complexity that emerges from the interactions of simple components without being explicitly programmed or designed. The book concentrates on the Sante Fe Institute, which was founded in 1987 to study complex systems and their applications in a wide variety of disciplines. See also [Levy, *Artificial Life*].]

Winograd, Terry and Fernando Flores. *Understanding Computers and Cognition.* Addison-Wesley, Reading, Massachusetts, 1986. [Winograd is the creator of a well-known artificial intelligence program known as SHRDLU. This book reflects his acceptance of some of the criticisms that have been leveled against the artificial intelligence enterprise.]

Index

T